149809

# SCOTT OF THE ANTARCTIC

# BOOKS BY ELSPETH HUXLEY

Scott of the Antarctic        1978
Gallipot Eyes: A Wiltshire Diary        1976
Florence Nightingale        1975
Livingstone        1974
The Kingsleys        1973
The Challenge of Africa        1971
Love among the Daughters        1968
Their Shining Eldorado        1967
Brave New Victuals        1965
A Man from Nowhere        1964
With Forks and Hope        1964
Back Street New Worlds        1964
The Incident at The Merry Hippo        1963
The Edge of the Rift        1962
A New Earth        1960
The Flame Trees of Thika        1959
No Easy Way        1957
The Red Rock Wilderness        1957
Four Guineas        1954
A Thing to Love        1954
The Sorcerer's Apprentice        1948
I Don't Mind If I Do        1950
The Walled City        1948
Race & Politics in Kenya (with Margery Perham)        1944
East Africa        1941
Atlantic Ordeal        1941
Red Strangers        1939
Death of an Aryan        1939
Murder on Safari        1938
Murder at Government House        1937
White Man's Country: Lord Delamere and the Making of Kenya        1935

# Elspeth Huxley

# SCOTT

## OF THE

## ANTARCTIC

Atheneum NEW YORK 1978

Library of Congress Cataloging in Publication Data

Huxley, Elspeth Joscelin Grant, 1907-
    Scott of the Antarctic.

        Bibliography: p.
        Includes index.
            1. Scott, Robert Falcon, 1868-1912. 2. Explorers
        —England—Biography. 3. Antarctic regions.
    I. Title.
    G875.S35H88    1978    919.8'9'040924    [B]    77-23662
    ISBN 0-689-10861-3

*For Cousin Peggy*

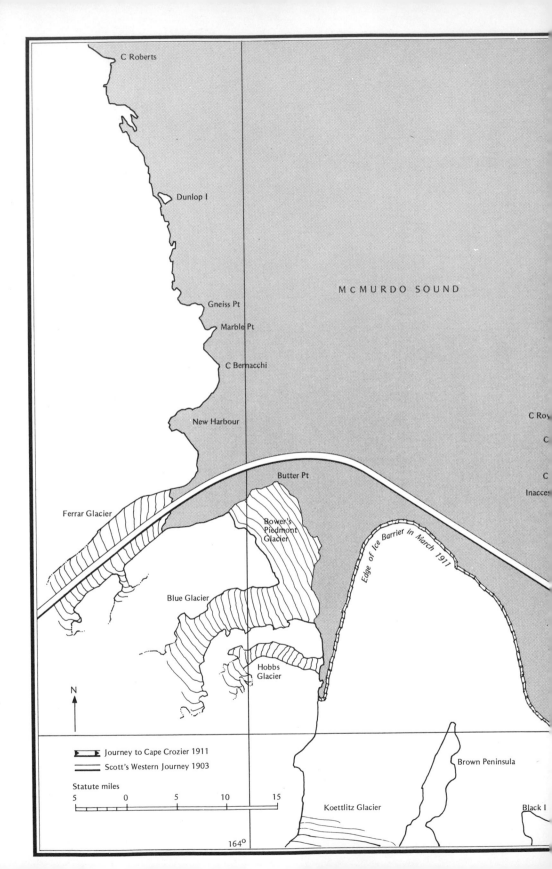

C Roberts

Dunlop I

Gneiss Pt

Marble Pt

C Bernacchi

New Harbour

MCMURDO SOUND

C Roy

C

C

Inacces

Butter Pt

Ferrar Glacier

Bower's
Piedmont
Glacier

Edge of Ice Barrier in March 1911

Blue Glacier

Hobbs
Glacier

N

Journey to Cape Crozier 1911

Scott's Western Journey 1903

Statute miles

5    0    5    10    15

Brown Peninsula

Koettlitz Glacier

Black I

164°

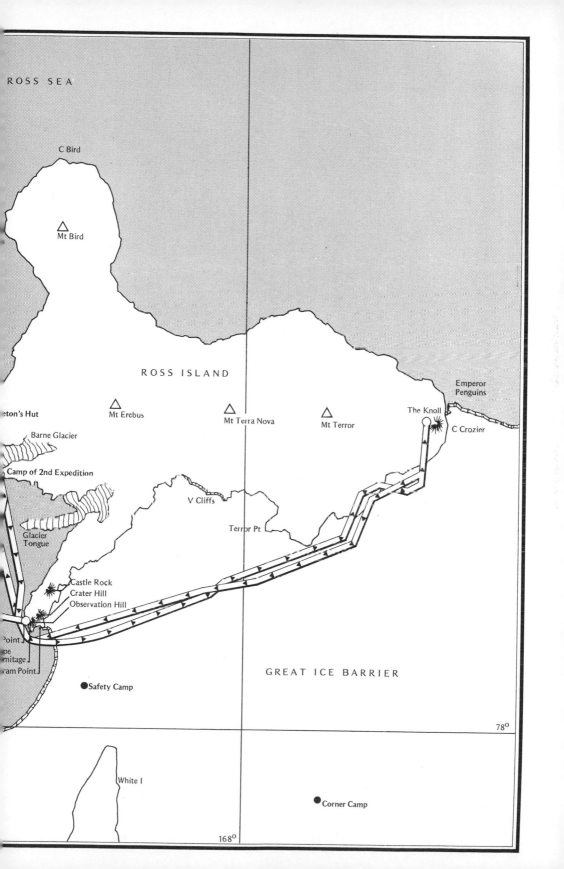

# Contents

# Illustrations

# Preface

What qualities does a man need in order to become a national hero? He must, in general – there are always exceptions – be a man of action; he must be brave; he must be bold; and it is a great advantage, if not a necessity, that he should die in the attempt to reach his goal. There is a touch of Icarus about many national heroes of the Western world. By such standards, Robert Falcon Scott qualifies for his place in this select company.

Each generation regards its national heroes in a different light, and for this reason, if for no other, his story bears retelling. The time that has elapsed since he and his companions died in the snow is very short historically, but measured by ideas and outlook, with two world wars in between, it is immense. To be first to plant your country's flag at the Pole no longer seems an aim worth dying for, much less to endure atrocious hardships in the attempt; so we seek subtler motives, buried in the character of the man himself. The quest for the Pole, or for some other harshly guarded natural feature, so the argument runs, is in reality a quest for self-knowledge. This theory can, I think, be pushed too far, and love of country as a motive be unjustly belittled.

Scott himself was anything but the simple, straightforward sailor-man, glamorous in his naval uniform and single-mindedly devoted to the cause of King and country, that he may once have seemed to be. He was a complex, self-questioning character more at home in Doubting Castle than in the performance of those deeds of derring-doe extolled by his mentor, Sir Clements Markham. So it is as a reluctant hero that he has appeared to me, but a hero nevertheless, since courage, endurance and steadfastness in achieving whatever aim has been set must be heroic, even by the standards of a generation which has down-graded heroism. His was the conquest of the self, a feat perhaps more admirable than the conquest of the Pole. I personally came to respect Scott but also to feel sorry for him mainly because of his self-dissatisfaction. It was, of course, his death that gave him stature. Had he returned safely from the Pole, the runner-up and not the winner, he would not have been awarded a place in the national gallery of heroes.

As Scott himself often stressed, the story of the two polar expeditions is not the story of one man, but of groups of individuals of forceful personalities and widely differing natures who succeeded in working together in their teams. Their mutual reliance in the strange, artificial and greatly testing isolation of the Antarctic is a subject of such depth and dimension, that only the fringe can be explored.

At the end of this book I have made acknowledgement to the many who have helped me, although by rights they belong at the beginning. To avoid confusion, all distances are given in statute miles (5280 feet); the explorers themselves often used geographical miles (6084 feet, equal to one minute of a degree of latitude) but had no fixed rule about it. Temperatures have been given in Fahrenheit throughout and money in the pounds, shillings and pence of Scott's day.

# Personnel of the British Antarctic Expeditions

## The 'Discovery' Expedition 1901–4

### R. F. Scott, Captain

OFFICERS

Albert B. Armitage, *Lieut., RNR*
('*The Pilot*')
Charles W. R. Royds, *Lieut., RN*
('*Charlie*')
Michael Barne, *Lieut., RN* ('*Mike*')
Ernest H. Shackleton, *2nd Lieut.,
RNR* ('*Shackles*')
George F. A. Mulock, *2nd Lieut.,
RN*
Reginald W. Skelton, *Lieut. (E) RN*
('*Skelly*')
Reginald Koettlitz, *surgeon and bot-
anist* ('*Cutlets*')
Edward A. Wilson, *surgeon, artist,
vertebrate zoologist* ('*Uncle Bill*')
Thomas V. Hodgson, *biologist*
('*Muggins*')
Hartley T. Ferrar, *geologist*
Louis C. Bernacchi, *physicist*
('*Bunny*)

WARRANT OFFICERS, RN

Thomas A. Feather, *boatswain*
James H. Dellbridge, *2nd engineer*
Fred E. Dailey, *carpenter*
Charles F. Ford, *steward*

PETTY OFFICERS, RN

Jacob Cross, *PO*
Edgar Evans, *PO*

William MacFarlane, *PO*
William Smythe, *PO*
David Allan, *PO*
Thomas Kennar, *PO*

SEAMEN, RN

Arthur Pilbeam, *LS*
William L. Heald, *AB*
James Dell, *AB*
Frank Wild, *AB*
Thomas Williamson, *AB*
George B. Croucher, *AB*
Ernest E. Joyce, *AB*
Thomas Crean, *AB*
Jesse Handsley, *AB*
William J. Weller, *AB*
George Vince, *AB*

MARINES

Gilbert Scott, *RMLI*
A. H. Blissett, *RMLI*

CIVILIAN

Charles Clarke, *cook*

STOKERS, RN

William Lashly, *LS*
Arthur L. Quartley, *LS*
Thomas Whitfield, *LS*
Frank Plumley

# The 'Terra Nova' Expedition 1910–12

SHORE PARTIES

Robert Falcon Scott, *Captain, CVO, RN* (*'The Owner'*)

Edward R. G. R. Evans, *Lieut., RN* (*'Teddy'*)

Victor L. A. Campbell, *Lieut., RN* (*'The Wicked Mate'*)

Henry R. Bowers, *Lieut, RIM* (*'Birdie'*)

Lawrence E. G. Oates, *Captain 6th Inns. Dragoons* (*'Titus', 'Soldier'*)

G. Murray Levick, *Surgeon, RN*

Edward L. Atkinson, *Surgeon, RN, parasitologist* (*'Atch'*)

SCIENTIFIC STAFF

Edward Adrian Wilson, *BA, MB (Cantab)., Chief of the Scientific Staff, zoologist* (*'Uncle Bill'*)

George C. Simpson, *DSc, meteorologist* (*'Sunny Jim'*)

T. Griffith Taylor, *BA, BSc, BE geologist* (*'Griff'*)

Edward W. Nelson, *biologist* (*'Marie'*)

Frank Debenham, *BA, BSc, geologist* (*'Deb.*)

Charles S. Wright, *BA, physicist* (*'Silas'*)

Raymond E. Priestley, *geologist*

Herbert G. Ponting, *FRGS, camera artist*

Cecil H. Meares, *in charge of dogs*

Bernard C. Day, *motor engineer*

Apsley Cherry-Garrard, *BA, Asst. zoologist* (*'Cherry'*)

Tryggve Gran, *Sub-Lieut, Norwegian, NR, BA, ski expert*

MEN

W. Lashly, *Chief Stoker, RN*

W. W. Archer, *Chief Steward, late RN*

Thomas Clissold, *cook, late RN*

Edgar Evans, *PO, RN*

Robert Forde, *PO, RN*

Thomas Crean, *PO, RN*

Thomas S. Williamson, *PO, RN*

Patrick Keohane, *PO, RN*

George P. Abbott, *PO, RN*

Frank V. Browning, *PO, 2nd class, RN*

Harry Dickason, *AB, RN*

F. J. Hooper, *steward, late RN*

Anton Omelchenko, *groom*

Dimitri Gerof, *dog driver*

SHIP'S PARTY

Harry L. L. Pennell, *Lieut., RN*

Henry F. de P. Rennick, *Lieut., RN*

Wilfrid M. Bruce, *Lieut., RNR*

Francis R. H. Drake, *Assistant Paymaster, RN (retired), secretary and meteorologist in ship*

Dennis G. Lillie, *MA, biologist in ship*

*and 27 officers and seamen*

# SCOTT OF THE ANTARCTIC

# 1                 Markham's
                    Choice

On 1 March 1887, a middle-aged geographer, Clements Markham, watched from the bridge of HMS *Active* a number of midshipmen preparing to race their cutters across the bay at St Kitts in the West Indies. The boats lay at anchor with awnings spread; the midshipmen, each in charge of a crew, had to get them under way and make sail, beat up for a mile round a buoy, down mast and sail, and row back to the starting point. 'The race tested several qualities,' Markham wrote, and it was a close thing between Tommy Smyth of the *Active*, Hyde Parker of the *Volage* and a young man from the *Rover*, aged eighteen, called Robert Falcon Scott. By a narrow margin, Scott won the race.

The four ships of the Royal Navy's Training Squadron to which the *Rover* belonged were cruising in the Caribbean, and a few days later their Commodore, Albert Markham, invited the victor of the cutter race to dine on board the *Active*. Here young Scott met his Commodore's guest and cousin Clements, who was much taken with the midshipman's intelligence, enthusiasm and charm of manner. 'My final conclusion', Markham wrote, 'was that Scott was the destined man to command the Antarctic expedition.' Destiny, in the shape of this vigorous gentleman with Mutton-chop whiskers, had laid its finger on young Midshipman Scott.

There was no such thing, in 1887, as an Antarctic expedition for Scott or anyone else to command. It was an idea – or more than an idea, a fixed intention – in Clements Markham's mind. If ever a great enterprise owed not only its conception but its whole existence to one individual, that enterprise was the National Antarctic Expedition of 1901–4, and that individual was the Fellow of the Royal Geographical Society, later to become its President, who stood beside his cousin on the *Active*'s bridge in the year of Queen Victoria's Golden Jubilee. And if young Robert Scott had not won the race he would have ended his career as he began it, a competent naval officer unknown alike to the outside world and to posterity.

The span of Markham's life overlapped the whole Victorian era. As a boy he saw Victoria when she was still a princess, 'at a great dinner given by William IV'. (His father, vicar of Stillingfleet in Yorkshire, was also a Canon of Windsor, and had no doubt installed his young son in a spectator's gallery.) When he was thirteen years old one of his aunts, the Countess of Mansfield, invited him to dine at Langham House. Here he so favourably impressed a distinguished guest, Admiral Sir George Seymour, that he was invited to join the Admiral's ship, HMS *Collingwood*, flagship of the Pacific Squadron, as a naval cadet.

Such invitations were then a normal method of recruiting officers into the Royal Navy. The procedure had changed little, if at all, since the days of Pepys, who had restricted the entry of 'Captain's servants' to four per hundred of the ship's company, or eight per hundred if the Captain was a nobleman; he also imposed a lower age limit of thirteen, or eleven in the case of an officer's son.

So young Markham quitted Westminster School to submit himself to a form of examination introduced only about five years earlier. Told to write out the Lord's Prayer, he got halfway when the examiner said, 'That'll do, boy.' A doctor punched him in the midriff and grunted satisfaction, and Markham was accepted as a future officer. On 20 July 1844, his fourteenth birthday, HMS *Collingwood* sailed for the Pacific where she was to remain for four years. The Admiral took his wife, four daughters, a six-year-old son, a full complement of servants, and a cow.

Soon after HMS *Collingwood* returned from the Pacific, a naval expedition – one of many – was fitted out to search for the remains of Sir John Franklin and his men who, in the vessels *Erebus* and *Terror*, had left England in 1845 to seek the North-west Passage, never to return. Despite expedition after expedition, the mystery of how and where Franklin and his company had perished was to remain unsolved for fourteen years.

Clements Markham was a restless youth who had formed the ambition of becoming an explorer. In 1851 he was serving as a midshipman in HMS *Assistance*, commanded by Captain Erasmus Ommaney, which in company with HMS *Resolute* sailed into the Arctic to continue the search for Franklin's remains. On board was Lieutenant Leopold McClintock, who devised techniques of sledging later to be used by Scott and others in the Antarctic. McClintock was a brilliant leader, sledger and explorer, and to the twenty-one-year-old midshipman Markham he became a hero, mentor and later a lifelong friend. His conclusions, based on great experience, were through his disciple Markham to have a profound influence on future British ventures into ice and snow. One of these conclusions was that, for long and gruelling journeys, trained, disciplined and fit men were more reliable draught animals than dogs. He did not reject dogs, and took them as auxiliaries, but reliance in the main on man-hauling, and the laying out of depots in advance of the main sledging parties, were two principles of his polar technique.

After repeated attempts to trace their missing ships and men the Admiralty gave up the struggle, but Franklin's widow did not. In 1857 she fitted out the little *Fox*, a steam yacht of 170 tons, and McClintock took her north into the maze of frozen inlets, bays, straits and islands beyond the Arctic circle to continue the search. Two years later, a party from the *Fox* encountered Eskimos who had in their possession silver plate, buttons and other articles that had belonged to Franklin's men. McClintock had hit the trail; skeletons were discovered, guns, a boat, fragments of embroidered slippers, and finally a record left by Franklin's second-in-command, Captain Crozier, which enabled them to piece together the tragic story. The two ships had been imprisoned by ice for two winters, supplies had run out, the leader – by then a man of sixty – had died on board, and the 105 survivors had set out on a hopeless attempt to march to the mouth of the Great Fish River on the mainland. In the words of the Eskimos, 'they fell down and died as they walked along' until the last man had perished. The mystery solved at last, McClintock with small, lightly equipped sledging parties carried out a remarkable series of explorations in the course of which he charted 1800 miles of coastline and travelled over 8600 miles without the loss of a single man.

On his return from the Arctic, Markham left the navy to pursue in earnest his career as an explorer, starting in Peru; but the sudden death of his father, which left him penniless, obliged him to abandon all his hopes and take a dreary job as a junior clerk in the Legacy Duty Office of the Inland Revenue. Undaunted, he got himself transferred to the precursor of the India Office, proposed the introduction of the Peruvian cinchona tree (from whose bark quinine could be extracted) to India, and managed to resume his travels by collecting and establishing the seedlings. Then he was loaned as geographer to the British military expedition under Sir Robert Napier, which marched across Abyssinia to the Emperor Theodore's stronghold at Magdala. There it inflicted a crushing defeat on the forces of the Emperor, who had imprisoned a number of British subjects in a fit of pique because Queen Victoria had failed to reply to a fraternal letter. (The Foreign Office had mislaid it.) Meanwhile Markham had married and been elected a Fellow of the Royal Geographical Society, to which he was to devote most of his immense energies for the rest of his active life.

In the last half of the nineteenth century the Royal Geographical Society reached the zenith of its power and influence, largely through its sponsorship of great explorers such as Burton, Livingstone and Speke. All over Africa, minor mountains, lakes and waterfalls were being named after its presidents while the major ones were assigned to royalty. Africa was all the rage in geographical circles, but Markham's interest held fast to earth's still undiscovered poles. He did not think much of African explorers anyway. Of Livingstone he commented, 'his expression was lowering and disagreeable. I did not think he improved on acquaintance.' Moreover he was 'not an accomplished traveller'. As for Stanley, he was 'a howling cad', and when a fellow-geographer protested that the Society was 'going down down down in public estimation' because it had given Stanley the cold shoulder, he replied, 'damn public estimation, the fellow has done no geography'.

Indifferent geographers or even howling cads as these explorers might be, they packed the lecture-halls when they returned to report their discoveries to the Society which, if it had not actually sent them forth, numbered amongst its Fellows leading authorities on every region of a world still only half-revealed to men of European nations. Hugh Robert Mill, its scholarly and distinguished librarian from 1892 to 1900, described its heyday in these words:

There was a rich fullness of life in the Royal Geographical Society in the early nineties of the nineteenth century . . . Sir Clements Markham, as President, over-flowing with enthusiasm like a boy, used to stage a series of brilliant evening meet-ings to commemorate the deeds of Prince Henry the Navigator, Columbus, Franklin and others on appropriate centenaries. The annual dinners, where Cabinet Ministers, great ambassadors, poets and social lions of every kind did honour to the Society under the perfect management of the unrivalled toast-master of the Hotel Metropole, were at first the glory of the year, though later the quality of the fare and the eloquence of the speakers began to pall, and the feast became a duty to attend. Best of all the functions was the annual Conversazione in the Natural History Museum, where the President received the Fellows and their ladies, and the Council appeared in all the glories of Knights Grand Cross or even in the awful dignity of the Orders of the Garter, Thistle and St Patrick. And in those days few of the Council could not mount at least the insignia of a modest CMG or CIE. Truly the Royal Geographical Society seemed then a goodly company; it was an honour to belong to it as a Fellow, a privilege indeed to serve as a senior member of the staff.

After twenty-five years as secretary, Markham was elected President in 1893. On assuming office he 'resolved that the equipment and despatch of an Antarctic expedition should be the chief feature of my term of office'. This decision he announced in his first presidential address in November 1893, and an Antarctic committee was appointed under his chairmanship. Years of discussion, propaganda and the writing of learned papers had preceded the setting up of this committee, and years of discussion, propa-ganda and detailed planning followed.

The question of a leader was obviously crucial, and for years Markham turned it over in his mind. About two things he was clear. Polar exploration had been a naval affair since the days of Frobisher and Davis,* and a naval affair it must remain. The leader must be a naval officer. And he must be young. Throughout his life, Markham had an almost obsessional belief in the importance of youth in matters of action. 'The fatal mistake', he wrote in his *Personal Narrative*, at the age of seventy-three, 'has been to seek for experience instead of youth. Both cannot be united, and youth is absolutely essential. Elderly men are not accessible to new ideas and have not the energy and capacity necessary to meet emergencies.' Moreover Markham saw the main object of the proposed expedition as 'the encouragement of maritime enterprise and to afford opportunities for young naval officers to acquire valuable experiences and to perform deeds of derring-doe'. The advancement of science he saw as a collateral objective, but 'geographical discovery and opportunities for young naval officers to win distinction in time of peace' were to come first.

Markham's friendship with his cousin Albert provided him with opportunities to meet and assess young naval officers in their early stages of development.

I knew well that it would be a dozen years at least [from 1887] before an Antarctic Expedition could be actually on foot. The midshipmen of the Training Squadron were, therefore, the future gunnery and torpedo lieutenants from among whom an efficient Commander of the Expedition must be selected. I cultivated their acquaintance . . . I believed Tommy Smyth to be the best man in the *Active*, though wanting ballast, Hyde Parker in the *Volage*, and Robert F. Scott in the *Rover*.

Tommy Smyth scored a black mark for throwing potatoes at his naval instructor. Not that Markham was against a display of high spirits, but Smyth's fault was that 'if anything happens, he takes the heaviest and biggest thing at hand and hits out', clearly an undesirable reaction on the part of a polar explorer. Robert Scott had committed no such indiscretion.

* Sir Martin Frobisher, first English Arctic explorer, who in 1576 discovered the bay that bears his name in Baffin Island, and made two subsequent voyages in search of the North-west Passage. He was knighted for his part in the defeat of the Armada, and died of wounds after an attack on Brest, then held by Spain, in 1594. John Davis, who on his first Arctic voyage in 1585 gave his name to the strait between Baffin Island and Greenland, on his second surveyed the western coast of Greenland and on his third reached a latitude of 72° 12′N. Markham wrote that he 'converted the Arctic regions from a confused myth into a defined area . . . He lighted Hudson into his strait. He lighted Baffin into his bay'. He was killed by Japanese pirates off Sumatra in 1605.

# 2 Going to Sea

By the time Scott joined the training ship *Britannia* in 1881, aged just thirteen, the system of entry into the Royal Navy that had prevailed in Markham's day had been revolutionised. After 1857, when examinations were introduced and an old three-decker sailing ship converted into a training vessel, cadets were put through strenuous courses in seamanship, navigation, elementary physics, astronomy, geometry and trigonometry, and in a few general subjects such as divinity, French, geography and English dictation.

This was a narrow, strictly practical curriculum, designed to turn out competent sailors and not educated men. Classical studies, literature, history, the arts in general were ignored. Scott worked hard and proved himself an able pupil. Shortly after his fifteenth birthday he passed out with a first-class certificate in mathematics and seamanship and a second-class in French and 'extra subjects'. The final report assessed his conduct as 'very good' – there was one higher category, 'exemplary' – and he was rated midshipman without further examination.

Life in *Britannia* in the 1880s was spartan, strenuous and spiced with danger. Sail remained the dominant theme. Cadets carried out exercises aloft in the rigging 120 feet above deck. They slept in hammocks; bathrooms were unknown; instruction was brusquely imparted by warrant and petty officers; as among all boys, there were bullies and baiters; punishments included beatings as well as extra drill. The price of survival was complete suppression of a boy's natural feelings of fright, home-sickness and lack of self-confidence. He had to learn to bear pain without flinching, to obey orders smartly, and generally to put away childish things. For a boy coming from a comfortable, indulgent home, such a plunge into the *sauve-qui-peut* of a naval training vessel must have been a traumatic experience indeed.

From all that can be gleaned of Robert Falcon Scott's childhood, he came from just such a home. His father, John Edward Scott, was the youngest of eight children. One of the four elder brothers died young, two went into the Indian army and one became a naval surgeon. Poor health as a boy exempted John from this Service tradition and he inherited a small brewery in Plymouth which his father had bought, in partnership with a brother, for £4782 out of prize money received during the Napoleonic wars. Both these brothers had been pursers, a branch of the navy more lucrative than glamorous; in their generation there were four brothers, and all became naval officers.

This particular branch of the Scott clan had been settled in Devon for about a hundred years. Tradition had it that a great-great-great-grand-father, Robert the first, fought for Prince Charles Edward at Culloden, and after the defeat fled with his wife to France. On the way, it was said, a son, Robert the second, was born in a fisherman's cottage near Leith. Some thirty years later this Robert returned, not to his native land, but to Devon, where he started a small school. He married a girl twenty years his junior by whom he had the four naval sons, including the purser Robert the third, who died in 1863 after siring his family of eight and leaving the brewery to Robert Falcon's father.

John appears to have been an amiable, self-indulgent character who enjoyed pottering round the home and garden which, like the brewery, he had inherited from his father, Robert the purser. This was a house called Outlands near Stoke Damerel, just outside Devonport, which had been enlarged into a miniature country property, with a creeper-covered house, a stream at the bottom of the garden, three large greenhouses, appropriate dogs, a peacock on the lawn and an adequate staff of maids and gardeners. John Scott held the office of churchwarden, took part in a day's sport with the guns in the company of his neighbours now and then, and cherished the heated greenhouses with their peaches, grapes and house-plants whose culture was dear to his heart. Altogether he enjoyed a respect-able social position and an income from the brewery which, while modest, appeared to be adequate for the needs of his family, and whose permanence and stability it occurred to no one to doubt.

In 1861 he had married Hannah Cuming, daughter of William Dennett Cuming of Plymouth, a Lloyd's surveyor, Commissioner of Pilotage, Commissioner for the Catwater Improvement, and a member of the Chamber of Commerce, one of a thoroughly respectable, solidly con-servative and reasonably well-to-do Plymouth family. The sons of such Devon families took to the sea as birds to the air. One of Hannah's brothers, Harry Cuming, became a Vice-Admiral. So there was a naval tradition on both sides of the parentage of young Con, as his family called him, from the last syllable of his middle name.

John and Hannah's family led off with two girls, Ettie and Rose, and then came Robert Falcon, the eldest son, born at Outlands on 6 June 1868. After him came a girl, Grace, then another boy, Archie, and finally Katherine. Con's education followed lines normal for a boy of his time and class. At first he shared a governess with his two elder sisters and then, at the age of eight, rode a pony to a small private day school at Stoke Damerel along deep Devon lanes innocent as yet of tarmac, motor cars and tourists. His sister Grace recalled seeing one day, from the nursery window, 'a small disconsolate figure, very tired, coming up the path'; his pony had run away while he was leaning over a gate, lost in his thoughts, admiring the view. Throughout his childhood, day-dreaming was a habit he strove to overcome; everyone, himself included, regarded it as a shameful weakness. He had another weakness, even more reprehensible: squeamishness at the sight of blood and of suffering in animals. This failing he never overcame, though he learned to conceal it.

As a boy, Con Scott was not particularly robust – 'shy and diffident, small and weakly for his age, lethargic, backward, and above all, dreamy' one of his biographers unflatteringly relates. Nevertheless his childhood was a happy one. The first five children were born within nine years and had no need to look beyond the family circle for playmates. Their pleasures were simple ones: climbing over a high, locked gate to reach the village sweet-shop, navigating the stream at the bottom of the garden in a tub, swinging from a branch of a holly tree to land on a parapet of the stables. It would be safe to assume that John Scott was an easy-going father, although subject to fits of temper exacerbated by over-crowding; Outlands had to accommodate not only the six children and numerous servants, but also an aunt who lived to be ninety-six, and Hannah's ailing parents, whose nursing taxed her strength and stole her time. When everyone was at home, the population of Outlands numbered seventeen. Con's Cuming grandfather died in his eighty-fifth year.

Hannah Scott won the devotion of all her offspring. To Con, she was always 'the dear Mother'. Some years later, after the family's security had collapsed, he wrote to her, 'If ever children had cause to worship their mother we feel we have, dear; you can never be a burden, but only the bond that keeps us all closer together – the fine example that will guide us all our lives.'

It is a pity that so little is known of what lay behind this stereotyped image of the good wife and mother. Hannah Scott had strong religious principles, never questioning the teachings of the Church of England and worrying sometimes about the spiritual condition of her eldest son. 'My own dearest Mother,' Con wrote on his departure from New Zealand on his last journey in 1910, 'I quite understood and anticipated your anxiety concerning our spiritual welfare.' The Bishop was to hold a farewell service on board and 'I read the Church service every Sunday on our voyage to Melbourne and I propose to do the same with equal regularity throughout the voyage. You need not have any anxiety on this point.'

She was a handsome woman and photographs display a strong, finely-shaped face with a wide forehead and a firm chin. It is difficult to see much resemblance between her and Con, except perhaps in the shape of the head and the wide, deep brow. John Scott shows in his photographs a spade-shaped head and a face lacking in authority. That Hannah, in her unobtrusive way, ruled the roost at Outlands there can be little doubt. Con's two elder sisters also had strong characters. This feminine influence dominating his childhood must have made Con's plunge into the starkly male, comfortless and harshly disciplined world of the *Britannia* a grim ordeal. It was sink or swim with a vengeance. There was, however, an intermediate stage when he left his beloved Outlands, his pony, the garden and the affectionate sisters, to undergo what might today be called a crash course at a naval cramming establishment at Fareham. This was Stubbington House, generally known as Foster's, which he left at the age of thirteen on passing into the *Britannia*.

He joined his first seagoing ship in August, 1883. She was HMS *Boadicea* (Captain Church), flagship of the Cape Squadron, and in her he served as midshipman for two years. For the first time he was earning money, about £30 a year, but was far from being a charge on the state, as his father continued to pay the Admiralty £50 a year for three years after his first appointment, and to find his uniform. Admiral Sir Mark Kerr, who passed out from the *Britannia* four years before Scott, wrote that in his first ship the messman was allowed one shilling a head a day to feed the gunroom mess, and that the diet was salt beef and salt pork (both mainly fat), pea-soup, cabbage and potatoes, plus cocoa and biscuits which were always weevily. Cooking was not regarded as a skilled job; it was not until 1905 that a system of regular full-time cooks was introduced into the navy.

Midshipmen were still pupils, with naval instructors as their uniformed schoolmasters. But they were also being initiated into the business of running a warship, and, above all, of accepting responsibility and discharging it quickly, efficiently and without fuss. As a fifteen- or sixteen-year-old, a midshipman might be put in charge of a shore-leave boat manned by ratings who would have to be rounded up, possibly in a drunken and bellicose condition, and returned safely to their ship, together with the boat and its gear. Should the weather change suddenly, he would have to decide whether it was safe to pull for the ship or whether to wait on shore, keeping control of the men, and on returning to the vessel he would have to justify his decision. If any harm came to the boat, he was in deep trouble. At an age when modern boys are practising sex rather than seamanship, he was discharging responsibility for the safety of men and of Admiralty property. Any uncertainties, perhaps panic, that he might feel had to be ruthlessly concealed. The ability to make quick decisions, self-control, courage and a nice balance of caution with boldness – these were the lessons a midshipman had to learn in order to survive.

These young officers got to know their men better than most of their contemporaries in the army, even more than those in civilian careers, were able to do. In *The Fleet That Jack Built*, Admiral Sir William Jameson wrote that midshipmen were 'up aloft in all sorts of weather and away for long hours in boats under oars and sail. In spite of rigid barriers, young officers learnt the lower deck point of view in a way which is often difficult to achieve in these more democratic days.' That Con Scott learned the lessons of his training thoroughly and well is indicated by the comments of his various commanders and his steady climb up the lower branches of the naval tree. The captain of the *Boadicea* noted that he had served 'with sobriety and entirely to my satisfaction'. After a brief spell in the brig *Liberty*, whose commander considered him 'a zealous and painstaking young officer', he served a year in HMS *Monarch*, whose captain also considered 'Mr Scott a promising young officer'. At the end of 1886 he joined HMS *Rover*, to be rated by her captain 'an intelligent and capable young officer of temperate habits'. These are standard comments, like those in school reports, but do suggest that Scott's character was being moulded to fit a system that was turning out, in the last quarter of the nineteenth century, young men of courage, integrity, resource and a strong sense of duty, fit to officer an institution that commanded the respect and admiration of the world.

The navy was then in an awkward transitional stage between sail and steam. Although by this time steam had conquered, members of the Board of Admiralty were still fighting a rearguard action on behalf of the sailing vessels in which their active lives had been spent. The handling of a sailing ship, they firmly believed, called forth in men qualities of nerve, courage, physical fitness and sheer guts seldom demanded of men in steamships. Shovelling coal into a furnace below decks was no substitute for testing a man's strength, wits and fortitude aloft in the rigging in the teeth of a hurricane. Also there were practical reasons for sticking to sail. The wind was always available, or nearly always, and it was free. Coal had to be transported to distant places which might be vulnerable to enemy action, and it had to be paid for. Considerable areas of the globe, the polar regions among them, remained without coaling stations, and so could be reached only by vessels able to fall back on sail when their coal supplies ran short.

The merchant navy abandoned sail with even more reluctance than its senior sister. In 1890, when Scott was a full lieutenant in a steam-propelled warship, his future companion Shackleton went to sea as an apprentice in a full-rigged clipper, and not until 1894 did he serve in a steam-propelled merchantman. The fact that Scott had done no sea-time in a sailing ship was advanced as an argument against his fitness to command an Antarctic expedition; he was the first naval explorer whose apprenticeship had not been served under sail. He was not altogether without experience, however, for HMS *Rover* and her fellow training vessels, while steam-powered, were also masted, and could be made to look, and behave, like sailing ships, by lifting their propellers out of the water and lowering their funnels out of sight.

After nine months in HMS *Rover*, Scott spent the winter of 1887–8 at the Royal Naval College at Greenwich, and in March 1888, when not yet twenty, he sat for examinations for his lieutenancy. He was awarded first-class certificates in pilotage, torpedoes and gunnery, and got the highest marks of his year in seamanship, coming first in a class of nineteen. He was commissioned as a sub-lieutenant and at the end of 1888, after leave and further training, he was instructed to join the cruiser *Amphion*, then stationed near Vancouver.

He had to make his own way across North America, completing the last stage of the journey, from San Francisco to Esquimault, British Columbia, in a tramp steamer which ran into heavy winter seas. Her passengers were mostly miners and their families bound for Alaska, who were either drunk or prostrated by sea-sickness, or both, and lay on the floor of the saloon in conditions of horrible squalor. One of Scott's cabin-mates – there were five in a single-berthed cabin – was a fellow-countryman named Courtauld-Thomson (a future peer), who, twenty-five years later, sent his recollections of the voyage to Sir James Barrie. His companion, he wrote, 'the jolliest and breeziest English naval lieutenant', organised a small body of volunteers and 'dressed the mothers, washed the children, fed the babies, scrubbed down the floors and nursed the sick', generally restoring order out of chaos and now and again quelling belligerent miners with his fists. 'Practically day and night he worked for the common good, never sparing himself, and with his infectious smile made us all think the whole thing was jolly good fun.' A quarter of a century no doubt added enchantment to the view taken by the future Lord Courtauld-Thomson of the sub-lieutenant's Boy Scoutish breeziness and *joie de vivre*. Scott himself did not find storms at sea, even in the comparative comfort of a cruiser with no drunken miners on board, to be jolly good fun. One of the few surviving letters of this period, written to his father from HMS *Amphion*, reported:

Everything on board was miserable. I was cold, I was dirty, I was slightly sea-sick, very homesick, hungry, tired and desperately angry – the wardroom was

upside down, my cabin was chaotic and stuffy.* In dull despair I sat myself in
an armchair in the wardroom and determined not to move until the weather
moderated. I should have kept my promise if the chair hadn't broken. I was
cursed by the infuriated owner.

This letter, and a fragment of an almost still-born diary, suggest a
different nature altogether from that of the sunny young sub-lieutenant
with his infectious smile and cheerful shouldering of responsibility
depicted by Courtauld-Thomson, and by J. M. Barrie in his oft-quoted
introduction to Scott's posthumously published last journals. This scrap
of diary, written in a log-book of HMS *Amphion* – thus dating it between
December 1889 and April 1890, when Scott was twenty-one – indicates
a deep malaise verging on self-hatred, a state of mind familiar to many
intelligent young men and women searching for certainties and getting
only dusty answers from an indifferent world.

'After many more or less futile attempts, I again decide on starting a
diary,' he began. The question was, what kind of diary? It could concern
itself with actions, or with thoughts. With youthful pomposity, he recorded
his decision.

It being therefore my wish in starting such a work (for work in the sense of labour
it undoubtedly is) merely to please myself, I make the experiment of transcribing
my thoughts, hoping that the disappointment that will necessarily meet me in the
inefficiency of my pen, will in some measure be compensated by the interest stored
up for future years, when the mutability of time, ideas and sentiments will have
undergone their common evolution.

Curiously enough, what most distressed him was not worries about his
career, about inability to cope with responsibilities, or to get on with his
fellow-officers, or about the lack of women and of almost any intellectual
interest or sensual pleasure, but about what he called the 'inefficiency of
my pen' – in other words, a lack of literary talent.

How much have I often felt the restriction. How I have longed to fix some idea,
only so that I may build from it – but though the words or general meaning may
remain in what is written, the attraction has vanished like some will-o'-the-wisp
and I find myself sitting idea-less and vacant . . . It is in the face of such difficulties
that I summon up my energy to control my pen. The vague argument that something must be done at some time to encourage an ability to express myself on paper
even as an ordinary gentleman should, urges me on; there comes too a growing
fear of my own thoughts; at times they almost frighten me . . . What a pleasure it
must be when the right word is forthcoming at the right place, or when without
trouble argument succeeds argument.

* Scott's appointment as acting lieutenant had by then come through; he had
therefore been promoted from the gunroom to the wardroom, and from a hammock
slung amidships to a cabin, albeit a very small one, of his own.

The rest of the page on which this was written has been torn out. The diary continues:

It is only given to us cold slowly wrought natures to feel this dreary deadly tightening at the heart, this slow sickness that holds one for weeks. How can I bear it. I write of the future; of the hopes of being more worthy; but shall I ever be – can I alone, poor weak wretch that I am, bear up against it all. The daily round, the petty annoyances, the ill health, the sickness of heart – how can one fight against it all. No one will ever see these words, therefore I may freely write – what does it all mean?

Either this heaviness of spirit, this sense of desolation, stifled the young man's resolve to get his thoughts on paper, or he destroyed the rest of the diary, somehow overlooking the first couple of pages.

How much this gloominess was due to the ill-health to which he refers, and what caused that ill-health, no one can say. But, despite appearances, this self-questioning, self-distrust and sense of doom ran like a deep current underneath the stream of action and the rapids of success for the remaining twenty-three years of his life. Concealment was possibly the hardest of his achievements. He had to learn to conceal, or to overcome, so much – as a boy, his dreaminess and dread of pain and blood; as a young man the terrible homesickness that (as this diary shows) had not been overcome; later, his poverty, the near-destitution of his family; always, his quick temper; and a streak of indolence which he believed he had inherited from his father. He was not a born sailor and leader of men; he learned to be one. Although he schooled himself to become an efficient officer, his disenchantment with the navy was no passing mood. 'The naval officer', he wrote some five years later to his father, 'should be provided by nature with an infinite capacity for patiently accepting disappointment.'

'What does it all mean?' A question almost everyone has asked in youth and whose answer was traditionally sought, in western society, in the teachings of the Christian faith. Evidently by the age of twenty-one Scott had ceased to find these answers adequate or convincing. A cousin who knew him well observed that he had never heard Con speak of God, only of providence. That he came eventually to believe human destiny to be ordered by some force or power beyond human comprehension is suggested by his writings, but he was never explicit; nor did he refer to a deity, or to personal survival after death, or to the great events of the Christian calendar. He seems to have occupied an uneasy stance between the agnostic and the believer.

Here was something else to be concealed, most of all from his mother, who had her suspicions which he did his best to dispel. Never a rebel, Scott took part in the religious observances forming part of naval routine without, so far as we know, any qualms. In any case he accepted the Christian ethic, whatever he may have thought of the Christian story. Sunday service was part of national and naval tradition and he believed wholeheartedly in both of these. In a percipient character analysis Louis Bernacchi, one of his *Discovery* team, wrote: 'Truth and right and justice were his gods, and these did not come from any religious sense. They were something within himself. He led a decent human life because he was a decent human being.'

To use a phrase of Samuel Palmer's, Scott was one of those who are 'double-minded – inconsistent with themselves', not through hypocrisy or shallowness but because the rationalist in him was at odds with the conformist. It is perhaps significant that among the few possessions he was to pack for his first southern journey – possessions so carefully rationed for weight that he had to choose between a pair of socks and their equivalent weight in tobacco – Darwin's *Origin of Species* was the book that went into his kit.

# 3 Family Disaster

After Scott's service in the Pacific came a brief spell in the Mediterranean in HMS *Caroline*, and then leave at Outlands, and the company of 'the dear mother', his four sisters and his brother Archie, newly commissioned in the Royal Artillery. Archie was a cheerful, good-natured, nice-looking young man, an extrovert in contrast to his introspective brother.

This summer leave in 1891 was probably the most carefree time of Con's life. On his lieutenant's salary of £182 10s a year (finding his own uniform) he felt himself at last independent and, while certainly not rich, able to dress decently and pay his own way. The brothers played golf together, took up riding, and with their sisters played tennis and sailed an eighteen-foot boat in Plymouth harbour and up the Devon rivers. Both brothers were proficient small-boat sailors and the girls took to it with enthusiasm, coached now and then by their uncle Admiral Harry Cuming.* Con at this period was 'very impressionable', his sister Grace recalled. 'The sailor's life and his romantic nature caused him to idolise women . . . His affections were easily caught though not easily held.'

He had decided to specialise in the navy's newest weapon, the torpedo, and in September 1891 reported on board the torpedo training ship at Portsmouth, HMS *Vernon*, for a two-year course. This was the kind of work he liked: precise, practical and forward-looking. He emerged with first-class certificates in all subjects and was appointed to HMS *Vulcan*, an experimental torpedo depot-ship stationed in the Mediterranean. She bristled with torpedo-tubes and other armaments, and carried six torpedo-boats on her upper deck. This made her unwieldy, and officers in more conventional warships looked on her as a bit of a joke. But Scott was enthusiastic. He was becoming an expert, and this gave him a new self-confidence. 'I look on myself now', he wrote to his father in 1894, 'as an authority on the only modern way of working a minefield and suchlike exercises.' Now, at twenty-five, he could begin to think of promotion. Competition was stiff and he was afraid of being passed over in favour of men better connected ('Stanley is a godson of the Queen, and son of the Earl of Derby'), or better at putting themselves forward. 'I am a poor

* Vice-Admiral W. H. Cuming (1832–96).

diplomatist ... Meanwhile things constantly annoy and irritate one – but as you see, I work for a larger than ordinary stake.'

Before the end of 1894, promotion had become not a matter just of gratification, but almost of survival. His mother had to break the news that the family was virtually bankrupt. John Scott had sold the brewery in Hoegate Street a few years before, retired to his garden and greenhouses and was living comfortably, as everyone thought, on the interest. In fact he was drawing on his capital and probably – though there is no precise information on this point – he made an unwise or an unlucky investment. Suddenly, the safe and ordered world of this united, mildly prosperous family collapsed. Outlands had to be given up and John Scott, in indifferent health and at the age of sixty-three, was obliged to look for a job. Hannah's reaction was, to an almost incredible extent, that of the dutiful, uncritical Victorian wife. In a fragment of diary she wrote:

On the 23rd October [1894] a crushing blow came of heavy losses. At once we decided to let our house and hope that some occupation will come that will please my dear husband and bring him comfort in the loss of his old house. On November 12th our dear Rose commenced work at Nottingham Hospital, under three weeks after the loss. The others all anxious to be up and doing are only restrained by the occupation at home in getting things in order for letting the furnished house. From Con comes a fine manly reliable letter offering help ... Truly sorrow has many compensations and with God's help we shall yet if He wills it return to our old home.

The house was let and John Scott actually did find a job, as manager of a small brewery near Shepton Mallet in Somerset. After an interlude on a Devon farm where, according to J. M. Barrie, when he was on leave Con got up concerts in which he sang comic songs, the family moved to Holcombe House near Shepton Mallet which they rented for £30 a year.

The three remaining sisters soon followed Rose's lead in seeking their own careers. The eldest, Ettie, aged thirty-two and still unmarried, despite good looks and considerable vivacity, had taken part with some success in amateur theatricals. She chose the stage, a profession not only, then as now, precarious, but by no means altogether respectable. She found a place in a touring company whose leading lady was Irene Vanbrugh. Not surprisingly, Hannah Scott was apprehensive and had to be urged by Con, who thoroughly approved of Ettie's venture, to go to a performance and 'yourself see her life'. The two younger girls, Grace (Monsie) and Kate (or Kitty) chose the more conventional trade of dressmaking, but even that had its dangers; they set up on their own in London and later spent some months in Paris. Once again Con had to urge acceptance on his mother. He was glad, he wrote, that you are beginning to appreciate that by this honest hard work the girls are anything but sufferers. The difference in them since they have been about, meeting all manner of people and relying on themselves, is so very plain to me. They have gained in a hundred points, not to mention appearance and smartness ... I honestly think we shall some day be grateful to fortune for lifting us out of the 'sleepy hollow' of the old Plymouth life. I am longing to see old Arch and tell him how hopeful I think it all.

The financial disaster of 1894 was followed, three years later, by a greater blow. In October 1897, John Scott died of heart disease at the age of sixty-six, leaving his family without even the support of his small salary. He had, it seems, no life insurance, and had taken out no annuity for his widow. Hannah had to leave Holcombe House and the family became, for a while, both penniless and homeless. Monsie and Kate had taken rooms over a shop in Chelsea; here their mother joined them, and the burden of supporting her fell upon her two sons, themselves struggling to live on very meagre Service pay which most young officers were able to supplement by parental allowances or private means.

Archie was in West Africa. After the family's financial collapse he got himself seconded from the Royal Artillery to the post of ADC and private secretary to the Governor of Lagos, Sir Gilbert Carter. The pay was better, and living expenses less. A year later he transferred to the Hausa Force, then a small body, less than a thousand strong, engaged in bringing law and order to warring tribes of the interior of the Oil Rivers Protectorate (now part of Nigeria); this was the precursor of the West African Frontier Force. After his father's death, Archie contributed £200 a year to his mother's support. Con's entire salary was little more than that, and, after paying his mess bills and finding his uniform, there can have been very little left. Nevertheless, he paid £70 a year towards his mother's support.

The period of extreme financial stringency on which he now entered must have pressed very hard upon a young man ambitious in his career, and with an appetite for enjoyment, companionship and moderate pleasure normal to everyone of his age. He had always been abstemious, but now so closely must his mess bills be watched that even a glass of sherry in the ward-room must have been an impossible extravagance, and the mildest of shore-leave carousels out of the question. Nothing would have cut a normal young man off from his companions more than inability to pay for a round of drinks or for his share in some outing or pleasure. If a game of golf was proposed, he would have to consider the green-fee; to take a girl out to dinner would have been impossible.

There was also the question of dress. Smartness to Scott was not a foible, it was a part of naval tradition, and to look shabby would have been harmful to his career. Whether or not it was true, as Barrie wrote, that the gold braid on his uniform grew tarnished, he must have had to darn his socks. To wear his clothes until they were threadbare must have been humiliating in a Service whose senior officers were in many cases rich and privileged, in nearly all were critical, and in some sartorially perfectionist. (In his day in the *Britannia*, Admiral Sir Humphrey Hugh Smith recorded – eight years after Scott served his cadetship in her – the lieutentants wore diamond tie-pins in their black satin neck-ties. Sir Algernon Heneage, when Commander-in-Chief of the Pacific Station, always sent his shirts to London to be washed, as did his Flag Captain James Hammet; neither of them wore the same shirt two days running.)

Poverty – and real poverty it was – can only have forced Scott to withdraw into himself; it cut him off from his contemporaries and encased him in a shell of reserve. 'Do you remember I warned you that secretiveness was strongly developed in me?' he was to write, years later, to his future wife; and again: 'Don't forget that at forty the reserve of a lifetime is not easily broken. It has been built up to protect the most sensitive spots.' The sensitive spots were his lack of self-confidence, his sense of inferiority, of frustration and of isolation, born of his youthful inability to hold his own with his peers because of lack of money. But never by any recorded word of his did a complaint escape him. Self-pity was not among his faults.

One factor remained constant, and was to remain so throughout his life: devotion to his family. After the financial crisis of 1894 he applied for a transfer to the second of the navy's torpedo training ships, HMS *Defiance*, stationed at Devonport, in order that he might be on hand to help arrange the lease of Outlands and his mother's and sisters' removal to Somerset. When they were safely settled he applied for another seagoing post and was appointed torpedo lieutenant in HMS *Empress of India*, a battleship in the Channel Squadron whose standards of smartness and efficiency left a good deal to be desired. The Admiral's inspection, he reported to his mother (November 1896), had been in general scathing, but flattering to him. 'It was remarked (though not by the Admiral) that the only clean parts of the ship were the torpedo department, and that also at drill etc: the torpedo department shone by a mere absence of doing wrong. Altogether I am pleased with my own show.' He had sixty men under him, and when he read the riot act to them 'they responded altogether'; they cleaned up their quarters and when exercises took place 'we are always first there. Nevertheless it is sad to belong to a ship which is so exceedingly backward and to feel that the main causes of the slackness still remain.'

Despite the ship's backwardness, life on board was by no means glum. 'I take the part of the *principal lady* in *Bombastes Furioso*,' he wrote, again to his mother. 'What do you think of that? A gorgeous golden wig complete with a complete dress made on board, stays, silk stockings, buckled shoes, sleeves with lace – splendid – you should see – and also you should hear – the rich falsetto voice.' The young naval officer in drag offers an unfamiliar glimpse of the future hero.

His appointment to HMS *Empress of India* lasted less than a year, but in the course of it he once more encountered Clements Markham, who was again on a cruise in the Mediterranean with his cousin. The by now elderly geographer had not forgotten the victor of the cutter race at St Kitts. 'I was more than ever impressed by his evident vocation for such a command' [that of an Antarctic expedition] Markham noted in his journal after this second meeting, which took place at Vigo in Spain.

In the summer of 1897 Scott was appointed torpedo lieutenant to the flagship of the Channel Squadron, HMS *Majestic*, a change in every way for the better. She was one of the navy's crack battleships, completed only two years earlier, of 14,900 tons displacement and of a class considered superior to any warship of any nation then afloat. She carried a complement of 722 men and her captain, when Scott joined her, was Prince Louis of Battenberg (later Lord Mountbatten). He was succeeded by George (later Sir George) Egerton, a man of great charm and excellence, who came to think highly of his torpedo lieutenant. When Markham asked his opinion of Scott's capacity to lead an expedition, he replied, 'He is just the fellow for it, strong, steady, genial, scientific, a good head on his shoulders, and a very good naval officer.' Egerton himself would have been Markham's first choice – 'the beau ideal of a polar commander, a born leader of men' – but for his age, at the time forty-six. Another officer Markham favoured was Commander John de Robeck, but Scott was described in his notes as 'the best man next to Egerton'.

Two of Scott's messmates in the *Majestic* were Lieutenant Michael Barne, of Sotterly Hall in Suffolk, and Engineer-Lieutenant Reginald Skelton. It was on Scott's suggestion that both these young officers were subsequently invited to join the expedition, together with the assistant engineer, Warrant Officer J. H. Dellbridge, and two petty officers, Edgar Evans and David Allan.

It was while Scott was serving in the *Majestic* that his father died. His eldest sister Ettie had married, a few months before, a promising politician, William Ellison-Macartney, MP for South Antrim and Parliamentary Secretary to the Admiralty. This was a 'good' marriage – better than anything she was likely to have achieved had the family remained at Outlands – and her husband reinforced the family's rescue team; he advanced a loan to enable Monsie and Kate to study fashion in Paris, and contributed a small sum towards his mother-in-law's support. Meanwhile Rose had taken the bold step of going as a nursing sister to the Gold Coast, later called Ghana, but then known as the White Man's Grave. She was to 'bank her own money for her own rainy days'. Some two years later (in 1899) she married Captain Eric Campbell of the Royal Irish Fusiliers, one of her brother's fellow-officers in the Hausa Force.

In the autumn of 1898 Archie came home on leave and Con took him for a cruise off the Irish coast in the *Majestic*. Con was enormously proud of his brother – 'so absolutely full of life and enjoyment and at the same time so keen on his job'. Archie was intending to transfer to the civil side of the administration; he had passed examinations in Yoruba and was hoping to become a district commissioner. 'He deserves to be a success,' Con wrote to his mother. 'Commissioner, Consul and Governor is the future for him I feel sure.' Little more than a month later Archie was dead. He went to Hythe to play golf, contracted typhoid fever and died within a week.

Bitter self-reproach worsened his mother's grief. She thought that his health had been undermined by going to West Africa in order to help her and her daughters. Con wrote to console her. 'Don't blame yourself for what happened, dear. Whatever we have cause to bless ourselves for, comes from you. He died like the true-hearted gentleman he was, but to you we owe the first lessons and example that made us gentlemen. This thing is most terrible to us all but is no penalty for any act of yours.'

The whole burden of the family support now fell on Con – or nearly the whole burden, for his brother-in-law helped as best he could. But he was not a rich man, his political hopes were to be disappointed and soon there were children to cope with. The first of the three children, a daughter Phoebe, was born in 1898 and when Con, on leave at the time, called at his sister's house at No. 4 Walton Street, Knightsbridge, to enquire for news of the confinement, he rang the bell and fainted from anxiety on the doorstep while waiting for a reply.

It was while he was serving as torpedo lieutenant in the *Majestic* that his third and decisive encounter with Sir Clements Markham took place. The incident is best related in his own words. When on leave in June 1899, 'chancing one day to be walking down the Buckingham Palace Road, I espied Sir Clements Markham on the opposite pavement, and naturally crossed, and as naturally turned and accompanied him to his house. That afternoon I learned for the first time that there was such a thing as a prospective Antarctic Expedition; two days later I wrote applying to command it.'

Sir Clements Markham recalled in his journal the young lieutenant's application in these words: 'I was just sitting down to write to my old friend Captain Egerton of the *Majestic* about him [Scott] when he was announced. He came to volunteer to command the expedition. I believed him to be the best man for so great a trust.'* Scott certainly needed two days to think over a proposition coming out of the blue and put to him, one may be sure, with great force and persuasiveness. 'I may as well confess', he was to write in *The Voyage of the Discovery*, 'that I had no predeliction for polar exploration.' His sister Ettie confirmed that 'he had no urge towards snow, ice, or that kind of adventure'. At this period, she added, he had grown restless in the navy and 'wanted freedom to develop more widely'. He had 'developed great concentration, and all the years of dreaming were working up to a point'.

Doubts of his own capacity must have plagued him during those two days. He was junior in rank, inexperienced, the Antarctic meant no more to him than Patagonia or the Mountains of the Moon. He had commanded men, but only as a cog within the great naval machine; as commander of a still unformed expedition he would have to design, programme and control the whole engine. Perhaps, in his heart, he would have preferred to continue in the well-oiled grooves of his chosen career. Yet, as his sister said, he was restless, and to turn his back on such an opportunity would have been, quite simply, an act of cowardice. For that reason, if for no other, he really had no choice. In any case, Markham's invitation might well come to nothing. The expedition was a project merely, not a going concern, and might be still-born. All he was being asked to do was to volunteer; others would certainly apply, and someone else might be chosen. Perhaps he half hoped that this would be so. The 'deeds of derring-doe' so romantically envisaged by Sir Clements had not, even in childhood, attracted him. To play for safety was the lesson life had taught. But he put in his application, went back to the *Majestic* and, so far as anyone can tell, thought little more about the matter for the best part of a year.

* There is some ambiguity about this. Scott said that he wrote to apply, Markham that he called in person. Probably Scott called to discuss the matter after sending in his application, and the two actions got telescoped in Markham's mind. Markham wrote his journal some years later and was by then an elderly man.

# 4 Markham's Battle

The story of Markham's struggle to mount an Antarctic expedition is one of hard slogging, frustration and delays. An explorer *manqué*, he found himself bound like Gulliver among the Lilliputians in a tangle of committees, deputations and intrigues. His aim was clear and simple. 'A dash to the South Pole is not what I advocate, nor do I believe it is what British science desires. It demands rather a steady, continuous, laborious and systematic exploration of the whole southern region, with all the appliances of the modern investigator. This exploration should be undertaken by the Royal Navy.'

What little had been found out about the Antarctic – and it was very little indeed – had mainly been the navy's doing, and Markham regarded this vast southern region as a naval preserve. Captain Cook in HMS *Resolution* (462 tons), accompanied by HMS *Adventure*, had been the first to cross the Antarctic Circle in 1773, sailing beyond the 70th parallel and, by the circumnavigation of Antarctica, exploding the myth of *Terra Australis*, a fabulous southern continent, the home of peculiar beasts and even, perhaps, of tropical forests. Cook's 'farthest south' record was beaten in 1832 by James Weddell, a sealing captain employed by the firm of Samuel Enderby and Sons.

In 1841 the navy's James Clark Ross, 'discoverer' of the North Magnetic Pole, commanding HMS *Erebus* and HMS *Terror*, became the first to buffet a way through the drifting pack-ice that surrounds the continent and emerge into the open water of what is now the Ross Sea. Beyond lay the rim of the great Antarctic continent which he claimed for Britain, and named Victoria Land. Rounding Cape Adare he saw, glittering in the unsetting summer sun, mountains which he named the Admiralty Range. As he sailed southwards, scattering names like the plates dropped from Antony's pocket, innumerable peaks, capes and inlets, seen for the first time in history by human eyes, came into view: Herschel, Northampton, Paget and Christie after 'eminent philosophers of the Royal Society'; Wheatstone after 'the inventor of the electric telegraph'; Daniell after 'my much lamented friend the late professor of chemistry of King's College'; another series after a number of academic clergymen; he named them all. (Ross was a devout man; the scenes he witnessed, he wrote, could hardly fail not only to delight the eye but to improve the mind; 'for how was it possible thus to admire the stupendous and magnificent fabric, without our thoughts rising in adoration of the Author, and Maker, and Preserver of all?')

Pressing south and naming more natural features as he went (Coulman Island after his future father-in-law, Cape Anne after his fiancée, Cape Wadworth after her uncle, others after secretaries, treasurers and plain members of the Royal Society and the British Association), on 28 January 1841 he sighted that active volcano belching smoke within whose sight Scott was to make his winter quarters. He named it Mt Erebus after his ship, and its inactive companion Mt Terror. On the same day the Great Ice Barrier – now called the Ross Ice Shelf – came into view, 'a mighty and wonderful object, far beyond anything we could have thought of or conceived', but a great disappointment; it blocked his way to the south as effectively as the cliffs of Dover would have done. This Barrier has often been described, but Ross's first impression can scarcely be bettered.

It presented an extraordinary appearance, gradually increasing in height as we got nearer it, and proving at length to be a perpendicular cliff of ice, between 150 and 200 feet above the level of the sea, perfectly flat and level at the top, without any fissure or promontories on its even, seaward face. What was beyond it we could not imagine.

No one was to find out until Scott's first southern journey.

Hoping to find a way through, Ross sailed eastwards along its cliff-face for some two hundred miles before turning back and passing by the bay which he named after one of his officers, Archibald McMurdo. After an attempt to reach the South Magnetic Pole he was obliged to relinquish 'the perhaps too ambitious hope I had so long cherished of being permitted to plant the flag of my country on both the magnetic Poles of our globe'.*

He returned to Tasmania, but only to refit; this indomitable sailor, said to be the handsomest man in the Royal Navy, made two more attempts in *Erebus* and *Terror* to find a way through or round the Barrier. On both

* A brief explanation of the magnetic Poles in simple non-scientific terms seems virtually impossible to formulate, beyond saying that they are the two spots on earth's surface, one in the Arctic and one in the Antarctic regions, where the end of a freely suspended compass needle will point straight down. The major source of earth's magnetic field stems from an electrical current system within the core of earth itself, but owing to little-understood variations in this system, magnetic Poles move about. The current South Magnetic Pole is in the coastal region of George v Land, but in a few years' time it will have moved on. The magnetic Poles are not diametrically opposite each other. Variations in the field have a connection with sunspots. Much still remains to be discovered about this very complex subject.

voyages his little ships encountered fearful storms and dense pack-ice, but their crews battled on undismayed, spending New Year's Day in 1842 moored to an ice-floe on which they played strenuous games ending in a fancy-dress ball. But the Barrier and the pack-ice, a thousand miles of it in places, defeated them, and they returned to Folkestone in September 1843.

Some thirty years later (1874) Captain George Nares RN took the first steam vessel, HMS *Challenger*, across the Antarctic Circle and through the pack; he was mainly concerned with oceanographical research and made no landing on the continent. A lull followed; attention was focused on the north polar regions. But Markham, together with several former naval colleagues, never let the matter drop. In his unpublished *Personal Narrative*, written in his spidery hand with frequent underlinings in red ink, he described the various efforts made to get an expedition under way, most of which foundered on a refusal by the Treasury to grant any money.

'At this time', he wrote [1894], 'I made a most serious mistake by inviting the Royal Society to join the RGS in their Antarctic project.' The prestige of this Society, founded by Charles II more than two centuries earlier, was immense. The right to put FRS after their names was the highest honour to which most scientists aspired, although a good many added other letters, or noble prefixes, as well. But prestige did not, as Markham had expected, bring in money. It led merely to additional trouble. Top-flight scientists were proud and prickly and unhappy in collaboration with lesser fry such as Fellows of the RGS. Their first response was to play 'a scurvy trick', in Markham's view, by sending a deputation, without informing him, to urge upon the Chancellor of the Exchequer the importance of a magnetic survey 'in the southern region'. The Chancellor 'snubbed them well and sent them about their business', but Sir Clements was snubbed too, first by the First Lord of the Admiralty and then, much worse, by the Prime Minister, Lord Salisbury, who 'regretted that he was unable, under existing circumstances, to hold out any hope of HMG embarking upon an expedition of this magnitude'.

Markham battled on, writing papers, addressing meetings, lobbying his naval friends, but all in vain. The Treasury would not budge an inch. He grew seriously alarmed lest other nations should rush in where his own was too niggardly to tread. Already there were ominous signs. In 1895, the Norwegian Henrik Bull, financed by the inventor of that deadly weapon of whale destruction, the harpoon gun, had landed a party from his whaler on Cape Adare; they thus became the first men to set foot on the Antarctic continent. Amongst them was a young man called Carsten Borchgrevink. Three years later, a Belgian expedition led by Lieutenant Adrien de Gerlache in the *Belgica*, with the Norwegian Roald Amundsen as mate, explored parts of Graham Land and spent a miserable year frozen into the ice of the Bellingshausen Sea. Then in 1898 Borchgrevink returned to Victoria Land in the little *Southern Cross*, 276 tons. He built a hut near Cape Adare, wintered there, landed on the Great Ice Barrier and made a short sledge journey inland to set up a new farthest south record at 78° 50's. A young Tasmanian physicist, Louis Bernacchi, later the physicist on the *Discovery*, was among his team.

Markham was incensed because Borchgrevink had persuaded George Newnes, the proprietor of *Tit-Bits*, to put up the money for his expedition. Here was a penniless Norwegian nobody – he had been a school-master in Australia – securing good British money, while all the illustrious geographers, scientists and gold-braided admirals had failed; it was intolerable. He was most unfair to Borchgrevink, calling him evasive, a liar and a fraud. The Norwegian got no thanks for having named an island after Markham. Evidently he had an unfortunate, aggressive manner – 'no one liked him very much' Mill remarked – and scientists recoiled from the bragging note sounded in articles (probably written for him) published in Newnes' popular magazine. He took with him seventy dogs, with two Finns to manage them. He had to wait thirty years for recognition by British geographers, when he received the RGS Gold Medal. He died soon afterwards.

Despairing of Government aid, Markham turned to private sources. In April 1897 the Council of the RGS, after some demur, authorised its President to appeal for funds, promising a generous £5000 of its own. For some time, fund-raising hung fire. Markham 'kept on writing letters to rich people' until suddenly one of them responded with an offer of £25,000. This was Mr Llewellyn Longstaff, a paint manufacturer living in Wimbledon. 'This noble conduct altered the whole posture of affairs,' Markham noted. The Prince of Wales, who had 'declined to connect himself with the expedition until public feeling was manifest', jumped on the bandwagon and became a patron, and the Duke of York followed suit. The bandwagon began to roll and the First Lord of the Treasury, Mr Arthur Balfour, made signs that he was prepared to climb on board. At last 'the Chancellor of the Exchequer yielded'. Mr Balfour received a deputation, shepherded by Markham, of distinguished men, and in July 1899 the Government announced a grant of £45,000, provided that private sources matched it with an equal sum. The fund then stood at £42,000. Markham appealed to the RGS Council and 'that enlightened body' agreed to find the extra £3000 needed to secure the Treasury grant. Thus did the pertinacity of one man, by then in his seventieth year, achieve the aim.

Unfortunately he now agreed to a step which turned out to be even worse than a serious mistake; it was a 'fatal error'. A joint committee of the two Societies was formed to plan the expedition, acquire a ship, assemble the personnel and direct the whole business. Its first meeting was held on 26 June 1899. The committee was much too large; the membership was thirty-three, and the Royal Society had managed to gain the edge with an extra member, seventeen of theirs and sixteen from the RGS. The chairman, Lord Lister, President of the Royal Society, was 'always courteous, never taking a decided line, and caring nothing'. The committee proved not only cumbrous but far from amenable, and Markham soon found that it harboured a number of snakes in the grass.

From the start, this joint committee was split down the middle on the vital matter of the expedition's primary aim. The scientists saw it as an opportunity for valuable research. Markham's view, shared by most of his RGS colleagues, was defined in his *Personal Narrative*. 'Collateral objects would be the advancement of the sciences of magnetism, meteorology, biology, geology; but these are springes to catch woodcocks. The real objects are *geographical discovery* and *opportunities for young naval officers to win distinction* in times of peace.' Fellows of the Royal Society did not see themselves in the role of snared woodcocks, nor the Antarctic as a sort of adventure playground for the navy's young men.

This difference, of course, involved the leadership. Markham had laid down in advance his qualifications. 'He must be a *naval officer*; he must be *in the regular line* and not in the surveying branch, and he must be *young*. These are the essentials.' Added to that he must have imagination and enthusiasm, be cool in temperament yet quick and decisive in action; he must be a man of resource, also of tact and sympathy. Markham believed that he had found such a paragon.

He now had to fight on two fronts. The Royal Society wanted a scientist as overall leader, but the Admiralty, or certain influential members of its staff, wanted a naval surveyor. Markham was against this because he considered surveying to be a naval backwater; up-and-coming young men went into the executive branch, and then might specialise in gunnery or torpedoes, where prospects of promotion were best.

It soon became clear that Markham was not going to get acceptance for his nominee without a serious struggle. The scientists joined forces with the 'hydrographic clique', headed by the chief Hydrographer to the Admiralty, Sir William Wharton, and backed up by his assistant Captain Tizard ('a man with a most forbidding countenance') to put forward their own choice. They did not object to a naval officer as commander of the vessel which would get the expedition to its winter quarters; but their plan was that, once there, he should land a party on the ice, build a hut and leave the scientists to get on with the job while he would sail back to winter in Melbourne, and return the following summer to collect the scientists. The commander's role, in such a case, would be reduced to that of skipper of a ferry-boat taking the expedition to and fro.

Their choice to fill the post of Director of the Scientific Staff was John Walter Gregory, an eminent geologist. A self-taught boy from Stepney in East London, the son of a wool merchant, Gregory had made his name by exploration of the Rift Valley in East Africa. At an early age he had become director of the geological department of the British Museum and had recently been appointed to a chair at the University of Melbourne. Markham, ironically enough, had not only supported his application for the chair, but had actually suggested him for director of the expedition's scientific staff. He was 'a little man with a very low voice, always nervously pulling at his moustache', according to Markham, 'and does not inspire confidence; but his scientific ability is undoubted'.

He may not have inspired confidence in Markham but he did among members of the Royal Society, and he was far from being an armchair professor. He had not only been on safari in East Africa's Rift Valley when it was a wild, unmapped and dangerous region,* he had scaled Alpine peaks and explored in Spitzbergen within the Arctic circle. Clearly he was particularly well qualified for the task in hand.

When H. R. Mill, offered a chance to visit Spitzbergen, sought permission to take his annual leave at a time when the RGS Council was in session, Markham refused in the words 'The proper place for a librarian is in the library'. Similarly, he thought the proper place for a scientist was in the laboratory, not out among the ice-floes in command of polar explorers. Always a romantic, he romanticised the navy and saw in the pick of its young officers fit successors to Cook and Ross, Franklin and Parry, or looking back farther perhaps to Drake and Raleigh. Such men were certainly not to be relegated to the position of skippers of ferry-boats at the beck and call of professors. Moreover, an expedition of this kind could have only one head. The recipe for failure, he wrote, was divided command.

The joint committee began its deliberations in the same month (June 1899) that Markham invited Scott to apply for the post of leader. Seven sub-committees were appointed, and the whole machine was soon bogged

---

* In 1893 he led an expedition of forty Africans from Mombasa across Masailand to Mt Kenya, which no one had as yet attempted to climb. In difficult conditions he reached the snow-line (at one point, at an altitude of about 15,000 feet, he carried a frozen Zanzibari porter on his back up an icy mountain face) and he made the first surveys of its peaks and glaciers. His small expedition set up a record by marching 1650 miles in just under five months, including the mountaineering episode. In a tribute to the steadfastness of his men he admitted, 'I had been relentless, and insisted on the caravan going on and on, stopping for neither rain nor flooded rivers, hostile tribes nor fear of famine.' His habit of collecting as he went earned him the native name 'loaded pockets'.

down in academic argument and irrelevant detail. At Markham's insistence, an executive committee of four with himself as chairman came into being. The Royal Society's representatives were the forbidding Captain Tizard and Professor Poulton from Oxford, a strong partisan of Gregory's, whose subject was 'the mimicry of butterflies'. Markham thought him 'a dull stupid man with a genius for blundering, and totally ignorant on every subject that could possibly come before the committee'. In the wings lurked Sir Michael Foster,* one of the Royal Society's joint secretaries, in Markham's view a born intriguer who would go to any lengths to keep his own Society on top and the RGS in its place.

Gregory was appointed Scientific Director in February 1900, four months before Scott became the expedition's naval commander. He himself was in Australia. Markham then sent a request to the First Lord of the Admiralty for the release of two young officers, one to lead the expedition, and the other to be number two.

The work involved in the stress of contest with the mighty powers of Nature in the Antarctic regions calls for the very same qualities as are needed in the stress of battle. Our application is that a young Commander should be allowed to take charge of its executive work . . . Youth is essential in polar service. No efficient leader of discovery in icy seas has ever been over forty, the best have been nearer thirty.†

Markham followed up his general appeal to the First Lord (Goschen) by a note to the First Sea Lord, Lord Walter Kerr, who was a personal friend. He put forward three names: Commander John de Robeck, aged thirty-eight, Scott, thirty-two, and Charles Royds, twenty-four. 'Lord Walter replied that the names were noted,' and consulted two of his Admirals, who opposed the release of de Robeck. The release of the two younger men, both considered to be 'excellent officers', was agreed. 'Lieutenant Scott would in the natural course be considered for promotion before long and would do well to command the expedition,' ran a minute initialled by Lord Walter Kerr. His release, together with Royds', was approved on 5 April 1900.

* Sir Michael Foster, FRS, 1836–1907, professor of physiology at Cambridge, and biological secretary of the Royal Society from 1881–1901. Later he became MP for London University. An impressive teacher, he was also an ardent gardener and bred hybridized irises.

† Cook was forty-five when he began his three-year Antarctic voyage, Ross forty-one when he discovered the Great Ice Barrier, Franklin was sixty when he disappeared in the Arctic; Markham thought his age to be the main cause of the catastrophe. Parry was under thirty when he led his first expedition into the Arctic, McClintock thirty-one when he set out on his first Franklin search, and forty when he solved the mystery. Nansen was thirty-four when he made his attempt on the North Pole, Peary fifty-three when he reached it – but that was to come later.

Sir William Wharton was extremely angry. He resented Markham's high-handed assumption of authority and his habit of settling matters with friends in high places over the heads of the joint committee, and said so in no uncertain terms in an Admiralty minute.

There is, as I thought, much indignation on the part of those responsible for the Antarctic Expedition at Sir Clements Markham's action in writing to the Admiralty on his own responsibility asking for certain naval officers. Markham has told the remainder of the Committee, of whom Tizard is one, that he did not name the officers, and that the Admiralty selected them themselves ... It is absolutely necessary to nip at once this assumption of supreme authority on the part of one man or we shall be led we know not where and come to grief.

Nipping Markham's activities was, as Wharton should have known by then, much easier said than done. An attempt was made at a meeting of the joint committee on 18 April 1900, when Markham informed its members that the Admiralty had agreed to release Scott and Royds. Tizard became 'very insolent . . . and then broke out against Scott, declaring that he could not survey, and that he was quite unfit . . . This was rather more than I could stand. In the evening I wrote Tizard a letter, giving him a piece of my mind.' He also wrote to Scott, still in the *Majestic*, warning him of what was going on. 'Of course they [Wharton and Tizard] cannot undo what has been done, and what all good men approve, especially the Geographical Society.' But they could make trouble and cause delays. Markham asked Scott for ammunition to refute the charges of unfitness and incompetency.

Scott's appointment now hung in the balance. At the next meeting of the joint committee (4 May 1900) 'a regular row' ended in the appointment of yet another committee, consisting of naval officers only, to settle the matter. It was equally divided: six on Markham's side and six of the 'hydrographic clique', who would 'strive to secure a job for the survey department with obstinate perversity'. He was quite right: when the sub-committee met, Wharton and Tizard 'put forward the names of officers in their Department, four, one after the other, who were unfit, who had not volunteered, and had not been asked if they would volunteer'.

The matter was now completely deadlocked and Scott, at sea, must have reckoned very little of his chances. As Markham observed in his notes, the only way the matter could be resolved was by the absence from a meeting of one or two of its members. Almost, it seemed, as if by the hand of providence, this happened at the very next meeting (24 May 1900). According to Markham, 'some of the clique were ashamed and stayed away'. This sounds unconvincing, and there may have been other reasons. At any rate, it worked. The committee divided and Scott's appointment went through. The fight was over. Next day, the joint committee unanimously approved a recommendation, proposed by Markham and seconded by Lord Lister, that Scott should become the commander of the expedition. On 9 June 1900 a letter was despatched, signed by both presidents, informing him of the decision. All Wharton could do was to add a stiff minute to the file (15 June 1900).

It must be distinctly understood that My Lords, in consenting to allow the two officers named by Sir Clements Markham to serve in the Antarctic Expedition, are not to be considered as making themselves responsible either for their selection, or that they are specially qualified for this particular service.

An admiral does not haul down his flag if he can help it, and while Wharton had lost the battle he was quick to see that, by joining forces with those among the scientists who did not accept an overall naval commander, a flank attack could be mounted which might well encircle Markham's forces and so win the war.

Three years earlier, a Set of Instructions to the future commander of the projected expedition, making his position as absolute boss crystal clear, had been drawn up by Markham. 'The scientific work will be under your immediate control, and will include the magnetic and meteorological observations, the astronomical observations, the surveying and charting, and the sounding operations.' He had followed almost word for word the instructions issued to Sir Wyville Thomson, chief scientist in Nares' expedition in *Challenger*; these had worked smoothly then and he saw no reason why they should not do so on the present occasion. Now his enemies, spotting their opportunity, began to re-write these instructions, eroding away the powers to be given to the naval commander.

In December 1900 Professor Gregory arrived in Britain to organise his side of the expedition. He, for his part, had no doubt but that he had been invited not only to direct the scientific programme, but to take command of a landing party equipped for wintering in the Antarctic with huts, dogs and sledges, while Scott was to spend the winter in Melbourne. Having written from Australia to the executive committee summarising his understanding of the situation, he had received a cable 'approved', and therefore regarded the matter as settled.

In London, he soon found that it was not. According to Markham, instead of busying himself with his scientific programme, he spent his time plotting with the hydrographers, the professor of butterflies and others to emasculate Scott's powers and virtually hand the whole expedition over to the 'conspirators' of the Royal Society, who were 'trying to burn *our* house down, to roast *their* eggs'. As to Gregory, 'I now found that he was a man of very nervous temperament, that he still suffered from tropical fevers, that he had neither experience nor qualifications for the command of men, that he had no head for organisation, and that a serious mistake had been made.' Gregory himself was annoyed because Scott had ordered scientific instruments without consulting the Scientific Director.

In the stately purlieus of Burlington House, scenes took place more appropriate to the managing body of an unsuccessful football club than to national leaders of science and exploration in conclave on matters of high import. These culminated in a tempest; Markham threatened to leave the room, there were shouts of 'then go!' and eventually he stalked out – to attend another meeting, that of the governing body of Westminster School, 'an assembly of gentlemen, such a difference' – leaving the conspirators in possession of the field. Gregory, newly elected an FRS, went back to Melbourne in April 1901 thinking his position secure.

Markham was no more prepared to haul down his flag than Admiral Wharton had been. He had behind him his Society which had put up nearly all the non-government money; it lay within their power to wreck the whole enterprise by withdrawing their support. Three admirals, including Markham's cousin, resigned in protest from the joint committee, and Markham refused to sign the new Set of Instructions, not only obnoxious in themselves but couched in 'damnably bad English'. Finally he called in Sir George Goldie, the founder of the state of Nigeria, who was to succeed him as president of the RGS,* to sort out the whole matter. This he did with skill; Sir Michael Foster, the devious secretary, deserted Poulton and 'ate his leek', and yet another committee was set up to write another Set of Instructions. These turned out to be identical with the set originally drafted by Markham.

So victory was complete. Before the conspirators were finally routed, however, there was an animated scene, with 'Poulton up and down like a jack-in-the-box, the bird of prey [a physicist called Buchanan] and the scowling villain [Tizard] on their legs, Sir George Goldie quietly dropping a little oil into the flames now and then. But the good ship was safe.' In May 1901 Gregory was informed by telegram that a new Set of Instructions was placing him under the orders of the naval commander, and asking whether he agreed. He did not.

* Sir George Goldie, FRS, (1836–1907). A Manxman who started his career in the Royal Engineers, he first visited the Niger region in 1877 and introduced orderly methods of administration throughout the territories. In 1900 these were sold to the British Government for £865,000, and became the Protectorates of Northern and of Southern Nigeria. There have been few more self-effacing imperialists than Goldie. Hating publicity, he wrote that the 'principle that has remained unaltered ever since I began to think' was 'L'oeuvre, c'est tout; l'homme n'est rien.' True happiness was to be found only in doing good work, in however small a sphere. 'Self-advertisers', from Caesar to Napoleon, he regarded as the worst enemies of the human race. Markham admired him immensely.

According to this [Markham's] theory, the position of the scientific staff is accessory and subordinate . . . Were I to accompany the expedition on these terms there would be no guarantee to prevent the scientific work from being subordinated to naval adventure, an object admirable in itself, but not the one for which I understood this expedition is to be organised.

So he resigned. In his place was appointed Dr George Murray,* head of the botanical department of the British Museum, on the condition that he would go only as far as Melbourne to give scientific advice and training to the other scientists, and then return to his duties at the museum.

Although Professor Poulton considered the loss of Gregory's services a 'disaster to the interests of science', and although the man who replaced him as geologist (though not as director) was not, professionally, in the same class, Markham was surely right in his main contention, that an expedition cannot have two heads and that divided command would have wrecked it. Gregory was an older, much more experienced man than Scott, in his field an eminent man, and one accustomed to running his own show; it was unlikely that he would have taken orders from Scott, and certain that Scott would not have taken orders from him on any matter affecting the safety and well-being of the men for whom he was made responsible. Nor would Scott have agreed to go at all on condition that the *Discovery*, built at considerable public expense for the purpose of Antarctic exploration, was merely, as a letter from the geographers on the joint committee put it to Sir William Huggins, 'to land Dr Gregory, leave the Antarctic regions altogether, and return to embark him again'.

Gregory may have been disappointed, but his career did not suffer. After a term in Melbourne he returned to occupy the Chair of Geology at Glasgow University for twenty-five years. He was drowned, at the age of sixty-eight, while crossing a river in Peru. Markham's unfavourable opinion was not shared by the *Dictionary of National Biography*, whose contributor described him as 'tireless in body, tenacious and indomitable in purpose, an indefatigable worker with a rare memory. As a teacher he was supreme and students thronged to hear him, whilst his stoutness of heart, enthusiasm and geniality made him almost fanatically loved by those who knew him best.'

Gregory died unknown except among geologists. Scott's name was to become a household word.

* Not to be confused with Sir John Murray, FRS, naturalist in the *Challenger*, who in 1893 read a paper to the RGS on the need for a new attack on the Antarctic, which Markham used as ammunition in his campaign to get support for a British expedition.

# 5 The Joint Committee

After his meeting with Markham in June 1899, Scott had gone back to sea, where he found his duties as torpedo lieutenant in the flagship of the Channel Squadron thoroughly congenial. He liked and admired his captain, Egerton, who was to become a lifelong friend, and found the admiral 'a very cunning person' with 'lots of sense, lots of nerve and means to be thought energetic'. Moreover the admiral had been 'exceedingly nice' about the torpedo lieutenant's conduct of an ambitious exercise involving an attack on the fleet by torpedo boats directed from stations secretly set upon shore. 'I am quite pleased with myself because it is the first time anything of the sort has been done for about four years,' he wrote to his mother from Port Mahon in the Balearic Islands, where he was at last 'getting really decent exercise . . . rushing about over the island on our bikes'. He added, 'Having now established myself as a competent torpedo man, my policy is to show myself able to do the general service duties.'

All his hopes were of promotion – might there be a chance that when the *Majestic*'s First Lieutenant was promoted, he would be 'shoved in as No. 1'? He appeared to have put the Antarctic project out of his mind, or at least not to have mentioned it to his family except in the oblique remark, 'I have my eye on another thing which I fear is a bit out of my reach.' He added (to his mother), 'I trust and hope that June will bring me to a greater dignity and a prospect of helping matters more actively than has been possible heretofore.' June was the month when naval promotions were normally announced and he was hoping, as indeed came to pass, that he would be raised to the rank of Commander.

By then he had been notified that the wider command was no longer out of his reach but suddenly, and probably alarmingly, within his grasp. What his feelings were we do not know. The waywardness of fate, the simile of fortune's wheel, must surely have come into his mind. Had it not been for that small, half-forgotten triumph at St Kitts twelve years earlier, and then for that accidental encounter in the Buckingham Palace Road, this extraordinary opportunity would not have come his way. Like a roulette ball, he had come to rest in a slot not of his own seeking. The hand that spun the wheel was Markham's. Any other man would have compromised with the scientists and the hydrographers long ago. The fight took a year but Markham won it, at no small cost to his health. In the middle of all the fuss he passed his seventieth birthday, recorded in his journal in the rather grumpy note, 'This is my birthday, aged 70, weight 86 kilos. No notice taken of it by anybody.' We may hope that his wife Minna* was exempted from his implied stricture, since they were a devoted couple. She had accompanied him on many of his botanical travels to Peru, India and Ceylon, and for holidays to Norway. To Norway he repaired to recuperate when the battle was over, drawing 'a long breath of thankfulness'.

Two days after Scott received his letter of appointment, dated 9 June 1900, he wrote a brief, formal letter of acceptance, saying all the right things: his awareness of the honour done to him, the hope that he would justify the joint committee's confidence, his gratitude to the Admiralty, and his belief that he could 'confidently leave in your hands my interest in a profession to which I am devotedly attached'. It was respectful without being obsequious, confident without being arrogant – exactly right.

A fortnight later, the two Presidents received from Scott another letter couched in very different terms. Instead of gratitude and dutiful hopes of being found worthy, there is a brusque, peremptory list of conditions to be accepted in advance of the assumption of his duties. These were:

1  I must have complete command of the ship and landing parties. There cannot be two heads.
2  I must be consulted on all matters affecting the equipment of the landing parties.
3  The executive officers must not number less than four, exclusive of myself.
4  I must be consulted in all future appointments, both civilians and others, especially the doctor.
5  It must be understood that the doctors are first medical men, and secondly members of the scientific staff, not vice versa.
6  I am ready to insist on these conditions to the point of resignation if, in my opinion, their refusal imperils the success of the undertaking.

Hardly the letter, one would think, of a diffident young naval officer newly presented with a plum which a few months ago he had thought out of his reach. He was threatening to throw away the plum before he had even tasted it. The intuition of a detective is not required to deduce the authorship of this high-handed set of demands; even the actual words in

* Minna Chichester was a great-great-great-great-niece of the explorer James Bruce of Kinnaird, who discovered the source of the Blue Nile in 1770. The Markhams had one daughter, born a year after their marriage, then no more children. The daughter never married, devoting her later years to good works in London's East End.

one case – 'there cannot be two heads' – are those of his sponsor and champion.

Scott's appointment came at a time when the joint committee's kettle was coming up towards the boil. The pro-Gregory faction was still endeavouring to procure for their man the necessary powers to make him the *de facto* overall commander. 'I was glad to find', Markham wrote, 'that Scott was quite resolved, from the first, to allow nothing of the sort.' Scott's letter laying down conditions 'gave me the greatest confidence in his firmness and clear insight' – hardly surprising if he had drafted it.

The matter settled, and his appointment to the rank of Commander gazetted (30 June 1900), Scott went on leave for a few weeks, and then started work by taking a course in magnetism at Deptford under the eye of one of the less excitable of the joint committee's members, Captain Creak. He then took up his duties first at the RGS headquarters and, soon after, at an office in Burlington Gardens which he shared with Cyril Longhurst, aged twenty-one, whom Markham had appointed secretary at £100 a year. Despite his inexperience, Longhurst was a level-headed young man who had evidently summed up his explosive, dictatorial but warm-hearted chief pretty accurately. 'You know the dear old man,' he wrote to Mill. 'When once he goes off there is no stopping him; he must say what he thinks and the damage is done. He is like a "doubtful" bottle of soda water.'

Scott was living with his two sisters and his mother over the shop in Chelsea, and started the day by trotting across Hyde Park for exercise in his tweed suit, high stiff collar – the fashion then – and well polished boots. He found himself plunged into a confusing world of administrative detail, ordering an extraordinary variety of stores and equipment, trying out samples, procuring scientific instruments, deciding on the best kind of pemmican, finding out where to get reindeer-skin boots – all unfamiliar, all bewildering affairs. He must have been conscious all the time that nearly half the members of the joint committee had strenuously opposed his appointment, distrusted his ability, and were still trying to force him into the resignation that he had, rashly perhaps, threatened if he did not get Markham's way.

Markham noted the effect of this unrelenting strain. 'It would have driven most men out of their senses. It had a visible effect on Scott, but he bore it all with a most wonderful prudence, tact and patience.' H. R. Mill, by no means an easy man to impress, thought that Scott 'if anyone, could bring order out of the chaos which had overtaken the plans and preparations'. The young commander, he added, had a most sympathetic character 'and we were friends at once'. Later, Scott was to write to Mill thanking him for kindness when he (Scott) was 'a stranger in a strange land'. The RGS's librarian noted with appreciation Scott's quickness in grasping the essentials of the sciences in which Mill himself was an expert, oceanography and meteorology, his industry in reading and absorbing everything that had been written about the Antarctic, and his energy in hurrying off to Germany to inspect progress in fitting out a scientific expedition under von Drygalski which, together with another under Otto Nordenskjöld of Sweden, was to go south about the same time as the British venture.

In October 1900 Scott and the Markhams went to Christiania (Oslo) to consult Nansen, then at the height of his fame and prestige. His vessel, the *Fram*, had returned intact with her crew after drifting with the polar current right across the Arctic from the Siberian sea to emerge, after thirty-five months, north of Spitzbergen, thus proving the Arctic region to be not a continent but an ocean. The *Fram* had been built to a revolutionary design, roughly like a saucer, on the principle that the ice, instead of crushing her, would lift her above the floes. This theory had been triumphantly vindicated and there had been talk of building Britain's new exploring vessel to the same design. But to reach the Antarctic the vessel would have to buffet through vicious seas, cross the 'roaring forties' and force her way through hundreds of miles of pack-ice, not drift along like a fly in amber; for this, naval experts considered that a sturdy whaler type of vessel was required, rather than a floating saucer. No one doubted the soundness of this judgement until Amundsen borrowed the *Fram* from Nansen and sailed her down to the Antarctic and right into the Ross Sea.

Nansen was courtesy itself to Scott, showing him his ship the *Michael Sars*, discussing equipment, telling him where to get it made or where to procure it. To Nansen's inventive powers were due most of the recent improvements in sledging equipment, such as lighter and more manageable sledges, better clothing, and the Nansen stove which excelled above all others in lightness, efficiency and economy in fuel. He was modest about his own achievements and wrote of the older generation of British explorers, 'Most of what I prided myself upon, and what I thought to be new, I find they anticipated. McClintock used the same thing forty years ago . . . No one has surpassed and scarcely anyone approached them.'

The two men took to each other at once. Of Nansen, Scott wrote to his mother, 'He is a great man, absolutely straight-forward and wholly practical, so our business flies along apace. I wish to goodness it would go as well in England.' Later, Nansen was to write of Scott, 'I see him before me, his tight, wiry figure, his intelligent, handsome face, that earnest, fixed look, and those expressive lips so seriously determined and yet ready to smile – the features of a kindly, generous character, with a fine admixture of earnestness and humour.' If Nansen was practical, he was also a romantic and a dreamer, and his writings are full of self-questioning, of mystical longings, unfulfilled hopes, and a kind of cosmic gloom often associated by non-Scandinavians with northern silences and Arctic winter dark. Such semi-philosophical musings would perhaps have been too fanciful for Scott, but he also had his dreams and visions overcast with self-questionings and perplexity. 'Ugh! these everlasting cold fits of doubt!' Nansen wrote. The same cold fits attacked Scott, who would have echoed Nansen's conclusion, 'Without privation there would be no struggle, and without struggle no life, that is as certain as that two and two make four.' The two men found themselves on a common wavelength. Only seven years separated them in age.

Scott absorbed with gratitude everything that Nansen told him and followed his advice. Many of his ideas came from Nansen – a windmill, for instance, for generating electricity, which was to fail in the *Discovery* but had worked well in the *Fram*. Nansen advised him to get dogs and he got dogs. He was later criticised for not getting enough of them, for getting the wrong kind, and for being half-hearted in his use of them. In fact he did what Nansen had done himself, and bought them in Russia. It was suggested that he should have got Greenland dogs, which were bigger and better. The fact was that Greenland dogs were by that time very hard to acquire. The many Arctic expeditions of the past fifty years had drained the supply and Eskimos were reluctant to sell. (Ten years later Amundsen, who achieved so many impossible things, got a hundred of them.) Nansen himself had sent to eastern Siberia and bought forty dogs which travelled for three months across northern Siberia with a herd of reindeer, crossed the Ural mountains, and arrived at Kharbarova, where the thirty-four survivors were taken on board.

Through an agent in Archangel, a Mr Wilton, the Russian who had collected Nansen's dogs was commissioned to buy twenty for the British expedition, in addition to a large number he was to get for a projected American venture to Franz Josef Land. He bought them from the Osiak and Samoyed tribes of Siberia and took them to Archangel where Wilton, who had been promised the first pick, selected twenty dogs and three bitches, and sent them to the London zoo where they were cared for until they could be shipped to New Zealand in the charge of seaman W. J. Weller ('fairly good in singing comic songs and plays the mandolin' Markham noted). As was to be expected, some proved better than others, but there appears to have been too high a proportion of duds. Scott noticed that they fell into three distinct types: the first a big, strong-limbed animal with a thick, short coat, the best puller; the second a short-legged, thickset dog with a long, shaggy, black-and-white coat; and the third a wolf-like beast he thought timid, cunning, suspicious and uncertain-tempered. With no experienced dog-driver among the personnel, it is little wonder that the British sailors had difficulty in forming this polyglot collection into efficient sledge-pulling teams.

Moments of relaxation were allowed in Christiania; Scott and the Markhams heard a famous Portuguese singer, de Souza; they met the composer Grieg, and the Duke of Abruzzi; and Sir Clements read a paper on Inca civilisation. Scott went on to Copenhagen to arrange for a supply of pemmican, and then to Germany to see how Erich von Drygalski's preparations to sail the *Gauss* into the Antarctic were getting on. He was dismayed. Here was no joint committee, no unnecessary delay, no intrigues and umbrage, no hint of divided command – von Drygalski was himself a scientist, so a Gregory solution, as it were, had been agreed – and no financial stringency; the German Government had put up all the money without demur. He could not but feel envious, and afraid that the *Gauss\** would steal the *Discovery*'s thunder. After his return he wrote to Nansen:

> As you guess I have been a good deal worried, but beyond what you may guess there have been annoyances that would be incredible to anyone who is ignorant of the conditions under which our expedition was organised. For whilst I have been trying to carry out the equipment with due care and on the precepts you taught me in Norway, a committee of thirty-two scientific gentlemen have been quarrelling as to where the expedition is to go! and what it is to do!! 'Too many cooks spoil the broth' and too many scientific men on a committee are the devil. But about all this you will doubtless by this time have heard from Armitage.

Although Markham was resolved upon a predominantly naval expedition, he did not exclude men from the Merchant Navy if their experience was likely to be useful. So he had invited Albert Armitage, aged thirty-six, an officer in the P and O fleet, to serve as second-in-command and navigator. His appointment, dated 29 May 1900, slightly ante-dated Scott's. A Yorkshireman, he had been a cadet in the *Worcester* (the Merchant Navy's equivalent of the *Britannia*), and when his company were asked to suggest a first-rate man and reliable navigator to accompany the Jackson-Harmsworth Arctic expedition, his was the name they put forward.

Frederick George Jackson was an adventurous young Englishman who had managed to persuade Alfred Harmsworth, proprietor of the *Daily Mail*, to put up the money for an exploration of Franz Josef Land, then

---

\* The *Gauss* sailed within a few days of the *Discovery*, to reach the Antarctic coast early in 1902. She was caught in the ice, and the magnetic observatory with which she was equipped had to be set up on an ice-floe. After great difficulty she was freed and returned to Cape Town intact in April 1903, without making the important geographical discoveries that had been hoped for, but having done valuable scientific work.

thought to be part of a continent which might, or might not, extend to the
North Pole. In 1894 Jackson had bought a ship, sailed to Franz Josef
Land, and landed a party of eight who spent three years in a hut within
the 80°N circle, shooting polar bears in prodigious quantities and carrying
out some scientific observations. Jackson took thirty dogs and four Siberian
ponies, but his attempt to approach the Pole was thwarted by the discovery
that Franz Josef Land was not a land at all but a series of scattered islands
that had been faultily mapped by their discoverer, Julius Payer. Armitage
was one of the land party, so he had three polar years to his credit. One
day, taking a walk with field-glasses, he spotted a dark object on the snow.
Scarcely believing his eyes, he dashed back to tell Jackson. A ragged scare-
crow covered in oil and grease, black from head to foot, was approaching
on skis. This was a much more unlikely encounter than that between
Livingstone and Stanley, but the interchange of remarks (as recorded by
Jackson), no less uninspired, achieved no immortality. 'I'm immensely
glad to see you,' Jackson said. 'Thank you. I also.' 'Have you a ship?'
'No, my ship is not here, only one companion at the ice-edge.' After a
pause, 'Aren't you Nansen?' Jackson enquired. 'Yes, I am.' 'By Jove, I'm
d–d glad to see you.' Nansen had left the *Fram* and her crew drifting slowly
westwards to make a dash, with one companion, for the North Pole.
Forced to turn back, they wintered in a tiny hut living entirely on bear-
meat in a latitude of 86° 13′N, the farthest-north record that was to stand
until Peary reached the Pole in 1909. They then proceeded on skis, dragging
sledges and two kayaks, having eaten all their dogs by then, across some
seven hundred miles of ice, hoping to reach Spitzbergen where whaling
vessels occasionally called. Instead they came upon Jackson's camp, which
saved their lives – seas unnavigable in kayaks lay between them and Spitzbergen – and they returned to civilisation in July 1896 in Jackson's *Wind-
ward*.

Armitage was therefore able to greet Nansen as an old friend when he
followed up Scott's visit to Christiania in order to obtain sledges, fur
clothing and sleeping bags. 'Armitage is splendid,' Markham wrote.
'Quite unperturbed whatever happens, he goes his way without hurry or
excitement, but with the most painstaking exactitude. He is universally
liked and respected.' Because of his polar experience and seniority,
Armitage had thought that he, and not Scott, should have commanded
the expedition, and for that reason he had rejected Markham's first
approach. Markham persuaded him to see Scott before reaching a final
decision. He dined with the family in Chelsea (May 1900), was charmed
with his host, and accepted. 'I never met a more delightful man than Scott
to work with,' he wrote. At first he appeared to bear no resentment for
having to accept a subordinate position, which he agreed freely to do;

yet concealed on those broad, square shoulders lay a chip that never disappeared, but on the contrary, as years went by, grew heavier and more burdensome.

The doctor on Jackson's expedition had been Reginald Koettlitz, over six feet tall and with drooping moustaches, of German extraction but trained at Guy's Hospital and afterwards in practice in Dover. His appointment, made in 1900 when he was thirty-nine, also ante-dated Scott's. Markham thought him 'a very honest good fellow, but exceedingly short of commonsense', and with no sense of humour. Koettlitz's views on the major medical problem of all polar expeditions were in line with orthodox opinion at the time. Scurvy, he believed, was caused by a poison resulting from the putrefaction of preserved food, and the way to guard against it was to make sure that the food was absolutely pure, and the tins absolutely airtight.

Far and away the most successful polar explorer in avoiding scurvy amongst his crew had been Captain Cook. Fresh lemons are generally thought to have been his main prophylactic, but he also insisted on his men eating onions, fresh meat and vegetables when available, and sauerkraut. His method of persuading the men to take to unfamiliar sauerkraut was typical. He had it served only to officers, who sang its praises so effectively that the seamen began to clamour for it too, and liked it so well that it was soon being rationed. His well-known kindness and consideration had an occasional lapse, however; two men were flogged for refusing fresh meat.

By Koettlitz's time, medical opinion about scurvy, despite Cook's experience, held to the theory of contamination by some 'taint'.* In a letter to *Guy's Hospital Gazette* (March 1901) Koettlitz averred that there were no such substances as anti-scorbutics, and that it was waste of time to look for them; all that was needed was to use food free from 'scorbutic properties'. In the same journal and in the same year Dr G. Newton Pitt suggested as the cause of scurvy an absence of some essential property in food, not the presence in it of a 'taint'. Jackson's land party, he wrote, Koettlitz included, had avoided scurvy by eating plenty of fresh bear meat, not by avoiding 'tainted' food. It was, perhaps, a pity that Dr Newton Pitt

* The suspicion that certain diseases, scurvy among them, resulted from deficiencies in diet, was not confirmed until experiments with living animals were devised. In 1912, symptoms of scurvy were produced in guinea pigs by withholding fresh plant food. Sir Gowland Hopkins (1861–1947) is generally considered to be the principal discoverer of vitamins; in a paper published in 1912 in the *Journal of Physiology* he gave precision and focus to the various theories of deficiency diseases. The isolation of an anti-scorbic compound (ascorbic acid) by C. King and W. Waugh did not occur until 1932. Most animals can synthesize vitamin C for themselves, but not men, monkeys or guinea pigs.

was not appointed surgeon in place of Dr Koettlitz. However, most polar explorers, including Scott and his men, reached the right conclusion for the wrong reasons, and came to insist on fresh meat.

For the post of assistant surgeon, the choice fell on a young man, recently qualified at St George's Hospital, with a singular talent for drawing and painting in water-colour, a deeply religious temperament, and a passion for birds. This was Dr Edward Adrian Wilson, son of a Cheltenham doctor. Too much bird-watching at night in wet woods and on chilly commons, too much starving himself to give money to beggars or to buy books, too much burning midnight oil to make up for time spent in art galleries, and possibly too much smoking, his sole self-indulgence, had ruined his health. He contracted pulmonary tuberculosis and spent two years in Norway and then in a Swiss sanatorium, which arrested the disease; but no sooner had he begun his duties as junior house surgeon than blood poisoning resulted in a dangerous and acutely painful abscess in the armpit. He met Scott in November 1900 with his arm in a sling. Scott engaged him on the spot but he still had to pass an Admiralty Medical Board. His first attempt failed and the second Board, held only a few weeks before the *Discovery* sailed, reported, 'Mr E. A. Wilson unfit on account of disease in the right lung'. There is a note in Markham's papers, 'nevertheless Scott said he *must* have him and took him'. Wilson himself was determined to go. 'I quite realise it will be kill or cure, and have made up my mind that it will be cure.'

The three naval officers – Charles Royds, Michael Barne and Reginald Skelton – were appointed about the same time as Scott, but three scientific posts remained to be filled. That of 'naturalist' was offered to a Scot, W. S. Bruce, but he was organising an all-Scottish expedition of his own and refused. (This sailed in the *Scotia* in 1902.) An experienced marine biologist, Thomas Vere Hodgson, director of the marine biological laboratories in Plymouth, was chosen. ('Young to have a polished bald head,' Markham noted, 'sometimes needing a skull cap, but otherwise apparently strong and healthy.') By contrast the geologist had no experience at all. Hartley Ferrar, aged twenty-two, was just down from Cambridge with an honours degree and a cap for rowing; in fact he was at Henley regatta when the telegram appointing him arrived. Irish by birth, brought up partly in South Africa, he was, Markham thought, capable, but 'very young, very unfledged, and rather lazy'; if sufficiently sat on by 'the young lieutenants', he might be 'made into a man in this ship'.

The physicist was Louis Bernacchi, aged twenty-five, such a last-minute appointment that he could not sail with the *Discovery* but joined her in New Zealand. His had been a tough, adventurous boyhood spent on a mountainous island uninhabited save for his family and their dependants, which his father, a silk merchant from Lombardy, had bought from the Tasmanian Government for £20,000. He had studied physics and astronomy at the Melbourne Observatory and, alone among the party, possessed Antarctic experience, having spent two years with the suspect Borchgrevink in his hut on Cape Adare. 'Always grown-up – never a boy' was Markham's comment.

Finally there was Ernest Shackleton, another Merchant Navy officer, another Irishman, another doctor's son, another young man – twenty-six. But, unlike the others, no one had invited him to volunteer. He pushed his way in. Having gone to sea at the age of sixteen as an apprentice in a sailing vessel – her captain considered him 'the most pig-headed, obstinate boy I ever came across' – he had worked his way up to the position of third officer in a Union Castle liner, become engaged to be married, and told his future father-in-law 'my fortune is all to make but I intend to make it quickly'. An Antarctic expedition might not make his fortune, but it was an opportunity to make his mark, a way out of the rut. He was very ambitious. Like Scott, he had no special interest in the polar regions; unlike Scott, no predilection for scientific research. He applied to join the expedition but was turned down. It so happened that Llewellyn Longstaff, who had been the first to give financial backing to the expedition, had a son who was a passenger to Cape Town in the liner in which Shackleton served. During the voyage the two men became friendly and, through young Longstaff's intercession, Shackleton secured an interview with Armitage. The second-in-command took to him and recommended him to Scott, who in February 1901 appointed him third lieutenant in charge of holds, stores, provisions and deep sea water analysis. 'His brother officers considered him a very good fellow,' Armitage wrote, 'always quoting poetry and full of erratic ideas.' Markham at first thought him 'a marvel of intelligent energy'. Later, Shackleton was to sink in his estimation very nearly, if not quite, to the level of a howling cad.

That completed the tally of officers and scientists. In addition the navy, with considerable reluctance, released three warrant officers and six petty officers, including Edgar Evans and David Allan from the *Majestic*. For the ratings, Scott's method of selection was simple but effective. He wrote to friends in the Channel Squadron asking them to call for volunteers, and then to select one or two of the best. By this method Scott ensured that he would get not only good men, but men accustomed to naval discipline. He admitted frankly that he did not trust his own ability to command men of any other background. The *Discovery* was to sail under the Merchant Shipping Act, whose rules of conduct were considerably less strict than those imposed in warships by the Naval Discipline Act. He believed that if he had a naval crew, they would go on behaving as if they were still under naval discipline, and he proved correct. 'We lived exactly as though the ship and all aboard had been under the Naval Discipline Act', he wrote, 'and as everyone must have been aware that this pleasing state of affairs was a fiction, the men deserve as much credit as the officers, if not more, for the fact that it continued to be observed.'

# 6   Scientists and Sailors

The *Discovery*, meanwhile, was being built at Dundee. She was the first ship ever purpose-built in Britain for scientific work. It would have been cheaper to buy and convert a whaler, but not so satisfactory; the *Discovery* was to be something special. She was the sixth of her name.

To build her was by no means easy. To start with, she had to be a wooden ship. Wood will give before the pressure of ice, while steel will buckle. The skills of building wooden ships were all but forgotten – the men who knew how to build them were either dead or very old. She had to be basically a sailing ship, with auxiliary engines. No such vessel had been laid down for years. It was a formidable task, but one that Markham relished. Like most old sailors, his heart was in sail. He called into being a committee consisting of Sir Leopold McClintock, Sir Anthony Hoskins, his own cousin Albert and other old salts, and they entrusted the design to Mr W. E. Smith, Chief Constructor at the Admiralty, who had built wooden ships before.

The ship was to be exceptionally strong, built of a variety of timbers: English oak for the frames, eleven inches thick; Riga fir for the lining, eleven inches; Honduras mahogany, pitch pine or oak for the four-inch-thick lining, all sheathed with two layers of planking – twenty-six inches of solid wood in all. Her enormously strong projecting bow was designed to force its way through pack-ice, acting as an ice-breaker; some of the bolts running through the wood were eight and a half feet long. An overhanging stern gave protection to the rudder and screw.

An added complication was the provision on deck of a magnetic laboratory. No steel or iron was to be allowed within thirty feet of it in any direction. Copper had to replace the iron normally used; part of the rigging had to be made of specially woven hemp; even iron-shod cushion buttons had to be removed in favour of lead ones. There was to be a moment of consternation in New Zealand when it was discovered that a parrot was hanging in an iron cage within the magic circle. Fuel, oil, coal – 350 tons of it – fresh water, dog-food, medical supplies, scientific instruments (lent, no doubt with reluctance, by Admiral Wharton), axes and saws, a sectional wooden hut, a piano, a library – there was no end to the things that had to be made room for in a vessel 172 feet long and 34 feet wide, of 485 tons register and a displacement of 1620 tons.

Tenders were invited but only two received. These were thought to be outrageous and the managing director of the most likely company was summoned to London, to be beaten down to an estimate of £43,750. On 14 December 1899 a contract with the Dundee Ship Building Company was signed. The ship's keel was laid on 16 March 1900 and her final cost, with engines, came out at £49,277. Scott delegated the task of keeping an eye on the building to Skelton and Royds, but visited the dockyard from time to time. On one occasion, he escaped death literally by inches. A cable snapped and a heavy pulley crashed down on to the spot where he had been standing until a moment before. Mr Smith had just advised him to step aside.

By November 1900 Markham had decided that the cluster of sub-committees spawned by the hated joint committee must go, leaving the commander free to do his job without interference and delays. After consulting with Markham, Scott drew up a detailed plan of how the sum available, some £93,000, was to be spent, under six different heads: the ship, the ship's engines, wages and salaries, provisions and clothing, travelling and shore equipment, and ship's furniture. Against each head a sum was fixed and Scott was given power to spend up to that sum, supervised only by a finance committee of four, two from each Society. This streamlined system worked well and Scott was now free to go ahead and get the expedition ready in a little over six months, a truly monumental task.

He was still nagged by insecurity. Opposition to him was mounting. Gregory arrived from Australia and it looked more and more as if he might have to make good his threat to resign. 'Scott's position was not safe,' Markham noted, 'and he was kept on tenter-hooks of anxiety.' On 9 February 1901 Armitage received a message asking him to come to Scott's home at 80 Hospital Road, Chelsea. 'Things are now in a condition from which I can see no way out but resignation,' Scott wrote. 'I should be glad therefore to explain the situation to you.' Armitage found him 'very much depressed', and resolved to hand over to his second-in-command and withdraw from the scene. Armitage persuaded him to think it over and meet himself and Markham next day, when, as Armitage recorded, they 'had a pow-wow over it, and the two of us got Scott to stick to his guns'.

He did stick to them, but cannot have enjoyed it. This year of tribulation strengthened his self-control, stiffened his shell of reserve, sharpened his powers of concentration. It did not sour him. Markham, of course a partial observer, wrote of him at this time,

Scott had an unprecedentedly difficult task before him. A young officer, with everything to learn, he showed a grasp of the general problem, as well as of all the intricate details, which was most remarkable. He brought to the work a very able and capable mind, a sound and clear judgement, and an excellent memory. He showed unfailing tact and most conciliatory bearing, combined with firmness and resolution when necessary. He is an admirable organiser, a born leader of men, sympathetic, and full of forethought and anxiety to meet all the reasonable wishes of his gallant companions. Above all Scott has the instincts of a perfect gentleman.

Even his relaxations cannot have been very relaxing. In the midst of the turmoil he was a guest at a grand dinner arranged by Markham for 270 Fellows of his Society and sat next to the Duke of Northumberland. In one respect, at least, his anxieties were lightened. His salary as the expedition's commander was £500 a year on top of his naval pay, at a reduced rate while on 'harbour time' until the expedition sailed, and then at full 'sea time' rates. He was thus able to help his mother to an extent which prompted her to write, when on holiday in Normandy, 'you have surrounded me with all the comfort I can possibly want, and I have the constant knowledge of your great love'.

On 21 March 1901 Lady Markham, with a pair of golden scissors, cut the tape and the *Discovery* slid into the Tay, 'a beautiful sight' in her husband's eyes. Early in June the vessel berthed at the East India dock in the Thames. Then came the tedious business of getting everything sorted and stowed. There was a lot to stow. Forty-seven hefty men eat, drink and need a lot in three years, and there was to be no question of short commons on board: 150 tons of roast pheasant, 500 of roast turkey, whole roast partridges, jugged hare, duck and green peas, rump steak, and frills like wild cherry sauce, celery seed, blackcurrant vinegar, candied orange peel, Stilton and Double Gloucester cheese. Nor were they to go short of drink with twenty-seven gallons of brandy, the same of whisky, sixty cases of port, thirty-six of sherry, twenty-eight of champagne. Also lime juice, 1800 pounds of tobacco, a great deal of pemmican (a mixture of dried lean beef and lard), raisins, chocolate and onion powder. The tinned food was examined with meticulous care and a good deal was rejected – tins labelled plaice were found to contain onions, parsnips to be masquerading as plum pudding, and many had just gone bad.

Small but important items were the sledging flags. Each officer and scientist was to have his personal swallowtail pennant with motto, designed by Markham. These were relics, Markham said, of the days of chivalry, and previous polar expeditions had attached flags to their sledges when they set forth on their journeys. The motto he provided for Scott was 'Ready, Aye Ready'; for Royds, 'Semper Paratus'; for Shackleton, 'Fortitudine Vincimus'; for Koettlitz, 'Nil Sine Labore'; Wilson's struck a gayer note with 'Le Bon Temps Viendra'. Markham also drew up pedigrees. Shackleton's went back no farther than 1610. Royds' did better, leading through the female line to a John Rawson whose family had owned land in Yorkshire before the Norman Conquest. Barne's, however, was the champion; his mother was Lady Constance Seymour, a daughter of the Marquis of Hertford, and his pedigree went right off the top of the page and down the other side to arrive at Alfred the Great. No one else, Scott included, could provide material for a family tree.

While the *Discovery* was being made ready, visitors poured on board to see her. Two former colleagues of Sir James Clark Ross were among them: Sir Erasmus Ommaney, aged eighty-seven, who had sailed with Ross into the Arctic in 1835, and the famous botanist Sir Joseph Hooker,* who urged upon Scott the desirability of taking a balloon to make aerial surveys. No one had previously thought of a balloon, but advice from such a quarter could not be ignored, and with considerable difficulty an extra £1300 was found – an appeal to the public produced only £80 – a balloon was bought from the army, and Skelton, Shackleton and two ratings went to Aldershot for a brief course in its management.

Then there was a Godspeed service on board conducted by the Bishop of London, and a farewell dinner given by the Athenaeum Club. Last-minute possessions were taken on board – Shackleton brought a typewriter, a make-up box and conjuring tricks. At length, on 31 July 1901, the *Discovery* weighed anchor, paused at Spithead to 'swing ship' to correct her compasses, and proceeded to Cowes, in the midst of a royal regatta, to receive the royal blessing. The new King and Queen, not yet crowned, came aboard; the King made a short speech and Hannah Scott pinned the Victorian Order (fourth class) to her son's tunic. Markham placed a copy of the Instructions, thirty clauses signed by the two presidents, in Scott's hands. The Queen's pekinese fell overboard and was rescued by a sailor; one must hope that it was not being chased by Scott's Aberdeen terrier Scamp, who accompanied his master as far as New Zealand and became a general favourite. (Three kittens also went.) Next day, 6 August 1901, the *Discovery* passed the Needles on her way to the unknown. 'Truly, they form the vanguard of England's chivalry', Markham eulogised her captain and crew. 'No finer set of men ever left these shores, nor were men ever led by a finer Captain.'

---

* Hooker (1817–1911) had served as naturalist in Clark's *Erebus* and *Terror* Antarctic expedition of 1839–43, producing as a result a learned study, *Flora Antarctica*. This was followed, after travels in the Himalayas and elsewhere, by an equally authoritative *Flora Indica*. In 1865 he succeeded his father as director of the Royal Botanic Gardens at Kew and became the most famous botanist of his generation. He was awarded the Order of Merit in 1907, and lived to the age of ninety-four.

The thoughts of the Captain, who must have been worn out, were more sombre. 'Before us lay new scenes, new interests, expanding horizons; but who at such times must not think sorely of the wives and mothers condemned to think of the past in silent patience for the future, through years of suspense and anxiety?' For himself, he had his mother, so dependent on him, in mind. Armitage's wife was to give birth to their first child nine weeks later; Wilson had married his Oriana Souper, a colleague in the Battersea mission in which he had worked, only three weeks before the ship sailed.

Sorrows of parting soon gave way to an immediate need to get the ship into order. She was heavily laden, clumsy and extremely slow. 'She is really awfully dirty and very untidy indeed' Royds noted in his journal. Her masts were stubby and her spread of canvas small. Even with favourable winds she could not make much more than seven knots in the Bay of Biscay, no brisker a pace than an ordinary cyclist can achieve. Obviously it was going to take a long time to reach New Zealand, some 14,000 miles away, at the pace of a cyclist. Intentions to practise techniques of sounding and dredging in deep water as they went along had to be abandoned.

None of this damped the spirits of the young men on board. They were at the start of a great adventure and as gay as larks. The second oldest and most sober of the scientists, Hodgson (aged thirty-seven), startled everyone by appearing at dinner in the wardroom, as the saloon was by courtesy called, in a red wig brought by Shackleton. Of all the scientists, Hodgson most closely matched the layman's idea of a boffin. One day, excited by a discovery in his small laboratory which had been rigged up on the afterdeck, he dashed out excitedly exclaiming, '*muggiaea!*' Thereafter he was known to his messmates as Muggins. Before long Scott had to expostulate on the disgusting state of his laboratory and 'feared there were still pangs to be endured from his untidiness and want of hygienic perception'. Hodgson admitted to 'a holy stink in my lab, Scott is frightened of the stink'. Probably he paid little more regard to his commander than he had to his Sovereign's consort, when, at Cowes, Queen Alexandra and her ladies looked in to find him bottling spiders. He concluded a dissertation on the habits of spiders with the remark, 'Now you women had better get out or you may get your frocks spoilt.' Royalty withdrew.

Apart from the regular complement, two extra scientists crowded into the narrow wardroom, which had a stove at each end and ten cabins opening out of it. One was Dr George Murray, bound for Melbourne, the other Hugh R. Mill who had been invited to go as far as Madeira to give instruction in meteorology and oceanography. 'It was a very happy party in the wardroom,' he wrote. 'Scott waived the seclusion which is the right of a captain, and took his turn with the rest to preside at table.' One day Scott asked his advice as to the best route to follow in order to penetrate as far as possible into the Antarctic continent. He sat for three hours in Scott's cabin, oblivious of the noises around him, concentrating his thoughts, and reached the conclusion that a landing should be attempted at the head of McMurdo Bay. It was to this bay – or sound, as it proved to be – that Scott shaped his course.

At Madeira they took on more coal, dropped Mill, gave Scamp a run and sent back a lot of mail. All the officers wrote to Markham, praising the ship for her comfort and buoyancy to set against her slow speed and other defects, and saying how much they liked each other. 'During the ten days there has not been a jarring note anywhere,' Mill affirmed. Scott wrote to his mother that he liked all his companions and Wilson, Skelton and Barne most of all – particularly Wilson, who was 'a little more serious than the others'. Everything he was to learn about this young artist and doctor strengthened his first impression. With Wilson he was to form the strongest, perhaps the only, deep friendship of his life. Wilson's impressions of the commander were also favourable. 'The Captain turns out with all of us and shirks nothing, not even the dirtiest work,' he wrote to his wife.

There was dirty work in plenty after leaving Madeira. Horrid smells came up from the bilge and inspection showed that the holds were flooding and ruining many of the provisions. Everything had to be got out of the holds, when a sad state of affairs was revealed: stinking rotten cheese, rusting tins, mouldy flour. What could be dried, was dried, the rest thrown overboard, the holds pumped out and everything cleaned up: but it was impossible to stop sea-water seeping in. This was the famous 'Dundee leak' which was to cause so much trouble. Other faults came to light: 'disgraceful cheap iron work' in Royds' words, which caused the spars of the lower topsail yards to be carried away. In the passage through the tropics other damage was done, unobserved at the time, to the dried fish, to be used as dog-food, stored in bundles on deck. This was to prove the most serious damage of all.

Cape Town was reached on 3 October 1901, just eight weeks after leaving Cowes. The Boer War was pursuing its melancholy course up-country, but the hospitality for which the Cape was famous was by no means inhibited. It was altogether too much for some of the crew, after eight boring weeks at sea. Practically everyone got drunk, and Royds wrote despairingly in his journal, 'They say that the grievance on the mess-deck is through there being merchant and naval men together; goodness knows what it is . . . things are too much of a good thing and can't go on.'

From Simon's Bay, Dr George Murray went home, taking the marine collections. Owing to the *Discovery*'s slowness, Scott had decided to cut out Melbourne and make for Lyttleton, New Zealand, his last port of call. Had Dr Murray gone on to Lyttleton, he would have overstayed his leave from the British Museum. There was to be criticism of Dr Murray's premature departure; Scott, it was hinted, was taking the opportunity to get rid of him. 'We were late in reaching the Cape and Murray left us on that account and *not* because tempers got upset in the tropics or elsewhere,' Scott wrote to Mill from Lyttleton. But his own comments on Murray suggest that he was not sorry to see the Scientific Director go. In a letter sent to Markham from Lyttleton Scott wrote:

I have now had to take the whole direction of the scientific work into my hands. My principle is to give each man a maximum amount of freedom in his particular job, and I find it works admirably . . . There is a feeling with Hodgson and Koettlitz that in some quarters at home it is intended that they should ultimately be treated merely as the collectors of any interesting collection they may make, and that somebody will step in with authority and grasp such scientific kudos as may be got. Of course they mean Murray, though they do not say so . . . My own opinion of Murray's executive capacity is very poor, and I feel sure that if he again gets a finger in the pie, he will make a mess of it.

He had, he went on to say, no personal animus; Murray was a decent enough man, but also,

the sort of man who would fly out and join the ship immediately on our return to civilisation, and so come home as fast as the expedition. I do not intend that this shall happen. Meanwhile I have complete loyalty from all. They are now my personal friends, and thoroughly understand that all must work for the common good.

Scott's remark that there was no personal bad feeling is borne out by Murray's own farewell note to him after leaving Cape Town (November 1901). 'I have all kinds of things to say – and frankly don't know how to say them – you know however what I mean. I shall "play the game" right through – that sums it up . . . Goodbye old chap. Yours affectionately – give Scamp a pat for me.' Previously he had written to Markham from Dundee 'I admire immensely Scott's powers of organisation even among affairs that must have been unfamiliar to him.'

Scott was touchy about the scientific work because he knew that the expedition's enemies in the scientific world had by no means laid aside their disapproval. 'One constantly hears gloomy forebodings as to the scientific work of the Expedition,' a Fellow of the Royal Society wrote to its President before any scientific results had even been received. Scott knew also that he had a light-weight team, not one of whom had a national, let alone an international, reputation, while in at least one important field, meteorology, the man in charge was not a scientist at all but a naval officer. Wilson summed it up when he wrote to his wife, 'With the single exception of Hodgson we are all intensely ignorant of anything but the most elementary knowledge of our several subjects. I am certainly no ornithologist . . .' Scott knew enough of science to know the limitations of his men and was all the more resolved that, from this motley collection, should come properly conducted work that would be taken seriously by the pundits of the Royal Society.

Soon after leaving Cape Town the ship encountered savage storms and proved, while rolling like a pig, to be thoroughly seaworthy; her sails were so small that there was no need to shorten them in the worst of storms, and one day she made a record run of 223 miles under sail. But it was a rough passage; everything broke loose and the piano careered about – 'it was a rather unsatisfactory instrument, as one could get no sound out of it', Royds wrote with restraint. The Captain, Barne and Wilson were swept off their feet and very nearly carried overboard.

For the Captain it was certainly no rest cure. He had taken over his command without a day's break, scarcely even an hour's, after an exhausting year of detailed preparation passed under a cloud of uncertainty as to whether he would ever sail in the *Discovery* at all. No sooner had he stepped on to the bridge than difficulties caused by the ship's own shortcomings were upon him. Then there was the strain of the shaking down together, in a very cramped space, of eleven oddly assorted individualists, a potentially explosive mixture of men from the Royal Navy, the Merchant Navy and the spheres of science and of medicine, ranging in age from forty (Koettlitz) to twenty-two (Ferrar). The scientists were unused to any form of discipline beyond that imposed by their profession; the naval officers were moulded to the rigid hierarchical system of their Service. In addition Scott had to get to know the men on the mess-deck, and smooth out signs of incipient friction between bluejackets and merchant seamen.

On top of all that lay the great weight of responsibility for the safety and well-being of nearly fifty men, for the ship into which had been put so much public and private money, for the hopes reposed in the whole enterprise which now was his to make or mar. He was heading into a region where there would be no charts and no advice to guide him. The ship could be crushed by ice and no one would know; in those days before radio no help could be summoned; on all this great lifeless continent, no human being found.

It is difficult to realise, knowing the outcome, how intimidating and how anxious the outlook must have seemed to this young man with no experience, no advisers, no knowledge, who had already been under great strain for a year. One is tempted to think that Scott had merely to set his course on the right meridian of longitude and he would arrive somewhere in the Antarctic where he could establish a base and take to the land. It was not nearly as simple as that. Between him and the continent lay a deep band of moving, changing pack-ice, no one knew quite how deep, innumerable icebergs, and a zone of fearful storms. As he sailed southwards, three other expeditions were in, had recently returned from, or were advancing upon the Antarctic. All were failures. There was the well-equipped, well-led German venture in the *Gauss*. There was the party led by Adrian de Gerlache in the *Belgica* which was caught in the ice for over a year, while her crew suffered horribly from scurvy and exposure, and several died. There was Bruce's venture shortly to sail in the *Scotia* to the Weddell Sea; this, too got trapped in sea-ice and returned without ever reaching the land.

The odds were against Scott's faring better, and he must have had many unhappy, apprehensive thoughts in his small cabin, puffing at his pipe, though in the wardroom he put on a cheerful, optimistic front, approaching as near to a hail-fellow-well-met bonhomie as such a naturally reserved, unbonhomous man could get. Markham had noted that the anxieties of the year in London had marked him, and this can be seen in photographs; the freshness of youth in earlier likenesses has given way to the lineaments of a sombre-eyed man with receding hair and slightly drooping mouth. It is the face, with its wide forehead, of a thinker whose thoughts are not predominantly glad.

Not surprisingly, his naturally quick temper now and again escaped control. When a fire broke out, due (Royds wrote) to a 'poor blameless oilskin' left on a shelf above a lamp, Royds, as officer of the watch, received a blistering reprimand. Scott cursed and swore when water used to swill down the decks swept into his cabin. The scientists irritated him sometimes, especially when a tow-net designed to trawl for deepsea creatures got tangled up or carried away due to Hodgson's carelessness. 'Certain of our men of science', he noted, 'seem to take no interest in actually capturing the beasts but only in those that are captured.' Skelton shared the Captain's views. When 2500 fathoms of wire was let out it got 'all kinked up through Hodgson not putting on enough swivels'. 'These scientific people', he added, 'may be all right at looking through a microscope and making theories, but as a rule they are devilish little good at the practical work, or catching their specimens. The Skipper was very sick.' Hodgson himself cheerfully admitted that he had misread the barometer, bunged up the Dyne's anemometer and smashed an electric lamp.

But as a rule a friendly, relaxed atmosphere prevailed in the wardroom with everyone resolved not to get irritated by other people's idiosyncrasies, such as Shackleton's Irish volubility and his habit of quoting thick slabs of poetry. Unfortunately, as most of his messmates came to think, his fiancée had given him as a parting present a volume of Browning, and he soon became a compulsive quoter of that poet's verse. Not everyone appreciated this. Bernacchi (who joined the ship at Lyttleton) recorded how, when being relieved on the bridge on a dirty night, Shackleton 'in his wheedling Irish voice kept me from my waiting bunk ranting endless verses in the voice and manner of an old-time tragedian – "one moment, old son," he wheedled as I edged towards the gangway, "have you heard this?" and he would quote Browning, his favourite poet – obscure lines that neither Browning nor Shackleton understood, much less a cold and yawning physicist.'

Shackleton made a buoy out of a Dutch cheese tin for measuring the height and speed of waves. Skelton was sceptical. 'For my part I can't see there is much to be gained by any information on the subject. A more perfect knowledge of waves would hardly be likely to alter the form of ships.' A difference in outlook between the scientist seeking knowledge for its own sake and the sailor respecting it only for its practical use divided the wardroom, and might have fatally divided the expedition's aims had it not been for Scott's understanding of both points of view. He was a naval officer certainly, but with an exceptional grasp of the physical sciences. Markham, in picking a good sailor, had chosen better than he knew.

In mid-November 1901 the ship, Scott wrote, 'arrived in an extremely interesting magnetic area, and I decided to steer to the south to explore it more effectively'. This detour through stormy seas took them as far south as latitude 62° 50's, within 200 miles of that part of the Antarctic mainland discovered in 1840 by the French naval officer Dumont d'Urville.* On 16 November the men in the *Discovery* had their first sight of pack-ice, mostly in small pieces two or three feet thick. Scott wrote,

What light remained was reflected in a ghostly glimmer from the white surface of the pack; now and again a white Snow Petrel flitted through the gloom, the grinding of the floes against the ship's side was mingled with the more subdued hush of their rise and fall on the long swell, and for the first time we felt something of the solemnity of these great Southern solitudes.

* Jules Dumont d'Urville, 1790–1842, a versatile naval officer, who, discerning merit in an old statue he noticed lying about on a Greek island, persuaded the French Ambassador in Constantinople to get hold of it; it turned out to be the Venus de Milo. In 1837 he set out with the *Astrolabe* and the *Zelée* with the intention of reaching the South Magnetic Pole. In the following year he planted the tricolour on an islet off Adélie Land which he named after his wife. He, his wife and child, on an outing to see the fountains at Versailles, were burnt to death in a train crash in 1842.

Every polar expedition left in its wake a trail of death, blood, suffering and destruction among the local fauna, and the *Discovery* was no exception. The men had to live off the country insofar as they could, and an additional reason for destruction was provided by the needs of scientific research. These southern seas were rich in bird life, and some of the men became adept at catching albatrosses, several species of petrel, Cape Pigeons and other birds on baited lines, or by entanglement in long thread streamers. Before reaching Lyttleton they landed on Macquarie Island, about 600 miles south-west of New Zealand and found two penguin rookeries, both very smelly. Each King Penguin carried a single egg balanced on its feet, and each bird was balanced on a stone to keep clear of the liquid guano. The birds refused to budge, and Wilson picked one up by its neck and carried it with the egg still resting on its feet. 'Poor things, they were very trusting', he noted, 'I am glad to say that not a bird was killed more than we actually needed.' Seals were equally trusting, and two seamen went on battering one bewildered animal about the head with a stick until Skelton came up and seized the stick and Barne put it out of its misery with his revolver. Most of the men, Scott noted, were 'wild and mustardy' and kept blazing off at anything they could see with their firearms. Everyone collected birds, eggs, plants, insects, shells, and Skelton noted that Shackleton 'produced the usual nondescript assortment unlike anything anyone else had got'.

At the end of November the *Discovery* berthed at Lyttleton, where the leak at last received attention, costing a disturbing amount of money. Hospitality was even more lavish than at the Cape. 'Not a single sober man on board,' Royds glumly observed. 'The men are rushed at as soon as they get ashore', he wrote to his twin sister, 'and all good Service feeling is lost and I have awful times. Better men never stepped a plank whilst they are at sea, but in harbour they are nothing but brute beasts, and I am ashamed of them, and told them so, and penitent indeed they are, but only until they are drunk again.' Scott was equally fed up with them. The drunken men 'disgust me, but I'm going to have it out with them somehow. There are only a few black sheep but they lend colour to the flock.' A few of the flock, one syphilitic, were discharged and replaced, including the cook. His replacement proved even worse, and a troublemaker into the bargain.

The arrival of these bronzed, healthy, dashing young sailors, nearly all bachelors – so young they were christened 'the babes in the wood' – naturally caused a stir. Officers and men alike were welcomed into New Zealand homes, sometimes with lasting results. The handsome Skelton (also 'very well-bred' according to Markham) was much taken with a family called Meares, especially with the youngest daughter Sybil, still at school. Mrs Meares made him a lampshade; some years later, Sybil became his wife. Ferrar also met his future wife in Christchurch. Royds was virtually adopted by a young couple with two small children; in company with their attractive mother he picked sweet peas, threw bean-bags, sang songs and conducted an enjoyable flirtation; on parting, he 'really felt awful low saying goodbye to dear Mrs R'. Michael Barne, Scott noted, 'made a fool of himself' and a warning had to be sent to his mother in Suffolk. Scott was entertained at gubernatorial level and Wilson had a gloomy time blowing penguins' eggs full of embryo chicks – 'a most awful job' – strong words for Wilson.

Scott received one piece of good news. There had been talk, before he left, of the need to send a relief ship the following year to find out if all was well with the *Discovery*, to return with news of her doings and to take additional supplies. Markham pressed for this with his usual vigour, but the problem, as always, was money. When the *Discovery* sailed, he was busy trying to drum up more contributions. In May 1901 the munificent Mr Llewellyn Longstaff offered another £5000 on condition that no body other than the RGS should have the power to spend it.

In September 1901 Markham went to Norway and, on his own initiative, bought a whaler, the *Morgenen* – the strongest ever built in Norway, he wrote, except the *Fram* – for £3880. She was re-named the *Morning*, sailed to England to refit, and Markham appointed to command her Lieutenant William Colbeck, RNR, who had been with Borchgrevink in the *Southern Cross* as magnetic observer. All this before the money to refit her had been raised, but Markham thought the chance too good to miss.

When this news reached Lyttleton one load, at least, was lifted from Scott's mind. He had been worrying about how completely the expedition's retreat would be cut off should no relief ship be sent. 'Our movements and the risks we could rightfully take must be greatly limited, if the loss of the ship of necessity implied the loss of all on board.' Now he could start for the south knowing that 'a line of retreat is practically assured to us'. Markham was able to make good his word about the *Morning*, but when he wrote to Scott at Lyttleton only a modicum of the money had been raised: £9500 by February 1902 and she had to leave in July. He must have been disappointed when the Prince of Wales gave only £50. It was like pulling teeth; but at last a splendid tooth from a financier, Mr Edgar Speyer, yielded £5000, and the *Morning* was able to sail. The Admiralty's sole contribution was to lend two young officers: Sub-Lieutenant George Mulock, who had taken a surveyor's course, and Lieutenant Edward Evans, who was so keen to go that he called on Markham, whom he had never met, at 21 Eccleston Square, and, sitting on a park bench in the sun, talked him into agreeing. Evans was appointed second officer of the *Morning*.

In Lyttleton the *Discovery*, her leak by no means cured, was loaded to the limit with stores, coal, equipment and livestock; the dogs were collected from the quarantine island where they had been waiting; and a flock of forty-five terrified sheep, a present from New Zealand farmers, was driven on board. Her decks were so packed with paraphernalia that there was scarcely room for the helmsman to stand. As Scott wrote with his customary restraint, 'the ship was not in a condition in which one could look forward to crossing the stormiest ocean in the world'. The Bishop of Christchurch invoked God's much needed blessing, and on 21 December 1901 they were off, escorted by two warships, HMS *Ringarooma* and HMS *Lizard*, past gaily dressed steamers and to the roar of cheering crowds and the music of bands.

In the midst of this stirring scene came disaster. A young seaman, Charles Bonner, had climbed to the top of the mainmast. He stood up, waved, and pitched forward on to the deck below, dashing his head to pieces. There was a stunned silence; some of the men wept. Bonner had taken a bottle of whisky with him into the rigging. Two days later, at Port Chalmers, Bonner was buried with naval honours; and a seaman called Sinclair, who had joined the ship at Cape Town, stole a suit of civilian clothes and deserted. It was he who had handed Bonner the bottle of whisky. The tragedy was thought by some to be a bad omen but it did not prove so. Only one man failed to return from the Antarctic.

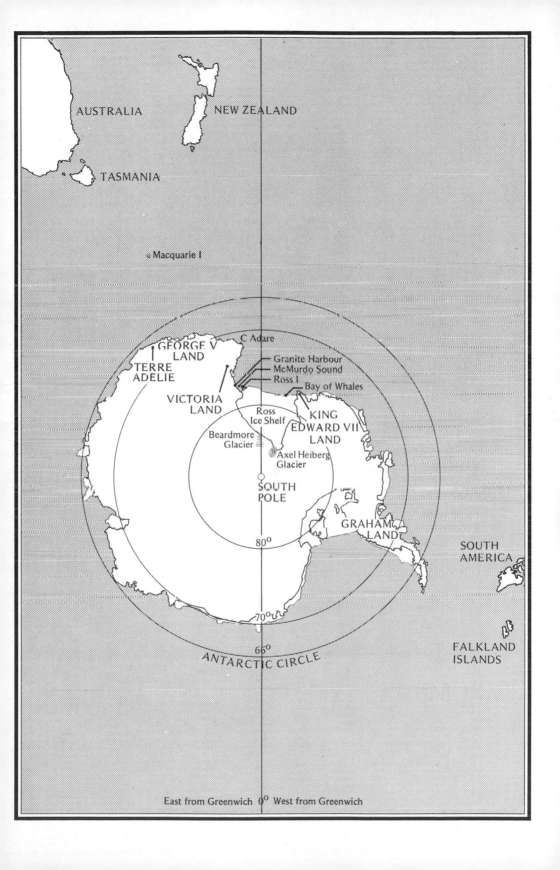

# 7 McMurdo Sound

The *Discovery* was fortunate on her southern voyage to cross the stormy ocean without a storm. Within a fortnight, in latitude 65° 30's, her company sighted their first iceberg, and by evening there were seventeen in view. These southern bergs were different from their Arctic counterparts: much bigger, and more uniform in shape, having flat tops and wall-like sides. Some were enormous; the largest seen from the *Discovery*, later on, was estimated to be seven miles long and 200 feet high. Scott thought that they had broken quietly away from a large ice-sheet, probably from the Great Ice Barrier for which the ship was heading. Next day she crossed the Antarctic Circle (66° 33's).

Bird life was abundant. In the open sea, the Wandering Albatross, with a wing-span of over eleven feet, followed the ship in considerable numbers, and none of the Ancient Mariner's feelings of guilt disturbed the *Discovery*'s crew, who caught and skinned them. Several other kinds of albatross and of petrel, the Cape Pigeon, the big, predatory skua and other species were noted, sometimes killed, and sketched by Wilson who was enchanted by it all and was scarcely seen without his pencil and sketch-book; he worked up his quick impressions afterwards into water-colour drawings. As they approached the pack-ice, albatrosses disappeared, to be replaced by the Southern Fulmar, the Antarctic Petrel and the small Snow Petrel, white all over save for black feet and bill.

Soon after crossing the Antarctic Circle they entered the pack. Royds described this as 'pieces of ice loosely packed, seldom exceeding twenty or thirty yards in diameter, with a smooth flat surface; having here and there small irregular prominences or hummocks, the whole of snowy whiteness'. It was constantly on the move, and required great skill and unflagging wariness in navigation to take advantage of every opening, or lead, and keep clear of larger floes that were constantly, and alarmingly, grinding against the ship's sides. Here again the *Discovery* was lucky. Ross had been obliged to sail through eight hundred miles of pack and it took him forty-six days. The *Discovery* was clear of the pack for the time being (there was plenty more to come) and into open water in five.

Now they were among the seals, and in a few days the ship became, in

Scott's words, 'a regular butcher's shop'. In the water, seals were wary enough, fearing attack by Killer Whales or by the giant of their own tribe, the Sea Leopard, but once on an ice-floe they had no fear, since they had no natural foes. Once man arrived they had, indeed, the deadliest foe of all, but knew it not. Shooting unsuspecting seals from a whaleboat was therefore child's play, but hauling them on board, skinning and flenching them – removing the thick layer of blubber between skin and flesh – was harder work and by no means pleasant. Wilson, helped by seaman Walker, skinned the first (a Crabeater)* and Royds noted that the mess and smell was 'truly awful'. The slaughter went on briskly and the meat was hung in the rigging for future consumption – the Antarctic provided a permanent deep-freeze. 'I spent the whole day from breakfast till dinner time skinning and cutting up seals, bathed in blood from head to foot,' Wilson recorded. He never complained, it was part of the job, but the reader of his diary can sense the abhorrence he felt. A few days later he saw three Crabeaters on a floe beside the ship but wrote 'I didn't dare call the Skipper again, as we had killed so many crabbers and he hates the sight of our butchers' shop.' Wilson noted the beauty of the living seal 'when a little alarmed and gaping at one with head erect and mouth open, big dark eyes and distended nostrils, and red tongue and white skin and teeth'.

Shortly before midnight on 8 January 1902, Royds, the officer of the watch, sighted land on the port bow. 'The sky was a lovely clear azure blue, with the most brilliant sunshine.' This was Victoria Land, fringed by a chain of magnificent mountains. So clear was the atmosphere that the ship was 120 miles away when land was sighted. 'The water was a mass of quivering colour' Bernacchi wrote 'and a phalanx of deepest purple clouds marshalled in the path of the sun gave an unearthly radiance to all around.' They were heading for Cape Adare at the mouth of Robertson Bay, where Borchgrevink's party had wintered, and here they landed on a pebbly beach at the foot of a rocky cliff-face rising to 1000 feet and swarming with Adélie Penguins (*Pygosceli adeliae*), which had their nests in pockets in the rock right up to the summit.

The birds were constantly proceeding up and down to the sea, walking upright, and Scott estimated that it must have taken those with the highest nests an hour each way to clamber up and down – all time lost from the day's fishing. The young were relentless in their demands for food, rushing about with open beaks, knocking each other over in their headlong search for a food-laden parent, and squawking urgently. The stench was abominable.

* Four species of seal were encountered. Much the most common was the Crabeater, *Lobodon carcinophagus*, whose stomach was nearly always full of shrimp-like krills. The others were the Weddell, *Leptonychotes weddelli*; the rare Ross Seal, *Ommatophoca rossi*; and the Sea Leopard, *Hydrurga leptonyx*, who is particularly partial to Adélie Penguins. All winter in the Antarctic or sub-Antarctic regions.

Many of the young perished and were disembowelled by gory-throated skuas. Each parent, of either sex, returned from the sea with a crop full of fish to be disgorged into the open beak of its young until all was gone, when it hurried back to the sea. Here was a scene of ceaseless activity. In winter, these penguins migrated northwards, to return in the Antarctic spring to their rookeries, and start the process over again.

More or less in the middle of the rookery was the hut put up by the *Southern Cross* expedition. Inside was a letter left by Borchgrevink and addressed to the commander of the next expedition, which Scott opened and read out. His companions found it ridiculous – 'full of bad spelling and punctuation, there wasn't a word of use to anybody, not even an approximate list of stores,' Skelton wrote. 'One only wonders how such a man can ever have impressed anybody with his fitness to command an expedition.' The letter claimed the discovery of a new species of seal and an island named after the Duke of York. Skelton commented, 'The first is of course the well-known Ross Seal, and the latter does not exist.' Nearby was the grave of Nikolai Hansen, the expedition's zoologist. Bernacchi climbed the hill to pay his respects to the memory of his former colleague. He disagreed with his present ones about Borchgrevink, with whom he had got on very well.

Next day, after a cylinder containing a record of progress to date had been left in the hut, the *Discovery* nearly foundered before her work had begun. Thick pack-ice hemmed her in and carried her towards a chain of grounded bergs; 'we could see and almost hear the heavy floes grinding and over-riding one another against these barriers,' Scott wrote. 'For the first time we faced the dangers of the pack, and became aware of its mighty powers.' Push her engines to the utmost as her engineers and stokers might, the ship was helpless, and appeared doomed. All this impressed itself so deeply on Scott's memory that three years later he wrote in *The Voyage of the Discovery*,

Above us the sun shone in a cloudless sky, its rays were reflected in a myriad point of the glistening pack; behind us lay the lofty snow-clad mountains, the air about us was almost breathlessly still; crisp, clear and sunlit, it seemed an atmosphere in which all Nature should rejoice; the silence was broken only by the deep panting of our engines and the slow, measured hush of the grinding floes; yet beneath all ran this mighty, relentless tide, bearing us to possible destruction . . . it was difficult to persuade oneself that we were completely impotent.

Most of the crew were asleep and unconscious of the danger; 'that they were not told,' Scott added, 'bears testimony to the fact that a fuss was seldom made in the *Discovery* unless there was some good reason'. Just when all seemed lost, the tide gradually slackened and the ship gingerly pushed her way through to open sea. Once again, her luck held.

From Cape Adare she pursued a course almost due south along the eastern shore of Victoria Land. Although it was midsummer, the weather worsened, a ninety-mile-an-hour gale lashed her rigging as she threaded a way through bergs and pack-ice, and it became so cold that sea water froze as it was hurled on to the deck by mountainous waves. Following Ross's course, they passed Possession Island where he had gone ashore to claim the land in the name of his Queen, and, after a twenty-four-hour-long struggle with wind and high seas, landed on Coulman Island to leave another cylinder on a post with instructions for the relief ship to pick up the following summer.

On 15 January 1902 they came to an inlet in the land's icy cliff-face. The ice was shot with superb colours from rays of the unsetting sun reflected off the floes. The inlet harboured, Wilson thought, about two hundred basking seals. 'It was a perfectly beautiful sight, and the absolute stillness and peace, a sort of eternal peace that could never be disturbed, seemed to hang about the cold clear air. I shall never forget it.' So had it been, peaceful and beautiful, white basking seals, stately penguins, prismatic colours, blue sea, for countless aeons, undisturbed by man. Within a few minutes of man's arrival, the eternal peace was shattered and crimson added to the colours on the floe. Thirty seals and ten Emperor Penguins were killed. 'I had to supervise the whole of this beastly butchers' work,' Wilson wrote, 'a duty much against the grain, and I worked till 2.30 a.m.' Scott's reaction was the same. 'It seemed a terrible desecration to come to this quiet spot only to murder its innocent inhabitants and stain the white snow with blood ... Some of us were glad to get away on our ski.'* Others enjoyed the *battue* as an opportunity to exercise their marksmanship, but no one was able to justify it on the ground of self-defence. Charging seals and savage penguins have not, as yet, been introduced into the sportsman's mythology.

This, however, was not sport, it was necessity. Despite the putrefaction theory of the cause of scurvy, fresh food was recognised as essential, and the only fresh food available was the flesh of seals and of larger birds such as penguins and skuas. The big Emperor Penguins (*Aptenodytes forsteri*), peculiar to the Antarctic, were very handsome in their glossy black plumage with a purplish tinge, and clean white shirt-fronts; they stood over four feet high and weighed up to ninety pounds. All penguins were full of curiosity and would come right up to human beings to see what on earth they were, bowing their heads like courteous old-fashioned gentlemen and calling to their companions to come and see this strange new phenomenon. Louis Bernacchi wrote of the Emperor Penguin (*Saga of the Discovery*):

* All the explorers wrote 'ski' in the plural without a final 's', which was added at a later date when the word became anglicised.

Possessing the manners of a perfect gentleman, the Emperor receives human explorers with great politeness and much ceremony. Waddling up to them, his mode of address is stately, and accompanied by many grave welcoming bows until the beak almost touches the breast. Keeping his head bowed, he will make what appears to be a speech in a muttering manner . . . The Emperor Penguin is not only a strange bird of great antiquity and rare intelligence, but, having lived for endless generations, he may have left behind him all the foolishness in which we humans today are involved and have acquired, in that germ-free and healthy atmosphere, a quiet philosophy, tolerance, a curiously open and interested mind, and, above all, excellent hospitality and courtesy to others. Apparently they have no vices and their virtues are simple. Nevertheless, the Emperor has a topsy-turvy breeding arrangement, for instead of laying its single egg in the summer it chooses the middle of the fiercest winter on earth, when it is dark and temperatures fall to —80°F.

Because their skins would be ruined by bullets, penguins destined to be stuffed and distributed to museums could not be shot, so generally the Emperors were surrounded, driven like sheep by several men into a huddle, and then caught and knifed. Hodgson said that 'the only way to do it is to jump on them from behind catching them at the same time by the scruff of the neck'. Misses were frequent, often the catcher would fall in the snow and the bird would halt and turn 'asking what the devil is the meaning of it all. It is generally explained.' Sixty years earlier the humane James Clark Ross had evolved a better method; he found that a tablespoonful of hydrocyanic acid would despatch the bird with no fuss and only a brief moment of pain. This tidier method does not seem to have been considered in the *Discovery*.

The well-known British conservatism in matters of diet must have caused anxiety; would the men take easily to seal steaks and penguin stews? They proved quite ready to adapt, with one or two exceptions. Scott confessed to 'a weak stomach in these matters' but was 'much rejoiced by the excellent spirit shown by the crew'. Almost everyone came to relish, especially, seal liver, a delicacy served as a rule at breakfast. Penguin eggs were also a treat when they could be found at an early stage of incubation, but as time went on the men became less squeamish about embryo chicks. Seal blubber had a most unpleasant, clinging smell and much depended on the trouble taken to scrape it off the flesh. The cook, a surly Melbourne man, caused many grumbles and at one time the Captain had him put in irons – for insubordination, not bad cooking. 'He is a wretched specimen of humanity.'

That was the only recorded use of this old-fashioned naval punishment. To begin with, a few of the men had to be disciplined, but the usual penalties were fines and loss of leave to take effect on their return to civilisation, and immediate cuts in the rum ration. If anyone defied a superior or started fights, Scott was strict, but in other ways he was an easy-going commander.

Once the ship was secured for the winter, he aimed at getting the routine work done by mid-day, so leaving the men free after that to do as they pleased. Off-duty they could smoke anywhere in their quarters. He tried to persuade them to take exercise, without making it compulsory; officers and men alike enjoyed football on the frozen snow, and later hockey, whenever conditions allowed it. Once the sledging started, distinctions of rank grew blurred and officers and men got to know each other as well as it is possible for human beings to know each other, by the equal sharing of everything from hunger, danger and exposure to meals and sleeping bags.

They made now for Cape Crozier on the north-eastern tip of Ross Island, where a third cylinder with despatches was to be deposited. Here was another enormous Adélie Penguin rookery and the post was erected in its midst, Scott reflecting on the unlikelihood of anyone finding it. With Royds and Wilson he climbed to 1350 feet and saw the Great Ice Barrier stretching as far as the eye could see to the south and east: level, smooth, barren, enigmatic. How far did it go? What lay beyond? Was it a great mass of ice afloat on water, a sort of monster floe, or was it part of the continent and grounded on rock? These were among the questions to which they hoped to find an answer. 'For the first time in its long history,' Royds wrote, 'the Great Ice Barrier has been looked down on by human eyes.' Scott noted that 'the very vastness of what lay at our feet seemed to add to our sense of mystery'.

Scott's decision to land at Cape Crozier was taken without prior warning to his officers, and Wilson noted, 'the Captain is strangely reticent about letting a soul in the ship know what even his immediate plans are'. Hodgson made a similar comment, 'the only objection to the work is that the Skipper is so very capricious and no one knows what is to be done till five minutes before it is done'. These might be taken for civilian comments – naval officers were seldom in the habit of consulting their subordinates before taking a routine decision – but Royds had made the same complaint at Cape Town; he was expected to be ready to sail at any moment without being warned in advance.

Capricious perhaps; but possibly this reticence sprang rather from preoccupation, from a long-standing habit of going into a brown study and not emerging until action could no longer be postponed. (Several minor instances of this absent-mindedness have been given; his steward Hare related that he once sprinkled sugar and poured milk over a plate of curry; Barrie how he turned up several hours late for a dinner party, having forgotten all about it and dined by himself.) When it came to long-term planning, as opposed to immediate action, he did take his colleagues into his confidence. A week or so after leaving Cape Crozier, he called his officers together and outlined his programme for the next year. 'The plan is excellent,' Royds considered. Probably Scott did not carry out often enough this public relations exercise, but brooded too long in solitude in his cabin with his pipe and his charts, and jerked himself out of his reverie to take a quick decision.

From Cape Crozier they steamed slowly eastwards along the Barrier's edge. The cliff's height varied from a few feet to about 240 feet. Here they saw the birth of icebergs: big pieces broke off the Barrier's edge, sending up fountains of spray, and slowly drifted northwards towards open sea. Ice-floes ground and pressed against the sides of the vessel. This was menacing, but the beauties of the subtle, ever-changing colours constantly delighted the eye. Here is one of Wilson's descriptions:

In these cliffs were the most wonderful bright blue caves, and the whole face was hung with long thin icicles which made the most fantastic grottoes, with pure blue depths in the caves and cracks ... We had a bright rainbow round the sun in patches shortly before midnight, and the most beautiful lights on the sea and clouds and icebergs. A *very* peaceful scene and very cold too. All day I had been skinning birds. It is a cold job as the birds are all lumps of ice, only they keep well.

On the sixth day they steamed into undiscovered waters. Every spar and yard of the ship sparkled with fog-crystals. A heavy snow-storm produced a white-out, but on 30 January 1902 rocks loomed ahead and a sounding of a hundred fathoms confirmed that the Barrier was merging into continental land. 'But what a land!' Scott exclaimed. Everything was hazy, indeterminate or invisible, and all around lay grounded bergs. A thick fog came down. They groped their way forward, sounding continually and no doubt praying, for danger from pack-ice and grounded bergs was acute. At last, patches of undoubted rock could be discerned about 2000 feet above them. They had reached the eastern extremity of the Barrier, over 400 miles from Ross Island at its western end. As Ross had done, Scott named this new land after his sovereign.

King Edward VII Land (now part of Byrd Land) tended to the north and they were forced seaward in a confusing situation, which led to their going round in a circle in a bay full of bergs and young ice beginning to form, harbinger of approaching winter. The *Discovery* must seek her winter quarters if she were not to share the fate of many predecessors, and successors too, and be caught in the ice and almost certainly destroyed. With regret, but with undoubted prudence, Scott decided to retrace their course to McMurdo Sound. As they steamed westwards the fog cleared, and their newly discovered land stood out plainly with high hills, gentle rising slopes and bare rock in places. They were never to see it again.

By the following evening, the whole sea was covered with new ice, so there had been no time to spare. They did, however, pause in a little bight to send up the balloon, and make a first, brief trial trip with a sledge. Scott elected to go up first in the balloon, and very nearly disappeared into the blue. At 500 feet he hurled out all the sandbags and shot upwards like a rocket, but fortunately the weight of its chain halted the balloon at a little under 800 feet and he was able to descend. Shackleton followed. They could see a long way from their elevation but saw nothing new, just an endless sheet of snow, rippled here and there by *sastrugi*, snow-waves brought about by wind. Wilson was most annoyed about the whole episode. 'I think it is perfect madness to allow novices to risk their lives in this silly way,' he wrote crossly. 'If some of these experts don't come to grief out here, it will only be because God has pity on the foolish.' The expedition's luck held in that the balloon did not come to grief, but it developed a leak and never went up again.

Scott had by now decided to winter in McMurdo Sound which seemed to offer what, in Antarctic terms, was a snug harbourage, though snug is not the word most people would apply. In Royds' opinion it was almost ideal.

No signs of any pressure anywhere, under the lee of the land against the pre- vailing wind, enormous scope for exploration to the south, and in fact to all quarters, close to that great conundrum, the Barrier, and very handy to the spot where the relief ship has to come, namely Cape Crozier. The only disadvantage that I can see is the fact of it affording no shelter to any winds from the north, but from all accounts they are seldom, if ever, known to blow.

After a good deal of difficulty the ship was secured by ice-anchors alongside an ice-foot in a small bay, and here Scott decided that she should remain. On shore was a level site suitable for the hut, which had come in sections from Australia – 'a fairly spacious bungalow of a design used by outlying settlers'. It was about thirty-six feet square, and surrounded by a covered veranda more suitable as a shelter for those quaffing the iced beer of the antipodes than for those withstanding the icy blizzards of the white south. The hut's main purpose was to serve as a shelter for returning sledge parties, should the ship break free of her moorings and be forced by storms out to sea. This never happened, and the hut was used mainly as a recreation centre, where Barne mounted a play and Royds a nigger minstrel concert, enjoyed by audiences muffled up against the cold in zero temperatures.

Two smaller asbestos-covered huts were put up to house the magnetic instruments which were the constant preoccupation of Bernacchi and Armitage. The dogs were moved into kennels, delighted to get exercise at last, the men equally pleased to clean up the deck. For relaxation there was football and practice on unfamiliar skis, which gave rise to a good deal of hilarity, many bruises and one broken leg.

It was growing colder. Ice was forming, the southerly winds were bitter, and the pumps, which were still being worked daily to cope with the *Discovery*'s leak, froze. Royds wrote despairingly that after ten hours' continual pumping, not a drop of water had come through. 'May the men who threw this ship together have bad dreams, and preserve me from ever again being in a ship that leaks.' Royds at least had an escape from the routine's irritations; he played the piano, which had by then been put in order, for an hour or so after dinner almost every night.

Wilson in particular appreciated this, and came to like Royds more and more. Shackleton, at first, had been his chosen companion; Wilson admired the Irishman's witty, sparkling conversation and remarkable memory from which an anecdote could be extracted at any moment to suit any occasion. 'He is still my best friend,' Wilson wrote to his wife that winter, 'but I have a great admiration for Royds' character, a most simple, honest, lovable soul, full of high feeling for all that is good . . . He is a marvel of patience as a rule, though it is a "Service" patience, which takes any amount of snubbing from superiors, is very considerate to inferiors, but very hasty and stern sometimes with his equals.' Royds had only one effective superior, so it must be assumed that snubs from the Skipper sometimes came his way. 'The Captain and I understand each other better than anyone else in the ship, I think,' Wilson added. 'He has adopted every one of my suggestions.' Wilson spoke his mind more openly to Scott than any of the others felt free to do. 'I admire him immensely, all but his temper,' Wilson wrote to his father.

He is thoughtful for each individual and does little kindnesses which show it. He is ready to listen to everyone too, and joins heartily in all the humbug that goes on. I have a great admiration for him, and he is in no Service rut but is always anxious to see both sides of a question, and I have never known him to be unfair. One of the best points about him too is that he is very definite about everything; nothing is left vague or indeterminate. In every argument he goes straight for the main point, and always knows exactly what he is driving at. There will be no fear of our wandering about aimlessly in southern regions.

Scott listened to Wilson's opinions but not always to those of others. Bernacchi wrote of his one and only experience of the Captain's sharp temper – not perhaps a bad record in three years. He drew attention to the risks of leaving the ship's boats on land without shelter, and Scott snapped back that when he wanted advice he would ask for it. Unfortunately he did not do so, and the boats got frozen in, sank under the weight of the snow and were very difficult to free in the spring.

Wilson won for himself a special position with everyone. He was 'Uncle Bill', and people came to tell him their troubles, certain of his sympathy, humour and absolute discretion. He had the gift of making those who sought his company feel better, calmer, less aggrieved. Scott unfolded his opinion of his colleagues in a letter, franker than most, to Admiral Albert Markham, which was posted in Lyttleton (5 November 1901).

Koettlitz may be described as a rather good-natured duffer, Hodgson a very rough diamond, but a good biologist, Ferrar has the makings of a good chap but wants gunroom discipline and he is getting it to the great benefit of his character from the young lieutenants, but the best of the civilian staff by chalks is Wilson – a first-rate doctor, an excellent artist and a charming messmate, always to the fore and always practical and with the keenest of intellects – I hope and think he will make a great name some day.

On 16 February 1902 the sun dipped below the horizon for the first time and for several hours, at sunrise and sunset, a soft pink light bathed the scene, blending into a deep purple on the distant mountains. Beyond the huts, the land rose sharply to a height of about 750 feet and this, named Observation Hill, became a favourite climb for those seeking exercise. From its summit a magnificent view of hills and mountains, with the smoke of Erebus, 13,375 feet high, rising to the north, beckoned the imagination; 'eyes are turned towards the south – the land of promise', Scott wrote.

It was too late in the year for long-distance sledging but he planned a few short practice trips to test the equipment and break in some of the men. The dogs also: these had been divided into two teams, one under the charge of Armitage, the other of Bernacchi, the only two with some experience – in actual fact, very little – of dog-driving. Armitage believed in harsh discipline and the whip, Bernacchi 'in persuasion and coaxing. A trial was staged, each man selecting his own team. Neither method worked noticeably well; the dogs fought, got tangled up in the traces and at first refused to pull at all, but eventually Bernacchi's team dashed off up the slope, leaving its breathless driver behind.

There was much hilarity, but this was the first of many hard lessons which taught them that dog-driving was not just a matter of harnessing the animals, cracking a whip and away the sledge would go. Sledge-dogs, whether Siberian or from Greenland, were wayward, capricious and often vicious beasts and had already displayed their unpleasant habit of rounding suddenly, for no apparent reason, on one or other of their number and literally tearing him to bits. Often the victim was a dog that had been singled out for praise or for affection by a human being. The dogs themselves then singled out that animal for death. It took the men some time to realise that any dog who had been separated from his fellows, even for a day or two, would be looked on as a stranger, and therefore as an enemy, when he rejoined the pack. 'The "king dog", Skelton noted, 'puts up the number of the dog in disgrace, and even if he escapes for a few days or even longer, he is finally killed.' Their king dog was Nigger, a remarkably fine animal. 'In peace he was gentle and dignified,' Scott wrote, 'but in war, as we knew to our cost, he was swift and terrible.' Another unforeseen complication was that these dogs, natives of the Arctic, shed their coats in the northern spring. In the Antarctic, this moult took place at the onset of winter, so that they were in their worst condition when they should have been at their strongest, and sweated in thick winter coats in the Antarctic summer.

Wilson, Shackleton and Ferrar were selected for the first trial trip, a short journey to a spot named White Island which looked to be about five or six miles to the south. No dogs were enlisted; the three men hauled a sledge themselves, and took a tent, sleeping bags and three days' food. It would be easy, they thought, to reach the island in half a day, and here came another lesson: the deceptiveness of shape and distances in these southern latitudes. Everyone constantly under-estimated distances. It took the three men two days' hard hauling to reach a peak on the island 2300 feet above sea-level. A blizzard engulfed them, faces and feet got frostbitten, the sweat of their feet lined their boots with ice, and tea froze in water-bottles worn beneath supposedly frost-proof clothing. It was early autumn; winter had not yet set in. Their reward was to see an unsuspected, unnamed range of mountains, and two unknown bays. They returned to the ship 'so bubbling over with their experiences that it was some time before we could get answers to our eager questions', Scott wrote. Skelton identified the bubbler as Shackleton, 'who immediately started in with tremendous accounts and hardly stopped talking until everyone had turned in'.

This three-day trip taught them how little they knew, and something of the dangers of ignorance. The weather had not been, by Antarctic standards, at all severe, but by marching on for too long in a snowstorm the three novices got so exhausted that they were almost unable to pitch their tent and cook their meal, and disaster all but overtook them.

The next venture was more ambitious. Four officers and eight men were to proceed with four sledges north-eastwards across part of the Barrier's surface, skirting Mt Terror, and thence to Cape Crozier, to deposit in the penguin rookery another canister containing directions as to how to find the expedition's winter quarters. Scott was to have led this party himself, but he fell when ski-ing and injured a knee. Royds replaced him. He drew one sledge with Stoker Arthur Quartley, an American from Baltimore; Able Seaman George Vince from Dorset; Able Seaman W. J. Weller and Frank Wild, a wiry, tough little Yorkshireman who claimed descent from Captain Cook. The other sledge was drawn by Barne and Skelton with Petty Officer Edgar Evans from South Wales; William Heald, son of a prison warder in Lancashire; Stoker Frank Plumley from Somerset; and Clarence Hare from Christchurch, at twenty-one the youngest man on board, who had joined the ship at Lyttleton and become a steward. Each sledge had four dogs.

There was nothing ship-shape and Bristol fashion about the loaded sledges. No one knew just how much food would be needed and in what proportions, how to use the cookers, how to put up the tents, or even how to put on their clothes correctly. Nothing had been tested, the art of packing sledges was unattained. Armitage and Koettlitz should have had some expertise, but do not seem to have employed it. 'Armitage is inclined to talk in a very superior way of his knowledge of sledging, although I am sure he would not have done it any better,' Skelton wrote.

On the morning of 4 March 1902 they started by hauling their sledges up an 800-foot-high ridge, then unpacking them, and carrying everything over the rocks to be repacked the other side. The dogs did hardly anything but fight, one of the cookers refused duty, frostbite attacked; the snow was so soft that they sank in well above their ankles, progress so slow that on the second day they advanced only five miles. The rations in food-bags got mixed up so that a mush of sugar, cheese, butter, soup tablets and chocolate had to be cooked all together. Most of the dogs went lame, the men were dead beat, and on the fourth day Royds decided to push on with Koettlitz and Skelton, wearing their only three pairs of skis, and send everyone else back to the ship under Barne.

Five days' hard going, dragging one light sledge, brought them to the edge of the Barrier, and early on 14 March 1902 they set off with alpine rope, crampons for climbing and the despatches, to look for the penguin rookery where the canister was to be deposited. They scrambled down about five miles of steep rocky slope which tore to ribbons their finneskoes (reindeer-hide boots with the fur inside), sustaining heavy falls, in a sub-zero temperature and driving wind. They failed to find the rookery and had a hard struggle to get back to camp. Next morning, Royds decided to return to the ship; there was only seven days' food left, the tent was shaky, one leg of the cooker was broken, their finneskoes were barely usable and the weather atrocious. Skelton and Koettlitz wanted to make another attempt next day, but Royds over-ruled them.

Later, Koettlitz was to accuse Royds of 'funking' the job and turning back before there was need to. Skelton, asked for his views by the Captain, spoke of Royds' poor spirit – the discomforts he caused in others by his awkwardness and 'girlishness' – how he had gradually 'edged away from the ridges'. As the ridges below Mt Terror were full of deep crevasses, some bridged by a thin layer of snow which gave way before a man's weight, as the sledge was constantly skidding and visibility poor, this

edging away may have been prudent. Royds was 'very much afraid of an
ankle going or some such accident which would have put us in a very nasty
position'. (He thought perhaps of Scott's injured knee.) What form his
'girlishness' in the tent took we can only imagine.

The line between prudence in one responsible for the lives of others,
and over-caution which might be called 'funking', is bound to be a narrow
one. Skelton's conclusion was that 'if he [Royds] does not actually funk
sledging he is next door to it and in fact is never feeling happy – too
girlish'. That seems an incongruous word to use of this hard-working naval
officer, much respected by the men, who had won early promotion for
saving the life of a sailor who had gone overboard in the Baltic, and who was
to end his days as Assistant Commissioner of the Metropolitan Police.

Royds freely admitted that he did not really enjoy the hardships of
sledging, an opinion the great majority of his fellow-men would have
shared; but he put up with them. Was his piano-playing a little suspect in
Skelton's mind? Skill at the piano, in those days, was regarded as a feminine
accomplishment, except in the case of professionals who were always
foreigners. If Royds was not an aesthete in the then accepted meaning of
the word, he and Wilson were, of all the company, the most perceptive of
the finer shades of life. Shackleton might quote poetry, but Royds and
Wilson, the musician and the artist, came nearer to feeling it. Royds loved
the company of women, was devoted to his family – above all to his twin
sister – and took pleasure in subtle changes in colour of the bowls of his
meerschaum pipes. Prudent or 'funking', he turned back without finding
the rookery and got his party safely home, experiencing on the way −42°F
of frost which kept them awake all night shivering in their tent.

# 8 Antarctic Winter

Royds and his companions made the return journey in four days with little food to spare – on one day they covered only four miles through deep, sticky snow – to be greeted by news that brought home to them how quickly disaster could punish mistakes.

Barne's returning party, eight in all, had arrived in good order within four miles of the ship at a hill called Castle Rock. When they reached its summit, a blizzard got up and reduced visibility almost to nil, so they pitched their tents. They could not get their cookers to work, so could make themselves no hot cocoa, and all but two of the men had on ski-boots, not finneskoes, so that frostbite started to attack.

Experienced men would have stayed where they were whatever the discomforts, but they were not experienced and had to learn at a price. The wrong decision was made, they left their tents and gear to make their way on foot to the ship, and soon found themselves on a steep slippery slope where to keep a foothold was almost impossible. Petty Officer Evans stepped on to a patch of bare ice, fell, and hurtled out of sight. Barne sat down and slid after him, vainly trying to check his speed with a clasp-knife. Quartley followed. All three men, as by a miracle, were arrested by a patch of soft snow on the edge of a precipice at whose foot the sea pounded. A yelping dog flashed past and disappeared into the swirling storm.

One of the seamen, Frank Wild, took charge of the party left at the head of the slope and led them in the direction in which he thought the ship must lie. Suddenly he saw the cliff at his feet and the dark sea far below; another step would have taken him over. His cry of warning halted all but Vince, one of those wearing finneskoes which had no grip on slippery ice. Like the dog, he vanished into the abyss.

Wild, with Weller, Heald and Plumley now faced an agonising climb up the steep slope through the blizzard; their lives depended on each foot-hold, one slip and they were gone. Hare, also finneskoe-booted, had vanished. Wild led his party through the darkness guessing at the ship's direction. This episode brought him to the fore as a leader and so he remained thereafter. Also he guessed right. Through the whirling snow-storm, the ship came into sight. Twelve men had set out, four now returned.

Search parties hurried out and that led by Wild came upon Barne, Evans and Quartley wandering about the slopes of Castle Rock, dazed and lost, and Barne so badly frostbitten that when he reached the ship the doctors feared that all his fingers would have to be amputated. That evening Royds brought in his party, so then it seemed that only two men were lost. Vince, they knew, was gone for ever; the other missing man was Clarence Hare. He had last been seen making his way back towards the abandoned sledges to get his ski-boots. The searchers found no sign of him and he was given up for lost.

Two days later, a figure was seen walking down the hill towards the ship. The others could scarcely believe their eyes when they saw that it was Hare, weak but perfectly sound and not even frostbitten. His story was a strange one. He had wandered about aimlessly until, exhausted, he had fallen down and simply gone to sleep. The snow covered and preserved him and he slept unharmed for thirty-six hours. When he woke he recognised his surroundings, and 'came aboard quite naturally as if nothing was amiss' Royds recorded. He had been without food for forty hours and was understandably indignant when given only warm milk. Inexperience, it was now apparent, was the enemy. Even in such vital matters as avoiding frostbite, experience alone could help them. It was not true, Scott observed, that people grew hardened to cold, they merely learnt how to cope with it; for instance, if you had to handle cold metal, you learnt how soon you must return your hand to its warm mitt before your skin stuck to the metal.

There was one more sledging journey to be made before winter finally set in: Scott himself wanted to gain experience, together with as many as possible of the others. A second objective was to lay out depots towards the south, for the use of sledging parties in the spring. They could not start until the ship was securely frozen in for the winter. This took longer than expected; no sooner did a layer of young ice form than gales dispersed it. At last, the sea froze in earnest and gloomy weather gave way to clear, sunlit days of great beauty, the snow flamingo-pink, the mountains purple, the sky blood-red. These scenes brought out a vein of poetry in Scott. 'This is the season of flowers,' he wrote on Easter Sunday (30 March 1902), 'and behold! they have sprung up about us as if by magic: very beautiful ice-flowers, waxen white in the shadow, but radiant with prismatic colours where the sunrays light on their delicate petals.' He went on to explain them scientifically; the mathematical precision of their structure appealed to him as much as their delicate beauty. They resulted from the exclusion of part of the salt when the sea froze. While they had a perfectly logical explanation it was curious, Scott noted, that they should reach their greatest perfection on Easter Day.

On Easter Monday, Scott started off with Armitage, Wilson, Ferrar and eight men divided into two teams, each with three sledges and nine dogs, and supplies for three weeks. Weights had been worked out on the basis that each man could haul up to 200 pounds and each dog 100 pounds, and 'the first discovery we made was that the dogs entirely refused to work on our theory'. Some of them had to be dragged along in their traces and progress was dismal, a mile an hour at best. Temperatures were wicked: down to —47°F when, exhausted, the men crawled into their sleeping bags. The dogs whined and howled all night. The men's fur garments froze as stiff as boards and 'once in, one can do literally nothing but lie as one falls in the tent,' Wilson wrote. 'Reindeer skin hairs get in your mouth and nose and you can't lift a hand to get them out.' At night the men lay in a puddle; sweat which had frozen underneath their garments thawed, and day by day the puddle grew worse, since nothing could be dried. 'In the morning you put on frozen socks, frozen mitts and frozen boots, stuffed with frozen grass and rime ... There's a fascination about it all, but it can't be considered comfort.'

Two more days of this and Scott decided that it was hopeless to go on. They dumped their stores and four of the sledges and sped home in one day, the dogs pulling for all they were worth with only two lightly loaded sledges. Altogether Scott's first sledging trip was a fiasco, but it was not his fault that it had been left until too late in the season. Bit by bit everyone was learning.

On 23 April 1902 the sun vanished over the horizon in a glow of many colours, not to reappear for more than four months. The long Antarctic winter was upon them. These months of darkness were thought to have a depressing psychological effect on men cooped up in ship or hut, often compelled by blizzards to remain indoors for days or weeks at a time with the elements gone wild and savage all about them. Antarctic snow was quite unlike the gentle flakes Englishmen were used to; it was hard and gritty, like fine sand 'which gets into every button-hole,' Wilson wrote, 'through your clothes, under your waistcoat, almost into your watch.'* Depression of the spirit affected health; there had been talk, in relation to other expeditions, of suicide and madness. Scott was determined that nothing like that should happen and knew that the way to avoid it was to keep everyone busy.

A winter routine was established, each man having his special task.

* 'At —40°c the size of ice 'plates' may be less than one millimetre in diameter and they have the consistency of fine flour. At temperatures higher than —5°c the crystals agglomerate into familiar snowflakes.' (*The Antarctic* by H. G. R. King.)

Royds was in general charge of the seamen and petty officers, who were employed on routine activities such as 'watering ship' every few days by hacking out blocks of ice and taking them on board to be melted in the boiler. Every two hours throughout the day, he went out to the meteorological screen to read the instruments. The screen was about a hundred yards from the ship and to reach it in pitch darkness in a blizzard could be a hazardous affair. A rope attached to posts ran between ship and screen, but frequently both rope and posts were buried in snow, as was the screen itself, and even in a hundred yards a man could lose his bearings in the driving, gritty snow and vicious gale. This indeed happened to Skelton and Bernacchi, who lost their grip on the buried rope and groped for two hours on hands and knees along a tide-creek, only twenty yards from the ship, before they found her by touch – they felt her before they could see her.

In temperatures of −40°F and lower Royds had to take off his mitts to wind clocks and change papers on recording drums, and frostbite was a frequent occurrence. At night, each of the eleven men in the wardroom took it in turns, the Skipper included, to take the two-hourly readings. It was not worth while to go to bed between-whiles so the man on duty sat by the stove reading, writing, mending his clothes and doing other odd jobs and making himself a snack in the small hours; sardines on toast was the favourite. Wilson volunteered to take the 8 a.m. readings throughout the winter.

One of Barne's tasks was to measure the movements of the tides with an ingenious gauge devised by the Captain, and made by the engineers. Scott's devices usually worked, unlike those of Shackleton, who devised a new form of sledge consisting of a rum barrel on wheels which gave rise to much hilarity. Barne accompanied Hodgson to holes in the ice made, at some distance from the ship, in order to let down his traps and draw them up at regular intervals with specimens of marine fauna. These ice-holes froze immediately, and opening them up in darkness and sub-zero temperatures was hard and chilly work. Hodgson was one of the smallest and oldest men on board (thirty-seven at the start), but one of the toughest, despite shortness of breath, which earned him the name of Windy among the men, and obliged the doctors to forbid him any but the shortest of sledging journeys. He proved to be one of the hardest workers in the team – although no one could surpass Wilson's industry – and eager to share his discoveries with anyone who displayed an interest. The noxious smells went on, however, and so did his carelessness in breaking instruments.

A continuous record of the earth's magnetic pull, recorded by delicate instruments bought in Germany and housed in the two asbestos huts, was the responsibility of Bernacchi, with the help of Armitage. Wilson had a dozen tasks. He was always at work sketching, even in darkness – though brilliant moonlight often illumined the marvellous beauties of the mountainous landscape – and working up his sketches by lamplight, which was hard on the eyes. There were many birds to be skinned, and routine medical tasks like the sampling of every tin of food and milk consumed on board, and regular inspections of the men. Gums and joints were looked at with especial care to detect the first overt signs of scurvy – swollen, discoloured gums, and swellings round the knees and ankles.

Skelton was constantly at work mending damaged instruments, or making new ones; he was a most ingenious, neat-fingered engineer, although sometimes a disgruntled one. He had a difference of opinion with the Captain over the windmill which had been intended to generate electricity. A storm blew it down and smashed the blades, which provoked one of Scott's outbursts of temper; it had been left running during a storm when it should have been disconnected. Skelton and his assistant Dellbridge reluctantly put it together again, but another gale blew it down a second time, and that was the end of it. 'Why we should have all the trouble of messing about with other people's fantastic ideas I don't know,' Skelton complained in his journal.

Everyone kept a diary, some confined to a brief record of events, but some acting as useful escape valves for pent-up feelings inevitable among men in a confined space rubbing up against each other's personalities. Scott's diary, in general, fell into the first category, Skelton's into the second. The engineer-lieutenant was more critical than most of his colleagues. Koettlitz incurred his displeasure for wasting oil to heat his bacteria incubator when there were no bacteria in it. 'It is the old game, his at any rate – wants everyone to wait on him.' Armitage was guilty of 'singularly bad taste' in getting in a dig at Scott at dinner; he thought 'the Pilot', as Armitage was known, was 'not always genuine'. Shackleton, who irritated him, was 'just an ordinary gasbag', but Skelton repaired the gasbag's typewriter.

Exercise was a problem; blizzards and extreme cold sometimes kept everybody ship-bound for days on end. So was replenishment of the larder. Many of the seals had retreated under the ice, where they could be heard rumbling and sighing. All the birds had gone north except the Emperor Penguins. One day a group of these was sighted, walking sedately across the ice. Despite a blizzard that was blowing, a party left the ship with a roll of wire netting, drove them into an improvised pen and despatched them by stabbing them with penknives in the back of the head. There were thirty, averaging seventy-one pounds. Next morning, four more came up, quite unsuspecting – 'hanging about for their dead pals I suppose', wrote Skelton, who had enjoyed the 'sport'.

Sir Clements Markham had presented the mess with a book in which he had noted the birthdays of all the officers, wedding days (only Wilson and Koettlitz), and other anniversaries such as the launching of the ship, St George's Day, his own birthday and, of course, that of the monarch. All these dates were marked by special dinners served with appropriate beverages, such as champagne, port, wine or brandy. Scott insisted on a certain measure of formality in the little wardroom. Each officer took it in turns to be president for one week, equipped with a gavel with which he rapped the table before proposing toasts. Following naval tradition, the president imposed fines – generally a glass of wine or port all round – for every swearword and every bet. Shackleton was often in trouble for betting.

Some of the non-naval members considered this formality overdone, but Scott believed it important in sustaining morale and standards of behaviour. This view was shared by Bernacchi, who as an Australian and a scientist was quite detached from the traditions of the Royal Navy. He thought that the comparative formality of dinner 'helped to preserve an atmosphere of civilised tolerance such as has seldom been found in polar expeditions'. In the trivialities of day-to-day living, he said, naval tradition was 'of infinite benefit'.

Observance of this tradition included divine service every Sunday. The whole ship's company was paraded in two ranks and inspected by the light of a lantern held aloft by the boatswain, Thomas Feather. 'Somewhat unnecessary in the circumstances,' was Wild's comment, 'but as one of the sailors remarked, "Oh well it pleases him and it doesn't hurt us."' Then came the service taken by the Captain; Royds played the harmonium and the men sang lustily. An inspection of the men's quarters followed, then Sunday dinner with New Zealand mutton, a great treat so long as it lasted. On weekdays, the meat diet was nearly always seal.

Exactly the same victuals were served to the men as to the officers. The only difference was that the men had beer, plus a tot of rum after mid-day dinner, the officers wine. Wilson, although a teetotaller, was put in charge of the drink, and commented on how abstemious everyone was. 'Wine constantly goes round the table without a glass being poured out, or but one or two at the most' on special occasions. A lot of whisky and wine went back in the *Discovery* untouched. Scott was, as ever, almost an abstainer, but Hodgson remarked that after an especially festive dinner to celebrate Midwinter Day (22 June 1903) 'the Captain was quite as much excited as was necessary for his dignity'.

Bernacchi could not recall a single open quarrel in the mess, but Wilson, separated after only three weeks of marriage from his partner, sometimes found the under-currents almost intolerable. 'God knows it is just about as much as I can stand at times,' he wrote to his Ory, 'but I don't intend to give way.' In his diary he burst out, 'I never realised to such an extent that "familiarity breeds contempt" as in the last year during which I have seen a little of the inside of the Royal Navy. God help it.' He thought the navy 'an unfortunate necessity' because it 'spoils many otherwise excellent characters'. He did not say which characters; not those of Scott or Royds, both of whom he admired. He was at times irritated by Barne, who was young and high-spirited and whom he called 'a thoughtless youth' in his diary.

The disappearance of the sun coincided with the first appearance of the *South Polar Times*, edited by Shackleton. All were invited to contribute, and could slip their compositions into a box outside the editor's sanctum, made by screening off part of a coal-bunker; *noms-de-plume* were the rule. The first copy was formally presented to the Captain at dinner and a bottle of cherry brandy opened to drink to its success. Contributions stuck pretty closely to daily experience, with informative articles about seals and penguins, the behaviour of ice, the best clothes for sledging and so on. There were neat silhouettes by Royds, and Wilson's delicate sketches. Several of the men sent in poetry somewhat in the Newbolt vein ('Deeds that Won the Empire' was their favourite reading); Scott's contributions, typically, took the form of acrostics, which his companions found hard to solve.

It was easy to fall into a winter rut, Scott considered, talking shop after dinner or playing whist, bridge or poker. His first proposal to counteract this was for a series of lectures, but when Royds submitted a programme Scott 'strongly objected to sitting for two hours to hear old Dr K and Hodgson meandering on about plankton life and crustacea', so debates were substituted; some serious and technical, others in a lighter vein. The question whether 'women suffer any disabilities at the present day as compared with men' was answered with a ten-to-one 'yes', Hodgson being the odd man out. He was in a minority again on the question of whether 'the influence of sport was beneficial to the nation or not', although he had an ally in Wilson, who thought that sport was a 'relic of barbarity, certain to die out in time in any civilised nation', an opinion howled down by the young naval officers. 'Only the Captain had ever realised that the question of sport had another side to it,' he commented. Another debate concerned the respective merits of the poetry of Tennyson and Browning, with Bernacchi the champion of the former and Shackleton of the latter, with copious illustrations. The issue was decided by one vote, but the records differ as to which side won. After dinner Scott sometimes played chess with Koettlitz, but this did not go any too well. 'The Skipper is very critical and prefers what he calls the sporting game, which as far as can be seen at chess consists in having his own way,' Hodgson commented.

The observation that the Captain could be a bad loser was made more than once. Kind words were said about him too: that he was very fair, took great trouble to see to others' wants, did not attempt to stand on his dignity, kept a firm grip on the work. Irritable and quick-tempered as he often was, he could also be restrained. When Hodgson, so aptly named Muggins, lost a thermometer and twenty-five fathoms of wire down a fish-hole, 'the Skipper was more sympathetic than I expected, and thinks more of the value of the work than I suspected'.

The young steward, Clarence Hare, wrote that the Captain was not bad-tempered so much as abstracted, with his mind elsewhere. A considerate man to look after, Hare thought; for instance he always did his own wash-ing, whereas most of the others in the wardroom got it done for them. Washing was a problem in the *Discovery*, or rather drying; no provision had been made for this and socks and underwear were festooned over stove-pipes and other parts of the wardroom, adding to the dampness of the atmosphere. After a time no one noticed the incongruity of standing to drink a solemn toast to the sovereign with underpants dangling overhead.

Cramped as the quarters were, their occupants proved adaptable. Hodgson, hardly a pioneering type, wrote, 'we probably have the most comfortable winter quarters ever obtained by any polar expedition, which is saying a great deal'. Nevertheless he was patronising about the navy: 'The show has been about as well run as could have been expected in naval hands, but a great deal more could have been done.' This must have been an irritating attitude in one so prone to break and lose irreplaceable equipment. 'Last night it was old Hodgson's observations and he did most of them wrong,' Royds wrote in his diary. 'The Robinson's he read wrong every time; in changing the Dynes' sheet, he failed to put the pen hard up against the paper . . . He broke the electric lamp, and also smashed the glass of the hurricane lamp.' As a result, Royds' nose got frostbitten.

'The Skipper is endlessly planning out new theories, and new methods of observation,' Wilson wrote in his diary, 'an endless and difficult job . . . He has always got some new idea for obtaining new facts, an excellent man for this job, full of theories and ingenuity – and always thinking.' There was a lot to think about in planning sledging programmes for spring and summer, with all the detail this entailed. For want of a nail, the kingdom could be lost and, with the kingdom, everybody's lives.

Skelton wrote in his critical way that when practical preparations for sledging got under way, the wardroom became 'a simple nursery', with Shackleton 'gassing the whole time – ponderous jokes flying through the air – articles being weighed to one-hundredth of a pound – instructions being given not to beeswax thread or to go easy with brass eyelets on account of the extra weight'. Scott, he added, was right about the importance of weight, but 'is fussy about it and why he listens to Shackleton so much beats me'. Skelton could not abide Shackleton, but Wilson liked him and together they walked or skied almost every blizzard-free day to the top of Crater Hill, about three miles away and 1000 feet high, in darkness or moonlight.

With more regard for the pagan elements in the Christian calendar than for its Biblical tradition, Christmas Day was celebrated on 23 June 1902, midwinter day in the Antarctic. Paper streamers decorated messdeck and wardroom, ingenious creations made of ice lit by candles stood on tables loaded with goodies; before mid-day dinner the officers visited in turn the warrant officers', the seamens' and the stokers' separate messes, exchanging good wishes, sampling sweetmeats and generally exuding goodwill. Royds' mother had sent a present for every man. The wardroom repast included turtle soup, New Zealand mutton, plum pudding and mince pies with various extras, and two magnums of champagne followed by port and liqueurs. Then came singsong, and finally a cooling-off on deck under a full moon. 'Overhead a myriad of stars irradiated the heavens,' Scott wrote, 'while the pale shafts of the aurora australis grew and waned in the southern sky.'

This extraordinary phenomenon never lost its power to astonish and beguile. Like many of the wonders of the world it cannot be described, but many have tried, among them Nansen, whose words, written of similar displays in northern latitudes, attempts the impossible more poetically than most.

The aurora shakes over the vault of heaven its veil of glittering silver changing now to yellow, now to green, now to red. It spreads, it contracts again, in restless change, next it breaks into waving, many folded bands of shining silver, over which shoot billows of glittering rays; and then the glory vanishes. Presently it shimmers in tongues of flame over the very zenith; and then again it shoots a bright ray up from the horizon, until the whole melts away in the moonlight, and it is as though one heard the sigh of a departing spirit. Here and there are left a few waving streamers of light, vague as a foreboding – they are the dust from the aurora's glittering coat.

In part, the reason why an aurora is so hard to describe is that it takes so many different forms. H. G. R. King* writes of the 'drapery aurora in which the whole sky seems to be hung with waving luminescent curtains. Sometimes these are followed by strong waves of red and purplish light moving rapidly upwards, one following the other like a rolling tide of fire; an awe-inspiring sight and known as the flaming aurora.'

On this midwinter night the dogs howled at the moon, the aurora

* Librarian of the Scott Polar Research Institute at Cambridge, and authority on polar literature and research.

faded, and at a temperature of —30°F the watchers were frostbitten and 'retired within to contemplate, rather sadly, our extremities swelling as they thawed. Clearly under no conditions can one play tricks with our climate.'

Ten days before this midwinter feast, Scott had summoned Wilson to his cabin and asked him (as he recorded in his diary) whether he would go 'with every dog we possessed' as his companion on the most important sledging journey of all, the attempt to cross the Barrier to find out what lay beyond, and to advance as far to the south as they could get.

Wilson was astonished; it was too good to be true. He reminded Scott of his own previous physical weakness; if either of them broke down on this three-months' journey, neither would return. In reply the Captain 'said some nice things' and made it clear that Wilson was the man he wanted. Wilson suggested that a party of three would be better than two. Scott agreed, and asked, who should the third be? 'I told him it wasn't for me to suggest anyone. He then said, he need hardly have asked me, because he knew who I would say, and added that he was the man he would have chosen himself. So then I knew it was Shackleton, and I told him it was Shackleton's one ambition to go on the southern journey. So it was settled that we three are to go.'

It has often been said that Scott was determined to make this an all-naval expedition and to push out everyone else, but in picking his companions for the most coveted journey of all it was a merchant navy officer and a civilian whom he selected. Wilson, as a doctor and an artist, was an obvious choice. But why Shackleton? He was strong, he was keen, he was cheerful, he was adaptable; but so were others. In his diary, Scott makes no mention of this talk with Wilson, which took place nearly five months before the southern journey was to start; but in the *Voyage of the Discovery* he stated that Barne and Shackleton were his chosen companions. Nothing was said about the later substitution of Wilson for Barne; the damage done to Barne's hands by frostbite was probably a major reason. Shackleton, of course, was overjoyed when he heard of Scott's decision.

Several short preliminary sledging journeys were planned for the spring. The weather grew worse rather than better; in August a temperature of —62°F was recorded at Cape Armitage. This was followed by a blizzard which smothered in snow all the recording instruments, choked the ship's funnels and kept everyone a prisoner on board except Royds and Bernacchi, who had to grope their way out to the screen and the magnetic huts, and Wilson, who was still taking readings every day at 8 a.m. after sampling mouthfuls of sour tinned milk, 'not a nice job' he admitted. Royds' most unpleasant task was to climb to the cross-trees on the mizzen mast, gale or no gale, to read the Dyne's anemometer, often getting frostbitten in the process.

The ship's stoves smoked so abominably during blizzards that all fires had to be drawn, and wardroom and messdeck alike grew excessively chilly. The wardroom was the worst off in that respect because underneath it lay draughty coal-bunkers with steel sides; the caulking had fallen out of the deck, and nothing but a thin strip of linoleum separated the living quarters from the bitter cold. Moreover the cabins were exceedingly damp. Condensation froze on the walls and floor; Scott wrote that on occasion he had literally to chip away a layer of ice to get into his bunk. Moisture trickled on to the floor and froze there, sometimes in the form of stalagmites.

Temperatures were fickle and rose and fell to an extraordinary degree in a short space of time. Sometimes wardroom and cabins became too hot. In the morning Wilson, first up, opened all the decklights to let in fresh air – much too fresh in the view of Armitage and Koettlitz, who came in on one occasion muffled up in sweaters and gloves as a protest, 'growling about the cold and fresh-air faddists and so on'. All the rest, Wilson said, were on his side, including the Captain, who came in last, as he nearly always did, and said he hadn't noticed the cold. After breakfast, Wilson secured the Captain's authority to have his way about the ventilation; so now Wilson wrote, he could 'make these stuffy Arctic explorers breathe fresher air against their wills . . . I think they feel the cold more because they are a good bit older than any of us, but all the same, fresh air must be good for them, so they shall have it'. Good-natured, helpful, kindly as he might be, when Wilson had a principle he stuck to it without reservations. 'One learned never to swear in front of Uncle Bill,' one of the men who served with him recalled. Bill must have felt inclined to swear himself when he dug through snow into the coal chute, the only entry to the bunkers where his penguin skins were stored, to find almost every one ruined by coal-dust, damp and mildew. His written comment merely was, 'The work of a taxidermist is a little heart-breaking on a ship in this climate.'

# 9  Summer Sledging, Dead Dogs

So now the long winter, with its darkness and forced inactivity, was at an end. Although our faces looked pale and white in the glare of the returning day, beneath the pallor lay every evidence of unimpaired vitality; and believing ourselves to be in the perfection of health, as we were of spirits, all thoughts turned to the coming season and to prospects which could look nothing but bright and hopeful. (*The Voyage of the Discovery*)

Sledging was to start on 1 September 1902 – early in the season, too early as it turned out, but everyone was impatient to be off. Several short preliminary journeys were planned before the main effort. Armitage was to recover the depot laid in the autumn only eight miles to the south, and then lead a party to the west to see whether a way could be found through the mountains to whatever lay beyond in the direction of the Magnetic Pole. Royds was to go south-west to investigate a glacier which appeared to join the Sound and might perhaps offer a route inland towards the geographical Pole. Scott himself was to make a short journey to the north mainly in order to test a new form of dog-harness he had designed, and to gain experience in driving dog teams.

In fact, blizzards ushered in September, but Scott was not to be checked, and on 2 September started in atrocious weather taking four sledges, with four dogs each, and eight companions. They were back within three days, finding the conditions impossible alike for dogs and men. Armitage retrieved the depot, and set off a week later to the west with Ferrar and four men. Parties were leaving the ship now like bees going forth from their hives. On 10 September Royds got away with Koettlitz, Petty Officer Evans, Frank Wild and two leading stokers, William Lashly from Hambledon in Hampshire and Arthur Quartley. This time the party looked 'very workmanlike', with sledges well packed and everything in its right place, very different from the previous autumn's turn-out. Lessons had been learned, and a quick, effective camp routine worked out.

The discomforts of the sledging camp were described by nearly all the *Discovery*'s journal-keepers. The first stage was to put up a small tent just large enough for three men to lie down in. If a blizzard was blowing, as it frequently was, this might involve a long struggle with flapping canvas and a collapsing pole. Snow was piled round the outside to hold the sides down and a floor-cloth spread inside, while the third man – they hunted in trios – unpacked the sledge with its frozen contents, took the gear inside and got the cooker ready, sometimes 'burning' his fingers on the bare metal to which his flesh clung.

Changing from the day outfit, a windproof blouse and gaberdine trousers and leggings, into furs for night-wear, was a laborious business. (Woollen underwear stayed on from start to finish of the journey.) Each man first took off his finneskoes, taking care to leave them in the shape of his feet; the soft boots froze as hard as bricks in a few minutes and if he pulled them off carelessly, he could not get his feet into them next morning until he had managed somehow to thaw them out. Then he had to unlace his leggings which required bare fingers, pausing every minute or so to thrust his hands back into their mitts to avoid frostbite.

Three pairs of socks were pulled on: woollen bedsocks and human hair socks, both carried next to the skin all day to keep them warm, and an outer pair of fur socks, worn with the fur inside. Then came a pair of long fur boots reaching above the knee, then fur trousers, then last of all a big, loose fur blouse. Day-socks were often wrapped round the legs inside all this to keep them warm for next morning, together with the *saennegras*, hay that was stuffed into the toes of the finneskoes. Then came the one bright spot, hot supper prepared in the Nansen cooker by whoever was cook for the week. It consisted of hoosh, a 'beautiful mess' of mixed ingredients which might vary, but had a basis of pemmican, often with cheese added and extras like oatmeal and 'red ration', a compound of pea-flour and bacon. After some experiment, Scott settled on a ration of 35·5 ounces of food for each man. This was the bare minimum on which a man could perform the heavy labour of drawing a loaded sledge over rough terrain and at the same time keep up his body temperature in freezing conditions. It did not protect against scurvy – no concentrated, dry ration could do so, and the southern polar regions, unlike their northern counterparts, held no land animals to provide fresh meat. Appetites were always ravenous and the last mouthful was scooped from the cooker and from the pannikins which held each man's portion. After the hoosh there was hot cocoa, greatly relished. There followed the complicated process of settling in for the night.

The question of whether it was best to sleep three men in a bag or to have a bag each was much discussed. (Both kinds of bag were made of reindeer hide.) Scott at first came down on the side of three-man bags, because three men toggled up together kept warmer than three men in separate bags. But of course the discomfort was greater in a three-man bag. No one could move without disturbing the others. Often they were attacked by cramp, and anyone who has experienced this will know how agonizing it must have been to lie as still as they could endure to lie, instead of exercising the limb, which is normally the only way to stop the pain.

Condensation of breath was another trouble; after a few days the inside of the tent became covered with a layer of ice, and every time the wind shook it, a shower of ice and frost crystals fell on to the sleepers' faces. Also their breath froze in their beards and round the necks of their coats, producing a collar as hard as iron. Despite their exhaustion, sleep was generally disturbed and often elusive. Shivering fits lasted sometimes for hours. Next morning, the whole process had to be repeated in reverse, with day clothes frozen stiff as boards and a bitter wind howling.

Then came a ceremony to which none of the journals even refers, such was the reticence of the day. Bernacchi, writing twenty-five years later, when attitudes were not quite so prim, was more explicit. Latrines were ruled out because they took too long to dig and would fill immediately with drifting snow. So, 'feeling like a ham in a sack', after loosening his garments within the tent each man would go forth into the snow, facing the wind and 'watchfully awaiting a temporary lull'. The rest, he wrote, was a matter of speed and dexterity, but however quick you were your nether garments filled with snow and for the next few hours you must endure the extreme discomforts of a wet, cold bottom. No wonder he added 'it is a ghastly business'; and when, later on, some of the men suffered from dysentery, and blizzards raged for days on end, the mind boggles at the thought of their miseries.

On 17 September 1902 Scott started on a preliminary southern reconnaissance with Barne and Shackleton, thirteen dogs and a fortnight's provisions. On the second night out they omitted to pile enough snow on to the skirts of their tent, a blizzard got up and they might as well not have had a tent at all. They spent the whole of the next day in their sleeping bags resting on their elbows and clinging with frozen fingers to the skirts of the tent, while the wind strove relentlessly to whip it away; their bags were filled with half-frozen slush and the temperature fell to −43°F. (By comparison, that of the domestic deep-freezer is normally kept at −5°F.) Thus they lay, with one short dash to seize provision bags, until 6 p.m. when the storm abated somewhat and they managed to make the tent secure. All were frostbitten, especially Barne, whose fingers had never recovered from their injuries on the night of Vince's death. It was not surprising that, taking stock next morning, their clothes stiff with ice, everything wringing wet, they decided to return to the ship to get dry. The dogs had slept out the storm in hollows which they dug in the snow. Scott wrote that his trousers felt as if cut from sheet iron. A splendid sunrise, 'lighting

the east with brilliant red and bathing the western hills in the softest pink'
must have been a poor compensation.

Their respite on board ship was brief; five days later Scott was off
again with Shackleton and the boatswain, Thomas Feather, in place of
Barne, whose hands were still so swollen from frostbite that they looked in
the words of Wild (another victim), like 'bunches of ripe plums'. They
started south again over the frozen sea with a chain of mountains on their
right that formed the wall of Victoria Land. Passing between two islands,
named Black and White respectively, they headed for a long peninsula of
ice-clad land stretching eastwards, which they named Minna Bluff after
Lady Markham. Beyond it lay the unseen. Ridges made of deeply fissured
ice-mounds barred their way. The dogs took alarm, sledges capsized,
snow-drifts obscured the view; Feather disappeared down a crevasse,
but a trace attached to his belt held, and he was pulled out unhurt. Then a
sledge met the same fate. Feather was lowered down the crevasse on the
end of an alpine rope to unpack it, bit by bit, until it was light enough to
be hauled up. They pushed on, crossing innumerable crevasses by means
of snow-bridges whose thin crust might at any step give way. Looking
back on it, Scott wrote, their behaviour was extremely rash, but once again
their luck held. They could not get beyond the Minna Bluff, however, and
on 1 October 1902 established a depot there with provisions for six weeks,
marked it with a black flag, took careful angles and headed for home, eighty-
five miles away, which they reached in three days.

Back in the *Discovery*, they were greeted with grave news. Armitage and
his party had returned from their journey three days before and Wilson,
on examining the members, had found symptoms of scurvy in Heald,
Ferrar and Petty Officer Jacob Cross. Scott had always dreaded this, but
the regular consumption of seal-meat had been thought to be an adequate
preventive. At one blow, Scott wrote, this news upset all his sense of peace
and comfort.

Drastic action was immediately taken: the ship spring-cleaned from bow
to stern, the bilges disinfected, bottled fruit and limejuice increased in
the diet, and a party sent out to conduct a massive slaughter of seals.
Wilson was again in charge, with Barne and four men. Taking all the dogs
and most of the sledges they went north and slew a great many seals in
such intense cold that they had to thaw their mitts in the blood of their
victims to get them on and off. Soaked in blood and blubber, they returned
with over a thousand pounds of meat, leaving more to be fetched later.
Scott was then able to ban all tinned meat from the diet and seal was served
every day. (One large seal lasted the company for only two days.) These
measures banished all symptoms of scurvy within a fortnight.

Later, Armitage was to lay the blame for this outbreak on Scott's dislike of killing animals, saying that if more seals had been killed earlier, it need never have happened. Enough seals had in fact been killed to provide fresh meat at least twice a week, and when the men were in the ship this proved sufficient. No symptoms of scurvy appeared until they went on sledging journeys, subject to great strain and living mainly on pemmican. Moreover, as the cause of scurvy was believed to be tainted meat, and as the greatest care had been taken by Koettlitz and Wilson to see that every tin opened for consumption was wholesome, all should have been well. It was lack of scientific knowledge, rather than Scott's admitted reluctance to slaughter a great quantity of seals, that caused the outbreak.

Scott might have taken comfort, if he felt this to be needed, from the opinions of the predecessor whom he so much admired, James Clark Ross. Like Scott, Ross knew that animals had to be slaughtered, but condemned all needless killing. On a visit to the Falkland Islands in 1842 he was invited by the islanders to join in their favourite sport, a wild cattle hunt. The sight disgusted him, and he endorsed an observation made by one of his officers that, 'The death by violent means of any creature innocuous to man should excite sympathy in the well regulated mind, proportionally to the defencelessness of the sufferer; whilst the sight of one of the larger animals, helplessly weltering in its own blood, is not only painful but revolting.' No animal is more innocuous to man than a seal.

The scurvy dealt with, sledging was resumed. Royds went off with Skelton, Evans, Lashly, Quartley and Wild on a renewed attempt to reach Cape Crozier and find the penguin rookery that had eluded them before. On 10 October 1902, at the foot of Mt Terror, the temperature fell to −58°F which Royds believed to be a record for polar travel. (In fact on 7 August 1902, on Crater Hill, −62°F had been recorded.) Next day Skelton and Evans, equipped with ropes and crampons – Royds had sprained an ankle – clambered down the rocks to the beach, found the rookery, and deposited the canister.

Back in camp, a blizzard held them prisoner for five horrible days. Gale-driven snow buried their two small tents, forcing the canvas inwards until the three men in each were too confined to cook a meal or even to stretch their legs; in their wringing-wet sleeping bags they suffered agonies from cramp. When at last the blizzard subsided, Skelton with Quartley and Evans went to inspect and photograph the junction of the Barrier with the land. At the Barrier's edge, they looked down and saw, with great excitement, a cluster of about four hundred Emperor Penguins: the first rookery belonging to this species that anyone had ever seen.

The Ross Sea, which had been completely frozen over before the blizzard, was now entirely free of ice, except for the small bay on to which they were looking. Descending over dangerous pressure ridges, they found no eggs but about thirty chicks, three of which they brought back. Each chick was carried on the feet of a parent and protected by a loose flap of the adult bird's abdomen. Chicks were constantly falling off, and in the scramble to get hold of them by adults overcharged with mother-love, a great many – Wilson estimated three-quarters – were trampled to death, a drastic but efficient form of population control. 'I think the chickens hate their parents,' Wilson commented, adding that this was not surprising. But the parents so loved their chickens that Skelton had to fight them off when he picked up the little birds, and next day he was stiff and sore all over. On the way back to the ship he and Royds suffered from painful and persistent snow-blindness, as well as from frostbite and cold; but on 24 October 1902 all got back safely to the joys of hot baths, change of clothing, removal of beards, lavish meals and the congratulations of the whole ship's company.

'It is a treat to have Royds back,' Wilson wrote. 'He is a splendid chap and makes a great difference in the mess.' Despite tender fingers and painful eyes, Royds resumed his nightly sessions at the piano. But not for long. They were soon on the move again; in a few days Barne was to take further supplies to the depot Scott had laid, and then Scott himself was to follow, with Wilson and Shackleton, on their long-planned southern journey. Royds had volunteered to go back to the Emperor Penguin rookery to gather further information and to search for eggs. This he did, taking only Frank Plumley and Arthur Blissett, a lance-corporal in the Royal Mounted Light Infantry attached to the Royal Marines. On 8 November 1902 they reached the rookery to find the adult birds but not a single young one. What had happened to them was a mystery; they could not, in three weeks, have shed their down and grown adult plumage, and therefore would not have been able to survive in the water. Wilson thought they must have drifted northwards on an ice-floe, but could only guess.

Royds' disappointment was reversed when Blissett spotted an object embedded in the ice which proved to be a complete egg; the first, they believed, ever to be found. It was in fact the second; the French explorer Dumont d'Urville had brought one back from Adélie Land in 1840. That egg found its way, oddly enough, to the Norwich museum, whence it has moved on to Cambridge.

On 2 November Scott, Wilson and Shackleton set forth on their southern journey, the centrepiece of the show, together with a large supporting party under Barne. Everyone else gathered to see them off, take photographs and cheer; under an overcast sky and with a chill wind blowing, their five sledges took off drawn by nineteen dogs – every available animal. The total load was 1852lbs, just short of 100lbs per dog: a heavy load as Scott admitted, but the men intended to assist the dogs and the load would lighten as the journey went on. Wilson noted that Scott disliked his flag and did not want to take it; he did not say why. Perhaps Sir Clements' motto smacked too much of a scout-leader admonishing his troop.

When Wilson had been invited to join the southern party, he had written, 'Our object is to get as far south in a straight line on the Barrier as we can, reach the Pole if possible, or find some new land, anyhow do all we can in the time and get back to the ship at the end of January.' Scott himself nowhere expressed the hope of attaining the Pole on this exploratory journey, and those who had sent out the *Discovery* had studiously avoided any mention of it; Markham had always regarded attainment of the Pole as a red herring. To find out what lay beyond that immense sheet of snow-clad ice named by Ross was a sufficient objective. But hope will always outrun sober expectation, and these three young men in perfect physical condition, knowing by now what they had to face and equipped to do so by practical experience and a twelvemonth of meticulous planning, cannot but have entertained the vision of a triumphant return, leaving their country's flag flying at the extremity of the globe. That they might not return at all they well knew. All had left farewell letters: Scott to his mother, Wilson to his wife, Shackleton to his betrothed.

Wilson dated the day of their departure as the 23rd Sunday after Trinity. To him, the matter of their return was in the hands of the Almighty. Man proposes, God disposes; he stepped out beside the sledges believing implicitly that God would guide them as He willed to triumph or disaster. This faith was never shaken. A sacrifice demanded of a polar explorer that he deeply regretted was to be cut off for several years from receiving Holy Communion, and on Sundays he would find a time and place to read through parts of the Communion service in a solitude shared only with his Creator and his absent wife. But while Wilson was a religious man, he was also a scientist with a mind trained to measure, analyse and assess. His assessment of their chances of making important discoveries was realistic. A month before they left he wrote, 'Our prospects of finding land due south are not by any means bright. Still he [Scott] is bent on going on a long journey in that direction and I shall say nothing against it.'

'We did not expect a feather bed down here, and so *de rien*' was Shackleton's robust philosophy. The first part of his ambition had been realised; he was at the right hand of the leader of this great national enterprise, and there can be little doubt that his irrepressible optimism had carried them to the Pole and back before they had properly started.

Scott's hopes and fears were, as always, more enigmatic. His diary is business-like and laconic, confined mainly to the weather, position, times, distances, the day-to-day events of this gruelling journey. For him, much

more than for the others, this was the crisis of his career. The hard road
south across the Barrier could be for him a road to fame, public acclama-
tion, naval advancement and the security whose lack had haunted him for
so long. The first two he could do without; the other two were very close
to his heart. Should he fail, he would slip back into obscurity and worse,
branded as a man incompetent to grasp a great opportunity – not up to
the job.

For long hours in his cabin, he had brooded over every foreseeable
contingency; few expeditions can have been more carefully thought out in
advance. But no man can foresee contingencies that have never been
experienced, not merely by the man himself, but by any other human being
in history. The whole Antarctic continent was *terra incognita* in the fullest
meaning of the words. All that these three men could be sure of was the
blizzard's ferocity, the cold's intensity, the dangers of concealed crevasses,
the certainty of frostbite, snow-blindness and hunger. If you could, as
they knew, get hopelessly lost within a few yards of the ship, how could
you expect to march for hundreds of miles into the unknown and back
without disaster? On Scott rested the full weight of the responsibility.
The public money that had been invested, the trust of learned societies
and eminent men, the hopes of those who looked for a great national
triumph – all this now depended on his leadership, his guts, the correctness
of his decisions. But above all, of course, on that element which can be
called luck, providence, or the will of God.

'The dogs have never been in such form,' Scott wrote; they went away
at the gallop, and trotting men could barely keep up with them. Soon they
were slowed by sticky snow and deep *sastrugi*, and then for two days a
blizzard kept the men in their tents. Lying in their three-man sleeping-bag,
Scott, Shackleton and Wilson took it in turns to read chapters from the
*Origin of Species*. On the third day out, Shackleton started a persistent
cough. Wilson had never felt entirely confident about Shackleton, and had
written, 'For some reason, I don't think he is fitted for the job. The
Captain is strong and hard as a bulldog, but Shackleton hasn't the legs
the job wants. He is so keen to go, however, that he will carry it through.'

Beyond Minna Bluff, they were into the unknown and 'already appeared
to be lost on the great open plain'. It was a weird feeling; with overcast
skies and a fine drifting mist, everything looked grey and there was nothing
whatever, not a rock, not a hummock, to break the monotony. Scott referred
later to 'the terrible sameness of grey'. But at the 79th parallel the sun
shone again and spirits rose. Photographs were taken, and half Barne's
supporting party turned back. The rest pushed on for two more days until
they, too, turned back on 15 November 1902. The sun shone on their farewells and 'our hopes ran high for the future', the leader wrote.

From the next day, things began to go wrong. The snow was soft, the surface bad, but the main trouble lay with the dogs. All their initial vigour and enthusiasm seemed to fail. Instead of greeting their drivers in the morning with wagging tails and eagerness to be up and doing – especially the leader Nigger, a big black dog with tawny markings, a powerful chest and a deep throaty bark, of whom Scott wrote 'a more perfect sledge dog could scarcely be imagined' – they had to be cajoled and bullied into their harness, and were done by the day's end. From 16 November onwards Scott's diary makes sad reading, with the dogs daily losing heart and condition, and the men's hopes of making a heroic journey slowly fading away.

Supposing the loads to be too heavy, Scott resorted to the soul-destroying expedient of relaying. The loads were halved; each sledge took on a half-load and dumped it, returning for the second half; thus men and dogs must cover three miles for every mile they advanced. On the 18th, they gained five miles but had to march fifteen. This was extremely depressing; even more so was the fact that the dogs continued to lose condition rather than to recover with lighter loads. Ice crystals clogged the runners of the sledges and made the going very hard. On the 19th Wilson wrote, 'This is wearing us out and the dogs, and the exertion of driving the poor beasts is something awful.' On the following day they advanced only three and a half miles. The three men took the duties in turn. The first, harnessed to the head of the trace, led and shouted encouragement; the second pulled in silence behind him; the third, who did not pull, wielded the whip with as much brutality as he could summon, and shouted himself hoarse. 'It is all very heart-breaking work.'

The British love of dogs, and habit of regarding them as faithful friends of man rather than as beasts of burden, has been blamed for Scott's failures. It is true that he was fond of animals, dogs included, as were most of his followers. He was a humane man. It was not so much the need to use dogs as beasts of burden, or having to kill and eat them, that troubled him, as the cruelty with which they had to be treated while alive. He was not alone in these feelings. Fridtjof Nansen, like Scott a humane man and, like him also, unsuccessful in reaching his goal, had written of his dog teams:

It was undeniable cruelty to the poor animals from first to last, and one must often look back on it with horror. It makes me shudder even now when I think of how we beat them mercilessly with thick ash sticks when, hardly able to move, they stopped from sheer exhaustion . . . It is the sad part of expeditions of this kind that one systematically kills all better feelings, until only a hard-hearted egotism remains. When I think of all those splendid animals, toiling for us without a murmur, as long as they could strain a muscle, never getting any thanks or even so much as a kind word, daily writhing under the lash until the time came when they could do no more and death freed them from their pangs – when I think of how they were left behind one by one, up there on those desolate ice-fields . . . I have moments of bitter self-reproach.

And even Amundsen, as revealed by his writings less sensitive and introspective than Nansen, pleaded guilty to the same charge. 'The daily hard work and the object I would not give up had made me brutal, for brutal I was when I forced those five skeletons to haul that excessive load. Thor had to go till he dropped. When we cut him open we found that his whole chest was one large abscess.' He added, 'My only dark memory of my stay in the South – the over-taxing of those fine animals.'

It might be put to Scott's credit, rather than the reverse, that he hated the whole business and refused to carry it to the lengths deplored by the Norwegians. Walking behind 'a long string of depressed animals . . . showing an utter weariness of life', he would 'occasionally bring the lash down with a crack on the snow or across the back of some laggard'; this was 'sickening work but it was the only way'. Neither Nansen nor Amundsen was likely to have wasted energy in bringing the lash down on the snow.

Scott's failure sprang not from his compassion for the dogs but from faults in their feeding. Quite soon it became clear that something had gone wrong with their diet. He had originally intended to take dog-biscuit, 'but in an evil moment I was persuaded by one who had great experience in dog-driving to take fish'. His adviser might have been Nansen, who had successfully fed his teams on dried stockfish, which was exported in large quantities from Norway for human food. There was nothing wrong with the advice, nor with the stockfish when it was bought. Rolled in bundles, it was carried on deck and had to pass through the tropics. Scott concluded that during the voyage it had acquired the kind of 'taint' for which doctors so assiduously screened the human tinned food. In fact, it had probably got damp and over-heated and parts of it had gone bad.

With hindsight, it seems strange that no one thought of this hazard: neither Scott himself nor any of his officers – Armitage who had experience of feeding dogs, Shackleton who was in charge of stores and stowage, nor either of the doctors, especially Koettlitz who was a bacteriologist. It is always true, and always will be, that people learn by their mistakes and Scott paid dearly for this one. 'The lesson for future travellers in the South is obvious,' he wrote, 'in that they should safeguard their dogs as surely as they do their men.'

There was nothing to be done but to press on as far south as they could get so long as the dogs lasted, and then to do the hauling themselves. Scott described the failure of the dogs as 'a terrible calamity'. They would have made better progress had they killed off all the dogs as soon as they realised the position, depoting for the return journey the meat they could not haul, but they went on hoping against hope that somehow the animals would overcome the trouble and revive.

As it was, they decided to veer towards the high mountains on their right, farther away than they looked, owing to the nature of the atmosphere which could, on occasion, enable a man to see a mountain 300 miles away. Also the refraction of light produced strange mirages. Objects out of sight beyond the horizon would appear quite clearly, sometimes upside down, only to disappear as suddenly. Now and again these mirages helped explorers by displaying to their eyes a cairn or flag for which they were making, but which was still invisible. The most remarkable instance of this was to be experienced by Shackleton and two companions in 1909 when, on their last legs from hunger and exhaustion on their return march after their attempt to reach the Pole, they were searching for the depot on which their lives depended; it was out of sight, but a mirage projected the flag above the horizon; the flag disappeared just as they had taken its bearings. Shackleton always believed this to have been a divinely-inspired miracle; without it, they would have perished.

On 25 November 1902 there was a morsel of comfort; Scott's party crossed the 80th parallel, beyond which all maps were blank. 'It has always been our ambition to get inside that white space and now we are there the space can no longer be a blank; this compensates for a lot of trouble.' They read another chapter of Darwin. Their trouble now was principally hunger. Scott had cut the ration to 28·6 ounces per man per day, which included only 7·5 ounces of meat. Based on expert medical calculations, this was a perfectly adequate, indeed a generous, ration for ordinary purposes, but did not reckon with ravenous appetites resulting from man-hauling sledges hour after hour, in conditions of extreme hardship and cold. Wilson gave the day's menu just before rations were cut. Breakfast: chopped bacon fried with pounded biscuit, two cups of tea and a dry biscuit. Lunch: one biscuit, two cups of Bovril, a stick of chocolate, and four lumps of sugar. Supper: hoosh of pemmican, red ration, pounded biscuit, one soup square and powdered cheese, all boiled up together. A cup of sweetened cocoa rounded off the meal.

As time went on, the ration was progressively reduced and pangs of hunger became acute. Snow-blindness kept Wilson writhing in agony for a whole afternoon and evening. He had rheumatism as well, but in spite of it spent several hours each day, after they had camped, with sketchbook and crayons, attempting to capture the subtle colourings and, as they approached the mountains, distant views of glittering peaks. On 29 November a display of parhelia – mock suns created by refraction of light from myriads of tiny, many-faceted ice crystals suspended in the dry atmosphere – and wierd circles of light taxed his skill and sharpened the feeling that they were advancing like tiny insects into a strange, unearthly mystery, estranged from everything else in the world.

'We cannot stop, we cannot go back, and there is no alternative but to harden our hearts and drive,' Scott wrote. Luckily, he added, each man had to drive only one day in three, but even so, it was almost as bad to watch as to perform. 'Certainly dog driving is the most terrible work one has to face in this sort of business.' They took to night marches in the hope of easing matters for the dogs, but it made little difference. On 5 December he wrote, 'The events of the day's march are now becoming so dreary and dispiriting that one longs to forget them when we camp; it is an effort even to record them in a diary. Our utmost efforts could not produce more than three miles for the whole march.' One hot meal was cut out. Five days later the first death occurred among the dogs and his companions fell eagerly upon the corpse; 'there is a chance that this change of diet may save the better animals'. Their lives might well have been longer had he killed off the weaker animals at once and fed them to the stronger, without waiting for them to die.

On 15 December 1902 they made a depot of their dog-food, 'none too soon'; they had struggled on through deep snow, sinking in up to the ankles, every step so short that the heel of the advanced foot was seldom planted beyond the toe of the other; they covered only two miles. Heading now for the coastline to the west, they were halted by an enormous chasm. Near its brink they made a depot of most of their remaining food and with lightened sledges advanced without relaying, an inexpressible relief. With relaying, they had travelled 280 statute miles to advance less than two degrees of latitude. (A degree of latitude measures sixty-nine geographical, just under seventy-nine statute miles.)

Rations had been cut again and hunger was a torture. They thought and spoke of nothing but food. Scott was the best off, he reckoned, because he was the only smoker and his two pipes a day gave solace. 'Nearly every night now we dream of eating and food,' Wilson wrote. 'Dreams as a rule of splendid food, ball suppers, sirloins of beef, cauldrons full of steaming vegetables. But one spends all one's time shouting at waiters who won't bring one a plate of anything, or else finds the beef is only ashes when one gets it, or a pot full of honey has been poured out on a sawdusty floor. One very rarely gets a feed in one's sleep.' Though he did once eat a whole dream-cake, and part of a huge roast sirloin set before him by Sir David Gill at Cape Town during an examination in Divinity. The reality next day was 'a cold and meagre lunch of a piece of dried seal liver, a biscuit and eight lumps of sugar', followed by a chapter from Darwin read by the Skipper.

They had decided to try to save the best nine dogs by feeding them on the flesh of the others, and noted some improvement. Wilson volunteered for the job of butchering. Scott knew that he ought to take his turn but shirked it, 'a moral cowardice of which I am heartily ashamed'. The selected victim was led a little way off behind the sledges, and although the others raised enfeebled howls of anticipation, knowing that a meal was on the way, the victim himself wagged his tail and followed willingly, never suspecting his fate. 'We can only keep them on the move by constant shouting; this devolves on me,' Scott observed. 'Stripes and Brownie doing absolutely nothing and vomiting. Poor old Grannie pulled till she could pull no longer and lay down in the snow; they put her on a sledge and she soon died. The dogs take away all idea of enjoying the marches.' Scott began to wonder whether they would get back under their own unaided efforts; the dogs were dwindling fast.

Then came another blow. Wilson reported that Shackleton's gums were swollen, the first sign of scurvy. Bacon was abandoned and seal-meat increased a little, but the net result was even less food. 'Hunger is gripping us very tightly.' On 20 December Wilson lay awake all night from sheer hunger, but they pressed on and Scott wrote glowingly of the beauties of the mountains ahead. He was looking for a glacier coming down from 'the interior ice-cap – if there is one' by means of which a party of men, not this one certainly, might climb up to the plateau – if there was one – above the mountains and find a way to the Pole.

In their desperate craving for food absolute fairness in its distribution was essential, and Shackleton invented a game of 'shut-eye' to achieve this aim. One of the three divided the food into equal shares; a second man turned his back; the first asked 'whose is that?'; the second named its consumer; and so on until the three portions were allocated by chance, not judgement.

At last there came a break in the dreary routine. On Christmas Day the sky was cloudless, the sunshine gloriously bright, the distant mountains sharply defined, the snow sparkling and the smell of breakfast cooking in the tent beyond words enticing. For some time they had restricted themselves to one hot meal a day to conserve their dwindling supply of paraffin but on this day they let themselves go. Breakfast consisted of a pannikin-full of biscuit and seal-liver fried in bacon and pemmican fat, followed by a spoonful of blackberry jam. They covered six miles before lunch, dragging the sledges themselves while the dogs walked along with slack traces. For lunch they had hot cocoa with a whole biscuit, and more jam.

Although the temperature was below freezing point, they found the heat uncomfortable. Nevertheless they made their best march since the dogs

had begun to fail: eleven miles. Supper was a feast: hoosh into which
they put double portions of everything, so thick that a spoon stood up in
it, followed by cocoa which for once was hot. Shackleton had stowed away
in the toe of a spare sock a miniature plum pudding, the size of a cricket ball,
which was heated in the cocoa and decorated with a crumpled spray of
artificial holly. For the first time for weeks they went to bed replete and did
not dream of food.

Next day their troubles began again; Wilson's eyes were so painful that
even he could not conceal it. Shackleton performed the butcher's task on
Brownie; 'poor little dog he has been a decided nuisance to us and probably
an equal one to himself during the last week'. Yet optimism was not to be
put down. 'With so much new land and so much matter for discussion one
begins to think that our trip will really find a corner in polar history. If
so, one's hard work and short commons will be repaid.' And again: 'Ever
before our eyes was the line which we were now drawing on the white space
of the Antarctic chart.' They were by now abreast of a sharp conical peak
which they named Christmas Mountain. Steep red cliffs sweeping away to
the south-east marked the coastline, and the limit of their vision was a far-
distant, lofty peak, 'the most southerly land to which we should be able to
apply a name' Scott wrote; Mr Longstaff was commemorated in this
*ultima thule* of the south.

Wilson was in agony from snow-blindness which even cocaine could not
alleviate. The victim of this horrible complaint felt as if his eyeballs were
being tattooed by red-hot needles, or bombarded by gritty sand. In Wilson's
case it was caused by leaving off his goggles in order to sketch. Next day
he hauled his sledge on skis blindfolded, 'his head literally in a bag', and
they all approached nearer to the coast by ten miles. 'Nothing could have
been nicer than the way I was treated,' he wrote of his companions. As he
walked along he day-dreamt of beechwoods on Birdlip Hill. The swish-
swish of the skis were 'as though one's feet were brushing through dead
leaves, or cranberry undergrowth, or juicy blue-bells. . . . it was delightful.'
Despite the pain and hunger he had begun, like his leader, to feel that it was
all worthwhile.

Although we shall not have done a good record towards the South Pole, we shall
have had the unlooked for, hardly expected, interest of a long new coastline with
very gigantic mountain ranges to survey and sketch, a thing which to my mind has
made a far more interesting journey of this than if we had travelled due south on a
snow plain for so many hundred miles and back again.

As Wilson hauled blindfolded, Scott described to him more mountains
that were coming into view, even farther south than Mt Longstaff, more
lofty, more magnificent. Within their field of vision the range culminated

in a 'gloriously sharp double peak crowned with a few flecks of cirrus cloud'. This dwarfed all the mountains they had hitherto seen. They named it Mt Markham, and estimated its height at 13,000 feet.

Scott had decided to turn back on the last day of the year. Two days were left in which to push on as far as they could, but a blizzard followed by fog kept them in their tent, frustrated and famished. They had reached their farthest south at 82° 17's. Although still about 480 statute miles from the Pole, and some 115 from the glacier by which all three were to ascend to the plateau in years to come, they had advanced over 300 miles farther south than any other mortal. The dogs were too far gone, Scott sadly remarked, to show even a spark of excitement when they turned towards home; 'it almost seems that most of them guess how poor a chance they have of ever seeing the ship'.

By the afternoon of 31 December 1902 the weather had cleared and the three men made a dash on skis for the cliff face to gather samples of red and black rock for the geologist. But their way was barred by a deep chasm which, with ropes and ice-axes, they endeavoured to descend. It was a chaos of ice, Wilson wrote; on all sides were crevasses with sheer ice cliffs and 'not a sign of any of them until one of us went down and saw blue depths below to any extent you like . . . one was always expecting to see someone drop in a hole, and while keeping your rope taut in case that happened, you would suddenly drop in a hole yourself'. Progress, as he observed, had 'an element of uncertainty about it'. When they reached the bottom of the chasm they were confronted by a sheer overhanging ice wall ahead, impossible to surmount. Once again Scott was disappointed, but Wilson was enthralled by the beauty of the scene. The prismatic colours of ice crystals formed what looked like a carpet of snow glittering with gems of crimson, blue, violet, yellow, green and orange, 'of a brilliance that would put any jewel in the shade'. That night the hoosh pot was upset and the ravenous men scraped up every morsel from the floorcloth, and wasted none.

They had food enough to last a fortnight and must average better than seven miles a day to reach the nearest depot before it ran out. That did not seem much, but they must march considerably farther on good days in order to allow for fog and blizzards, and they were not as strong as they had been. Scott admitted a mistake in having under-estimated the amount of food they needed to keep up their strength. It had been a false economy. Not only did the dogs assist them no longer, they were a hindrance. There was a strong vein of obstinacy in Scott's nature. He had determined to get some, at least, of the dogs back to the ship, although he had constantly to revise his estimate of the number likely to survive by feeding on their weaker companions. Several were carried on the sledges, too weak to move, to be despatched when camp was made. A dog a day was dropping dead or being slaughtered. Bismarck was killed on 4 January 1903 (Epiphany Sunday, Wilson noted, 'good juicy brown beef dripping is one thing I long for, and a large jugful of fresh creamy milk in Crippetts' dairy'). Boss dropped behind and never reappeared. 'He must have sunk like the rest from sheer exhaustion, but with no one by to give him the last merciful *quietus.*' When Kid caved in, Scott wrote that he could almost weep; 'he has pulled like a Trojan throughout, and his stout little heart bore him up till his legs failed beneath him, and he fell never to rise again'.

When finally they gave up even trying to drive the few remaining dogs and let them follow free, the relief was immense. 'No more cheering and dragging in front, no more shouting and yelling behind, no more clearing of tangled traces, no more dismal stoppages, and no more whip.' He would prefer ten days of man-hauling, he wrote, to one spent in driving a worn-out dog team. Now, instead of shouting at the animals, they could talk to each other, and found that time passed a great deal quicker as a result.

All the same it was a dispiriting march, relieved whenever possible by hoisting a sail and scudding before the wind. Wet, soggy snow clung to the runners, and the men were permanently wet themselves owing to the mild weather and hot sun. In his sleeping-bag Wilson 'steamed like an engine'; no one had taken off his clothes since the ship had been left behind. Now there was anxiety as to whether they would find the depot in this immensity of greyness. When they were down to one day's remaining rations Scott, taking a meridional altitude, casually swept the horizon with his telescope and spotted the black flag: a tribute to the accuracy of his navigation. That night they had a lavish 'fat hoosh', but next morning (14 January 1903) there was another blow. Symptoms of scurvy had re-appeared, especially in Shackleton; not only were his gums red and swollen, but his throat was congested, his breath short, and he started to spit blood.

Next morning they re-organised, jettisoned everything they could, and started back with two lightly loaded sledges. But that evening Wilson, getting Scott alone, told him that the situation was more serious than he had said in Shackleton's presence. A total breakdown might not be far away. Scott now made up his mind to abandon his hope of charting the western coast-line and faced the necessity of despatching the last two dogs. It went to his heart to give the order but he did. Nigger and his companion Jim were killed. 'I think we could all have wept', he wrote, 'at this finale to a tale of tragedy; I scarcely like to write of it.'

Now there were only two men to pull the sledges. Shackleton had to walk beside them avoiding exertion insofar as he could. Even so, that night violent paroxysms of coughing attacked him and he gasped for breath. The grey, overcast, gloomy weather echoed and intensified their mood. No land, no mountains, nothing to see as they plodded on. 'One cannot see one's own footsteps in soft snow in this light.' Wilson, indomitably sketching in a bitter wind, was again attacked by snow-blindness and, despite a doubling of the seal-meat ration, hunger still gripped them all. He and Scott were dragging over 260 lbs each. Despite all this, as they trudged along they 'had long talks on every subject imaginable and indeed he [Scott] is a most interesting talker when he starts'.

Shackleton was still coughing, spitting blood and feeling dizzy; 'with his excitable temperament', Scott wrote, 'it is especially difficult for him to take things quietly . . . It is all very dreadful to watch, knowing that we can do nothing to relieve him.' But the extra seal-meat was having its effect and both Scott and Wilson were much better. The overcast weather made navigation without landmarks a very tricky affair. 'It is difficult to describe the trying nature of this work,' wrote Scott, 'for hours one plods on, ever searching for some definite sign.'

On 18 January 1903 Shackleton gave out; a bad attack of breathlessness forced them to camp. 'He is very plucky about it, for he does not complain, though there is no doubt he is suffering badly.' Two days later he was better, then worse, then better, until on 28 January they reached Depot A, only sixty miles from the ship. 'At length and at last we have reached the land of plenty.' So greedily did they stuff themselves with sardines, marmalade, pea-soup, prunes, port and other luxuries that their over-loaded stomachs kept them on the go most of the night. Naturally this exacerbated Shackleton's condition; next day it took them twenty minutes to get him on to his skis, and later he had to travel on one of the sledges. Nevertheless, they covered fifteen miles that day with the help of their sail, and for the rest of the journey Shackleton's condition improved although he continued to spit blood, had a fall from giddiness, and could do no hauling.

Soon White Island came into view, then the mountains Erebus and Terror. 'We are as near spent,' Scott admitted, 'as three persons can be.' Next day (3 February 1903) they saw two specks on the snow which they took to be penguins, but which resolved themselves into the figures of Skelton and Bernacchi coming to meet them. Soon they were back on board, the ship adorned with flags to greet them, handshakes and congratulations all round. The relief ship *Morning* had arrived a week before. 'All the news was good about everything,' Wilson recorded, 'except that there are still eight miles between ship and the sea.' Only now did he realise how filthy they were, 'our faces the colour of brown boots, except where lamp soot had made them black'. There was a great celebration, but 'instead of drink and noise and songs and strangers,' Wilson recorded,

'I know I was longing to lie down on my bunk and have a long quiet yarn with Charles Royds'. They had been away for ninety-three days and had covered 960 statute miles. 'If we had not achieved such great results as at one time we had hoped for,' the leader concluded, 'we knew at least that we had striven and endured with all our might.'

Shackleton
Goes Home

The *Morning*, commanded by William Colbeck RNR, had left Lyttleton on 6 December 1902. On the way to Cape Adare this elderly vessel, considerably smaller than the *Discovery* – only 150 feet long – and not nearly as robust, almost collided with a small rocky island. After extricating her, Colbeck and two companions went ashore, hoisted the Union Jack, claimed the island in the name of King Edward VII and called it after Captain Scott. The Captain himself had been becomingly modest in the matter of names; all his officers were by now commemorated by capes, points, inlets, glaciers and so on, but this unimportant island way out in the middle of the southern ocean was the only natural feature to receive his name.

On 24 January 1903 the *Morning* made fast with ice-anchors to the floe off Hut Point. Armitage and a party of twelve hurried across with sledges to bring back the mail for which everyone was eagerly waiting. The mail, however, did not come, and on enquiry a signal from the *Morning* ran, 'Detained by ice'. Those in the *Discovery* wondered whether it was really ice that was detaining Armitage's party or the hospitality of the *Morning*'s company of seven officers and twenty-two merchant seamen, drawn from whaling and sealing vessels. Royds, left in the *Discovery* to cope with restless discontent among the men awaiting their letters, endeavoured to administer a prod with a signal asking for 'latest news'. The reply, 'King crowned last year', did not seem adequate in the circumstances. More than forty-eight hours after the relief ship's arrival, a party from the *Morning* delivered bags of mail which made up for the frustration; Royds alone had sixty-two letters and a splendid cake, 'like a blooming wedding cake,' together with some new music, from 'dear Mrs R.' in Lyttleton.

All the talk was of whether the eight or nine miles of ice that penned in the *Discovery* would break up, and be carried out to sea by wind and current, in time to enable her to return to Lyttleton with the *Morning* – or indeed to return at all that season. Colbeck dared not risk leaving his departure until later than the end of February, but it was possible that the *Discovery* might yet break free during March. Every day the *Morning* edged in a little closer, but the pace was disappointingly slow until 10 February, when a mile of ice broke away. But next day the weather changed again and the ship's chances of getting out before winter looked remote.

There was a lively celebration on board when the southern party returned: a gala dinner with champagne, attended by Colbeck and others from the *Morning*, who contributed fresh mutton and potatoes. Wilson had brought back Nigger's fangs for Able Seaman Ernest Joyce, a coast-guard's son from Sussex, who had been his keeper: these were 'the only remains of our pack of dogs'. Skelton as mess president proposed a silent toast to those who had died in the cause of science: 'our dogs'.

Of the three men, Scott had come through with least damage. All had scurvy in its early stages. Scott's legs were swollen and his gums sore and he was overcome, for several days, with an overpowering lassitude. Wilson had strained a leg which had swelled badly, he was exhausted, and retired to bed for ten days. Shackleton was still an invalid.

To read reports from other sledging parties that had gone out during his absence was Scott's first task: a pleasant one, since there had been no disasters and all had made important finds. The first was the Emperor Penguin's egg brought back by Royds' party; a champagne and liqueur dinner had been held in its honour, the egg had been repeatedly photo-graphed and Corporal Blissett said that he was anticipating a knighthood.

A more ambitious party had left the ship on 29 November 1902 with the object of crossing McMurdo Sound and scaling the mountain range that ran along the coast of Victoria Land and disappeared far inland to the south. It was a continuation of these great mountains that Scott's party had traced to 83°s. This western party was led by Armitage and numbered twenty-one at the start, divided into four teams. Armitage was in the first team with Skelton and four men. Between them they had ten sledges, all man-hauled. After a send-off breakfast including a rare treat – mustard and cress grown by Koettlitz under a skylight – the cavalcade set off with sails set, before a spanking breeze. They carried eight weeks' provisions at the rate of thirty-six ounces per man per day.

When they reached the mountains beyond the Sound they had to haul their sledges with block and tackle up to a plateau lying between two peaks. On 10 December 1902 half the party returned to the ship. The others, led by Armitage, pushed on trying to climb the mountains, and at 6000 feet were halted by an unscaleable cliff. Turning back, they descended by a different route and at one point, roped together, glissaded down some 4000 feet to land at the foot of a glacier which Armitage named after Ferrar.

This gave them their route inland, not an easy one; the glacier was heavily crevassed and they crossed ugly cracks by means of insecure snow-bridges. Beset by snow-drift, biting winds and low cloud, by Christmas they had nevertheless reached the top of the glacier at 8200 feet, and celebrated by a meal of fried cheese, bacon and horse-radish sauce. Soon afterwards one of the men, Petty Officer William Macfarlane from Forfar in Scotland, collapsed, and several others were too spent to go on. Armitage, Skelton and the rest left them in a tent to recover while they themselves went on to reach the summit of the ice-cap at just over 9000 feet, a hundred miles from the coastline of Victoria Land. Here they turned back.

On the return journey Armitage fell twenty-seven feet into a crevasse; his harness held and he was hauled back. To everyone's surprise Hartley Ferrar, the strong young rowing blue, gave in, lay down in the snow and lost consciousness; his life was saved by a seaman, William Heald. Ferrar sank down in the snow and went to sleep on three occasions. Heald woke him each time and managed to keep him going till they saw the light from a lamp erected by Cross on a bamboo. The temperature was −45°F all this time. On his return Ferrar's legs and hands were exceedingly swollen and Heald's legs swollen also. Both had symptoms of scurvy.

The party got back to the ship on 19 January 1903 after an absence of fifty-two days. They had pioneered a route up the Ferrar glacier by which to climb the western mountains to the plateau on which, many miles to the north-west, lay the South Magnetic Pole. Specimens of fossil plants had been found at 8000 feet, and the skeleton of a crab-eating seal at 3000 feet, thirty miles from the sea. How and when it had got there was a mystery.

This western journey had resulted in important new discoveries and Scott had every reason to be pleased. Skelton, however, was not. He did not think that Armitage had done nearly as much as he could have done had he been more energetic and determined, and less obstinate in accepting other people's advice. Years later, he set out these views in a letter written after Armitage's death. 'We were keen,' he wrote of the rest of the party, 'but the marches were short and the day's work far too short – Scott would have been horrified . . . At the top of the glacier it was suggested to him to split the party in half and send on the fittest to the limit – he was again obstinate or nervous of responsibility – what a chance missed.' Perhaps latent scurvy and the shake-up everyone had received in glissading down to the glacier's foot might be some excuse. But if he had 'done some real pushing' Skelton believed, it would have made Scott's subsequent journey beyond the western mountains unnecessary, and other important explorations could have been made.

Meanwhile, Royds had spent a most frustrating time in the ship trying to free her whale-boats from the snow and ice in which they had become embedded – a contingency not foreseen, as no doubt it should have been, by the Captain, by Armitage or by any of the lieutenants. The operation was a slow and difficult one, involving the use of saws and explosives, but at last the boats were freed and damage done to them repaired. In other ways, those who remained on board enjoyed a peaceful interlude writing up journals, making scientific observations, developing photographs, now and again killing seals, fishing for skuas with baited lines and, of an evening, celebrating a good many anniversaries with wine, sing-songs shared with the men, and dancing the Lancers. (At least one of the anniversaries noted by Markham, that of the election of Dr George Murray to be a Fellow of the Royal Society, evoked scant enthusiasm.)

The Captain came back to a fortnight's uncertainty about the ship: would she, or would she not, get away? His instructions on this point were clear. Colbeck had brought a joint letter from Markham and Huggins instructing him to 'take what you want from the *Morning*, and extricate yourself from your winter quarters with as little loss of time as possible . . . You will return to Lyttleton in March or April 1903.' If funds were sufficient, the *Discovery* would return to McMurdo Sound for another summer.

After the *Morning*'s return to England, Scott was accused of disobeying orders and electing to remain in the south when he could, with sufficient exertion, have got away from his winter quarters. Predictably, several Fellows of the Royal Society took this line. Sir William Huggins wrote to one of them, 'I suspected all along that Scott had secret instructions from Markham to remain a second year. Were not our instructions to Scott clear and definite that he was *not* to remain a second year unless unable to extricate himself from the ice?' *The Times* ponderously remarked that Scott appeared to have followed a famous naval precedent by turning a blind eye on his orders. None of the records support this accusation. When Colbeck decided that he could wait no longer and the *Morning* sailed, five miles of ice separated the *Discovery* from the open sea. More ice then broke away and the distance was reduced to three and a half miles, but that was the minimum; after that, ice started to re-form and gave the ship no chance to break free. Personally, no doubt, Scott was not sorry; much unfinished business remained still to do. But it was the severity of the climate and not the duplicity of the Skipper that kept the vessel ice-bound for another year.

On 22 February 1903 he was still hoping, and tried blowing holes in the ice with explosives to crack the floes. This did no good. By the 25th he had accepted the fact that the *Morning* must leave without them lest she be trapped as well. The transfer of supplies from the relief ship had already started; her crew conveyed them on sledges to a halfway flag, and the *Discovery*'s crew dragged them the rest of the way. Fourteen tons of stores were man-hauled in this laborious way, and twenty tons of coal deposited on the ice. In Scott's praise for the way the men stuck to this boring task there is an undertone of scepticism about its necessity. The transferred supplies were 'none of them necessary to our continued existence in the south, but were such as added greatly to the comfort of our position'. They could, at a pinch, have lived on seals and penguins alone, but in any case had plenty of flour, biscuit, tea, chocolate, jam and other staples. However they were glad of extra frills like sauces, herbs, tinned soups and so on which filled 'minor deficiencies' and fresh New Zealand cheese and butter was much better than that in tins. An impression remains that he thought the sending of a relief ship at all was only marginally necessary, except for the welcome mail, and the opportunity to send back reports about the expedition's doings.

There was, however, one other useful purpose; to get rid of those individuals who had failed to pull their weight. In an address to the men, Scott had told them that a second winter in the ice was on the cards, and that anyone who wanted to go home in the *Morning* could do so. Eight applied, which he wrote was 'curiously satisfactory': these were the very eight men he wished to discard. It has been stated that all were merchant seamen, but four out of the eight were from the Royal Navy, and two of the others were civilians, namely Brett, the unsatisfactory cook from Melbourne, and Clarence Hare, the young New Zealand steward whose departure was generally regretted. Of the rest, Royds wrote, 'I doubt if they will be even missed,' and the Captain was glad to be rid of them.*

There remained the question of Ernest Shackleton. Scott had made up his mind that he must go, because he feared another breakdown when sledging was resumed. In his diary he wrote, 'On board he would have remained a source of anxiety, and would never have been able to do hard out-door work.' In this view he had the full support of Wilson, who had seen him when the breakdown was at its worst, and the rather half-hearted, less definite concurrence of Koettlitz, who examined him on his return. Koettlitz was inclined to think that no permanent harm had been done and that Shackleton need not go home. Scott pressed the point, suggesting that a level of health adequate for one of the civilian staff would not suffice for an executive officer subjected to the extreme test of sledging. As they all well knew, the breakdown of one man must jeopardise the lives of all his sledging companions. Koettlitz then put in writing his opinion,

Mr Shackleton's breakdown during the southern sledge journey was undoubtedly, in Dr Wilson's opinion, due in great part to scurvy taint. I certainly

* Those who returned in the *Morning* – apart from Shackleton – were: Brett, cook; Buckridge, laboratory assistant from the Cape; Duncan, merchant seaman from Dundee; Hare, steward from Christchurch; MacFarlane, petty officer RN who broke down on Armitage's western journey and was invalided; Page, stoker RN from Yorkshire; Peters, able seaman RN from Cork; and Walker, able seaman RN from Dundee.

agree with him; he has now practically recovered from it, but referring to your memo: as to the duties of an executive officer, I cannot say that he would be fit to undergo hardships and exposure in this climate.

That was as far as he would go. Wilson went further and wrote, 'It is certainly wiser for him to go home.' Petty Officer William Macfarlane was sent home for the same reason and was as disappointed as Shackleton, although his feelings were less publicised.

With modern knowledge, there would have been no need to have invalided Shackleton. Scurvy, provided it has not gone too far, need have no permanent effect upon the constitution. But modern knowledge was not available; no one knew what the effects might be, and Scott, who had seen for himself how near his companion had come to complete collapse, thought the risk too great. Both doctors, one firmly and the other marginally, advised against his staying. On the one hand Scott had to weigh the feelings of a young officer, on the other the safety of the men that officer would have as his companions. Even when the *Morning* left, Shackleton, after a month's rest and good feeding, had not recovered. Barne went with him to the relief ship and noted in his diary 'we went on very slowly, as poor old Shackles is still very shaky ... We stopped to rest several times on the way.' On the evidence, Scott would have been rash to make any other decision than to send Shackleton home.

Even before the *Morning* left, however, rumours were in circulation that he had other reasons. After a visit to the relief ship with Koettlitz, Hodgson wrote, 'I hear it is true, as I suspected, that personal feeling is the real reason for Shackleton's departure. We find our combined selves an awful crowd on board this ship.' Armitage disagreed with Scott's decision. In a letter written nearly twenty years later to H. R. Mill, who was writing a biography of Shackleton, he told this story:

Shortly after their return, Shackleton told me that Scott was sending him home, and asked me if I could do anything about it. He was in great distress, and could not understand it. I consulted Koettlitz and he informed me that Scott was in a worse condition than Shackleton. I then went to Scott, and asked him why he was sending him back. I told him there was no necessity from a health point of view, so after beating about the bush he said: 'If he does not go back sick he will go back in disgrace.' I told Shackleton, and promised to look after his interests...

During the winter, Wilson told me the following story, which Shackleton confirmed later. On the southern journey, Wilson and Shackleton were packing their sledges after breakfast one morning. Suddenly they heard Scott shout to them: 'Come here you BFs.' They went to him, and Wilson quietly said: 'Were you speaking to me?' 'No Billy,' said Scott. 'Then it must have been me,' said Shackleton. He received no answer. He then said: 'Right, you are the worst B F of the lot, and every time that you dare to speak to me like that you will get it back.' Before Shackleton left he told me that he meant to return to prove to Scott that he – Shackleton – was a better man than Scott.'

That Scott could be short-tempered and was a stickler for discipline is undeniable. Some incident of this sort may well have taken place. But Scott also had a strong sense of justice and knew his own faults. Whether he would have allowed Shackleton's defiance, insubordination as he would have called it, to sway his judgement is an open question, as the whole affair must be. And that Wilson, so renowned for his discretion and for smoothing over points of friction, should have told this abrasive tale to Armitage, does not ring true. Memory can play tricks within a week, and after twenty years it is seldom reliable.

Armitage was a man with a grievance that grew through the years. Its origins lay in the conditions of his appointment, also related many years later to Mill. After his initial refusal to serve as second-in-command, Markham and Scott between them had persuaded him, against his better judgement as he said, to change his mind. But he had made conditions which were somewhat vague, and not put into writing; he claimed that these were broken 'as I was warned they would be by two of his brother naval officers and by some of the Committee of the Expedition'. Twenty-four years later he did put them into writing, in his autobiography written after his retirement and published in 1925. He listed four conditions: that his appointment was to be independent of Scott's; that he was to be landed in the Antarctic with a hut, eight men including one of the doctors, and a team of dogs; that no restrictions were to be put upon his sledging activities; and that his pay was to be not less than £50 short of Scott's. In his book, he claimed that only the last of these conditions was fulfilled. On arrival in McMurdo Sound, he wrote, Scott implored him to forgo the others, saying that they would cripple his own efforts and that 'he could not do without me'. So Armitage reluctantly agreed.

Time has buried the truth along with the protagonists. That Scott, let alone Markham, would have agreed to such conditions seems, on the face of it, most unlikely. To do so would have been to give Armitage equal authority with the commander on sledging matters, and so resulted in the divided command to which Markham, backed up by Scott, was so inexorably opposed. Some record of so important an agreement would surely have been kept, especially as Armitage had been warned, according to his own statement, that it would be broken.

Several of Armitage's *post hoc* recollections lack the ring of truth. It was manifestly untrue that Shackleton was a fitter man than Scott at the end of the southern sledge journey. On the outward voyage, Armitage wrote, Scott had told him that 'he was afraid of Royds' naval influence and would soon settle that, as he was out to make all he could of the business for himself, especially his RN promotion and from a pecuniary point of view'. The first remark is obscure, the second unlikely. Even if Armitage had correctly stated Scott's motives, it was most improbable that such a reticent, secretive man would have revealed himself to a subordinate who was not even a personal friend.

Before the departure of the *Morning*, Scott suggested to Armitage that he might wish to go home on account of his wife and the child that he had never seen. Armitage was deeply offended. He took it as an insult; Scott was trying to get rid of him and he thought he knew the reason:

I had been told that Sir Clements Markham intended to make the expedition a great Royal Navy one *only*, but all went well with me for the first year, when Scott thought that he had enough experience to go on his own – *he had not* – then he endeavoured to rid himself of all the Merchant Service element. When he, in a most kindly manner, suggested that I should return in the *Morning*, I absolutely refused. But he never forgave me, as not only did I destroy the RN idea, but he feared that I would obtain kudos which he desired.

It was in fact Armitage who never forgave Scott. What he could not know, and probably never did, was the reason, or at the least another reason, that lay behind Scott's suggestion. It arose from some unedifying gossip relayed to Scott by his mother, and to Koettlitz by his wife in letters that came out in the *Morning*. Scott had evidently asked his mother to keep in touch with Mrs Armitage. 'I have neither seen nor heard anything of her for nearly a year,' Hannah Scott wrote to her son. 'She called on me last July and left her mother's cards . . . I made a point of returning her visit before leaving town and to my relief did not find either lady at home . . . I fear she is altogether impossible.' Lady Vere Hughes had 'rushed in one Sunday afternoon saying some friend of hers had been in Richmond at the police court, and that Mrs Armitage's name had been mentioned in connection with a quarrel at the lodgings, and she had been charged with drinking and flirting with the son and "many other things"'. Lady Vere urged Hannah Scott to succour Mrs Armitage 'for the honour of the ship', but Hannah was not having that; she was 'in no way justified in taking up the cause of a person I know so little of', and who had a mother of her own at hand anyway.

This tittle-tattle, true or not, must have seemed to Scott remote indeed from the great polar expanses and problems of survival with which he had been grappling. But clearly Armitage must be given an opportunity to go to the rescue of his wife, who had been left to cope with life on her own within a few weeks of her first baby's birth. Unable to give his true reasons Scott, however tactful, could not but give offence.

Some observations made by Skelton many years later, after Armitage's death, may be relevant in helping to account for 'the Pilot's' allegations against Scott.

I think Armitage's character was often rather soured – he did not think he got enough credit for his work – he was not popular in our Expedition nor in his own Service, the P and O. Scott was tactful with him and none of us had rows. He had that silly inferiority complex of the Merchant Navy for the Royal Navy. In his private life he had much misfortune, his brother in the RN, who I knew well, committed suicide rather than face a Court-Martial for a nasty crime. His wife was 'a hell of a woman' and poor old Armitage whom she made penniless was far too kind to her.

The last ten years of his life after leaving the P and O found him very impecunious and embittered by lack of appreciation by others . . . Personally I never had a row with him but never corresponded or got near to him and that goes for all of us in the *Discovery*. His books are not always accurate, and rather poor stuff – as you say he is inclined to claim too much.

Once it was realised that the *Morning* must sail alone, everyone got busy writing letters. (Royds wrote fifty-six.) Cheerful, reassuring letters; their writers had never been so fit, they were looking forward to another year on the ice. Scott alone had worries: would the ship be able to break out next summer, or indeed at all? If not, what then? Had this been an exceptionally severe season, or was it the norm? He kept these worries to himself and wrote to his mother, 'I have enjoyed the whole thing amazingly . . . All the crocks I am sending away, and am much relieved to get rid of. Except Shackleton, who is a very good fellow and only fails from the constitutional point of view.' He went on to give a rosy picture of his fellow officers. Royds had lost all his bumptiousness, allowing his solid good nature to come to the top. Michael Barne was tireless and always cheerful; there was no bottom to Wilson's pluck and endurance; Skelton was an all-round sportsman and just the man for the job; Hodgson 'the most solid, sound old person imaginable'; and even Ferrar, a conceited young ass to begin with, after a dressing down which reduced him to tears had ceased to be objectionable and become a nonentity, a step in the right direction. Scott wrote to Wilson's wife, 'Words always fail me when I talk of Bill. I believe he is really the finest character I ever met.'

Wilson, too, was enthusiastic. 'I like him [Royds] more than anyone else on the ship,' he told his wife. 'His music is a perfect godsend to us but in many, *many ways* which I cannot detail here, I feel that in him I have a friend who can understand things that others can't.' Royds wrote to his twin sister Jess, 'So far, so very good, and we are still on the best of terms with each other.' But, in his case, polar life was beginning to pall. Having had the experience, 'let me forever be where life is and plenty of it . . . I long to dance, to talk to others, in fact I'm nearly sick of my own sex.' But it never crossed his mind to elect to return in the relief ship. That would have amounted to disloyalty with the added suspicion of 'funking' – crimes literally unthinkable to the naval officer of the day.

On 1 March 1903 there was a farewell party in the *Morning*, which went on for half the night, with sixteen officers crowded into a space meant for seven. She was a very small ship, old and dirty, and Scott was critical. 'The general system is on Merchant Service lines . . . There is much we could learn without doubt, but on the whole I am entirely convinced that the naval discipline and routine is infinitely preferable, indeed I believe it would be a necessity for continuous polar work.'

On 2 March 1903 the *Morning* sailed. Scott drew a vivid picture of her departure. After snatching a hasty breakfast, overnight guests from the *Discovery* were mustered on the floe to shout their last farewells; the *Morning* slowly backed away, 'every rope and spar outlined against the black northern sky. Cheer after cheer was raised as she slowly gathered way, and long after she had passed out of earshot our forlorn little band stood gazing at her receding hull, following in our minds her homeward course and wondering when we too should be permitted to take that northern track'. Royds gave a slightly different account. The men, no less than the officers, had enjoyed a party. Breakfast in the *Morning* did not appear until eleven o'clock 'and it was by the greatest good luck that we managed to get something to eat'. Scott was reluctant to take his leave because it looked as if a blizzard was brewing, but by 2.30 p.m. sledges and men were on the ice and the ship moved off. 'The scene on board was not enticing and many men were too drunk to even stand, and some of our chaps on the ice soon began to feel the cool air and shew signs . . . Had rather trouble with Wild and Smythe, but by eventually securing them firmly to the sledge I managed to get along and arrived on board about 6 p.m.'

Shackleton had shed tears as he watched his friends and shipmates drop out of sight. In his place, Sub-Lieutenant George Mulock, aged twenty-one, transferred to the *Discovery*. His talent for surveying and cartography resulted in neat, accurate charts of the expedition's newly discovered lands and exploratory journeys. He took his share of the sledging, but it was left to Skelton, as usual criticial, to sum him up in equivocal terms. 'Mulock is distinctly peculiar for such a youngster, a mixture of sulkiness, attempts at sarcasm, great readiness to take offence where none is meant, a little conceit.' Skelton was not easy to please.

# 11    The Most Desolate
## Region on Earth

The winter of 1903 set in earlier and was much colder than the year before; by mid-March the bay was covered with young ice, and lingering hopes of a break-out had disappeared. Everyone settled down to the winter routine. Fresh meat every day was now the rule, normally seal, but now varied by skua which had been Skelton's idea. Royds thought it tasted like duckling. Over a hundred seals and 550 skuas had been stored in the snow-trench larder so that scurvy, everyone hoped, was now a thing of the past. The cooking, too, was much better as performed by Clarke, the former cook's mate and a trained baker. For exercise, they played hockey with home-made sticks and 'no time to consider the rules' at temperatures down to −39°F. The lighting was another improvement; acetylene cylinders had come out in the *Morning* and Skelton fixed up an excellent system to replace smoky paraffin lamps. Bernacchi became editor of the *South Polar Times*.

Midwinter Day 1903 found them all, Scott wrote, even more cheerful than they had been the year before; there was a sumptuous dinner with turtle soup, halibut, roast beef with artichokes and devilled wing of skua, plus champagne. Temperatures fell so low that all the recording clocks save one ceased to function and mercury froze in the thermometers. On 16 May 1903, −67°F was recorded on the thermometer at Cape Armitage, to which Koettlitz took a daily walk. Taking advantage of this habit Michael Barne, who enjoyed practical jokes, dressed up in furs to resemble a bear and with ferocious growls sprang out at the doctor as he was proceeding with his lantern to take the readings. 'Although he [Koettlitz] didn't mistake Michael for a bear,' Skelton wrote, 'he walked straight on and came back to the ship very angry. He can't understand a joke.'* Barne thought that 'Cutlets [the doctor's nickname] is the simplest man I have ever met' and looked ridiculous 'pottering about the edge of the floe with a muslin landing net like an old lady in her dotage, trying to catch diatoms'.

* There are, of course, no bears in Antarctica, indeed no land mammals of any kind; the largest land animal is a tiny wingless fly. There are practically no plants either, only a primitive lichen and one or two mosses round the coast. Thus Antarctica is infinitely poorer in life than the Arctic, which supports several land mammals, including bears and foxes, and over a thousand species of plant.

Muggins was equally vague and went shrimping on an ice floe; before he realised what had happened he was drifting out of the harbour and had to be rescued; but he had none of Koettlitz's stiffness and aroused protective feelings amongst the younger men.

Sledging programmes for the coming season were discussed and planned. Scott asked his officers what they would like to do. Royds said he wished to go again to Cape Crozier to look for more penguins' eggs. Armitage wanted to go south across the Barrier, more or less in Scott's footsteps. 'In my opinion,' Royds wrote, 'his sole wish is to beat the Captain's record. This the Captain wouldn't allow, though not for that reason by any means.'

This request by Armitage put Scott in an awkward position. If he refused it, he laid himself open to the charge that he wanted to keep to himself the credit of a 'farthest south' record and would not let a subordinate 'have a go'. This raised the perennial question of what the expedition was really for: discovery and scientific knowledge, or 'a dash to the Pole', or as near to the Pole as anyone could get. Scott had never wavered in his belief in the first-named objective. He did not think that, without dogs, Armitage or anyone else would get much farther south than he had, or add significantly to scientific knowledge if he did. International competition was one thing: rivalry between two members of the same expedition to set up a somewhat meaningless record would be a waste of effort. He did not believe that anything useful would be achieved by Armitage and a party of men trudging south across the Barrier with no hope, in the time and with the resources available, of climbing up the mountains beyond.

Nevertheless before turning down Armitage's request he consulted Billy Wilson, as, when in a difficulty, everybody did. Wilson wrote in his diary:

The Captain worked out the possibilities on paper and showed them to me, and I agreed with him in thinking it was far better to apply all our sledging energies to new work, rather than covering old ground with the chance of doing so little at the end of it. The upshot of it all is that Armitage is off the sledging list for this year altogether, though whether this is due to himself or anyone else I cannot say.

The resentment which Armitage had felt all along – against his subordinate position, against the Royal Navy, perhaps against his own failure to win popularity in this small group of men – was sharpened and deepened by this incident. Of Scott's decision he wrote in his account of the expedtion, which in general was most restrained; 'This was, I must confess, a sore disappointment to me, as I had set my heart on sledging over the Barrier to the south. However, I resigned myself to the inevitable' –

somewhat consoled, he added, by permission to explore the south-west portion of McMurdo Sound.

Was Scott acting in good faith, or was his true motive a determination to keep for himself the kudos of a 'farthest south' record? It can be argued either way. It could also be asked, what was Armitage's motive in wishing to go south, without dogs, across an ice-shelf whose mystery had now, more or less, been solved, with little or no chance of fresh discovery? It is hard to find in his desire any motive other than that diagnosed by Royds, to go one better than Scott. The expedition had not been raised to provide a forum for an endurance test between two of its members. Scott's decision would appear to have been manifestly right.

A further decision that he now reached cannot have eased relations between him and his second-in-command. During the winter, Skelton had told him of his poor opinion of Armitage's performance on the sledging journey to the west. There lay the polar ice-sheet, still unexplored, and Armitage had found a route to its summit. This was the most promising direction, Scott considered, in which to seek further discoveries. In particular, he was anxious to bring back geological specimens which would throw light on the region's remote past. Ferrar's discovery of fossil plants suggested that the ancient legends of a semi-tropical continent with lush vegetation buried now beneath literally miles of ice and snow might have a true foundation. The polar ice-sheet could not be reached, with the resources at their disposal, by going south across the Barrier; it could be reached, without too much difficulty, close at hand over the western mountains. The prospect excited his imagination and it was here that he decided to go himself. Nothing is known of Armitage's feelings, but it must have riled him that the Captain, while refusing to let him go south, was now proposing to go west himself in the footsteps of his second-in-command. Scott's reason, or excuse, was that he regarded Armitage's western journey more as a reconnaissance – as indeed his own venture to the south had been – than as a mission fulfilled. It is easy to see both points of view.

In August came the worst blizzard they had experienced; if a man ventured even as far as the deck he gasped for breath and half-suffocated, with eyes, ears and nose stuffed with gritty snow. Had he gone even a couple of yards from the ship he could scarcely have survived. A bitch who gave birth to a litter of pups in the after deck-house was found with her tongue torn out; it had frozen to the feeding tin. Wilson, dissecting a seal, discovered that it had suffered from gout.

When the blizzard subsided they could watch again, with wonder, the marvellous displays of the aurora australis which everyone agreed defied description, but which everyone tried to describe. Wilson wrote that the green of an emerald was dull and dirty compared with the green lights in

Scott's mother

Sir Clements Markham, originator
of the British Antarctic
Expedition of 1901-4

ABOVE On board the *Discovery*. (*left to right*) Lt Armitage, Lt Mulock,
Lt Shackleton, Dr Wilson, Lt-Eng Skelton, Capt Scott, Lt Royds, Dr Koettlitz,
Mr Bernacchi and Mr Ferrar

BELOW The *Discovery* and dog sledge team at Hut Point

ABOVE Winter quarters photographed from the north-west
BELOW Members of the crew celebrating Christmas on board the *Discovery*

ABOVE A sledge camp in morainic ice

BELOW Wilson's sketch of cramped conditions inside a tent

Sledging in April.
Camping after dark.

ABOVE The Emperor Penguin colony at Cape Crozier, drawn by Wilson on his visit there in 1902

BELOW Shackleton, Scott and Wilson celebrating Christmas 1902 on their journey south

Ernest Shackleton, the leader
of three subsequent expeditions
to the Antarctic

Kathleen Bruce, taken around
the time of her marriage to
Scott

Scott and his wife aboard the *Terra Nova*

ABOVE The dogs on the deck of the *Terra Nova*

BELOW Unloading the ill-fated motor sledge

Scott in his den. On the wall are pictures of Kathleen and the baby, Peter

The hut at Cape Evans and the western mountains, taken with a telephoto lens

The hut from the west, with Mt Erebus in the background

Wilson working on a sketch

ABOVE Oates and the ponies

BELOW Birdie Bowers and Victor

Ponting, the photographer, stroking an Adélie Penguin on her nest

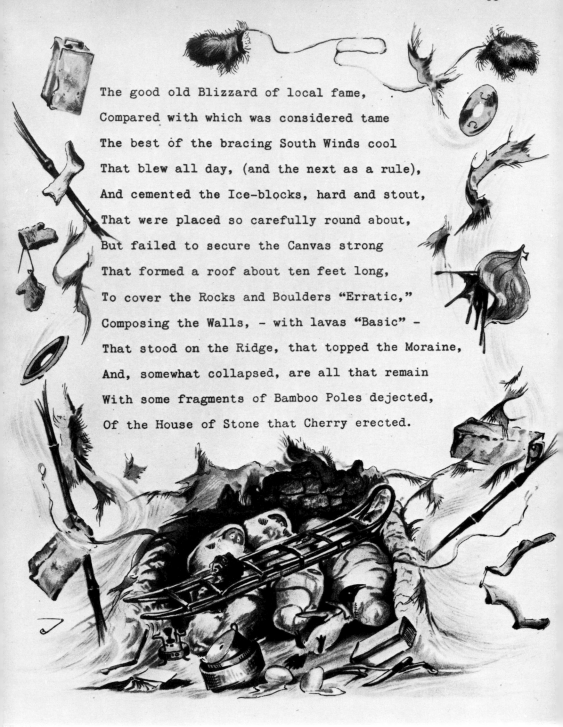

The good old Blizzard of local fame,

Compared with which was considered tame

The best of the bracing South Winds cool

That blew all day, (and the next as a rule),

And cemented the Ice-blocks, hard and stout,

That were placed so carefully round about,

But failed to secure the Canvas strong

That formed a roof about ten feet long,

To cover the Rocks and Boulders "Erratic,"

Composing the Walls, - with lavas "Basic" -

That stood on the Ridge, that topped the Moraine,

And, somewhat collapsed, are all that remain

With some fragments of Bamboo Poles dejected,

Of the House of Stone that Cherry erected.

A page of the *South Polar Times* describing the blizzard on the Cape Crozier expedition which nearly resulted in the deaths of Bowers, Wilson and Cherry-Garrard

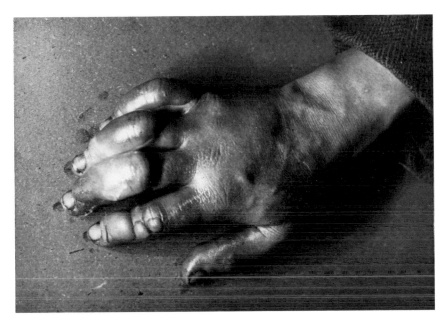

ABOVE Dr Atkinson's frostbitten hand

BELOW Camp under the Wild Range on the Beardmore Glacier

Midwinter Day dinner 1911. (*left to right*) Debenham, Wright (*standing*), Oates, Atkinson (*standing*), Meares, Bowers, Cherry-Garrard, Scott, Wilson, Simpson, Nelson, Lt Evans

the sky; 'neither lilac nor amethyst describe the colour I have spoken of as lilac, but the light of incandescent potassium does exactly'. As the winter waned, a deep red glow suffused the northern sky and against it stood out hills and mountains etched in black. Plumes of smoke from Erebus' volcano caught and held the blood-red light as it spiralled into a deep-blue sky. 'If a dozen rainbows were broken up and scattered in wavy ribands and flecks of curl and fleecy-like forms, to float against a background of dull grey,' Wilson wrote, 'you would get an idea of the colouring.' He was constantly at work trying to capture on paper impressions of these ever changing displays.

On 21 August 1903 the rim of the sun appeared for the first time over the horizon. Scott wrote lyrically of little warm, pink clouds floating about and, in the south, a rich flush over-spreading the darkness; to the north the smoke of Erebus rose straight up in a golden spreading column. 'All thoughts turned towards the work that lies before us.' Sledging programmes had been pinned to the notice board with exact times, loads, dates of departure and return worked out in detail. Everyone was to be back on board by 15 December 1903 so that all hands could unite in a concerted effort to extricate the ship, if possible before the return of the *Morning*.

There were to be two major ventures, each with a supporting party to lay depots and then return. The Captain was to go west up the Ferrar glacier as far as he could get; Barne was to explore an inlet that appeared to pierce the western mountains south of McMurdo Strait. There were also to be several unsupported journeys, five in all. This was a more ambitious, better-planned programme than that of the previous year, to be undertaken with partially worn-out and patched equipment and with no dogs, but with one over-riding asset: experience.

The first to leave the ship, on 7 September 1903, were Royds, Wilson and four men, bound for Cape Crozier including Corporal Arthur Blissett of penguin-egg fame, and Petty Officer Jacob Cross, whom Wilson had taught to be a useful taxidermist. They went away with flags flying on two sledges, carrying food for three weeks. By now sledge-packing had been brought to a fine art. In each tent slept and fed three men, and for each group of three was packed a canvas bag containing food for one week. In that weekly bag were smaller bags, each with a different kind of food: pemmican, oatmeal, pea-meal, cocoa, chocolate, red ration, sugar, frozen milk (cut into small cubes), pepper, salt, onion powder and tea. They had become adept at brewing hoosh in the shortest possible time. 'We are a most jovial party,' Wilson wrote, 'all six full of humbug over every discomfort.'

They reached their previous camp to find that a large chunk of the Barrier cliff had fallen off and driven away the frightened penguins – about a thousand of them, many with young – to a new rookery. Two live chicks, a number of dead ones and a collection of eggs were taken up the cliff by the roped and cramponed explorers. On their march back to the ship, temperatures fell to −61°F. They shivered sleepless in their three-man bags all night, and in the morning their clothing was so stiffly frozen that it crackled like a suit of tin armour when they moved. In addition most of them were frostbitten; Blissett's face was swollen like a bolster. Despite all this, the men kept up a constant flow of jokes and got back to an orgy of hot buttered toast on board, feeling that their job had been well done. Cross had carried the chicks in his sleeping jacket and they were still alive. One died soon afterwards, but the other was housed in Wilson's cabin and fed at four-hour intervals, night and day, on chewed-up seal-meat. Wilson was getting little sleep these days. Not only did he get up at 1 a.m. and then again at 5 a.m. to chew seal-meat and stuff it down the chick, he stayed up all night on one occasion to paint a fish found in the stomach of a seal.

Despite the Emperor chick's unpleasing habits – he was insatiably greedy, obstinate and vicious, 'losing his temper and guzzling in a most human fashion', Wilson grew devoted to him. The chick liked to stay up late looking at the candle, and got 'frightfully angry, struggling and chirruping in his box if I put him to bed early'. He was covered with grey, silky down and had a black and white velvety head, and 'flapped his little featherless wings like a little duck with his nose in the air, preening himself all over'. Surely there can never have been a more dedicated biologist than Wilson. All the eggs they had brought back contained putrid embryos but Wilson blew the lot: 'the smell was extraordinary, but the result was our first perfect egg, blown through a small hole'.

On 9 September 1903 Scott set out with Skelton and four others – Frederick Dailey the carpenter, Petty Officer Edgar Evans, Seaman Jesse Handsley and Leading Stoker William Lashly – to lay a depot preparatory to an ascent of the western mountains. Armitage had reported the inlet at the Ferrar glacier's foot, named New Harbour, to be impossible for sledges, but Scott wanted to see for himself. By picking a way among jagged ice cliffs and pinnacles, sometimes portaging their loads and sledges, they found a way up the glacier to a spot about 2000 feet above sea level, where they made a depot. Armitage had taken three weeks to reach that position; Scott did it in a week, including two days when they were held up by a blizzard.

They got back in three and a half days, averaging twenty miles a day hauling their now lightened sledges in temperatures that seldom rose above −50°F. 'We were inclined to be exceedingly self-satisfied,' Scott wrote, but their bubble was pricked by reports from Barne's party who had been out on the Barrier laying a depot south-east of White Island.

The mercury in their thermometer sank to −67·7°F and then broke; Barne was convinced that the temperature had fallen to −70°F and below − over one hundred degrees of frost, and the expedition's record. One of Joyce's feet got so badly frost-bitten that Barne and Mulock took it in turns to hold it against the pits of their stomachs and knead the ankle for several hours, thus saving the foot from amputation.

The Captain's team left for their main journey on 12 October 1903. The advance party consisted of Scott himself, Skelton, the boatswain Alfred Feather, Petty Officer Evans, Handsley and Lashly. A smaller party consisting of Ferrar, with Able Seaman Weller and Petty Officer Thomas Kennar, were to concentrate on geology, and the supporting party, led by Dailey the carpenter, with Able Seaman Thomas Williamson and Stoker Frank Plumley, were to lay the depots.

Scott wrote that he had 'some pride' in this journey; the difficulties they encountered would have defeated them the year before, but their experience and hardness of condition saw them through. 'I cannot but believe we came near the limit of possible performance,' he wrote. If he was able to look back on the journey with satisfaction, it was largely because there had been no dogs to spoil the memory of hardship endured and dangers surmounted.

With four sledges, hauling 200lbs per man, they reached New Harbour and dragged their loads up Ferrar glacier to a basin lying at about 4500 feet. Here they found that the German silver (an alloy of zinc and nickel) protecting the wooden runners of the sledges had split. Next day the damage worsened and the whole party was forced to turn back with three damaged sledges out of four. They were eighty-seven miles from the ship and 'came as near to flying as is possible with a sledge party', reaching the ship in three days; on the last day they marched a record thirty-six miles. Five days after their return a party of nine started out again with the repaired sledges. It is easy to imagine Scott's impatience and frustration at this delay, but he appears to have controlled his temper, while keeping everyone at work at full stretch.

The runners went on giving trouble but the men struggled up the glacier, passing two more seal carcases at 5000 feet; the mystery of how they got there remained unsolved. A violent squall of wind swept away some of their impedimenta including a small volume called *Hints to Travellers*, compiled by the RGS, which contained logarithmic tables vital to navigation across such featureless wastes as they knew they would encounter. Without these tables, they would have to proceed more or less by guesswork; as Scott put it, they would be 'marching into the unknown without knowing exactly where we were or how to get back'. He put the situation to his companions, who were unanimous in wishing to press on and take the risk. It was a gamble on Scott's skill and instinct for navigation, with long odds against success. The loss of the logarithms caused him 'many a bad half-hour'.

Like little ants, they toiled up those enormous mountains, whipped by a bitter wind, the sledge runners worn to shreds. Near the top they were caught by a blizzard which nearly buried them alive before they could find a small patch of snow, frozen almost as solid as the surrounding ice, on which to pitch camp. In their flimsy tents, hastily secured, they lay in sleeping bags for a whole week, the blizzard raging without intermission, everything enveloped in a thick fog of driving snow. It was the most miserable week of his life, Scott wrote. For twenty-two hours out of the twenty-four they were in their sleeping-bags, crawling out twice a day to roll up the bags, get the cooker going and eat a hot meal. They had one book with them: Darwin again, this time *The Voyage of the Beagle*.

Scott wrote up his diary with freezing fingers, scarcely able to see; 'for the greater part of the time we lay quite still with our eyes open doing nothing and simply enduring'. He makes no mention of what Bernacchi called the daily hygienic ceremony, and how it was achieved in the teeth of a blizzard next to impossible to stand up against, it is hard to imagine. 'Yet I do not believe we ever grew despondent,' he wrote. They named this Desolation Gap, nevertheless, and Scott feared that they had reached the end of their tether. But at last they got away, still unable to see more than a yard or two ahead, to clamber up an ice-fall criss-crossed by crevasses.

On the 14 November 1903 they reached the summit at 8900 feet to find themselves on a vast snow-plain with a level horizon. Heading due west, they plodded on through unrelenting conditions. Lashly kept a diary, and on 20 November noted, 'Dragging getting worse. Handsley's chest and throat gave out. Had to do relay work, this the Captain can't stand.' Two days later Scott sent one sledge back with Skelton, Feather and Handsley, and himself went on with the final pick of the bunch for sledging purposes: Edgar Evans and William Lashly. Evans had been a naval gymnastic instructor, had weighed 154lbs at the start of the journey and possessed tremendous muscles. Lashly's physique was not so noticeable but he was deep-chested, weighed 164lbs and was a teetotaller and a non-smoker – 'clean-living' as a subsequent companion (George Simpson) was to describe him, aged thirty-four, son of a farmworker and a married man. Scott was the lightest at 138lbs and felt that he did not deserve his ration. 'With these two men behind me our sledge seemed to become a living thing, and the days of slow progress were numbered.' A constant icy wind slashed their skin as if with a knife, and made their lips raw and bleeding. 'The wind seems to be very troublesome here,' Lashly observed.

On the last day of November they made their final outward camp, and turned back next day. 'I don't know where we are,' Scott wrote, 'but I know we must be a long way to the west.' He had been disappointed to find nothing but an endless snow plateau, the Barrier all over again but nearly 9000 feet above sea level, which made conditions worse. He was obsessed by a feeling of awe, deadness and futility. In all this 'silent, wind-swept immensity' there was no living thing, no bird or insect, no wisp of moss nor spore of lichen; so it had been for countless aeons, so it would continue for countless more. 'As long as I live,' he later wrote, 'I never want to revisit the summit of Victoria Land,' the most desolate region in the world.

Hunger, exhaustion, deep *sastrugi*, fog, snowdrift, frostbite, snow-blindness – it was a familiar story. Food dwindled, paraffin ran short, the fog was so thick that Scott could only guess at their position. 'My companions are undefeatable; however tiresome our day's march or however gloomy the outlook, they always find something to jest about.' In the evenings, they discussed naval matters. 'I learn a great deal about lower deck life more than I could hope to have done under ordinary conditions.'

'We have been struggling along very much in the fog, not knowing exactly where we were,' Lashly wrote, 'and we have also been on cold tea, cold lunch, and cold cocoa at night as our oil is getting short.' (5–10 December 1903) 'I am a little alarmed about our oil,' Scott admitted, 'so have decided to march half an hour extra each night.' Food-dreams began again. 'I think Evans' idea of joy is pork, whilst Lashly dreams of vegetables, and especially apples. He tells us stories of his youth when these things, and not much else, were plentiful.' They were pulling for ten hours a day. 'It is rather too much when the strain on the harness is so great, and we are becoming gaunt skeletons of ourselves. My companions' cheeks are quite sunken and hollow, with their stubby untrimmed beards and numerous frostbite remains they have the wildest appearance; yet we are all fit, there has not been a sign of sickness.'

On 14 December Scott faced the fact that they were lost. By now they had reached the edge of the plateau and were beginning to descend. Then Lashly slipped and started to slide on his back, whipping the others off their feet, and down they went, sledge and all, gathering speed as they bumped and bounced over rough, broken ice, 'much faster', Lashly observed, 'than we wanted to go'. A patch of soft snow halted them, miraculously there were no broken limbs, and when they had pulled themselves together Scott saw that, by another miracle it seemed, they had tumbled down the head of the glacier by which they had ascended. Also they had emerged from the snow-drift, could see familiar landmarks, and were only five or six miles from their depot.

But the worst was to come. In Lashly's words 'all of a sudden the

Captain and Evans disappeared down a crevasse and carried away one of the sledge runners, leaving me on top. It was now my duty to try and get them up again.' But he could not let go of the broken sledge. With great presence of mind, as well as strength, he held on to it with one hand and with the other pulled out a pair of skis and slid them underneath the sledge for extra support. Meanwhile Scott, with Evans just above him, was dangling at the end of the trace with blue walls of ice on either side and blue nothingness below. Providentially, on this day of miraculous escapes, his swinging feet encountered a thin shaft of ice on which he managed to get a grip with his crampons. Lashly could not pull them out, frostbite was rapidly robbing Scott's hands of their strength and feeling, and to climb the trace to safety called on his last reserves of will and muscle. He just made it, and then, with Lashly, pulled up Evans, whose sole comment was, 'Well, I'm blowed.' That night they reached the depot, and eight days later, on Christmas Eve, the haven of the ship. Scott worked out the figures. In fifty-nine days, for nine of which they had been blizzard-bound, they had hauled their sledge 725 miles, climbing to nearly 9000 feet, an average of fourteen and a half miles a day.

Only four men were in the ship to greet them; all the others were in a camp about ten miles away, sawing and blasting at the ice in the hope of accelerating the break-up of the floe and so the freeing of the vessel. Scott had a few days' rest and read reports of other sledging teams. All had come back safely. On the western mountains Ferrar had discovered a fossil leaf. Wilson had solved the mystery of how the Emperor chicks had disappeared from their rookery while still too young to fend for themselves. With their parents, they had gathered on the edge of the floe as it started to break away; pieces of it had detached themselves and floated northwards. Each piece carried a cargo of penguins, borne in the required direction without having to stir a foot or flap a wing, as if on some imperial palanquin. On his return to the ship, the first thing that had caught Wilson's eye was a small black cross, and 'I knew that my Emperor Penguin was dead. I was very glad indeed, for I think he was pretty miserable.'

Christmas fare after starvation rations brought on acute indigestion, but as soon as Scott recovered he and his companions made for the sawing camp to see how operations were getting on. They were scarcely getting on at all. Charges of gun-cotton sunk in the floe and detonated were making little or no impression. Sawing through ice eight or ten feet thick was gruelling work. Each heavy saw, about eighteen feet long, was attached to a tripod and the men pulled on ropes to lift or press down the saw with an action resembling that of bell-ringers. They worked in four-hour watches and, as Scott remarked, four hours of uninterrupted bell-ringing would be more than enough for most people.

The intention was to break up the floe by means of two parallel cuts. The ice between these two cuts had then to be disposed of, which involved further diagonal cuts; so, for every mile of advance, four miles of ice had to be sawn. An advance of nine feet an hour on a single cut was good going, and frequently the channels froze up again after sawing. Scott's orders to embark on the sawing operation had been based on the assumption that conditions in the summer of 1903–4 would be much the same as they had been at the start of the summer before, when eleven miles of ice had separated open sea from Hut Point. Conditions were not the same, however. When summer came, twenty miles of ice, not eleven, separated ship and sea.

Where ice and water had met the year before stood several islets, and this was the place Scott had selected for the start of the operation. Sawing would then proceed from the edge of the floe towards the ship in the hope of opening cracks which the movements of the tide would widen, until the whole floe would break up and the ship could work her way free. Now these islets lay halfway between ship and sea. This could not have been foreseen when Scott had left on his outward journey and handed over to his second-in-command. Armitage carried out his instructions to the letter. He established a camp beside the islets and started sawing not at the water's edge, but in the middle of the floe.

It was clear to the meanest intelligence that this was a hopeless proposition. It must have been equally clear to Armitage, but he failed to use his initiative and to adapt his instructions to the situation. He was, of course, strictly speaking, in the right: 'them's my orders'. Had he varied them, he could have earned a reprimand, all the more to be avoided because of his prickly relations with the Captain. If his rigid adherence to the letter rather than to the spirit of his orders was a way of getting back at the Captain, it misfired. Armitage was blamed, not Scott. 'The Pilot,' Skelton wrote, was 'entirely devoid of common sense, his only idea was to say that he had carried out orders . . . He also seems to have been making himself unpleasant to all hands especially Royds – absolutely tactless.' Royds wrote that the operation was 'absolutely futile' and that Armitage had 'twisted my words about and in general is trying to make a row'. Boatswain Feather asked to be taken off Armitage's watch and tension between 'the Pilot' and the scientists had become unpleasant.

Nevertheless the men in the camp were cheerful. 'There was never a healthier crowd of ruffians than the thirty unwashed, unshaven, sleepless, swearing, grumbling, laughing, joking reprobates that lived in that smoky saw-camp,' Wilson wrote. Their appetites were prodigious. Each watch of ten men, on coming off duty, fell upon their meal like wolves. Starting with enormous helpings of porridge, they went on to a stew made either with seal-meat or with Adélie Penguins who had been drawn to the camp by ill-judged curiosity; each penguin, Scott noted, was as big as a goose, and he watched ten men make light of a seven-penguin stew, going on to bread, jam and griddle cakes *ad lib.*

When he reached the camp on the last day of 1903 he found that twelve days of blasting and round-the-clock sawing had achieved two parallel cuts each 150 yards long. At that rate, someone had worked out, it would take 281·6 days of non-stop sawing in perpetual summer to cover twenty miles. Scott immediately called the whole thing off, remarking mildly in his journal that it had been an experience if nothing more. At least the men had been kept fit and occupied at a time when there was little else for them to do, and proof had been provided for those at home that the Antarctic climate, and not irresolution on the part of the men, was to blame for keeping the *Discovery* a prisoner. 'Twenty miles of ice hangs heavy upon me,' he wrote; he had reluctantly decided that preparations must be started to spend a third winter at Hut Point.

'The Captain is feeling the effects of his journey pretty badly,' Wilson wrote. By way of convalescence, both men dragged a sledge eight and a half miles to the open water. The Captain wanted to inspect the ice-edge and weigh the chances of a break-up. They were passed by bands of Adélie Penguins heading south in a tearing hurry, 'flippers outspread, heads bent forward, and little feet going for all they were worth', wrote Wilson. Then suddenly a band would wheel about and hurry back again without apparent reason. Next day they discovered a rookery on the rocks of Cape Royds, which they had missed for two years. They thought regretfully of all the eggs they might have enjoyed. After washing in a fresh-water stream brought to birth by the thaw and dining off fried penguin liver and seal kidneys, the two companions reflected that life in the Antarctic had its attractions.

On 5 January 1904 they were sitting in their tent with the flap drawn back when a ship came into view. At last, the *Morning*. A few minutes later, Wilson exclaimed, 'Why, there's another.' They were not seeing double; the second ship was larger than the first. 'We were dumbfounded,' Wilson wrote. Discussing what on earth this could mean – and never, Scott remarked, coming anywhere near the truth – they set off in search of four men who were encamped near by hunting penguins, to send them back to the *Discovery* with the news. They found the men finishing a hearty breakfast in the sunshine and preparing to go forth for an enjoyable day's hunt. These were among the men, Scott wrote, believed at home to be 'in dire straits and in need of immediate transport to civilised conditions'.

Wilson and Scott then made for the two ships, to be greeted at the ice-edge by four men speaking 'such perfect Dundee that we could hardly understand a word they said'. They were from the second ship, the *Terra Nova*, manned by Dundee men from whaling vessels. Soon Scott and Wilson were aboard the familiar *Morning* receiving their mail and hearing from their old friend William Colbeck why two relief ships, instead of one, were at anchor in McMurdo Sound.

# Markham's Downfall

The story of the *Terra Nova* was a tragi-comedy. Tragic, because it almost broke Sir Clements Markham's heart, aged and embittered him; comic, because it illustrated that unpredictable, semi-lunatic behaviour sometimes displayed by government departments, as if a March hare had got inside their bureaucratic skins.

When the *Morning* returned from the Antarctic early in 1903, Sir Clements metaphorically threw his hat into the air. The expedition – *his* expedition – had done all that had been hoped for and more. His faith in its leader had been abundantly justified. 'Captain Scott's journey to the south places him in the very first rank of polar explorers,' he exulted to Sir William Huggins. Moreover, records and collections were brought back by the *Morning* to silence those who had openly doubted whether anything scientifically valuable would result.

It was plain that a relief ship must be sent a second time, but scarcely any money was left in the fund. Time was too short to organise another public appeal, whose success would in any case be doubtful. It was now April; the ship must get away by early August at the latest. The Royal Society was as slow as ever and did not seem to realise the urgency. Three times during April Markham wrote to its officers in forceful terms. He, like others, had been badly jolted by mention of the scurvy outbreak, even though Scott had played it down. The *Discovery* had a year's provisions only, and unless relief was sent a 'terrible disaster' might occur. 'It is a matter of life or death.' In brief, the old man panicked. He was now almost seventy-four, subject to gout, and had suffered several attacks of nervous debility.

Eventually Markham roused Sir William Huggins to action and he and Markham jointly appealed to the Government in very strong terms (19 May 1903) for a grant of £12,000. At this point Markham gave a demonstration of the 'doubtful soda-water' qualities Cyril Longhurst had deplored. Instead of waiting for an official reply, according to a letter from H. R. Mill to Scott,

Markham assumed that they [the Government] would decline to contribute, and at the RGS annual dinner, and a little later at Liverpool, he used the most violent language as to the wickedness of the Government . . . If he had only been a little quieter in asking for more money in the spring he would have saved himself a world of trouble, and remained to reap his deserved reward.

As it was, the Government's reaction to Markham's emotional attack – those gallant men, he implied, were about to perish in the far south by reason of the parsimony and stony-heartedness of politicians – was a speech in the House of Commons delivered by the Prime Minister, Mr Balfour. In measured tones, he administered a smart rebuke to both Societies. He had always 'leaned towards the principle of extending limited aid' for scientific research, but only if the Government 'are able to feel absolute confidence that the scientific bodies . . . have placed before them all the information in their possession as to the estimated cost . . . That confidence has been rudely shaken.' Beneath these smooth official phrases was an accusation of sharp practice: Markham and Huggins had known all along that a relief ship would be needed for a second year but had lain low, and were now trying to bounce the Government into providing the money by emotional speeches about an impending national disaster.

If the Royal Society had been dilatory about appealing for funds, its officers moved like greased lightning to protest against this slur on their good faith. 'It is with pain that the Royal Society learns that the confidence of HMG has been rudely shaken,' Sir William Huggins immediately wrote. He set forth in detail the past history of the affair, concluding with a stab in the back for the RGS. 'The Royal Society have found the part of working in concert with another Society, having not wholly identical aims, a very difficult one.'

Mr Balfour took the point at once, contributing his own stab for good measure. 'I am glad to say that the facts thus brought before me exonerate the Royal Society from any responsibility for those incidents in connection with the original application for Government assistance to which I felt bound to allude in my statement in the House of Commons.' That left the RGS and its President to suffer the whole weight of the Prime Minister's rebuke. Markham had brought it on himself and did not get much sympathy. 'I believe it has aged him greatly,' wrote Mill.

There was worse to come. The Government now decided to take the whole matter out of the hands of the Societies and send the ship themselves. The Admiralty wanted to retrieve its officers and men from the *Discovery* without further delay, and suspected that if matters were left to the Societies – in effect to Markham – excuses might be found to keep them in the ice for yet another winter. They therefore urged upon the Treasury the need for action, saying that 'the safety of the Expedition is at stake'. On 20 June 1903 the Treasury agreed to foot the bill on condition that the *Morning* was handed over 'absolutely and at once', free of charge, to the Admiralty, and informed the two Societies of their decision.

Three days later a letter signed by both the Presidents went back accepting 'with great satisfaction' the Government's decision to send a ship, and adding that 'we frankly accept the condition' to hand over the *Morning*. Markham signed this letter but he can scarcely have known what he was doing, because on the same day he wrote independently to the Treasury, 'I regret that I cannot give you an immediate reply to the peremptory proposal of Their Lordships, as it requires careful consideration.' Their Lordships immediately requested 'to be informed which letter supersedes the other'.

Two days later, Markham climbed down. His personal letter did not supersede that which he had signed in his capacity as President of the RGS. His own Council, he wrote to Scott, 'apparently quite panic-stricken, without consulting me complied with the demand . . . They had no right to do this as she [the *Morning*] was a Trust for the subscribers. I protested strongly, but the thing was done.' To Longhurst he painted a dramatic version of his part in the affair.

After scuttling the ship the crew have left her in the long-boat and have abandoned the captain to resist the Royal Society, and Treasury pirates boarding her over the bows, quite alone. For the sake of Scott and the other dear friends, I will save the ship or go down with her. I am not the owner of the *Morning* to do what I like with her and give her to Mr Balfour or anyone else merely because he points an empty pistol at my head.

He fulminated, but the deed was done. A fortnight later, the Council of the RGS made over the *Morning* 'permanently and unconditionally' to the Government. The signature on the document was that of the acting President, G. H. Holditch. But on 23 July 1903 Markham wrote that he had 'signed that hateful document, under protest', and sent it to the Admiralty. What hurt him most about the whole affair was the defection of his personal bodyguard, the Council of the RGS. *Et tu, Brute* . . . 'I can never look on them in the same way as I once did, after that,' he later wrote to Scott. Longhurst said that the letters he got from Markham at this time were 'quite heart-breaking. The Treasury have acted in a most mean way and nobody can deny it. Personal spite goes a long way too.'

Neither he nor Markham had any difficulty in identifying the source of the personal spite. Few admirals take kindly to defiance by civilians and one, at least, had not forgotten Markham's defiance on the joint committee. An Antarctic Relief Committee had already been set up within the Admiralty to take over, refit and despatch the *Morning*, and its chairman was

Sir William Wharton, the hydrographer. He had not had to wait long for his revenge.

Wharton now made one of those decisions that seems, in retrospect, positively bizarre. Having strained at the gnat of a contribution towards one, existing, relief ship, the Admiralty engulfed a whole camel by deciding to send two. Doubtless the joint application for a Treasury grant by Markham and Huggins (19 May 1903) had put the idea into Wharton's head. 'It cannot be considered as certain that the *Morning* could get through single-handed,' the letter had said, 'and a second vessel, if a suitable one could be found, would be a great additional safeguard.' But an expensive one, they added. Wharton, blowing the expense, decided to send two.

It seemed almost impossible to locate, buy, refit, commission and despatch a suitable ship and get her to Lyttleton by the middle of November in the time available, little more than four months from the date of the decision at the first meeting of the committee on 22 June 1903. Wharton moved at a speed which, had it been customary in times of war, would have prevented many disasters. Before the decision to buy the ship had even been recorded, telegrams of enquiry were flying about the world. Wharton wired personally to Nansen, to sources in Germany and to all the major British whaling companies. Finally from St John's, Newfoundland, came a suggestion that the *Terra Nova* might do. She was the best vessel in the fleet of C. T. Bowring, a whaling firm, and considerably larger than the *Morning*: 744 gross tons, 450 tons register, 187 feet long and 31 feet wide. An urgent interchange of telegrams resulted in her purchase (6 July 1903) for £20,000 – as against £3800 paid by Markham for the *Morning*, and far above her value, it was generally thought. By the time both vessels had been fitted out, the cost came to over £35,000. Vice-Admiral Pelham Aldrich, one of the three members of the Relief Committee, went to Dundee to supervise refitting operations, and selected a crew from the Merchant Navy. Shackleton energetically assisted him.

Even with all this bustle, the season was too far advanced for the *Terra Nova* to reach New Zealand under her combination of steam and sail in time to proceed to McMurdo Sound with any margin of safety. So Wharton decided to have her towed much of the way. A series of naval vessels was alerted to carry out this unusual manoeuvre. HMS *Minerva* towed her from Portsmouth to Gibraltar; HMS *Vindictive* took her on to Aden; thence HMS *Fox* conveyed her to a spot 120 miles east of Socotra off the Persian Gulf, whence she proceeded under her own steam and sail to Hobart in Tasmania, not to Lyttleton, much to the annoyance of the people of New Zealand who had contributed £1000 to the *Morning* fund and regarded the men of the *Discovery* almost as their personal property, certainly as their personal friends. However, Hobart was nearer to the *Discovery*'s winter quarters and to Hobart she went, arriving on the last day of October, 1903, there to join forces with the *Morning*. The two ships proceeded together, Captain Colbeck in command, to McMurdo Sound.

This was a most efficient operation, conducted with remarkable speed; the only question was its necessity. Markham had no doubts on that score. Six ships, he pointed out, had negotiated the pack on about the same meridian without any difficulty; 'no ship that has tried has ever failed'. The *Morning* would have managed perfectly well and a second ship was a complete waste of public money. It escaped his notice that he, with Huggins, had originally suggested the scheme.

Everyone in the *Discovery* had been eagerly awaiting the *Morning*'s arrival, but the appearance of two ships dismayed them. Unaware of all the in-fighting that had gone on between Markham, Huggins, Wharton and others in London, Scott could only take it as a reflection on his own management of the expedition's affairs. Evidently he and his men were thought in London to be in want, difficulty and even danger and unable to extricate themselves. This did not indicate a well-conducted expedition under a competent commander. 'It was not a little trying,' Scott wrote with his usual understatement, 'to be offered relief to an extent which seemed to suggest that we have been reduced to the direst need. No healthy man likes to be thought an invalid.'

Colbeck brought despatches which explained the situation, taking a strong pro-Markham line. 'I feel more disgusted than I can say,' Longhurst wrote. (As secretary to the Admiralty's Relief Committee, at a salary of 7s 6d a week, he had followed events from the inside.) 'It is scandalous, when the poor old man has been slaving his hardest for the safety of the expedition, to be treated in this way.'

Scott was worried. His whole career hinged upon his getting promotion soon after his return. If it was thought at the Admiralty that his incompetence had landed the Government in this heavy expense, not to mention all the fuss and bother, his chances were probably ruined. A black mark on his record would remain until the end of his naval days. In a letter written from New Zealand on the way home he apologised to Sir William Wharton for the trouble and expense he had unwittingly caused. They had been victims of a most unusual season, he said.

I have been wondering whether my own reports led anyone to believe our position was at all dangerous or even serious. I can think of nothing, but I had little time to consider what I wrote. I had to mention such things as the scurvy for fear of garbled accounts through other channels, but I tried to point out that there was not the least chance of its recurrence . . .

The second winter passed in the most easy and comfortable manner possible and was far more comfortable than the first. In the spring and throughout the sledging season everyone remained splendidly fit and well, and before the relief ships arrived we had made some minor preparations for a third winter in a perfectly contented frame of mind. Except for the unfortunate home troubles, we all regarded the second winter as an unmixed blessing; everyone who has a particular scientific department openly rejoiced. The interest of the surroundings never flagged. We learnt to live in real comfort on the resources of the country, the sledging went like clockwork, each journey settled a string of doubts and we brought home a mass of fresh information, and I think we all felt some legitimate pride in the day's work.

Wharton's misgivings, and those of his naval colleagues, might well have been confirmed by this letter, rather than dispelled. The prospect of their officers and men remaining indefinitely in the Antarctic on full pay, feasting on seals and provisions sent at great expense in an annual relief ship, disturbed them as much as the apparently unlikely prospect of everyone dying from scurvy and privation. In July 1903 My Lords had it put on record that 'they could not consent to the officers and men of the Royal Navy being employed in any further expedition in the ice, even if sufficient private funds were raised for such a purpose, and that Commander Scott will receive directions to this effect'.

These directions were duly handed to him by Colbeck. If the *Discovery* could not be freed she was to be abandoned, and everyone was to return in the relief ships. Scott was appalled. In ordinary conditions 'a sailor would go through much rather than abandon his ship,' he observed, 'but the ties which bound us to the *Discovery* were very far beyond the ordinary'. For two and a half years she had been their home, their refuge, their source of comfort, and they loved her dearly. She was the finest purpose-built exploring ship that had ever sailed. And a captain who abandons his ship, even under orders, is like a partner in a broken marriage; it may not be his fault, but he has admitted failure. All the *Discovery* men would have to return 'as castaways with the sense of failure dominating the results of our labours'.

Twenty miles of very solid ice would have to disappear within six weeks if the ship was to be saved. It was now mid-January; the end of February was the very latest date by which the relief ships must leave. Captain Mackay of the *Terra Nova* thought that departure should not be delayed beyond 25 February 1904 and Colbeck agreed. Sawing had proved useless, so hitherto had blasting, and there was little to be done but pray for south-easterly gales, and to start to move the ship's gear, scientific instruments and collections into the *Terra Nova* and the *Morning*. In the *Discovery*, the ship's company was mustered and Scott read out the Admiralty's instructions. 'There was a stony silence. I have not heard a laugh in the ship since I returned.'

A half-way camp was established where men from the relief ships took over stores and impedimenta hauled to it by the crew of the *Discovery*. The scientific collections were enormous. Wilson alone had fifty seal-skins in good condition and hundreds of birds; Hodgson vast quantities of pickled creatures from the sea, the finest collections ever made of marine fauna from polar regions. A single sledge-load, drawn by fourteen men, carried 1300lbs of his gear. No one had worked harder than the bald-headed, short-winded, middle-aged and lion-hearted Muggins, and in these last few weeks he paid for it; he had a stroke which paralysed one side of his body and his power of speech. Tended by Koettlitz and Wilson he made a remarkable recovery, and a fortnight later, Skelton reported, 'got into the soup for doing too much, at which he kicked, but the doctors got the best of it'.

For the next five weeks, hopes and fears rose and fell like a see-saw. The ice was breaking up, but dreadfully slowly. Gradually, as chunks of ice broke away and drifted out to sea, the two ships anchored to the sea-edge of the floe moved in towards the camp below Cape Royds. Now the time came for an all-out attack with explosives. Royds moved over to the *Morning* to take charge of operations; in Colbeck's cabin he slept between sheets for the first time for two years, and found them 'cold and rather uncanny'. The sight of a house-fly made him shout with amazement.

Holes had first to be dug through the ice, still about six or seven feet thick, in which to insert large charges of guncotton, to be electrically detonated. Sometimes the explosions made a fair impression, at other times nothing resulted but a few small cracks and a large hole. Everything depended on elements so infinitely mightier, Scott wrote, than anything that man, with all his intelligence had devised. At times the whole exercise seemed futile, but it kept up the spirits of the company; while they could do nothing unless Nature came to the rescue, they felt that in a minor way they might be helping Nature on.

Scott's account of the last month at Hut Point reads like a commentary on a race run neck-and-neck between great cosmic forces, with the success or failure of a two-year enterprise as the stake. By 18 January 1904 the relief ships had moved between four and five miles farther in towards Hut Point, and on the night of the 22nd the ice broke away fast and the ships came in another mile. Royds in the *Morning* saw large floes drifting out to sea but eleven miles of ice still lay between her and her goal. On the 27th Scott wrote 'I fear, I much fear, things are going badly for us.' Royds, back in the *Discovery*, went up the hill to the lookout point and found everything hanging in the balance. 'It is perfectly sickening,' he wrote. 'Why doesn't it break up? What the devil is holding it? The prospects are as cheerless as they could be and I could simply scream at our absolute helplessness.' The thermometer fell to —14°F. Gloomily, the officers sat down to a sumptuous meal of roast beef and potatoes. The relief ships had also brought casks of stout, provided in a generous moment by the Admiralty, but both Royds and Scott found that it brought on rheumatism and reverted to claret.

They were woken up that night by a sound of creaking and groaning; the ship was moving for the first time. Next morning, the barometer of hope leapt upwards. The whole ice-sheet was heaving gently before the upward pressure of a heavy swell. Off Hut Point they could see water. But the relief ships were still a long way off, and the work of stripping the *Discovery* went on.

By 3 February the swell had gone and 'things look hopeless' Royds wrote. 'Everything is at a standstill.' New ice a good six inches thick had formed off Hut Point. Blasting was continuing near the floe's edge but the ice was thickening; between Hut Point and the ship the depth was fourteen feet. The charges made little impression on the floe but shook the ship tremendously. On 8 February the explorers noted, but did not celebrate, the second anniversary of their arrival at Hut Point, when the water had been clear; now there were still six miles of ice between the ship and her freedom. Scott returned from the *Morning* 'very down, as he thinks the chances of our getting out very small indeed'. They had champagne for their anniversary dinner and 'for a time forgot our troubles, but only for a time'. Scott's worst moment came two days later when he handed to Royds instructions for abandoning the *Discovery*. 'It turned me quite sick to have to read it and has given me the blight properly,' Royds observed.

Twenty-four hours later came an almost miraculous change. 'As I write' (Royds, 12 February) 'the *Terra Nova* is now only about two miles away and the ice continues to break away.' He was back in the *Morning*, digging and blasting. 'The ice was simply rushing out in huge lumps and floes, every blast sending more out, and cracking well behind.' They worked in watches through the night and the ships came in two miles in twenty-four hours.

St Valentine's Day saw the climax. In the afternoon, little change could be seen, but while the officers were at dinner they heard cheering from the men and one dashed in to say the ships were five hundred yards away. Everyone raced up to Hut Point and Scott described the scene.

The ice was breaking-up right across the strait, and with a rapidity which we had not thought possible . . . I have never witnessed a more impressive sight; the sun was low behind us, the surface of the ice-sheet in front was intensely white, and in contrast the distant sea and its forking leads looked almost black. The wind had fallen to a calm, and not a sound disturbed the stillness about us. Yet in the midst of this peaceful scene was an awful unseen urgency rending that great ice-sheet as though it had been naught but the thinnest paper . . . now without a word, without an effort on our part, it was all melting now, and we knew that in an hour or two not a vestige of it would be left, and that the open sea would be lapping on the black rocks of Hut Point.

The relief ships were racing side by side to reach the *Discovery*. The *Terra Nova*, stronger and larger, butted her way into the splintering ice but the little *Morning* took advantage of every lead and crack to nose her way forward like a terrier on a scent. The *Terra Nova*'s crew rolled her from side to side by rushing in a body to and fro from port to starboard. The men cheered wildly as each ship butted and twisted her way towards the pool of open water where lay the *Discovery*. At about 10.30 p.m. the *Terra Nova* broke through the last sheet of ice and the men on Hut Point ran up their silk Union Jack. It was a night to remember. Everyone rushed from ship to ship, everyone shook everyone else by the hand, and some 'reached that state which placed them in doubt as to which ship they really belonged to. Much can be excused on such a night.' Royds, however, collected some of the Merchant Navy officers from the relief ships and entertained them in the wardroom with sardines, his favourite delicacy. Next morning, the *Terra Nova* tied up to the *Discovery*'s capstan.

There followed a strenuous few days to get everything in order for departure; as all knew well, weather conditions could change radically within twenty-four hours. The first thing was to free the still ice-bound *Discovery*. A treble charge exploded near her stern lifted her bodily off the ice, the floe opened and she swung round slowly to face an easterly breeze. Cheer after cheer came from her crew and from the *Morning*'s as the blue ensign was run up and the vessel, after two years' imprisonment, 'came into her own again', as Scott wrote emotionally, with 'the right to ride the high seas'.

Next day, the ship's company carried out their last ceremony in the Antarctic, a memorial service and erection of a wooden cross to mark the grave of their only casualty, George Vince.

To have come through two years of such extraordinary perils and risks with the loss of only one life was indeed a piece of great good fortune. No man can command luck but the leader may have felt, as he looked back at Hut Point, that despite a good many mistakes he, like Cato, had deserved it. Throughout two and a half exacting years he had upheld among his men two vital factors: morale and discipline. In the last analysis, his only weapon was his personal authority. No laws prevailed in the Antarctic save those arising from a shared belief in the value of a common purpose, and in the leader's ability to achieve their common aim. The commander had a good lot of men but a mixed lot; he won their confidence, if not always their devotion, by his trust, and by never asking more of them than he asked of himself. 'You cannot bluff on an Antarctic sledge journey,' Bernacchi wrote. 'The Skipper seems to be more of a sticker than ever. I wish I could go as he does,' was Barne's comment. Lashly, toiling at his sledge, was heard to exclaim, 'If he can do it I don't see why I can't, my legs are as long as his.'

Scott himself wrote that the spirit of his men, who never jibbed at any order, was born of the principle of share and share alike. In outward forms, there was no equality. Wardroom, warrant officers' mess, messdeck; officers to order, men to obey. But in essentials there was an equality seldom realised, at that time, in British society, and never in the Royal Navy. When men trudge together in their harness, share a sleeping bag, starve together, fall down the same crevasse; nurse each other's frostbitten feet back to life in their bosoms; when every man's life depends on the fidelity of his companions; then class distinctions vanish, not by a conscious effort but in the natural order of things. That they could reappear, without objection on either side, in the more normal conditions of shipboard life, was a phenomenon that nobody questioned; that, too, was in the natural order of things. To preserve a balance between too strict a discipline and too lax a one must always be a test of leadership and Scott passed it in handsome style.

# 13 Homeward Bound

The *Discovery* was freed, the crew thought their troubles were as good as over, but their gravest peril was still to come. On the evening of 16 February 1904 a strong wind got up and the ship began to drag her anchors; her companion vessels made for the open strait. The Captain ordered steam to be raised and put the *Discovery* into the teeth of the gale intending to round Hut Point and reach safety in the open sea beyond. There was only about a quarter of a mile to go but wind and current swept her head-on aground a shoal, where she stuck with her masts shivering and wind and sea forcing her inch by inch further on to the shoal. 'I cannot find words to describe the horrible agony of the next eight hours,' Royds wrote. 'Oh! that awful bumping and ghastly grinding sound . . .' Sickening thuds shook her from stem to stern, she buckled and bent and big lumps of her false keel broke off and were tossed up by the waves.

'The poor Captain was most awfully low and gave the ship up for lost,' wrote Royds. In the middle of a mournful dinner which they thought might be their last, Mulock dashed in to say that the ship was moving astern. Full speed astern was ordered, all hands rolled the ship, slowly she began to work off and by eight o'clock was free. Over cocoa and sardines in the wardroom they compared their feelings, 'horrible thoughts,' Royds wrote, 'and there just above us was Vince's cross'. After taking off coal from the glacier and ice for water, and working all night to transfer coal from the *Morning*, on 19 February 1904 they left McMurdo Sound with all its memories behind. The three ships 'bounced along, one ship on each quarter, a fine sight for anyone knowing all the circumstances', Royds observed.

Scott had decided that instead of setting course straight for New Zealand, he would take the *Discovery* round Cape Adare and explore to the west, along the northern coast of Victoria Land, to see what lay beyond the farthest point reached by Ross in 1842. The *Morning* was to sail direct – or as direct as she could – to the Auckland Islands, where the three ships were to rendezvous before proceeding together to Lyttleton.

After two years inactivity, and the subsequent battering she had received, the *Discovery* was far from seaworthy; water started to pour into the holds, the pumps refused to work, gales sprang up, the rigging was recalcitrant, they bumped constantly into floes, the ship rolled heavily and almost everyone, land-bound for so long, was seasick. Then it was discovered that the rudder was so severely damaged as to be in danger of falling off altogether, and the spare one which they carried had to be shipped, but it was only half as big as the original and not nearly as effective. The farther west they penetrated, the worse the pack became, not only thick but entangled among icebergs, any one of which, had they failed to dodge it, would have holed the ship. They witnessed, at one point, an awesome sight; an iceberg turning turtle. It oscillated to and fro like a top, then with a mighty splash turned over and floated upside down.

Shortage of coal forced them to skirt the pack and seek open water where sail could be employed. This forced the *Discovery*, which had by this time lost touch with the *Terra Nova*, so far north that she missed the land altogether. The explorers could only re-discover the Balleny Islands, which looked quite different seen from the south, and prove by sailing over where it should have been, that the land whose existence had been reported by the American Charles Wilkes in 1838–42, was not in the position in which he had placed it. They netted more new marine species for Hodgson, and then headed for the Auckland Islands which they reached on 14 March 1904, with only ten tons of coal to spare. Neither of their companion vessels had arrived. Her men cleaned and painted the *Discovery*, making forays on the island to shoot anything that looked edible, including wild cattle and pigs, and rejoicing in their first sight of green and growing things for over two years. The New Zealand Government maintained a depot on these islands (called by sealers Sarah's Bosom) with emergency supplies for the use of ship-wrecked mariners. Among the graves surrounding it were those of a whole ship's company of sixty-eight souls wrecked on Enderby Island, a fate which the *Discovery*'s men might very easily have shared in this bleak southern ocean with its tempests, fogs, snowstorms and fields of enormous icebergs, deadly as a wartime minefield, which they had come through.

In due course their companion vessels kept the rendezvous, and three days' brisk sailing brought them to Lyttleton, which they reached on Good Friday, 1 April 1904, on a lovely morning, calm and hot. The welcome they received was anything but calm, and its warmth tremendous. Amongst the first on board was Wilson's wife, who wrote at once to Scott's mother to report how well everybody was; instead of appearing, as she had expected, older, thinner and more worn, they looked 'decidedly fatter', and were all brown and healthy as could be.

Reporters swarmed on board to interview the Captain who, in the course of these exchanges, made some remarks which either, as he forcibly averred, were falsified by the reporter, or, as Reuters claimed, fairly represented what he had said. Those who know how easily an unguarded remark made in a crowd of people all talking at once can be torn out of its context, blown up, distorted and then printed in big black letters on a front page, may think that Scott did make some indiscreet remark which he afterwards regretted. On the other hand these remarks may have been misheard or even, some reporters being what they are, not made at all, their purport having been picked up by newsmen from other members of the expedition and put into the leader's mouth. The *Discovery* men spoke with one voice about the absurdity of sending the *Terra Nova* to rescue them, and no doubt spoke freely. Moreover Markham's sister and brother-in-law, Charles Bowen, lived in Christchurch. Bowen held views in line with those attributed to Scott.

Whatever the truth of the matter, the publication in London of an interview criticising the Admiralty in the strongest terms naturally filled Scott with dismay. The story put out by Reuters' man in Christchurch, and given prominence in all the London papers, included the sentences:

Commander Scott emphatically protests against the despatch by the Admiralty of the *Terra Nova*, which he declares to have been a wasteful expense of money. He says that had the proper position of the *Discovery* been made known, it would have been obvious that she was perfectly safe, and no assistance beyond that which the *Morning* could render was requisite.

A more damaging statement from a serving officer could scarcely have been imagined. Unless the harm could be undone, Scott's chances of promotion would be wrecked. No wonder Royds, encountering his Captain in the streets of Lyttleton, noted that he looked disturbed by a telegram from London informing him of his publicised statement that the *Terra Nova* had been a useless waste of money. 'Although it was the truth,' Royds commented, 'he never said it.'

He would indeed have been a fool if he had, as he wrote to his brother-in-law William Ellison Macartney.

I have always been most careful to point out that we thoroughly understood the reason for the Admiralty's action in regard to the *Terra Nova*. There is here a dear old gentleman who is a brother-in-law of Sir Clements Markham's. With the best intentions in the world he has promulgated the doctrine that the *Terra Nova* was a waste of money. I found everyone ready to tell me so on arrival, but I always replied that the Government could do nothing less than make a certainty of the relief by sending a second ship . . . Altogether it was a very undeserved shock for there has been nothing written or spoken by me to countenance it, and as I say I have taken some trouble to put things straight.

This he did by issuing a denial to *The Times* and Reuters, and by telegraphing to the Admiralty and to the secretary of the RGS. 'I know how difficult it is to kill an impression of that sort' he wrote to his brother-in-law, adding philosophically,

However I suppose it will all be put right some day – meanwhile I foresee their Lordships will not be anxious to do much for me and they must do something or I shall be out of the running altogether. By Regulation I have two more years to put in [as Commander] and if that is adhered to I shall be a very antiquated post-Captain as things are going now.

Together with William Ellison Macartney, Scott was still supporting his mother, and in the background of that letter is the shadow of financial anxiety. His two dressmaking sisters were working hard but, his mother had written, 'it is really a bad season, and no money going'. Should he lose his chances of promotion then renewed poverty, as well as disappointment in his career, would be his reward for all the effort of the last three years. 'If they wait till we get home,' he wrote to his mother from New Zealand, 'then two or three persons will inevitably leap over my head. The question is whether they will pass me over in June. It is such a close thing that it must make a great deal of difference.'

Would the Admiralty believe his denials? In one quarter, at least, it appeared that they would. Anything that made Sir Clements Markham look a fool was pleasing to the hydrographer. It was Markham who, above all others, had been spreading in London prophecies of doom should relief not reach the Antarctic in time. Sir William Wharton's dislike of Markham appears to have outweighed altogether his disapproval of Scott's alleged criticisms. Far from being angry with Scott he was delighted, to judge by a minute (11 April 1904) remarking that 'The flat and public contradiction given to Sir Clements Markham by Commander Scott would cover with confusion anyone less irresponsible than that pachydermous gentleman.'

Wharton did not, of course, control promotions, but his influence was considerable when it came to an assessment of the expedition's work. Word was now beginning to get round that this had been outstanding, both in geography and in science. Markham could be expected to extol it, as he did with typical hyperbole in a letter to Longhurst (2 April 1904).

The news is magnificent. The second sledging season appears to have been as important, and energetically done, as the first. Taking both together, no polar expedition, Arctic or Antarctic, is to be compared with this as regards the importance of the work accomplished, the difficulties overcome, and the skill and ability with which the whole enterprise has been conducted.

While not prepared to raise a hearty cheer, the ranks of Tuscany ensconced in Burlington House were inclining towards a little mild applause. 'The professors I believe have woken up considerably since they heard news of your fossil discoveries,' Longhurst wrote to Scott, adding ponderously, 'Perhaps they will be able to trace their own birth period!' Longhurst urged him not to be so worried about shortage of money. Funds were so depleted that when they got to Lyttleton, Scott paid the crew of the *Discovery* but left the officers to fend for themselves, which in some cases meant borrowing from New Zealand friends. Necessary repairs to the ship were swallowing what little money remained. Together with Markham, Longhurst had been instrumental in getting a message of congratulation sent by the King, which clearly called for an acknowledgement. 'I hope it won't worry you to have to spend more money on cablegrams,' Longhurst commented.

Everyone wrote home from Lyttleton, and Royds and Wilson sent to Hannah Scott eulogies of her son. 'Without a doubt he has been the making of the Expedition,' Wilson wrote, 'and not one of us will but feel more and more grateful to him for the way he has acted throughout. Notwithstanding that it is a difficult thing, at least I imagine it is, for the Captain to make intimate friends with anyone, I feel as though we were real friends, and I need hardly say I am proud of it.'

The *Discovery* had to go into dry dock, her crew needed rest and leave, and rather more than two months passed before they sailed for home. Scott was fêted all over the islands, dined and wined by the Governor and other notables, played golf, and had to make a lot of speeches. 'We have had a very good time here,' he wrote to his mother, 'but it is high time we were off, as all our young men are getting engaged. Skelton is actually caught. I believe the young lady is very nice.' This was Sybil. Others were caught as well: Lieutenant Teddy Evans of the *Morning* and Ferrar among the officers, Blissett and Weller among the men.

Evans was married in Christchurch to Hilda Russell, and Michael Barne, his best man, enjoyed some tender exchanges with the bride's younger sister Rita, who worked a tablecloth and cushion with his crest on it for his cabin, cleaned his bicycle, and gave him a potted fern. He hung an enlargement of her photograph in his cabin and painted her name on a trunk she was taking back to her convent school. Cycling to her home in the dark to say goodbye, he met her pedalling towards the ship on the same errand; they collided. Next day he watched her waving from a train till it was out of sight; no wonder he was 'beastly sick' at leaving Christchurch. There had been a disappointment for Royds. The charming Mrs R. and her family were out of town; they gave him the run of their house and there he stayed, cosseted by 'old Nanny Sewle' who cooked him such enormous meals that even an appetite equal to post-sledging blow-outs quailed before them.

The Captain was less carefree. He and Royds were taken to court for shooting a bullock on Enderby Island; no one had realised that the cattle, although running wild, were private property; they were fined £5 with £1 8s od costs. They were back in a money economy again and he had his personal future to think about. 'How are we going to live when I get back to London?' he asked his mother. 'Is the shoproom I had before vacant? It would suffice.' But he thought it might be possible to afford a small house and pay a somewhat larger rent than the £80 a year he was finding for the Chelsea rooms. He asked her to look round for something suitable.

The expedition's scientists had hoped to be kept busy after their return classifying and writing up their material, a task of years, but there was nothing left in the *Discovery* fund to foot the bill. Their collections had gone to the British Museum of Natural History, their statistical material to the Royal Society. If they had hoped that these institutions, or any others, would support them while they put it all in order, they were disappointed. This was indeed a formidable task and ten years were to elapse before the publication of the final volume of the nine in which the expedition's scientific results were presented.

And so, back in England, the members of the scientific staff went their different ways. Wilson's huge collection of skins was housed at the Natural History Museum where he worked on them, unpaid, and at the same time, for a small fee from the publishers, on illustrations for new editions of standard works on British mammals and on British birds. He never went back to medical practice and remained completely indifferent to monetary reward. Fortunately, Ory was content to share his views.

The Service men had no problems about future employment. They could slip back into their grooves without loss of seniority, perhaps even with a small gain. Not that they were optimistic about this. Royds wrote that he expected promotion in about ten years' time, and looked for no advancement by reason of his Antarctic venture. Having private means and no dependants he could, unlike his Captain, accept this dreary prospect with comparative equanimity. He had made an accurate guess; he did not reach the Captain's list until 1914.

Reginald Skelton took an even gloomier view of his chances of advancement. In the rigid caste system of the Royal Navy, the executive branch constituted the Brahmins; engineers were, if not quite Untouchables, not far removed. Until very recently, in his day, officers of the two branches had not messed together, and they entered the Service by different routes. Engineers were looked down upon with the kind of snobbishness caricatured by Evelyn Waugh when he referred to anyone connected with the

BBC, from the Director-General downwards, as an 'electrician'. It was one
of the many reforms of Sir John Fisher to reduce the gap between engineers
and the naval Brahmins, a reform which took place while Skelton was
actually in the Antarctic.\* Lieutenants (E) were still very much on the
defensive when he wrote in his diary,

> Personally it [the expedition] must mean little or nothing to me. I have always
> recognised that. Nothing of any importance can be done by an engineer in the
> Navy, there is no appointment either lucrative or in any other way important in the
> whole branch, in fact once an Engineer RN one must be content to remain an under-
> paid nonentity . . . Personally, I would sooner have gone out to the colonies with
> £10 in my pocket and started as a labourer. I know enough now to say that any
> decent self-respecting Engineer RN can have only one idea of happiness and that is
> to get a decent job outside. Inside, well there isn't such a thing as success, one is
> always in a servile position.

It was ironical that the writer of these words should have been among
the first to disprove them. Skelton went back to make for himself a brilliant
career and occupy a far from servile position in the Royal Navy.

Scott, almost alone among the company, did hope for some personal
advancement. There were, he may have reckoned, three black marks, or
at least grey ones, against him at the Admiralty. One was the state of
destitution into which his expedition had, erroneously, been said to have
fallen, thanks to Markham's well-meant but misguided efforts. Then
there was the suspicion that he had not tried hard enough to extricate the
*Discovery* after her first winter, and might not have tried again had instructions not been sent to abandon her if he failed. Worst of all was the newspaper report from Lyttleton, which he hoped he had explained away. For
none of these matters did he believe himself responsible; the question was,
what the Admiralty believed.

The *Discovery* left Lyttleton on 8 June 1904, after a ball given by her
officers to 350 of their hosts and friends, and reached Spithead on 10
September. They had been away just over three years.

---

\* As Second Sea Lord, Jackie Fisher wrote, 'The real masters of the Navy were
the despised engineers, whose mammas were not asked to tea by other mammas.'
Far-reaching reforms introduced under the Selbourne Scheme in 1902/03 gave
engineer officers executive powers in their own department, which they had
previously lacked, and provided for a unified system of training. 'Making greasers
of us all' was how one Admiral described these much-resented reforms. It was not
until 1954 that a fully unified scheme abolished all the disabilities from which the
engineering branch, and other technical branches, had suffered for so long.

# 14    Penmanship
and No Medals

Sir Clements Markham and his wife boarded the ship off Spithead and were on the bridge when she steamed into Portsmouth harbour. 'All the men of war, and a line of boats sent from Whale Island, gave hearty cheers.' The warships were dressed, the *Discovery* herself was spick and span and her company, their faces mahogany-brown, 'all looked wonderfully well', Sir Clements proudly observed. A reporter noted that they spoke slowly and walked with deliberate movements.

The professors of the Royal Society had agreed to join the RGS as hosts at a welcoming luncheon held in a warehouse at the East India Docks. There was another congratulatory telegram from the King, but neither the First Lord nor any of the Sea Lords attended the 'luncheon in a shed', as a reporter scathingly called it. Scott, however, was not perturbed. He had received the news that he had hoped for at Portsmouth. His appointment as post-Captain was to take effect from the day of his arrival. In modern terms, this was the breakthrough; now, given reasonable luck and barring some blunder of his own, there was nothing to prevent him from one day hoisting his flag.

'Never has any polar expedition returned with so great a harvest of scientific results,' Markham pronounced in his speech of welcome on 16 September 1904 at the East India Docks. The tally was indeed impressive. A whole new land had been discovered, if not explored, to the east of Ross's Barrier, the Barrier itself had been penetrated and surveyed for some 350 miles, and the question settled as to whether it was afloat or part of the land. 'The greater part of it is afloat', Scott had stated; he would not say that it was all afloat because he had not completely traversed it. But from observations made by himself and his team it was plain that the Barrier was what it has since been named, an ice-shelf, a plain of floating ice fed by glaciers descending from great inland mountains, and anchored to land on each side; its sea-edge was constantly breaking off to form bergs which were carried northwards out to sea. As much as twenty or thirty miles, Scott reckoned, had broken off since Ross's visit sixty years before. Then, the range of mountains sighted by Ross in Victoria Land had been traced and charted as far south as the 83rd parallel, and penetrated to reach the polar ice sheet, at an altitude of about 9000 feet, on which both the geographical and the magnetic poles could be deemed to lie.

With the expedition's record of twenty-eight sledging journeys undertaken in the most severe conditions ever known; with the life history of the Emperor Penguin, the world's oldest bird, unravelled; with the discovery of fossil plant remains; with large collections of rocks and of hitherto unknown sea-creatures; with continuous meteorological and magnetic records kept for two years; with these and other discoveries and observations to the expedition's credit, Markham's claim was justified. Despite dissension among its organisers, despite a scratch team of scientists, the inexperience of all its men, the unknown nature of the problems it encountered, and the harshness of the environment into which it came, the expedition had been a notable success. Replying to the flattering things said at the luncheon, Scott disclaimed personal credit. 'An Antarctic expedition is not a one-man show, not a two-man show, nor a ten-man show. It means the co-operation of all . . . There has been nothing but a common desire to work for the common good.'

After the luncheon in a shed came a dinner given by the RGS in more elegant surroundings, and then everyone dispersed on leave. Before getting down to writing and lecturing, Scott treated himself at a West End tailor's to the first really well-cut suit he had ever owned. Next, he arranged for the transfer of his mother and two sisters to the house they had found at 56 Oakley Street, off the Chelsea Embankment. This was then a cheap, unfashionable neighbourhood of pleasant, early nineteenth-century houses, within earshot of the fog-horns of tugs moving up and down the river. This was to be Scott's home for four years. It still stands, marked by a commemorative blue plaque.

A newly discovered portion of Antarctica now bore King Edward VII's name, and Scott received the royal thanks in the form of an invitation to Balmoral, followed by appointment to Commander of the Victorian Order, a step up from the Membership which he already had. This was the only official honour he was awarded. There was nothing from the Government, not even a message of congratulation. This was remarked on sharply by the press; there was a feeling that Scott deserved a much better reception and at least an Order of the Bath, if not a knighthood.

On his return he had submitted a long despatch to the Admiralty, praising in the highest terms all his men. (He singled out for special mention Feather, Dailey, Dellbridge, Wild, Evans and Lashly.) Admiral Wharton wrote in his minute, 'Commander Scott and his staff have most magnificently maintained the high standard of efficiency of former polar explorers. I presume that steps will be taken about medals.' The First

Lord and the First Sea Lord concurred. A recommendation for awards must almost certainly have been submitted to the Prime Minister. If so, it was quite certainly ignored.

Markham had no doubt as to the reason. The serpent of the Royal Society had whispered into Mr Balfour's ear. Nor had Balfour forgotten the deceitful behaviour, as he had considered it, of the RGS in the matter of a relief ship. So Scott missed his medal.

At Balmoral, he was invited to lecture, and showed slides prepared from Skelton's photographs to a company including Their Majesties, the Prince and Princess of Wales, the Duke and Duchess of Connaught – and the Prime Minister. 'Intended an hour,' he wrote to his mother, 'but the King asked many questions and ran into 1¾ hours. All sorts of nice things said afterwards, none nicer than by the Prime Minister who said he regarded himself as the *Father of the Expedition*!!!! Don't give this away.' It was fortunate that Sir Clements Markham was not present.

Next day (29 September 1904) there was a grouse drive when 'the P. of Wales instructed me in the art and had the temerity to remain in the next butt. Shot 9 myself, less than most, more than some.' This was followed by a day's deer-stalking; the King shot three, the Prince two, Scott one. Altogether it was a great success, and to his relief Scott did not have to wear knee breeches or a frock coat.

Back in London, the real work began. Scott had sought the Admiralty's permission to deliver the lectures and write the book now expected of him. 'I have no wish to advertise myself,' he wrote to the First Sea Lord on 21 September 1904, but he asked for six months' leave in which to get the work done. This was granted, but he still felt anxious. 'I should be very sorry to do anything the Admiralty thought unbecoming to a naval officer. Except in this matter I have mentioned, I am trying to keep as quiet as possible.'

To keep quiet may have been Scott's intention but it was by no means Markham's. An exhibition at the Bruton Galleries, opened on 4 November 1904, drew an estimated 10,000 visitors to see a selection of Wilson's drawings and Skelton's photographs, a model of the *Discovery*, and sledging equipment and rations. Motor cars and carriages lined Bruton Street and Bond Street and persons of rank and fashion were marshalled into a long queue by a policeman. Society folk were not used to queues in those days and they protested that they had tickets; so had everyone, the constable replied, and kept them in line.

Three days later, Scott gave his first big lecture to 7000 invited members and guests of the two Societies at the Albert Hall. The Royal Society was still in a grudging frame of mind. A few days before the lecture, Markham had received 'a very nasty letter' from the secretary 'objecting to the officers of the *Discovery* lecturing or reading papers'. Markham ignored it. Despite the presence on the platform to support their leader of almost all the members of the expedition, the distinguished audience received the lecture tepidly with only 'gentle hand-claps'; but on the following evening a public lecture for which the audience paid admission aroused much more enthusiasm. In both lectures, Scott stressed again the point he always made, that this had been no one-man undertaking but a matter of team-work to which all contributed, with the advancement of knowledge, not do-or-die adventure, as the aim.

Markham presented Scott with a gold medal, specially struck; each of his officers received a silver replica and Captain Colbeck was not forgotten with a piece of silver plate. Medals, if not official ones, were now raining down on Scott. He had already been awarded the Patron's Gold Medal of the RGS, which his mother had received on his behalf while he was in the *Discovery*. Now, although not all at once, he was made a member of the French Legion of Honour and of the Russian Geographical Society, and received medals from the Geographical Societies of Phila-delphia, Denmark and Sweden, a decoration specially designed by order of the King which went to all his officers and men and, what pleased him most, an honorary degree of Doctor of Science from Cambridge University.

After London came Edinburgh with more lectures and the Royal Scottish Geographical Society's Livingstone medal. This was Shackle-ton's doing. He and Scott were on excellent terms. Shackleton had been one of the first to greet his former shipmates when the *Discovery* docked, and had stayed on board until one in the morning yarning with her Captain and with Markham, who had recommended him for the secretaryship of the Scottish RGS. 'Everyone is very pleased with Shackleton,' Scott wrote to his mother. 'He is showing great energy and business capacity.' In Edinburgh he was playing the part of new broom in the cobwebby premises of his Society, having electric light installed and even introducing a type-writer, regarded with deep suspicion by most of the Fellows. Scott went on to Glasgow and then to Dundee with Shackleton, who had been adopted as Liberal Unionist candidate for that constituency at the forthcoming election. He did not get in.

Gaining confidence as a speaker, Scott allowed a note of satisfaction to creep into his letters to his mother. The Synod Hall in Edinburgh was packed with 2300 people – 'they say there was a greater demand than at Nansen's lecture. My lecture came off. My first before a Scottish audience and I didn't take long to realise the difference. I never really felt that they were in sympathy but I contrived to exert efforts to please, and at the end I received a really big ovation'. Now a public figure, he had to take care of his appearance and asked his mother to send half a dozen collars, illustrating the shape – 'you will observe the flaps at the throat'.

On the platform, he presented a pleasing appearance. He was not exactly good-looking but appeared to his audiences as a slim, broad-shouldered, narrow-hipped man who looked taller than his five foot nine inches. He was dark-haired and clean-shaven, with remarkably clear, dark-blue eyes, and had considerable charm of manner. As time went on he learnt some of the tricks of the trade, such as running a hand in mock despair through his hair when a slide failed to come up at the right moment, and he brought in plenty of touches of humour of a dry, understated kind. In fact he turned into a workmanlike lecturer, although he spoke too fast. Bishop Wilberforce, remarked the *Manchester Guardian*, was generally conceded to hold the record as the fastest speaker in the kingdom, but Scott ran him very close. He spoke without notes, 'and though his words were all like competitors in a race they never overtook one another, but all stood out clearly and independently'.

He was now on half-pay, and travelled with the strictest economy: third-class tickets on the railway, and nights in cheap hotels. All his takings, less expenses, went into the expedition fund, which was still in low water. Markham had suffered another disappointment. He had invited the Government to take over the *Discovery*, which he felt now occupied a special place in British history, for purposes of research and future polar expeditions, but they had refused, and insisted on her disposal to the highest bidder. Markham sold her to the Hudson's Bay Company for £10,000, about a quarter of her original cost. He had been hanging on as President of the RGS until the return of the *Discovery*, when he almost immediately retired, to be succeeded by Sir George Goldie.

Despite continually quartering the country in unheated railway carriages, lecturing in draughty halls and sleeping in bare hotel bedrooms with Gideon Bibles in a drawer, Scott made a start on his book. Both Markham and Mill gave him sage advice: get it written, or as much of it as he could, before arriving in England, and published as soon afterwards as possible. For such a book, Markham wrote, he should be able to get a good sum. Mill advised him to keep it short, and have it illustrated with plenty of photographs.

To write a book while sailing a slow, small vessel through stormy oceans was a counsel of perfection that Scott had been unable to follow. 'Of all things I dread having to write a narrative,' he wrote to Mill, 'and am wholly doubtful of my capacity; in any event if I have to do it, it will take me a long time. I have not, like you, the pen of a ready writer.' By the start of 1905 the book was not nearly finished, and he applied to the Admiralty for another three months' leave. This was granted, but he knew he could not ask again.

'I have tied myself to a desk,' he wrote to Mill on 22 January 1905 from Oakley Street, his round of lectures more or less over. 'The resultant book will be very dull but it will not outstrip fact and I'm really rather indifferent to profits though by rights I can't afford to be.' The desk appears to have been at 22 Eccleston Square and not at Oakley Street. 'Scott comes every day to write his book in the old schoolroom and has lunch and tea with us,' Markham wrote in January 1905. Royds was staying in the house while compiling his report on meteorology, and Markham himself was busy downstairs writing a history of Peru. The day's work over, Sir Clements and Minna walked arm in arm in the Square, except on occasions when he was 'threatened by gout'. The company of the two young men, for both of whom he had a deep affection, brought solace to the old gentleman in his retirement from the Society he had served for over forty years and dominated for most of that time. Both young men, but especially Scott, had all the qualities he would have most desired in the son that he never had.

In the spring, Scott retreated to a hotel at Ashdown, whence he wrote to his mother, 'I cannot tell why I find it impossible to work in London but so it is, my ideas refuse to flow and I get a cramped inexpressive feeling that hampers me greatly,' But at Ashdown, in April, with woodland buds beginning to break, 'every now and again I can make a burst and get ahead'. So, with a good deal of painful effort, and with the active help of Reginald Smith, senior partner in the firm of Smith, Elder and Co, *The Voyage of the Discovery* took shape.

Reginald Smith was a well-known and well-loved figure in London's literary world, editor of the *Cornhill Magazine*, as well as a successful publisher. Respect for merit and kindness to authors were qualities for which he was famed. He would never publish a book that fell below his high standard merely because it was likely to make money, and he treated his authors as colleagues and often as friends, going to endless trouble to advise and help them. This he did for Scott, who submitted his book to him chapter by chapter as it was written, thinking each section worse than the last. Reginald Smith offered robust encouragement. He read the sledging chapters 'with delight and indeed emotion'. 'I can almost hear you speaking as you write.' When the book was completed, Smith, Elder's principal reader, Leonard Huxley, tidied up the prose and reported warmly in the book's favour. Scott's mind, he thought, was 'like wax to receive an impression and like marble to retain it'.

The book, in two volumes and illustrated by Skelton's photographs and Wilson's drawings, went through the press with, by today's standards, remarkable speed. Completed only in midsummer, it was published on

12 October 1905 in an edition of 3000 copies at two guineas a time. 'Sir Clements Markham, KCB, the Father of the Expedition and its most Constant Friend' was the appropriate dedication. Smith gave generous terms: three-quarters of the profits to Scott, one quarter to the publishers.

Scott need not have worried about his competence as a writer; the book was praised by nearly all the critics for its interest, straightforward presentation, vivid descriptive passages and its author's modesty. The *Times Literary Supplement* called it 'a masterly work' and a fellow-officer, Captain (later Admiral) Lewis Bayly, wrote that he held his breath when the author slid down a glacier and trembled when he dangled in a crevasse. Among his most appreciative readers were his former shipmates, every one of whom got a free copy – the author distributed in all nearly one hundred. Thomas Crean, an Irishman who had joined the Expedition from HMS *Ringarooma* in New Zealand, wrote a grateful letter, saying that it would remind him of being on the veldt again. (He had been invited to serve as coxswain when the Captain went back to sea.) Scott also insisted on sending Wilson a cheque for £100 as a reproduction fee for his drawings; Wilson protested, but was over-ruled.

*The Voyage of the Discovery*, while it got excellent notices, sold reasonably well and enhanced Scott's reputation, did not make a fortune for anyone. The first edition of 3000 copies sold out immediately, calling for a second printing of 1500 copies the following month. A cheque for £1569 14s 0d at the end of 1905 represented the author's share of the profits and made him a richer man than he had ever been before. That was not very rich. For a year he had been on half-pay, amounting to little more than the £200 a year he allowed his mother, and most of the pay which had accumulated while he was in the Antarctic, after the deduction of his mother's allowance, had gone in buying the lease of 56 Oakley Street and equipping the house with furniture.

After this initial success, sales dropped sharply. In 1906, Scott's share of the profits came to £228 2s 0d, in the following year to £26 2s 6d, and in the year after that to only £17 0s 6d. The lowest ebb was a sale of six copies in 1912.\* Probably the author was not unduly disappointed. Like many writers, he took little, if any, interest in the book when it was over and done with, and, in any case, had not written it for money. Writing for him was a labour not of love or of gain, but of duty.

Unchained from his desk, in September 1905 Scott went to stay with the

---

\* That was not quite the whole story; there was also a small sale in the United States which brought the author £184 5s 2d in 1905, then no more. In 1907, Smith, Elder brought out a cheap edition at 10s for which they paid Scott £21 15s 9d that year and small sums thereafter, adding a total of £47 3s 9d to his income before his death. Before the book went out of print in 1919, total sales of the two editions amounted to 5272 copies.

Reginald Smiths at their shooting lodge near Invereighty, Forfarshire. Here he enjoyed an unaccustomed round of gaiety and sport, including a grand party at Glamis Castle to celebrate the coming-of-age of Patrick, heir to the fourteenth Earl of Strathmore. His enjoyment of these social occasions was ruffled by a 'small worry in the shape of Armitage's book which, contrary to agreement, is advertised to appear immediately after my own. It is rather a breach of faith but I hope it will do little harm.'

The version given by Armitage some twenty years later was rather different. Scott, he wrote, 'tried, even, to prevent my lecturing or writing, and foolishly threatened my publishers, although I had the permission of the committee'. His book, *Two Years in the Antarctic*, came out in that same autumn of 1905, under the imprint of Edward Arnold. He wrote nothing in it derogatory to his former leader, but nothing in his praise either.

Back in London awaiting a posting at sea, Scott continued to sample social life. An eligible bachelor, attractive and good-mannered, modest, a sailor, something of a national hero, he was soon snapped up by London hostesses as an acceptable lion. London society was then a coherent and hierarchical body with a set of rules all the more binding for being un-written, and with such well-defined limits that people spoke of being 'in' it or not in it, as one might speak of being in a club, a cricket eleven or a zoo. (In New York, although not in London, there was even a published directory of those who were 'in'.) Naturally there was a hazy zone around the perimeter, like a moon's halo, where a deadly struggle took place either to get in or to avoid being dropped, a fate meted out remorselessly to those who broke the rules. All this naturally provided a rich storehouse of plots and themes for dramatists and novelists, denied to their successors today.

It also made the lionising process fairly simple. All that was needed was for one of the society hostesses, skimming perhaps through her newspaper, or exchanging gossip at a tea-party, to hear that Mr X had returned from the jungle after subduing single-handed a race of cannibals, or had won the vc in a feat of incredible daring on the North-West Frontier, or had ridden a horse from Vladivostok to Berlin, or had painted a controversial portrait hung in this year's Royal Academy; then a formal invitation would go out to request the pleasure of his company at luncheon or dinner. If he roared politely or amusingly, other hostesses would follow suit, and the lion would enjoy his hour of glory. No one expected this to last very long; the lion must go off to his hunting-ground and other lions replace him; but while it lasted the process was, on the whole, agreeable both to the lions and to their hostesses, providing opportunities for one-upmanship among the latter – for some lions, obviously, were better than others – which kept conversation alight.

Scott was, on balance, a good lion; his exploits had been internationally acclaimed, and the shyness that had once afflicted him had worn off. He was now thirty-six and without, so far as anyone knew, experience of a serious love affair – or even a casual one, unless an attack of calf-love, when a sub-lieutenant, for a married lady with a quick-tempered husband mentioned by his sister can be counted. There is no hint that any of the Christchurch ladies who caused such devastation among the *Discovery* men had engaged his attention.

Medals and honours were still arriving, speeches sometimes still required. 'I am sorry to say that my lines are cast in such places that in all probability I shall not return to those regions,' he said, referring to the Antarctic, at an RGS meeting in April 1906 when the gold medal of the American Geographical Society was presented. Yet in the same speech he all but contradicted himself by recalling in emotional terms 'those fields of snow sparkling in the sun', the pack-ice and bergs and blue sea, and 'those mountains, those glorious southern mountains, rearing their heads in desolate grandeur'. Sounds, too, came back to him: 'the movements of the pack, those small mysterious movements with the hush sound that comes across the water, and I hear also the swish of the sledge . . . I cannot explain to you, they will always drag my thought back to those good times when these things were before me'.

Time, in fact, was already playing its tricks, transmuting the lead of pain, fatigue and privation into golden memories. 'Those were golden days,' Bernacchi wrote years later, 'and their memories are fraught with joy.' Already Michael Barne, forgetting his frostbitten fingers, was trying to raise money for an expedition of his own. What were Scott's intentions? Outwardly, to pursue without further interruption his naval career, but increasingly he was feeling the contrary pull. The lure of the unknown, a sense of unfinished business, patriotic pride, personal ambition: many strands were twisted into the rope that pulled. Perhaps the strongest strand of all was the unspoken pressure of public opinion. 'England expects . . .' The duty expected of him was to go back and get to the Pole. In April 1906 he was saying that 'in all probability' he would not return; in the following September, J. M. Barrie wrote to him, 'I chuckle with joy to hear all the old hankerings are coming back to you. I feel you have to go out again, and I too keep an eye open for the man with the dollars.'

The diminutive Scots playwright James Barrie was a new literary friend. Scott and he were introduced, it has been said, by the novelist A. E. W. Mason at a dinner party in London. Barrie's version of their meeting has often been quoted. Having 'found the entrancing man I was unable to leave him'; after dinner they saw each other home throughout the night, back and forth between Adelphi Terrace and Oakley Street, unable to break off a conversation largely concerning 'a comparison of the life of action (which he pooh-poohed) with the loathly life of those who sit at home (which I scorned)'.

Barrie's admiration for Scott is easily explained. He had always idolised men of action; Joseph Thomson, the first European to march through the heart of Masailand, had been one of his friends and heroes. Scott, with the added glamour of the navy, brave and modest, clean-living and sensitive, was what Markham might have called the beau ideal of an explorer. The attraction Barrie held for Scott is less obvious. Perhaps it sprang from Scott's youthful but now abandoned ambition to express himself in writing, added to an interest in the stage first aroused by his sister's brief career as an actress, and to an almost wistful admiration for things of the mind rather than of the muscle. Scott was not the first man of action to think that he would rather write a great poem or paint a masterpiece than scale Mt Everest, or, in his own case, reach the South Pole.

If he over-rated Barrie as an artist, so did most critical opinion of the day. When their meeting took place, Barrie was at the peak of his fame. *Peter Pan* despite some adverse reactions (such as that of Anthony Hope who was heard to murmur 'Oh for an hour of Herod' as he left the theatre), had pleased the critics, and the public had taken the fantasy to its heart. James Barrie, little over five feet tall, pale and hollow-cheeked with a drooping black moustache – like Scott a heavy pipe-smoker – was possessed of a burning energy and, despite his whimsicalities and heavy-handed Scottishness, a charm which conquered even those unsympathetic to his brand of humour and predilection for fairies.

Through Barrie, Scott met a young American actress, Pauline Chase, then playing in *Peter Pan*, whom he took out to supper several times. No more came of that. Later, he went to stay with Barrie near Drumnadrochit in Inverness-shire where fellow guests included the theatrical producer Harley Granville Barker and the five young sons of Arthur and Sylvia Llewellyn Davies, whom Barrie unofficially adopted. Another of Barrie's friends whom Scott met in London was the former actress Mabel Beardsley, by then Mrs George Bealby Wright. In the 'nineties, she had toured with Irene Vanbrugh in whose company Scott's sister Ettie had played a minor role. Mabel Beardsley, best known as the sister of Aubrey Beardsley, the artist, was one year younger than Scott when they met. She 'took him up', he went quite often to her luncheons, and wrote her half a dozen letters after he returned to sea.

This he did in August 1906, as flag-captain to Rear-Admiral Sir George Egerton in HMS *Victorious*. 'The Egerton kindness is a thing never to be forgotten' he had written to his mother on hearing that the Egertons had taken her for a holiday while her son was in the Antarctic. Egerton invited

Sir Clements Markham for a cruise off the coast of Spain, and there were gay times on board with dinner parties every night at Gibraltar. Now freed of RGS responsibilities, the old man's health had recovered and he enjoyed a day's excursion on the island of Majorca, where they had an excellent omelette in a spotlessly clean inn. Scott may have found the dictatorial old gentleman a little trying. 'I'm afraid my experiences make it difficult for me to take kindly to being dependent on another person's movements and ideas,' he wrote to his mother.

Fresh family worries had come upon him. His brother-in-law Eric Campbell of the Royal Irish Fusiliers died suddenly of heart failure, leaving his sister Rose and a small daughter, Erica, almost penniless. Eric's family, Campbells of Barcaldine, were unwilling to help, and Scott wrote to his mother from the *Victorious* (21 October 1906) of new family arrangements. Rose and her daughter were to live with Mrs Scott at Oakley Street, Monsie was to be freed of all home duties and to devote her whole time to dressmaking. Scott's naval pay was to be even further stretched.

Meanwhile his mind was tending more and more to the question of a return to the south. Markham's visit may well have tipped the balance in its favour. 'His Discoverys all wished to follow their Commander,' Markham wrote. Disquieting rumours were in the air about foreign poaching in what Markham regarded as a British preserve. In particular, a Pole named Arctowski, who had been with de Gerlache in his *Belgica* expedition of 1897–9, was trying to raise the necessary cash. Not that Markham was unduly worried about him. 'Foreigners never get much beyond the Antarctic Circle,' Markham said.

# 15 Shackleton's Challenge

By early 1907, Scott had made up his mind to lead a second expedition to the south if the money could be raised. On 28 January he wrote to Scott Keltie, secretary of the RGS:

I saw Goldie and talked to him but I don't think he has any heart in the matter, though he has promised to do his best and keep sharp an eye to finding a possible millionaire . . . You were sanguine. You believe there will be little difficulty in raising funds with my name. I can't tell but I don't see how it is to be done at present without a general subscription – but I'd sooner have a single subscriber as you know . . .
There can't be a doubt but that the thing ought to be done. There is the finest prospect of a big advance in latitude that has ever been before a polar explorer. Rub all this in to Goldie – it's essentially the thing for a Geographical Society and remember what a future generation will think if you lose the experience combined with the will to go when they are at your command. It will soon be on record that I want to go and only need funds. I am pretty certain I could do the whole thing for £30,000. It won't look well for the Society if an inexperienced foreigner cuts in and does the whole thing while we are wasting time.

He was already in touch with several of his 'Discoverys'. Barne, Mulock and Skelton wanted to go south again, and Barne gave up the idea of leading his own expedition in favour of becoming Scott's First Lieutenant. Then a bombshell exploded. On 12 February 1907 Shackleton announced in the press his plan to lead an expedition towards the South Pole. A sum of £30,000 had already been promised and Shackleton asked for the patronage and practical help of the RGS. Its secretary wrote to Scott in some consternation asking 'what do you propose to do?'

This opened a rift between the two explorers that was never to be sealed. Since they had last met in Edinburgh, Shackleton's fortunes had been precarious. After resigning from the Royal Scottish Geographical Society to contest the Dundee parliamentary seat he found himself, on losing the fight, without a job, without resources, and with a growing family. He tried marketing a new brand of cigarette, then floating a steamboat company, then other projects of an equally speculative kind. At last his luck turned. A Clydebank shipbuilder, William Beardmore, took him on as a supernumerary secretary. Shackleton's enthusiasm, charm and eloquence soon had the Scotsman and his family in thrall.

Shackleton had by then made up his mind to go back to the ice. The strongest of his motives was to redeem his failure there. He wanted to make a name for himself, and he responded, even more strongly than Scott, to the pull of what Mill called 'the desire to wipe out *terra incognita*'. 'You can't think what it's like,' he wrote to his sister, 'to walk over places where no man has been before.' Mr Beardmore, being a cautious Scot, went no further than to guarantee an overdraft, to be repaid from money Shackleton was certain he could make on his return by writing a book, lecturing, and selling articles. His optimism in this respect, as in others, was unrestrained. He managed to persuade Heinemann to offer £10,000 for a book 'if we are successful' – presumably if he got to the Pole. In view of the sales of *The Voyage of the Discovery*, Heinemann were clearly optimistic too.

All through 1906 he had been busy with his plans. He intended to establish his base in McMurdo Sound, and to rely for transport mainly on ponies, with some dogs, and a specially designed motor car. When he set about recruiting staff he turned naturally to his former companions. In February 1907 he wrote to Mulock, who replied that he was already committed to Scott. This was the first, Shackleton stated, that he had heard of his former Captain's intentions.

He wrote also, on 12 February 1907, to Billy Wilson, inviting him to become his second-in-command. Wilson, reunited with Ory, had rented a small house in Bushey where he was working on his Antarctic bird report, and had started an investigation into the cause of a disease that was killing grouse in large numbers in the north. This was a long, laborious enquiry, very hard work for very bad pay (£150 a year plus expenses), which involved travelling all over Scotland and much of northern England, staying in cold, cheap hotels and carrying out his research in the roughest of conditions and without a laboratory. He dissected over 2000 grouse, and said that he went on skinning them in his sleep. Sometimes Ory read to him while he skinned and sketched. He, also, had made friends with the Reginald Smiths, and an occasional holiday at their lodge Cortachy was a bright spot in this drab existence. Scott stayed there during one of Wilson's visits and, when out deer-stalking, let a roe-deer pass unharmed, Wilson recorded, 'because it was such a pretty little thing'.

Like others, Wilson became deeply attached to the publisher and his wife Isabel, and they to him. Before his departure on the second polar expedition, the Smiths presented him with a wrist-watch. Wilson wrote a letter of thanks that could scarcely have been more gracefully worded.

From now onward till we return, successful, from the Pole, not a single day will pass but I shall be reminded by the simple inscription on the back of the watch of the friends whose friendship has made all but the highest principles in life impossible. It is a great thing to have a friend like that, and we feel that to possess the friendship of yourself and Mrs Smith is to possess something which will outlast watches, and will still be going when the last of them has stopped.

The grouse enquiry, directed by an official commission headed by Lord Lovat, was to take five years, and Wilson was only half way through when Shackleton's invitation came. He felt himself bound by his undertaking, and refused. 'Had I been free I should have gone with him,' Wilson wrote, and he told Lord Lovat that it was a great disappointment. His disappointment was nothing as compared with Shackleton's, who sent first one telegram, then another, imploring Wilson to change his mind. He even asked the secretary of the grouse commission to release him. The secretary replied, Shackleton wrote, 'that if I had asked for any other man they could spare him – *you* were unique! . . . Heaven knows how I want you – but I admire you more than ever for your attitude. A man rarely writes out of his heart but I would to you. If I reach the Pole I will still have a regret that you were not with me.'

The day after Wilson received this letter (16 February 1907), one came from Scott. He asked Wilson whether Shackleton had, as he now suspected, known of his (Scott's) intentions before announcing his own. Wilson replied, 'I have good reason to think that he knew nothing. I myself have never heard a hint of your going south again.' He remembered, he added, 'what you told me once in the south, that it would do you more harm than good with the Admiralty because it would put you out of date, and this has seemed so natural to me that I took it as certain . . . It had simply not occurred to me that you could spare the time and keep your position in the navy.' Shackleton, he suggested, probably thought the same. (Despite three years' intimacy in the Antarctic, the letter began 'My Dear Captain Scott.') He went on to attribute to Shackleton qualities of unselfishness he certainly possessed himself, but were possessed by very few others in a world that did not share his uncompromising Christian code of selflessness and duty. When Shackleton heard of Scott's intentions, he wrote, 'I believe he will throw the whole thing up and tell you that the last thing he would do would be to hinder you in bringing your work to a finish. Of course the work is yours, was yours to begin with and is obviously yours to finish . . . I cannot believe that Shackleton has been so misguided as to fail in seeing this.'

Scott at first half shared this view, and wrote to Scott Keltie (25 February 1907),

Of course it may be a coincidence but it looks as though he had an inkling of my intentions and has rushed to be first in the field. It looks like this yet I cannot quite believe it of him . . . Shackleton owes everything to me as you know, I got him into the Expedition . . . First and last I did much for him. Now I believe every explorer looks upon certain regions as his own, Peary certainly does, and I believe there are African precedents. I hold it would not have been playing the game for anyone to propose an expedition to McMurdo Sound until he had ascertained that I had given up the idea of going again; and I think I am justified in a stronger view when steps of this sort are taken by one of my own people without a word to me.

The view that an explorer may have, like birds and other animals, an exclusive right to his own territory, was shared by some others, for instance, the Frenchman Jean Charcot, who was also planning an Antarctic journey. 'There can be no doubt,' he stated, 'that the best way to the Pole is by way of the Great Ice Barrier, but this we regard as belonging to the English explorers, and I do not propose to trespass on other people's grounds.'

It was Shackleton's failure to give prior warning of his intention that rankled. Ordinary courtesy would require that he should have dropped a line to his former leader, if not to ask approval then to state that he intended to make his base in McMurdo Sound. This courtesy was overlooked. Shackleton was not methodical, his expedition was a one-man-band, and perhaps he never thought of writing; but it was a lapse that could have had another interpretation. It is most unlikely that he knew of Scott's plans before he launched his own. Their paths had not crossed for two years, and there had been no public statement. But Scott never shook off his suspicions, which Shackleton's subsequent behaviour could not but endorse, and they soured for good the relations between the two leading British explorers.

Scott made a genuine effort not to let his feelings stand in the way of goodwill towards the aims of Shackleton's expedition. He wrote to Scott Keltie (1 March 1907) expressing doubts as to its success but concluding, 'Meanwhile it is our duty to work together as Englishmen, I mean you, I and Shackleton and all concerned. The first thing is to defeat the foreigners. Whether Shackleton goes or I go or we both go, we must let Arctowski clearly understand that the Ross Sea area is England's and we will not appreciate designs on it.'

Shackleton now realised that in offending Scott he had offended others who might have helped him. Markham was forthright as ever; 'he has behaved shamefully, and it grieves me more than I can say that an Expedition which worked with such harmony throughout should have a black sheep after all'. The black sheep consulted Wilson, who wrote, 'I think that if you go to McMurdo Sound, and even reach the Pole, the gilt will be off the gingerbread, because of the insinuation which will almost certainly appear in the minds of a good many, that you forestalled Scott who had a prior claim on the use of that base.'

Shackleton was now in a dilemma, since the plans he had made public, and for which the money had been promised, stated quite clearly that he would winter in McMurdo Sound which offered – or so he believed, as it turned out wrongly – the best jumping-off place for the Pole. After, he said, several sleepless nights, he cabled to Scott 'Will meet your wishes regarding base please keep absolutely private at present as certain supporters must be brought round to the new position.'

The two men met in London and reached an agreement which Shackleton set forth in a letter dated 17 May 1907. He undertook to leave the

McMurdo Sound base to you, and land either at the place known as the Barrier Inlet or at King Edward VII Land, whichever is the most suitable. If I land at either of those places I will not work to the westward of the 170 meridian w and shall not make any sledge journey going West . . . I think this outlines my plan, which I shall rigidly adhere to, and I hope this letter meets you on the points that you desire.

It was mainly Wilson's soothing influence that had brought about this agreement. In view of the immensity of the Antarctic, the spectacle of two explorers arguing so vehemently about a pinprick on an unfilled map carries a suggestion of pomposity. Shackleton might have done better to have planned to strike out a new line of his own, Scott to have stood less on his dignity. Behind it lay personal incompatibility: they rubbed each other up the wrong way. The agreement was acknowledged somewhat stiffly by Scott: 'Your letter is a very clear statement of the arrangement to which we came. If as you say you will rigidly adhere to it, I do not think our plans will clash.'

Shackleton bought a small, dilapidated sealer, the *Nimrod*, laid in stores, and set about recruiting his companions. He failed to attract any of the *Discovery*'s officers but enlisted two men from the messdeck, Frank Wild and Ernest Joyce, who were so keen to go with him that they left the navy and gave up their pension rights. His second-in-command was selected in an unorthodox fashion. Standing one day on the roof of his house at Queensferry, almost under the Forth Bridge, he observed HMS *Berwick* coming in, and signalled in semaphore inviting the officer of the watch to dinner. Lieutenant J. B. Adams, RNR, the officer in question, accepted the invitation, and in due course a further one to go to the Antarctic and if possible the Pole. The *Nimrod* sailed from the East India Docks on 30 July 1907, taking a motor car, the first to be landed in Antarctica.

Meanwhile, Scott had encountered troubles of a different kind. On 1 January 1907 he had taken up an appointment as flag-captain in HMS *Albemarle*, a 14,000 ton battleship and second flagship of the Atlantic Fleet. The Fleet was on manoeuvres in February 1907 off the coast of Portugal, and HMS *Albemarle* was one of a line of eight battleships steaming, at night, in single formation. The ship ahead of her swung suddenly to starboard and

HMS *Albemarle* had to follow suit. HMS *Commonwealth* was too close behind to avoid a collision. It was 'a sickening sensation', Scott wrote to his mother, 'a jarring drag as though a colossal brake had been put on'. He had left the bridge just before the collision occurred. A change of speed had been ordered shortly before, and Scott subsequently wrote: 'It is arguable that the moment I chose for going below would have been more wisely deferred until after the ships had settled down from a change of speed.' Damage to the *Albemarle* was slight, but the *Commonwealth* was holed, and for a few moments there were fears of a terrible disaster. The fate of the *Victoria,* rammed and sunk by the *Camperdown* on a similar manoeuvre fourteen years earlier with the loss of more than half her men, must have sprung to his mind. His friend Admiral Markham had been in the *Camperdown* as second-in-command of the squadron and so involved in the subsequent court martial. But no one was injured on this occasion and the two ships proceeded safely to Gibraltar for repairs. There would have to be an official enquiry, although probably not a court-martial because 'it was difficult to know who to court-martial'. All the same, Scott might be censured, and his naval reputation harmed. The enquiry was held and no one reprimanded, but it had been an anxious time.

This was an anxious year altogether: Shackleton, the collision, family worries as always; and then, overshadowing all else, falling in love. Never once in all his letters to his family did he mention a woman's name, other than in general and impersonal terms, until he wrote to tell his mother that he wished to marry. So any previous affair of the heart – and the faculty of love is unlikely to have lain dormant until he was nearly forty – can be known only through the recollections not even of his contemporaries, but of their descendants. One episode deserves mention, because of the influence it may have had on his elusive character. The rock-like structure which Scott presented to the world was built upon an insecure foundation. A private income, property, a place in the country, a safe niche in the hierarchy, such powerful aids to confidence had never been his. He could be sure of nothing: of his future, of his family's well-being, of his ability to carry through to a finish the great enterprise that had been thrust upon him. He was vulnerable. When the hopes of such a man are disappointed, a sense of insecurity cannot but be deepened and he must all the more turn in upon himself.

There was living at this time, partly in London and partly in Paris, a young widow to whom the word enchanting could fairly be applied in the sense that links it with magic. Her looks, from all accounts, were striking, her intelligence exceptional, her background cosmopolitan, her accomplishments wide, her manner gay and unaffected. The genes of her inheritance were mixed and unusual. Her father was an Irish baronet of ancient lineage,

Sir Rowland Blennerhassett, her mother a celebrated German blue-stocking and wit, Countess Charlotte Leyden, author of the standard biography of Madame de Staël. At the age of eighteen their daughter Marie-Carola had married Baron Raphael d'Erlanger, a member of the famous banking family who had taken German nationality in order to occupy the Chair of Biology at Heidelberg University. He died young, leaving Marie-Carola with two small children, a boy and a girl.

Many admirers naturally sought her hand. She moved in what was then called high society, and international high society at that. French and German friends and relatives came and went; conversation might be carried on in several languages and be concerned with literature and drama, politics and the arts. Her guests would find the wit of the Paris salon rather than the stodginess of the London drawing-room. It was all a far cry from Oakley Street, the Channel squadron and memories of frostbite, pemmican and hoosh, and it might be wondered how Scott found himself in such an unfamiliar milieu.

The link was a brother officer and friend, Captain Rosslyn (known as Rosy) Wemyss.* He was four years senior to Scott and their paths had crossed on various naval occasions. Rosy Wemyss had conceived what his widow and biographer described as 'boundless admiration' for his younger colleague. When his appointment as the first Captain of Osborne College ended in September 1905, he urged his friend to succeed him, but Scott was seeing his book through the press and awaiting a sea appointment to the command of HMS *Victorious*.

Probably some time in 1907, Rosy Wemyss invited Scott to dinner and Marie-Carola, a friend of his wife's, was a fellow guest. For Scott it was a case of love at first sight. He became a frequent caller at her house, and perhaps suffered more torments than delights; without money or exalted social rank and with a mother to support, he had nothing to offer save a reputation for courage and endurance in polar regions which must have seemed little enough in the rich, sophisticated world into which he had strayed.

All that is known of his courtship are three impressions set lightly on a child's mind. First: a scene in a London Park on a summer's day. Marie-Carola was taking her two small children for a stroll. Instructing them, as they sauntered under the trees, in some point of geography, she paused to

* Born in 1864, Rosslyn Wemyss came of an ancient Scottish family. He passed out of the *Britannia* four years before Scott and climbed up the naval ladder at a pace accelerated by good connections and popularity with admirals and bluejackets alike. After an adventurous 1914–18 war he became First Sea Lord and a signatory of the Armistice on 11 November 1918. On his resignation he was promoted Admiral of the Fleet and created Baron Wester Wemyss. He died at Cannes in 1933.

draw a map in the dust with the tip of her parasol. A blue-eyed man came up behind her, smiled in amusement and lifted his straw hat. Second: the sourness of a French governess whenever she saw Scott's hat and gloves in the hall. It was not that she had formed a dislike for this particular suitor, but suitors spelled change; she did not want change, and feared as its harbinger the owner of that hat and those gloves. Lastly: after those garments were seen no longer in the hall, a tale of an unforeseen encounter between the two protagonists at a dinner party given by a mutual friend. They did not speak and, when dinner was over, Scott's linen table-napkin was found torn to shreds and scattered on the floor.

Rosy Wemyss and his wife were disappointed; despite the disparities, they had hoped for a match. Some years passed, and many suitors were discarded, before Marie-Carola married again. To her friends' surprise, she chose a kindly and conventional retired Colonel seventeen years her senior, former Governor of St Helena, Sir Henry Galway.* Appointed Governor of South Australia, he took his bride to Adelaide, where, in this unlikely setting, she became immensely popular and several 'streets' in ANZAC camps in Gallipoli were named after her. This marriage of opposites confounded prophets of doom by its success.

Scott went back to sea as Captain of HMS *Albemarle*, a first-class battleship with a complement of over 700 men. Life was hardening him; his clerk remembered him as a man bursting with energy, 'ardent and impatient' and none too easy to serve. Owing to a reorganisation of the fleet, his appointment ended on 25 August 1907 and he went on half-pay until appointed to the command of HMS *Essex* on 1 January 1908. On accepting this post, and so losing flag rank, his pay dropped by £100 a year, but he never noticed it until a fellow captain pointed it out on a country walk.

While living in Oakley Street between these appointments he was free to see friends and acquaintances, make new ones, and even to attend tea parties. It was at such a one, at Mabel Beardsley's, that he met for the second time a twenty-eight-year-old sculptor, Kathleen Bruce. Their first encounter had taken place about ten months before, also at Mabel Beardsley's, where Kathleen Bruce had taken note of a naval officer, neither young nor especially handsome, but healthy and alert; they had exchanged a few words, but neither had taken any interest in the other

---

* Born in 1859, son of a General and Colonial Governor, Henry Gallwey became Vice-Consul in the Oil Rivers Protectorate (now part of Nigeria) and in 1897 took a leading part in the capture and destruction of Benin City. He served in the Hausa Force and, after a term as Governor first of St Helena and then of Gambia, changed his name to Galway on receiving his knighthood and went, from 1914–20, to govern South Australia, where his popularity was as great as that of his wife; if she had streets named after her in Gallipoli, so did he in Adelaide. After his retirement in 1920 he was active in the affairs of the British and Foreign Bible Society. He died in his ninetieth year in 1949.

until Mabel invited them both to tea in late October 1907. Kathleen was then struck by his 'rare smile' and dark-blue eyes 'almost purple'. He saw a woman rather below average height with a mass of dark-brown hair, not very beautiful and not at all well dressed but, like him, healthy and alert and with a strong personality. She was attractive to men, and knew it. This time, Scott felt the attraction. He saw her home to her rooms in Cheyne Walk in rather an odd manner, for a sedate naval Captain, if her auto-biography is to be relied upon – 'laughing, talking, jostling each other, as we lunged along the riverside in hilarious high spirits'.

Scott was hooked. For the next ten days he laid siege to her, either with his presence or with a series of notes. Starting (2 November 1907) rela-tively mildly – 'I've tried to telephone you without result so now this is to ask you if I may take you out to dinner tonight. Dinner and the play, dinner and no play, anything you like but do let me come and carry you off.' He soon gave way to the lover's importunity – 'Uncontrollable footsteps carried me along the Embankment to find no light – yet I knew you were there dear heart – I saw the open window and, in fancy, a sweetly tangled head of hair upon the pillow within – dear head – it seems so long till Friday – give me all the time you can.' His time on shore would soon expire and Kathleen enjoyed, for those days, a free, emancipated life with many friends, perhaps suitors. 'I've been worrying about you – little vague worries centring about the thought that I may have hurt you in word or deed – dear if you knew I'm half frightened of you. I've so little, so very little to offer. Dear blue eyes they haunt me – sweet tangled head – if I could guess the thoughts within!'

Throughout November Scott's letters continued almost daily, sometimes twice a day, full of urgency and ardour but also of self-doubt and fear of his own inadequacy. 'I seem to have a million things to say to you yet a sense of the oppression of forty years of wrestling with hard facts, I fight myself. One thing dearest – there must be no sadness in that sweet face – never – that is the only fixed thought in me now.' (25 November 1907). He doubted his own capacity to make her happy but not for a moment his own love.

Once launched, this could be said to be a whirlwind courtship. Before the end of the month, marriage had been agreed and Kathleen had met Hannah Scott. 'You're in a fair way to capture my mother's head, she was full of you today . . . What did you say to her, do or say you little witch?' To which Kathleen light-heartedly responded, 'She's off – not on a broom-stick but only a turbine – to Paris – she'll be back again before you've had time to miss her.'

Kathleen Bruce's upbringing had been as unusual for the times as Con Scott's had been conventional. She was the youngest of the eleven children

of the Reverend Lloyd Stewart Bruce, a Canon of York, who was in turn
the son of a Scots-Irish baronet, Sir James Bruce of Londonderry. On her
mother's side she was descended from a Greek prince, Jacovaki Rizo-
Rangabe, whose daughter Rhalou, Kathleen's grandmother, married in
romantic circumstances a young Scotsman, James Skene. Her Greek
inheritance was strong in Kathleen, who enjoyed nothing better than to
vanish with rucksack and blanket to walk barefoot over the mountains of
Mediterranean lands, living on crusts and hard-boiled eggs. Her mother,
worn out by relentless child-bearing, died at the age of forty-two, leaving
the infant Kathleen to be brought up by a great-uncle, the Historiographer
Royal of Scotland, so firmly Presbyterian that, in his Edinburgh dwelling,
on Sundays the curtains were kept drawn until dinner-time.

Kathleen records in her autobiography that her female dolls were kept
permanently in bed with measles while the only male one, a sailor-boy with
brown curls, was her idol. 'So through life, let all females be kindly and
comfortably disposed of, so that my complete preoccupation with the male
of the moment be unhampered!' She never made a secret of her contempt
for women, an attitude which naturally made her enemies. She did have
some women friends, however – Mabel Beardsley was one and the dancer
Isadora Duncan another – but they were unusual women; the ordinary
kind she found dull, and said so.

The great-uncle died and Kathleen was pitchforked from the bleakness
of a strictly Nonconformist household into a Roman Catholic convent at
the other end of the religious spectrum. Here she had to take her weekly
bath in a chemise, and to attend chapel five times a day on Sundays. It
was not surprising that, in later life, she adhered to no religion. At the age
of twenty-three another traumatic change took place: she went to Paris to
study sculpture and lived gaily among students and artists, frequenting
the studios and cafés of the Left Bank. Such was her initial innocence that,
on the first occasion when she saw a nude male model, she rushed to the
lavatory to be sick.

For five years she studied in Paris, living on a shoe-string and, by her
own account, enthralling a number of students who were understandably
nonplussed when, having got on to the companionable footing usual in
this free-and-easy milieu, they found themselves, as it were, confronted
by a padlocked chastity belt. Her reason was even more unusual than the
behaviour itself. Most girls in her position kept their virginity, when they
did, in order to avoid having a son; she kept it because she wanted one.
But the son had to have the right father. When a girl companion remarked
that, with all these young men about, to achieve her aim should not be
difficult, she replied, 'I know, but none is worthy to be the father of my
son.' These young artists were unaccustomed to being judged like prize

bulls, and one of them, a handsome Swede, was so incensed that he lay in wait for her armed with a revolver.

After five years she returned home an accomplished sculptor and still without a son, or, as her memoirs indicate, without having taken the necessary steps to conceive one. In London, other suitors were put to the same test, among them the painter Charles Shannon, to whom she sat for her portrait, and the writer Gilbert Cannan, who subsequently married Barrie's former wife. No one was found worthy to be the father of her son until she met Scott. It took her only a few days to decide that here at last, in the person of this 'healthy, fresh, decent, honest, rock-like naval officer' was the sire for whom she had been searching. She reached this decision, she wrote, in Shannon's studio, and so informed him. Distraught, he rushed out and walked into a bus – fortunately without fatal results.

Before the end of the month (November 1907) Scott was writing 'I know we stand on such a trembling insecure foothold,' and of 'waves of difficulty washing all round our feet'. The difficulty was, put more simply, money. His pay, less Hannah Scott's allowance, plus the few guineas Kathleen made now and again from her work, were all they had. And both soon came to realise how different were their temperaments and attitudes to life. 'How little we know of each other,' he wrote, 'and yet how much . . . all serious thoughts go when I see that sweet face.' He was afraid that he was coming between her and her work as a sculptor. 'Dear my dear I see so little of you don't I. I'm very gloomy about everything tonight.' (2 January 1908) Two days later she wrote to him, 'Dearest Con. Don't let's get married, I've been thinking a lot about it and though much of it would be beautiful, there is much also that would be very very difficult. I have always really wanted to marry for the one reason, and now that very thing seems as though it would only be an encumbrance we could scarcely cope with.' He would be lonely, she knew,without her, but 'the relief of knowing that you need not worry or uproot your sweet little mother will compensate. If we had gone and done it right away, I would have gone through with it and made it all right, but now the more I think of it the more it seems to me I'd better stop. We're horribly different you and I, the fact is I've been hideously spoilt . . . let's abandon the idea of getting married and don't let's look at any more houses. There are things about it that I'm not sure I can face.'

Scott replied the next day with understanding, not despair.

I want to marry you very badly, but it is absurd to pretend I can do so without facing great difficulty and risking a great deal for others as well as for myself. If I was very young I should probably take all risks and win through. In facing poverty we should be living and believing in a better future. The old can only live in the present. My mother is 67, only a strand of life remains. She has had a hard life in many respects. I set myself to make her last years free from anxiety. I can't light-heartedly think of events that may disturb that decision.

He concluded, 'Little girl, if you care, be patient, and we'll pull things straight – have faith in me. But you must work with me, dearest, not against me. Dearest heart, I love you very much. So much that it is making me unhappy now to think how little it can mean to you.'

Hannah Scott was also understanding. Writing on the last day of 1907 to wish him well she said, 'You must never let me be a hindrance to your making a home and a life of your own.' She added a postscript, 'You have carried the burden of the family since 1894. It is time now for you to think of yourself and your future. God bless and keep you.'

She was not a possessive mother; she expected her son to marry one day but had hoped, as had his sisters, that he would choose a woman with at least some means. If he married a penniless woman he must face poverty, and the strain upon them both might wreck their happiness. Scott sent Kathleen an 'Estimate for 2 persons living in a small house in this year of grace.' It went into such details as £15 for coals, £25 for laundry, £6 for stationery, papers and incidentals, and allowed 10s a week per head for food. (Also, showing that poverty is always a relative term, a sum of £45 for a servant.) The total came out at £329. On top of his mother's regular £200 a year, he had to pay for her extra necessities. His naval income was less than £800 a year and, like all naval officers, he was often on half-pay for months at a time.

Kathleen Bruce may have charmed Scott's mother but was less successful with his sisters. An attitude that fell well short of enthusiasm prevailed at Oakley Street, not only on account of money. The usual question 'who is she?' could be satisfactorily answered, but what is described in police courts as 'character and antecedents' were dubious. She was an artist, she had lived alone in Paris for years, and what they knew of the friend who had introduced her to their brother can hardly have allayed their doubts. They were old enough to remember hearing, in hushed whispers no doubt, of the great scandal of 1895 involving Oscar Wilde. It had also involved Aubrey Beardsley, then art editor of *The Yellow Book* which had been closed down after an angry populace had stoned the windows of its publisher, confusing the magazine with a yellow book – a French novel – carried by Oscar Wilde on the way to his trial.

Aubrey Beardsley had not, in fact, been a friend of Wilde's, but he had moved in those homosexual circles, was rumoured to have had an incestuous affair with Mabel (who had produced an illegitimate baby, though probably not her brother's), and had left behind a reputation that could not have endeared Mabel to families like the Scotts of Oakley Street. On a more trivial level Kathleen's clothes, to which she was indifferent, could not have been approved of by Monsie and Kate, the skilled fashioners of court robes, although she could be sartorially creative in her own way. The first time that she was taken out to dinner, a convent-bred schoolgirl of sixteen, she bought for a few pence a length of coarse, unbleached calico, a square of dye and a bottle of gold ink, cut out a cloak, painted on it a bold design, and carried off the occasion with a panache that seldom, thereafter, deserted her.

The strong clerical tradition in her family might have counted in her favour with Hannah Scott – her father a Canon, one of her brothers a parish priest. But in the wide fold of the Church of England there were many kinds of sheep. Kathleen's elder brother, the Reverend Rosslyn Bruce, displayed certain eccentricities. He was a great lover of animals. Ferrets, lemurs and other small livestock peeped from his pockets; owls perched on his shoulder while he preached; once, conducting a funeral, he dropped to his knees by the graveside apparently overcome by grief, but observant mourners saw him grab a grass-snake and conceal it about his person. When raising money for a new church, he hired a circus to advertise it and toured Birmingham on a motor-cycle with a side-car containing a seal.

In animal circles he was famed for his success in the line-breeding of fox-terriers, on which he wrote a standard work. 'He breeds bitches for all the crowned heads of Europe,' was said of him. He supplied one to Queen Victoria, and another to Picasso, one of his friends. It was in the breeding of mice, however, that his greatest triumph lay. After producing – or causing the mice to produce – strains of lavender, apricot and red coloration, he persevered through fifty generations to achieve a grass-green strain of mice.

This lay in the future; at the time of Kathleen's engagement his genetic experiments were in their early stages. Kathleen's favourite brother was the sailor Wilfrid, but Rosslyn, who called her Kiddie, was the nearest to a father-substitute. When she underwent an operation for appendicitis and nearly died, the nurse asked her if she would like to see a priest. She summoned up enough vigour to say 'God forbid.' At that moment, Rosslyn arrived. Observing his dog-collar, the nurse tried to shoo him away. 'It's all right, it's my brother,' Kathleen said. 'I'd forgotten he was a clergyman.'*

When the courtship of Con and Kathleen seemed to be running on the rocks, she decided to go off on a walking tour with a cousin – not a woman, needless to say. She wrote to inform Con, uneasy about his reaction. His reply, in her words, was, 'Write to me often, and don't stay too long.' 'Oh this,' she thought, 'is a grand man; no self-pity, no suspicions, no querulousness, no recriminations! Perfect man.' She and her companion walked

* See *The Last of the Eccentrics* by Verity Anderson.

from Florence to Venice, carrying their blankets and sleeping out, washing in streams, and entertaining the peasants with songs accompanied on her companion's guitar.

Her fiancé was more prosaically employed, having taken over command on 25 January 1908 of HMS *Essex*, a battle cruiser of the Home Fleet. He was also, during and before his periods of leave, supervising the construction and testing of a motor-sledge designed for polar travel by an engineer called Belton Hamilton, of Finchley. Lord Howard de Walden was the financial backer. Hamilton's design was something altogether new, a fore-runner of the caterpillar track. Reginald Skelton and Michael Barne also paid frequent visits to Finchley to see how the machine was shaping. Scott had asked Skelton to go as second-in-command of his future expedition. The French scientist-explorer Jean-Baptiste Charcot* was also busy with the design of a polar sledge in Paris, and it was decided to test both prototypes, together with a third designed by Barne, in the snow.

The place chosen was Lautaret, not far from Grenoble, where Scott, Skelton, Lord Howard de Walden and Charcot with his party carried out the tests in March 1908. These were moderately successful only, and it was clear that a good deal more work needed to be done. Later that year Charcot set out in his ship the *Pourquois-Pas?* on his second Antarctic expedition. He went to Graham Land and its archipelago, deliberately avoiding the Ross Sea area so as to provoke no international rivalry.

Scott could not but contrast Charcot's behaviour with that of Shackleton. It was while he was in Paris, on the way to Lautaret, that he heard of a change of plan by his former colleague. The *Nimrod* had returned to Lyttleton with the news that she had failed to force her way through the pack ice to reach King Edward VII Land. Obliged to turn back, she had landed the explorer's party in McMurdo Sound to make their base close to Scott's old winter quarters, so contravening Shackleton's undertaking to Scott. In an emotional letter to his wife written as the *Nimrod* steamed westwards after her failure Shackleton wrote:

I have been through a sort of hell since the 23rd (January 1908) and I cannot even now realise that I am on the way back to McMurdo Sound and that all idea of wintering on the Barrier or at King Edward VII Land is at an end – that I have had to break my word to Scott and go back to the old base, and that all my plans and ideas have now to be changed – changed by the overwhelming forces of Nature...

* Jean-Baptiste Charcot was one of the most attractive of the early twentieth-century polar explorers. He made two expeditions to the Antarctic and several to Arctic regions, charting and making scientific records without seeking fame for himself. He forbade the wanton killing of animals and was one of the first to warn against the over-hunting of whales. An abstemious man, he waged 'unrelenting war against the *apéritif*, the curse of France'. He was drowned, with most of his crew, off Iceland in 1936.

I never knew what it was to make such a decision as the one I was forced to make last night.

Steaming eastwards along the Barrier, he wrote, they had reached a place he named the Bay of Whales, because of the many who were spouting there. He was searching for Balloon Inlet where he hoped a landing might be effected; it had disappeared. The pack-ice was thick about them, many drifting bergs menaced their fragile ship and Shackleton had concluded that a landing was impossible. Clearly great chunks of the Barrier had broken away in the last six years. 'I felt each mile that I went to the West was a horror to me. . . . I have only my word to Scott against my promised plans to the whole world and my forty comrades . . . My conscience is clear but my heart is sore . . . but I have one comfort that I did my best.' He established his base at Cape Royds on Ross Island, about fifty miles from Hut Point.

Had he been able to set it up in or near the Bay of Whales, he would have been about sixty miles nearer the Pole, which might have made all the difference. But the *Nimrod*'s captain, Rupert England, urged him in the strongest terms to turn back and Frank Wild wrote in his diary:

Shackleton was loath to return to McMurdo Sound and talked seriously of wintering on the Barrier itself. I strenuously objected to this, having seen 7 miles of Barrier floating away in the form of icebergs, and when my arguments were backed by the discovery that in places the edge of the Barrier was 8 miles further south than when we steamed along it in the *Discovery*, Shackleton reluctantly consented to return to McMurdo Sound.

Amundsen was to take a different view. It was in the Bay of Whales that he was to set up his base.

How genuine was Shackleton's dilemma? Eric Marshall, the expedition's doctor and cartographer, writing many years later to a friend, Dr John Kendall, referred to 'Shackleton's double-cross in breaking his promise to Scott by using his old base when other alternatives were available if he had had the guts to take a risk and land at the Bay of Whales.' While most of Shackleton's men were intensely loyal, Marshall had become disillusioned with his former leader. 'From the moment when Shackleton broke his word to Scott he was "suspect", and the final tragedy must be laid at Shackleton's doorstep. I have always been quite convinced that Shackleton never intended to land anywhere but at Scott's base. He was a very attractive crook.' This was a view shared by Sir Clements Markham, who never forgave him. Nor did Billy Wilson. Probably Wilson did not go as far as to think his former friend a crook, but to him a promise was a promise and that was that.

Scott thought the same. Shackleton's written promise, he told Kathleen, 'was a perfectly plain distinct statement absolutely binding him in an honourable sense. He definitely agreed not to approach my old quarters. I am bound to confess, in spite of his past behaviour, I thought he meant to abide by this, but, as you can see, he hasn't.' The change of plan 'is to me most important for it makes it definitely impossible to do anything till he is heard of again. These are far consequences. I won't discuss them now, but you can guess something of my thoughts. I shall of course get this sledge business as nearly right as can be, but then I really don't know.' He hated uncertainty and to this he was now condemned for about two years. If Shackleton reached the Pole, then he would either have to abandon his whole expedition, or find a new objective for it. The man who wanted to be master of his fate had become the slave of Shackleton.

# 16    In
# Love

'Kiddie is a quaint child,' the Reverend Rosslyn Bruce, also contemplating matrimony, wrote to his intended bride. Kiddie absolutely refused to wear jewellery of any kind and would not let Con give her any, not even a ring; nor, at first, could she face the idea of a conventional wedding. This made things difficult, Rosslyn conceded, for her fiancé, 'who has to think a little of what the navy considers *comme il faut*'. He added that she looked more beautiful than ever before. 'She's frighteningly in love with him I should think, but tells me that she never writes to him without saying let's put it off again and forget and forgive! What odd things girls really are.'

With a fierce torrent of emotion surging about in his breast and with Kathleen blowing hot and blowing cold, Scott was thoroughly bemused. His letters, too, became a torrent, and reflected anything but the happiness to be expected in a man about to marry the girl of his choice. Fear was tormenting him, fear that he would not make Kathleen happy, that their temperaments were too different, that she would find him a dull old stick, or worse still a burden, fear that he was too middle-aged and set in his ways to share her freedom of spirit and zest for life.

I'm sad tonight. It *is* difficult to know what to do and all the time I'm conscious of bringing unhappiness to you. It is *I* who make you cry. Disappointment in me I think, though your sweet generosity wouldn't admit it. Kathleen dearest don't let your happiness be troubled. Sometimes when all the obstacles loom large I wonder for the future, but always always I know that to take away that dear happy smile of yours would be the most dreadful thing in this world . . . Oh my dear my dear don't let me be a trouble to you.

In this long letter (11 May 1908) he analysed his own limitations and put very clearly the reasons why, despite all his devotion, *au fond* he doubted the success of their marriage. 'I love your splendid independence and the unswerving directness and candour of you. I love the unblinking courage that admits no difficulty yet shirks no responsibility . . . Kathleen dear, God being my witness there isn't a thought of mine that has held you lightly.' It was not Kathleen he doubted but himself.

Yet oh my dear there is another side to me, born of an hereditary instinct of caution fostered by the circumstances which have made the struggle for existence an especially hard one for me. Can you understand? I review a past – a real fight – from an almost desperate position to the bare right to live as my fellows. Is it strange that I should hate to look at all the consequences of a fresh struggle? My dear I know, as you will think, that this should be no attitude for the man deter-mined to conquer, but sweetheart, what I know and you do not, is our Service with its machine-like accuracy and limitations. It offers place and power but never a money prize, so that it must be poverty always. Dear heart, I'm a coward to write like this but it's late and I have been thinking much.

But just when he had argued himself into a frame of mind prepared to call it off, he realised that he could not do it. 'Withal and last comes the thought that I cannot give your sweetness up. It has grown too dear to me come what will and darling you are the only woman to whom I can tell things . . . Give me your patience.'

Kathleen was patient but puzzled; why was he inventing obstacles where none existed? She was one of the least money-conscious people in the world, caring little or nothing for the things it bought. The conventions that had moulded him were not hers. They would manage; she did not understand what the fuss was all about. 'Dear you really must not be so afraid – afraid of yourself and me and the future and all sorts of things. Nonsense Con, sweet one. Everything is perfectly harmonious and will be, why not . . . we are both perfect dears and together we shall be *splendid*, oh yes we shall.'

His mood fluctuated between despair of ever being able to break free of the machine he had once felt so proud to belong to, and hope that it was not too late for change.

Knock a few conventional shackles off me and you'll find as great a vagabond as you – but perhaps that won't do. I shall never fit in my round hole. The part of a machine has got to fit – yet how I hate it sometimes. Oh by nature I think I must be a freelance. Amongst uncertainties this is certain, I love the open air, the trees, the fields and seas – the open places of life and thought. Darling you are the spirit of all these to me though we have loved each other in crowded places. I want you to be with me when the sun shines free of fog . . . Be patient with all this foolishness.

Kathleen had been on her walking tour in Italy and wrote ecstatically of tramping back with her companion over the Simplon Pass, carrying twelve-pound packs on their backs, or in her case on her head:

. . . right over the snow and me bare-footed and oh it was so beautiful and we were so tired at the end, and we slept in the valley by a roaring deafening stream and foaming torrent, and it was good to live . . . and the sun shone, my Con, the sun shone always for us, and there was gentian and baby goats and waterfalls making rainbows and swallow-tailed butterflies and yellow violets and white white mountains and green and purple valleys, and joy in your vagabond's heart.

Her Con had pride but no jealousy, and he replied almost pathetically trying to match her mood. 'Why didn't I cross the Simplon with you? or meet you bare-footed and head-laden? Oh I love you and your free joyous outlook on life! but its disturbing sweet. I ask myself why must I dwell in this machine, the mill that grinds small.'

In Venice, Kathleen had encountered Isadora Duncan, the only woman she enthused about almost to the point of adoration. 'Dora is lying on the sofa and looking so wonderful and I wish you could see her.' In his mind's eye, Scott did see her, and the image sharpened his fear of the gulf between his world and Kathleen's. It was for him to reach out to her world, and he dreaded the possibility that she might be dragged down to his. He wrote a humble letter.

Do you realise that you will have to change me, change me, infuse something of the joyous pure spirit within you – a year or two hence it would have been too late. I should have been too set to admit the principle of change. It's something that I acknowledge my shortcomings! But oh dear me what a task you have before you. All this because you met Isadora Duncan and I see the great heart of you going out to her. I see you half worshipful, wholly and beautifully alive – and I love you for it. Here is the antithesis of all that's worldly and conventional. I know this, I say it to myself over and over, but oh the grinding effects of a mechanical existence – in the end I'm half fearful. Shall I satisfy you girl of my heart? . . . You'll have to inspire a dull person indeed.

There was more in this vein, contrasting her joy in life with his own plodding routine; yet a good word for the navy crept in. 'I find it a great fact, this enormous fleet with its wonderful collective organisation and underneath its myriad individual interests.' He ended on a note of sober hope, if not of confidence. 'I'll just do something with my life yet because there'll be a little lady supremely interested.' A few days later came a burst of optimism.

Kathleen dear you will marry me won't you? Don't change your mind. I just think of you always now . . . I've thought much of what was said of the lack of community of interest and at the end somehow I have a comfortable feeling that all is well. I believe we understand each other more than a little – far far more than those who marry normally do.

But he was too much of a realist to allow his hopes to soar into the clear skies where Kathleen's confident thoughts so often floated. 'We must trust each other infinitely, learn how beautiful life can be and then work, work, work till poverty is conquered.'

This emotional unburdening continued throughout 1908 until their marriage, but nowhere in his letters does he mention any ambition to conquer the Pole. As he himslf implied, these are not the letters of a would-be conqueror of anything except his own limitations. It was Kathleen who supplied the ambition. 'Write and tell me,' she admonished him (11 July 1908) 'that you *shall* go to the Pole. Oh dear me what's the use of having energy and enterprise if a little thing like *that* can't be done. It's got to be done, so hurry up and don't leave a stone unturned – and love me more and more, because I need it.'

Meanwhile Scott had another worry on his mind: the question of his mother's acceptance of his bride. At an early stage of the courtship he had written, 'Oh, I know, I know that all this is against your hopes, but don't judge till you know all the facts . . . So, dear, will you please ask Kathleen to come to see you as my future wife? Will you be kind to her?' He wrote urgently, asking for a telegram of reassurance. 'I ask myself how can we wait long. You know I am now 40. She is 28. Why should we wait till we lose so much that may mean all in the future? Goodnight dear Mother. I do not want to be selfish, indeed, indeed, and I know she does not.'

His hopes that his mother and his fiancée would make friends were only partially realised. Kathleen professed herself delighted with the '*sweetest* letter from your dear little mother . . . calling me Kathleen and wanting to "welcome me as a daughter" . . . I can't *bear* to be disliked and distrusted and I felt (foolishly maybe) that it amounted to that . . . She *shall* love me for I will love her and *make* her.' Con was relieved; he 'didn't think they'd all get over the money difficulty so easily'. Writing to her 'own best of sons', Hannah reassured him that 'with so attractive a personality as Kathleen's there is little need of fear, we shall all make her as welcome as you would wish if she does not mind entering a family who are and always have been very very fond of each other'. Despite these good resolutions on both sides, love was tardy in answering the summons. 'Indeed, I fear you don't understand her,' wrote the best of sons. 'My dear, she may not be all you wish but there isn't an ounce of jealousy in her frank nature . . . Try to be kind to Kathleen. She has lots of friends and people who love her, but she has never had a home.'

She was looking for one now, and depressed because those she liked were beyond their means. Con was back at sea in command of HMS *Bulwark*, flagship of the Admiral of the Nore Division of the Channel Fleet, but soon, with the departure of the Admiral, to become a 'private ship', that is, an independent command in the Channel Fleet. He told Kathleen that he was the most junior captain in the navy to fill such a post. And the extra £100 a year was restored. His mother was disposing of the lease of 56 Oakley Street. She was to move, with her daughters and Rose's daughter Erica, to Henley-on-Thames where a small house had been found. In due course Kate was to marry a surgeon in practice there, Harry Brownlow.

At last Kathleen's house-hunting succeeded. She was offered the remainder of a lease, twenty-seven years, of No. 174 Buckingham Palace Road for £50 a year – they would have to do their own decorations. It had 'lots of rooms and a studio and it's in perfect repair'. She was so excited that she wrote next day 'I'm really falling desperately in love with you,' and again a few days later, in the midst of a letter about furniture, to warn him that she would be irritable if he was absent-minded, and to order him to wear a hat as little as possible, especially in sunlight, as 'I will *not* have a bald husband'.

She was getting rid of her other suitors. First there was an ardent young law student 'teeming with vitality' who addressed her in impassioned notes as 'Dear Light o' the Sun'. She found it hard to dismiss him, but thought 'corn-coloured hair and a crooked smile, maybe, but not the father for my son'. Then she reported that 'the Frenchman who so loved me for all these many years is here. He cried rather at first, but now he's feeling better thank you and is prepared to be very good friends.'

Scott was still perforce watching the pennies. He sent Kathleen £5 to go towards wedding presents for two fellow-captains, Greatorex and Glyn. 'We are too poor to spend the whole sum on these presents, so get two little old silver boxes or something of that sort, and put the balance of the sum to our furnishing account.' Kathleen carried out these instructions so thoroughly that her fiancé had qualms. 'My poor friend Greatorex' (quite the ugliest man he knew) 'is 15s 9d enough for him?' Kathleen replied, 'I'm sorry about Greatorex but really they looked as if they'd cost *heaps*.'

He was worried too because if he died she would get nothing. He had no insurance, and what little money he possessed would go to his mother. All his widow would get would be a pension of £70 or £90 a year, he could not remember which. If he died, Kathleen replied, she would be no worse off than before unless there was a child, 'in which case it will have the £90 pension to live on, and since its mother has so thriven on a lesser sum, why should not it . . . Of *course* what you have must go to your little mother, she has nothing and I have quite as much as I need.' He still could not shake off his money worries which he described as 'the centre of my most sensitive spot . . . be sparing to my meanness when it peeps out'.

I cover myself with ridicule for the thought but there are moments when it is horrid to know that Mrs Scott cannot drive her carriage! . . . I want my mother to be happy and comfortable yet I know *we* must keep up some small state for the sake of my career – that's just the whole rub I know. We'll do it too.

Scott asked Kathleen to design a crest for the *Bulwark* to be painted on the ship's boats. With the drawings, she sent news of the house. 'Our house!' he replied. 'Oh I'm longing for the day when we shall just go inside and know there's nothing but our two selves . . . Whatever happens we must have a surveyor to make a definite report on the drains etc.' Then again the old doubts returned, the differences between them – 'what does it all mean?'

I'm afraid of what I shall be to you. Shall I always be trusted? Will it come natural to you to tell me things, or will you grow to think me only fitted for the outer courtyard of your heart? Will you come to see the limitations and be impatient of them, or worse, learn to tolerate with easy indifference – I'm stupidly anxious tonight.

He reverted to the subject of the navy, within whose system 'a fine thought of quality is condemned because it does not fit in'. The navy 'like nature itself atrophies the limbs for which it has no use however great their beauty'.

You must try to be long-suffering with me – and with all your might keep before you the conditions that have made me what I am and be merciful in expectation . . . Will many things be for one and not the other? Here I see the level, it is the dreamer, the enthusiast, the idealist – I was something of each once – and now it gives me the feeling of growing old! All has been so suppressed in me and yet in remembering I know that a hard life limited by practical fact was the only thing for me, the dreaming part of me was and is a failure . . . I want to be near your soul – and I pause to wonder if I have a soul that such a sweet free-thinking creature as you could ever find companionable.

If the self-torturing Con evokes sympathy so does Kathleen, who, in perceiving as she thought a strong, healthy, clean-living, dependable sire for her son, found herself involved with an introspective, self-doubting man struggling to crack the mould that had shaped him, yet knowing that, if he did so, only a malformed creature would emerge. She tried a dose of common sense to shake him out of it. 'Here I am a little ass of a girl who's never done a thing in her life allowing a real man to talk to her of superiority. My sense of humour can't do with it.'

Humble as he was before Kathleen, he ventured to suggest, as their wedding day drew nearer, that she might conform in one direction – a minor one – to the conventions of his world, which she so rightly despised. Clothes were of little interest to her and probably she looked 'a sight' in the eyes of the admirals' and captains' ladies with whom she would have to mix. (Years later, after her second marriage, James Lees-Milne was to describe her in *Ancestral Voices* as the worst-dressed woman he knew, adding that she rejoiced 'in a sort of aggressive no-taste in clothes and house'.)

The serious consideration is that when we are married you mustn't only look nice (which you can't help) but you must look as though there wasn't any poverty. You may say humbug but just let me put it this way. You've admired my clothes and just think of my feelings when I am so to speak 'expensively' dressed whilst your costume shows a saving spirit. It won't do for the present will it.

She was to look for some good clothes, buy them and then 'tell a very innocent husband exactly what he has to add to your banking account. Kathleen dearest I am dreadfully sensitive to appearances.' He added a postscript; he would be married in civilian clothes; and on reflection, 'Yes I think our individual energy has freer scope when there's many miles between us. Ought we to marry if that's so?'

Kathleen was not enthusiastic about his sartorial advice. 'I will get some clothes if you like, precious one, but they will always be little simple ones. I can't bear myself dressed up.' What was the use of filling chests of drawers with piles of underclothes that would never be worn? Much better 'get what one wants as one wants it'. She promised to dress up in a fashionable gown for their next meeting 'and you'll see what a fright I look'.

In the end she dressed up for their wedding in a conventional high-necked dress with veil and long gloves, and displayed in the photographs something of the look of a startled bright-eyed bird peering from a thicket. They were married in style on 2 September 1908 in the Chapel Royal at Hampton Court, where Kathleen's aunt Zoe, widow of a former Archbishop of Canterbury, had a grace-and-favour apartment. The solemnity of the occasion did not subdue her humour. The best man was a tall, handsome officer, and glancing at him she whispered to Scott 'Could I marry him instead?' Among those at the reception was the ageing sculptor Rodin who had come especially from Paris, where as a student she had watched him at work and entertained him to lunch in her own bare studio. On this occasion, to add a dash of colour she had put pomegranates on the table and apprehensively seen him eat them whole, hard pips and all. Later on she had watched him, in a looking-glass, at the open window shaking the pips out of his beard.

The couple went to Etretat, near Dieppe, for a short honeymoon which passed 'as confusedly and insecurely as most honeymoons', Kathleen recalled. Determined to adapt herself to the customs of the upper middle-classes, she had engaged as servants a married pair, and left instructions to have ready for the homecoming a good dinner with a shoulder of mutton. Everything in the new home was to be as snug and orderly as the most conventional husband could wish. After a bad crossing, they arrived to find the woman drunk and nothing ready. Kathleen shouted at the couple to be out of her sight within five minutes, but her husband exercised a calming influence, brought into play his tact by admiring the chintzes and saying how much nicer it would be to have the house to themselves, and walked her off arm-in-arm, and laughing, to a restaurant. 'We had only three hundred pounds a year to live on,' she wrote in her autobiography, 'and my husband had to be very much away; but all went very well indeed, and I was living in a state of exultation amounting to delirium; for the sublimation of my existence was now assured.'

# The Die
# is Cast

The lot of a sailor's wife in those days was generally pitied, with her husband away at sea for perhaps nine-tenths of their married life while she was left to bear the brunt of maintaining the home, rearing children, and enduring the loneliness of separation. The man, by contrast, was away in his ship having a rollicking time among his chums, carefree, well looked after, probably with wives in other ports. This was the popular image.

For Con and Kathleen, the reverse was true. It was he who was lonely in his captain's solitary splendour in the *Bulwark*, she who was living it up among a host of friends in London as well as beginning to make a name as a sculptor. She 'comfortably allowed her head to be gently gently turned' by the director of the Kensington School of Art, and in December 1908 sold a mask for eighteen guineas. 'You're not to tell me I'm not to make money by my work, I very much want to,' she wrote to her husband, who feared that she would prostitute her art because of their poverty.

They were not as poor as all that, she replied. She had settled all the expenses for £217, 'and there is not a single pennyworth of bills . . . our financial position is on a very sure footing for the moment. See? and I love you'. She was out almost every night. 'Yesterday I had a lovely day. First I made a statuette, then I went to the Pagets at Roehampton, I took my pianist cousin, there were heaps of people there . . . Then I went to a monster music party at the Wertheimers and then on to dinner at the Savoy.'

But she also had her moments of loneliness. In November 1908 she was in bed with pains which she thought (wrongly as it turned out) heralded the longed-for son, and wrote that she was as 'desperately, deeply, violently and wholly in love' as he was, and missing him badly. 'There's something so terribly real about you. I used to mend your trouser placquette hole and there's something grotesquely real about that. I never used to know anything about loneliness. Sir have you robbed me of my self-sufficiency?' The little house was getting barren; 'you must really come and strew about a few pipes and some ash . . .' She cheered herself up by going to the Caledonian market and buying for 9s 6d, an embroidered shawl, 'an exquisite Old Master drawing in an old frame, a real lace collar, two footstools, a looking glass, a little lace baby's cap and three beautifully worked tiny baby's chemises'. She gave the last away to a friend who had just had a baby.

There were brief periods together, sometimes twenty-four hours when his ship was in port, but for the first six months of marriage they had to get to know each other mainly through the medium of letters. This encouraged small misunderstandings and exaggerations, and had a bad effect on Scott. When they were together, her spontaneous gaiety infected him; apart, he brooded, his black moods deepened, all his misgivings came back. She wrote gay cheerful letters about the parties she had been to, dances, a mild flirtation with Lord Kilmarnock at a shooting party, new plays, and received replies that dwelt more than ever on his own inadequacies. He missed her constantly. 'Why can't I look up and see you? I'm impatient – it's being caged here; breakfast lunch and dinner all alone in this palatial prison . . . Pity me.' He added, more cheerfully, 'Yes do go in for marble, when I come home I can do some chipping. I love destruction with a barbaric delight.'

On the threshold of middle age he was taking stock of his own character and not liking it at all. Seldom can there have been a man so outwardly successful who rated himself so low. Now he was worried that Kathleen might be influenced by his personality, and he took it as axiomatic that such an influence would be deadening, a sort of damper on her flame of life and what he called her 'beautiful individuality'.

I've a personality myself, a mean poor thing beside yours, something that can neither inspire you nor content others, but yet has a tendency to dominate by sheer persistency . . . I hate it myself and hate the sense of responsibility it brings but I don't seem to have the power to make it different. And so dearest I've always the lurking fear that I shall influence you. Oh I know it won't be like the others, you're far too independent, in spite of this, small things I say, small attitudes to small conditions will be remembered and here and there a weed will take root.

The theme obsessed him; a few days later he wrote:

Don't allow yourself to be changed. Don't ever strike a note that doesn't spring from your dear natural self because you've an irritable man to please. It is you who must sway the man bringing him better and clearer ideas and (as you have done) showing him where his happiness lies.

She might not want to be changed but she did want to be educated; she had realised how little she knew. 'Correction of *ignorances* will in no way touch my personality.' She had been reading a book on political economy in the public library and suddenly had to ask the librarian for a map of County Cork. 'Of course it's absurd. But dearest you are the nicest husband I've ever had so what's to be done about it. I went to a ball last night, I danced every single dance from the very beginning to the very end and I loved it, and it apparently loved me.' Her husband meanwhile was having a 'tremendous shake-up of the ship', a matter much easier to deal with than his marriage. 'We shall be a man-of-war soon which is as much as to say that a boy will grow into a man but the point is to spell Man in capital letters.' Then he was back like a squirrel in a cage fretting at his unworthiness.

Oh girl, I don't think I'll ever be good enough . . . when I'm obstinate, despondent, pigheaded, dejected, there's something growing bigger inside that keeps shouting the greatness of you. Girl I could whip myself, why do I creep to knowledge? Why don't I grasp the fullness of it at once? . . . There never was there never could be anything more beautiful, and I'm a clod, a clown, a blockhead . . . oh darling you're somehow so exalted I can't *reach up*!

He put the matter in a nutshell when he wrote, 'Isn't this the position – to you it's You and I and a friendly world. To me it's You and I and the rest inimical?' He added, 'Tell me more and more of better things.'

As if this up-and-down existence of separation, brief reunion, separation again, was not enough to overstrain Scott's equilibrium, he found himself under attack from an entirely unexpected direction. In September 1908 the meteorological results of the National Antarctic Expedition were published by the Royal Society, with a preface by Dr Napier Shaw, director of the Meteorological Office, which sharply criticised the quality of the work and the competence of its authors. Scott could not but remember how, day after day throughout more than two years, Royds, or one of the others, had gone out to take the readings at the meteorological screen every two hours despite blizzards, frostbite, and 70° of frost. Not only was this arduous, conscientious work now questioned, but questioned, in Scott's opinion, in a most offensive way. Once the material had been handed over to the Royal Society, who passed it on to the Meteorological Office, not once had anyone concerned got in touch with any of the *Discovery*'s team to give Royds, or anyone else, an opportunity to clarify or explain doubtful points. Neither Scott nor any of his men had been shown the proofs before publication.

Tensed up as he already was, Scott lost his temper. From Bantry Bay, in the *Bulwark* (10 October 1908), he discharged a twenty-three-page broadside at Sir Archibald Geikie, who had succeeded Huggins as President of the Royal Society, protesting against the criticisms, in particular about remarks made by Dr Shaw under the heading: 'Miscarriage of Instructions.' What instructions? Scott demanded. Given by and to whom? He admitted only one mistake: a failure to remove the northern half of the sunshine recorder's bowl when the sun was very low in the north.

Geikie passed the letter to Napier Shaw, who found it 'very painful reading . . . the asperity of Captain Scott's letter goes beyond the limits of ordinary criticism'. He had not submitted proofs because 'my duty was to the Royal Society and not to Captain Scott or any member of the Expedition'. He was patronising about Royds. 'Mr Royds' introduction is a clear straightforward statement but it is obviously the work of an inexperienced meteorologist.' Scott was touched on the raw because it was plainly true that Royds was inexperienced. 'Captain Scott's letter,' Shaw went on to say, 'displays a resentment under *bona fide* criticism that would put an end to all scientific progress if it were indulged in by all observers.'

Briefed by Ferrar, Scott retorted with a list of mistakes made by the Meteorological Office; for example, 'south seems to have been printed for north' in five cases; the mileage of Skelton's sledge journey in 1902 was confused with that of the following year; and so on. He was not mollified by Geikie's reply, and demanded an enquiry.

Both Admiral Field, who had succeeded Wharton at the Admiralty as hydrographer, and the secretary of the RGS advised Scott that this would do more harm than good and damage the expedition in the eyes of foreign rivals. Although Scott still felt that it was 'preposterous to allow such enormities of mis-statement to go unchallenged', there was nothing he could do beyond reiterating his protests. His advisers were undoubtedly right. Among the papers of the expedition is a severe note addressed by Scott to Royds and Barne (September 1903) taking them to task for sloppiness. 'The log is a singularly incomplete record of the summer cruise of 1902. The dead reckoning is particularly inexact and unsatisfactory.' He listed seven instances of data insufficiently recorded in the log. Although these criticisms did not bear directly on the meteorological work, they would have reinforced the doubts of the professionals about the competence of Royds and other amateurs.

Scott had grown over-touchy. At this stage of his life a demon was sitting on his back and marriage had made it worse instead of better. What was the trouble? Self-mistrust, self-contempt, almost self-hatred: these were apparent. What lay beneath? 'Con dear are you still and always an unhappy man?' Kathleen asked. 'Oh what's the matter Con? What *is* the matter?' He could give no answer, although he searched for one in the recesses of his mind and heart. 'What does it all mean?' is a sentence that often occurred in his letters.

If he could give no answer, no one else can. But anyone may guess. Beyond a crisis of self-doubt, deepened by marriage to a woman of dominant character who possessed so many of the qualities he most admired but most lacked, lay, perhaps, a dread that had to be suppressed. The fates were crowding him into a corner and pointing with forbidding hands in a sinister direction. He could not escape another polar journey; Kathleen herself, let alone his colleagues and public opinion, had so decreed. Did a deep and unacknowledged dread of the ordeal lie at the core of his malaise? If self-distrust so greatly obsessed him, how could he hope to succeed?

At last, early in 1909, came good news – the event which Kathleen had so eagerly awaited. She was pregnant. 'My love my dear love my very dear love throw up your cap and shout and sing triumphantly for it seems we are in a fair way to achieve my aim.' And for goodness' sake, she added, don't start worrying, for 'we are agreed it is not wise to make life into Hell by anticipating things that may never happen, nor for that matter by anticipating things that most surely must happen, and so my sweet rejoice with me'. Rejoice he did, and rolled a fellow-officer on the floor of his cabin, but took her up for writing 'achieve my end' – it must be 'our end', surely.

The exultation did not last. Ten days later he was writing,

I'm obsessed with the view of life as a struggle for existence and then forced to see how little past efforts have done to give me a place in the struggle. I seem to be marking time, grudging the flying moments yet impotent to command circumstances. I seem to hold in reserve something that makes for success yet to see no worthy field for it, and so there's the consciousness of wasting and a truly deep unrest.

His black moods, he told her, were the outward signs of this inner frustration and he appealed again for her patience. For every lapse there was repentance; 'and how I long to be up and achieving things for your dear sake'. Kathleen replied that she understood but could do nothing about it. She never had these black moods because she was not ambitious. 'My funny little life is devoid of cares or worries or misfortunes.' She had named the child she was carrying Griselda, no doubt on the principle of not tempting the gods. Also she had hired a beautiful grand piano for 16s a month. Then there was a trip to Paris – 'Griselda simply loved Paris and is behaving beautifully.'

Fortunately, perhaps, for his marriage and his own equilibrium, early in 1909 an opportunity arose to spend nine months living at home with his wife like an ordinary mortal. Admiral Sir Mark Kerr had suggested that he might become Naval Assistant to Admiral Sir Francis Bridgeman, Commander-in-Chief of the Home Fleet, who was taking over as Second Sea Lord at the Admiralty. This would mean the creation of a new post. From a Service point of view, he wrote, the appointment would be 'good enough', though he would lose sea time, but that he would be with Kathleen for the best part of a year was decisive. The post was offered to him and he accepted. His pay would now rise to £950 a year. He took up the appointment at the end of March 1909.

The time had come when news of Shackleton could be expected. Having spent the English summer months of 1908 at Lyttleton, the *Nimrod* had returned to Shackleton's winter quarters at Cape Royds to await the re-appearance of the southern party consisting of Adams, Marshall, Wild and the leader, with or without news that they had planted the Union Jack at the Pole.

The announcement came through in March 1909 and was published in the London evening papers. Scott was travelling to London by train with his coxswain, Tom Crean, and ran along the platform with the paper in his hand to say to Crean, 'I think we'd better have a shot next.'*

Shackleton had not reached the Pole but he had made a magnificent journey. He and his companions had crossed the Barrier, struggled up a dreadful glacier which Shackleton had named after his patron Mr Beard-more, and, enduring all the hardships that the Antarctic in its cruellest mood could impose, had planted the flag at 88° 23's – 97 geographical miles and 113 statute miles from the Pole. There they had shot their bolt, and turned back after taking possession of the polar plateau in the name of the King. Everyone had got back safely, if only just. Another party, con-sisting of the Australians Professor Edgeworth David, aged fifty-one, and Douglas Mawson, with the Scots surgeon A. F. Mackay, had pushed on beyond the point reached by Scott on his western journey to plant another flag on the South Magnetic Pole and add by proclamation another icy plateau to the Empire.

Scott now had no choice. No medieval knight who threw his gauntlet at the feet of a rival could have given a clearer challenge than Shackleton had delivered. Scott had to go. (According to Armitage, Shackleton addressed an envelope to his former commander with a blank sheet of paper inside: the Pole was his if he could take it.)

First, there was his former lieutenant's triumphant return to be faced. The broken promise still rankled but Scott wrote to Major Darwin of the RGS, 'The private feelings incurred by past incidents cannot affect my judgement of his [Shackleton's] work. That excites my interest and admiration to an extent which can scarcely be felt by those who have no experience of polar difficulties.' On the day of Shackleton's return, 14 June 1909, he was found by Mill at the RGS 'gloomily discussing with Keltie whether he ought to go to meet Shackleton or not. He did not wish to go, but Scott was always a slave to duty, and we persuaded him that it was his

---

* Related by Dr E. L. Atkinson in a memorandum among the papers of the British Antarctic Expedition of 1910–13, SPRI, Cambridge. 'It is my impression,' stated Dr Atkinson, 'that this event settled the moment of the commencement of his preparations for his final expedition.'

duty to greet his former subordinate. He went with me to Charing Cross Station, and took first place at the reception.'

Cheering crowds lined the route along the Strand and through Trafalgar Square. 'I never saw anyone enjoy success with such gusto,' Mill wrote. 'His whole life was to him a romantic poem, hardening with stoical endurance in adversity, rising to rhapsody when he found his place in the sun.' By contrast, Scott hated cheering crowds and laurel wreaths. Mill admired both men in their different ways but had few illusions about Shackleton, who, he wrote, cared nothing for science nor for the Antarctic, and would just as soon have sought buried treasure on the Spanish main. 'An overmastering passion possessed him and raised his whole being on a wave of ambition which carried him to, and far beyond, the single goal he had in view.' With him in the carriage was his wife, to whom he remarked, 'I thought you'd rather have a live donkey than a dead lion.'

A few days later, Scott presided at a dinner given by the Savage Club to the explorer, gave unstinted praise and said 'the Pole must be discovered by an Englishman'. He added, 'Personally, I am prepared, and have been for the last two years, to go forth in search of that object, and before other countries can step in to take the credit of the results of these great works of Mr Shackleton, this country should come to the fore and organise another expedition.'

Shackleton was now receiving the full hero's treatment, including royal congratulations, a summons to Buckingham Palace and presentation of the Royal Victorian Order, a dinner attended by the Prince of Wales and 8000 guests, the RGS Gold Medal with silver replicas to his companions, and other honours and tributes. He was also knighted. There was comment as to why he should have received an honour that had been denied to Scott. Mr Balfour was no longer Prime Minister.

Shackleton's courage and endurance had not been matched by his managerial skill. The *Nimrod* had sailed with the expedition's fund still far short of its target and returned some £20,000 in debt. Shackleton wrote articles and gave lectures which drew enthusiastic crowds, but he had greatly over-estimated their pecuniary reward. There was not even enough money in the fund to pay off the *Nimrod*'s men. From this predicament, Shackleton was rescued by the Government, which made a grant of £20,000. By setting a precedent, this was to be of indirect help to Scott.

It has been said that the first quality needed in an explorer is to be a good beggar. Scott was now to learn the truth of this remark. With Markham gone, there was no massive support from the RGS, which gave only £500 and a qualified blessing – qualified because the new President, Major Leonard Darwin, and his officers, still held to the belief that scientific research and not attainment of the Pole should be the main objective.

Whatever they might think, the public had decided it was to be a race to reach the Pole, and it was the public who were being asked for money.

Before launching his appeal, Scott made sure that, on this occasion, there would be no misunderstanding. On 1 July 1909 he wrote to his rival, 'If as I understand it does not cut across any plans of your own, I propose to organise the expedition to the Ross Sea which as you know I have had so long in preparation so as to start next year.' With a stronger ship than the *Nimrod* and later in the year, he believed it would be possible to reach King Edward VII Land where he hoped to establish his base. 'I am sure you will wish me success; but of course I should be glad to have your assurance that I am not disconcerting any plans of your own.' Shackleton replied unequivocally that the proposed expedition 'will not interfere with any plans of mine'. He had at this time no plans, only vague intentions to attempt to march across the entire Antarctic continent, a project that did not reach the take-off point until more than four years later (December 1913) and then failed. 'Thank you for your letter of the 6th July, it is a very clear statement,' Scott replied; and on 13 September 1909 he announced his own plans. 'A simple direct appeal must be found,' and his announcement included the commitment, 'The main object of the expedition is to reach the South Pole and secure for the British Empire the honour of that achievement.' He needed the modest sum of £40,000.

His mind cannot have been focused wholly on the appeal, for on the day after its launching his son was born. Kathleen had prepared for the event in a manner then most unconventional, but which today would excite no surprise. She lived, she wrote, mainly on fruit and nuts, 'I walked and worked and danced and swam.' The 'gentle creature' with whom she had gone to Italy on a walking tour – Arthur Paget – had a caravan and tents on the Devon coast, and there she joined him 'triumphant with my burden' to enjoy wild raspberries and mushrooms, and sleep out on the beach wrapped in a blanket. A week before the child was born she swam out to sea on a calm moonlight night and thought 'My son will love the nights, and he will love the sea.' The fates were kind, and Griselda turned out to be Peter, as she had so passionately desired. He was called after Peter Pan, and had Barrie for one godfather and Markham for the other. 'And then a strange thing happened to me,' Kathleen wrote, 'I fell for the first time gloriously, passionately, wildly in love with my husband. I did not know I had not been so before, but I knew now.' Until then, he had been a probationer, a means to an end. Now she 'worshipped the two of them as one, father and son, and gave myself up in happy abandonment to that worship'.

# 18     Drumming
         Up Pennies

On 6 April 1909 Robert Edwin Peary, a fifty-six-year-old commander on almost permanent leave from the United States Navy, together with Matthew Henson, his Negro servant and companion, reached the North Pole on their sixth attempt: an event whose repercussions on Scott's life were to be momentous. With a persistance that can seldom have been equalled, Peary had been attempting for twenty-three years to gain the prize. (After his fourth expedition, he lost all his toes; he went back to the Arctic twice again after that and marched toeless to the Pole.) The event was noted with particular interest and some personal disappointment by Roald Amundsen, who was hoping to be the first at the Pole himself.

The North was won; the thoughts of polar explorers naturally turned towards the South. Several nations now began, or accelerated, preparations to capture the remaining polar prize. The United States at first seemed likely to take the lead. Soon after Scott launched his appeal, Peary announced in New York that an Antarctic expedition was to be formed, and put out feelers as to whether Scott would raise objections. Later, definite plans were published by the National Geographical Society to approach the Pole by way of the Weddell Sea, with Peary as the organiser if not the actual leader on the ice. Scott wrote to Peary welcoming the plan, but the British press played up the project as a transatlantic challenge, thus helping Scott's appeal.

Other nations were also showing signs of South Pole fever. A German, Lieutenant Wilhelm Filchner, had plans to march to the Pole by starting, like the Americans, from the Weddell Sea, and then continuing right across the continent to McMurdo Sound. The Frenchman Charcot, although he had renounced the Pole as an objective, was exploring in the region of Graham Land. Finally the Japanese had formed an expedition, led by Lieutenant Choku Shirase, to operate from a base in King Edward VII Land, the very region which Scott hoped to explore.

In retrospect, this international rivalry to arrive first across 'the stark and sullen solitudes that sentinel the Pole' at a point on the earth's surface fixed by scientific calculations and of very little use to anybody, seems rather absured. At least, on the negative side, it did no harm and involved no battlefields, holocausts or economic exploitation. When the Poles had been claimed, the contenders moved on to other natural objects like Mt Everest and, when the supply of these failed and the Olympic Games had been revived, to orgies of athletic competition in various urban centres, attended by a ballyhoo, bitterness and vulgarity wholly lacking in the days of 'the race to the Pole'. But of course deeper reasons lay behind the contest. A friend and shipmate of Scott's called Captain Nicolson, who had amused him and Kathleen by sending an unusual wedding present of skins, observed that Scott wanted 'only to show an example of enterprise and facing risks and hardships, much needed in these days'. That is just what he and his companions did, using to express their aim the symbol of the national flag.

Although the 'simple, direct appeal' of planting the Union Jack first at the Pole won support from press and public it failed to excite public generosity. No Longstaff, no Beardmore came forward with a massive donation. The nearest approach was Sir Edgar Speyer, the City financier who had given £5000 towards the purchase of the *Morning* and became Honorary Treasurer of the British Antarctic Expedition's fund. (He was also one of the founders of the Whitechapel Art Gallery.) He gave £1000. No other single contribution in Britain matched even this not very munificent sum.

Subscriptions came in dribs and drabs after Scott had addressed meetings, often poorly attended, in hired halls in dreary industrial centres, endeavouring to fire the somewhat damp imaginations of a populace to whom the Pole was merely a symbol of remoteness. 'Between £20 and £30 from Wolverhampton' – '£40 today' – 'nothing from Wales' – 'this place won't do, I'm wasting my time to some extent' 'I don't think there is a great deal of money in the neighbourhood' – 'things have been so-so here' 'I spoke not well but the room was beastly and attendance small' – 'another very poor day yesterday, nearly everyone out'. In the bigger cities there was more encouragement – £2000 from Manchester, £1387 from Cardiff, £740 from Bristol – but it was still like pulling teeth. The question was continually posed 'what's the use of it?' Scott knew that the answer he himself believed in, the advancement of scientific knowledge, would not inspire his audiences. Mutterings came from the mayors and business magnates in the industrial north about unemployment, local welfare needs, the low priority of polar adventures. Scott tried his best by mentioning the possibility of discovering pitchblende, a substance used in the protection of boats after caulking, and calling attention to the gold in Alaska, although he did not anticipate a gold rush up the Beardmore Glacier. But pitchblende did not generate a strong appeal.

It would be hard to imagine a more hateful ordeal for a man of Scott's temperament than this money-begging tour. How often, in cheap hotel bedrooms on cold nights, on platforms facing unenthusiastic audiences and flanked by Town Hall worthies who 'couldn't see the use of it all', he must have felt near to despair. Never one for *bonhomie*, he had to force himself to simulate qualities he despised, knowing that he could not do it very well. How he must have envied Shackleton, to whom putting on an act was second nature, *bonhomie* a strong suit, and lecturing a congenial art. Mill remembered his 'deep, husky voice rising and falling with the movement of his story, and sometimes raised . . . to a rafter-shaking roar'. The *Nimrod* came up the Thames in a blaze of publicity a fortnight after Scott's appeal was launched. In November 1909 Shackleton got the knighthood Scott had missed and his book, *The Heart of the Antarctic*, was published; inevitably he stole much of the thunder of the National Antarctic Expedition, as Scott's project had been named.

Moreover, Scott was back in the cage of poverty from which he had so briefly half-escaped. In December 1909 he went on half-pay and now he had a child to support as well as his other family commitments. On top of all this his small son contracted whooping-cough. There was, however, one bright spot. In January 1910 the Government announced a grant of £20,000, the same sum as had been given to Shackleton. Although still far short of its objective, the fund now looked a good deal healthier and was adequate to buy a ship. Scott had wanted the *Discovery*,* but the Hudson's Bay Company refused to part with her and, after considering several others, he bought the *Terra Nova* for a down payment of £5000 and a promise of a further £7500 when the cash could be found.

He was also able to push ahead with his experiments with motor sledges. There were three, one designed by Michael Barne, whose hands had never quite recovered from the frostbite; added to that, early in 1909 he was receiving treatment for a 'bent rib'. With great reluctance he resigned from Scott's shadow team. To his letter of withdrawal Scott replied (10 June 1909)):

My dear old Michael,
It would be difficult to tell you how sad I felt at getting your letter. Not that it is certain the chance would have come but at the knowledge of what it must have cost you to resign it. If all were certain I think that even then I wouldn't accept the resignation without a discussion. For the present there is nothing to be done – but my dear old chap you need never fear that I should not keep you informed of anything I do . . .

Three months later, Barne's engagement was announced and he was married before the *Terra Nova* sailed.

* After her service with the Hudson's Bay Company, the *Discovery* was chartered to the French Ministry of Marine Commerce, and then in 1916 put at the disposal of the Admiralty to help in the rescue of Shackleton's *Endurance* crew stranded on Elephant Island. She then carried grain to France, until she was bought in 1923 by the Crown Agents for use in scientific research in the South Seas. She was subsequently taken over by the Boy Scouts Association for the training of sea-scouts, and now lies in the Thames below Westminster Bridge, open on certain days and times to the public.

Early in March 1910 Scott went to Norway with Kathleen, Reginald Skelton, two mechanics and a 'motor expert', Bernard Day, to test the experimental sledges. At Fefor, at the foot of the Jotunheimen mountains, the tests were carried out with encouraging results. The top speed of the sledges was three-and-a-half miles an hour and Scott did not expect wonders of them; they were to be auxiliaries, to be used in conjunction with ponies and dogs. They were ungainly objects, proceeding by means of a spiked track much as tanks do today, steered by ropes, with no brakes and no reverse, but they were precursors of such sophisticated modern vehicles as the Polaris motor-sledge which can draw a ton of baggage over ice and snow.

In Christiania, Nansen met the party and introduced them to a young man, aged twenty-one, an accomplished skier, who was planning an expedition of his own towards the South Pole. Tryggve Gran was enthusiastic, strong and well off, and after he had taken the English party on a skiing trip Scott invited him to join the projected British expedition as a ski expert, and he agreed to shelve his own plans. As his pay was to be a shilling a month, he presented no financial problem to the fund. The sledges, on the whole, continued to look promising. Skelton naturally expected to continue his supervision of the experiments, and believed that he was booked to go south as second-in-command. The formal invitation never came.

Lieutenant Teddy Evans, who had talked his way into his appointment in the *Morning*, had started to raise funds for an expedition – yet another – of his own. This was before Scott's plans were announced. Some financial support had been promised in London, in his native Wales and in New Zealand, the native land of his wife. When Scott announced his plans, Evans offered to abandon his own, and to transfer his promised support to the National Antarctic Expedition – at a price. This was the position of second-in-command.

Scott could not afford to turn down so substantial a windfall. Evans was a most energetic and persuasive young man. The upshot was that Skelton was discarded and Evans given more or less a free hand to engage the non-scientific staff. Skelton was deeply hurt, and wrote angrily that Evans had been poisoning Scott's mind against him – in what way is not made clear. 'I am astounded, absolutely defeated,' he wrote, 'that you believe any danger exists from my side.' His rejection was a bitter pill to swallow.

If Evans acted the part of cuckoo in the nest, at least he proved a very pushing bird. Unlike Scott, he was good at fund-raising; 'it's no good talking to business men about magnetism, geology, metereology, or any of that scientific stuff', he observed. The refitting and equipment of the *Terra Nova* at the West India Docks fell to his charge. After her Antarctic voyage the ship had reverted to whaling and sealing and was in a filthy condition, stinking of whale oil and blubber. With energy and despatch, he got the vessel cleaned up.

Although people were proving slow to part with their money, offers of their persons were coming in from all over the world. More than 8000 volunteered. Among them were a number of 'Discoverys', and five were accepted: Petty Officers Thomas Williamson, Edgar Evans and Thomas Crean, also Chief Stoker William Lashly and William Heald.

The choice of scientists was crucial. Criticisms of the meterological work in the *Discovery* still rankled, and Scott was determined to secure for the *Terra Nova* fully qualified men whose work would be above reproach. 'We must have a considered programme of work,' he wrote to Major Darwin, 'and must not be the dumping ground of scientific freaks as the *Discovery* was.' (27 September 1909).

From the outset, he had been resolved on Edward Wilson as his Scientific Director. As early as March 1904 Wilson had written:

Can you really mean that you would like me to go south again with you? If you do may I tell you that nothing in the world would please me more, and my wife is entirely with me . . . As for your good opinion I can only say that there is nothing I would not do to deserve it, or to show you that I feel really grateful to you for it. I think I will not write more. You will understand that I would very much like to go with you, and at present I see nothing in the way of my doing so. We leave it open. You may well come across someone more fitted for the work.

In the intervals of the prolonged grouse enquiry, by 1910 nearing its end, the Wilsons had stayed with the Scotts in London, and in one of his bread-and-butter letters, dated soon after the Scott's marriage, Wilson wrote, 'We were simply delighted by her [Kathleen's] kindness and abundant hospitality and welcome. You have been a good friend indeed to me, no one ever had a better or a truer, and for such a friend I have no better wish in the world than that he should find a wife as well suited to him as mine is to me.'

Wilson consulted the Royal Society, the RGS and other bodies and took much care in the selection of his team. Instead of one geologist, as in the *Discovery*, there were three: two Australians, Frank Debenham and T. Griffith Taylor, plus Raymond Priestley, a Tewkesbury man who had been in Shackleton's *Nimrod*. A young Canadian, Charles Wright, was the physicist and George Simpson, whom Scott knew and liked, came from the Indian meterological service. There were two qualified biologists: Edward Nelson and D. G. Lillie. The physicist who didn't go was the young lecturer from the University of Adelaide, Douglas Mawson. Like so many others, he was forming Antarctic plans of his own, in his case to explore a 2000-mile-long unmapped stretch of coast and country west of Victoria Land, which had been named George v Land. Mawson had no intention of trying for the Pole. He suggested that his project might be fitted into the programme of the

British Antarctic Expedition, but Scott was by now too deeply committed to an attempt on the Pole to deflect his resources towards a programme of scientific research to be carried out in the opposite direction. In a letter to Griffith Taylor (15 February 1910) Mawson wrote:

I am almost getting up an expedition of my own – Scott will not do certain work that ought to be done – I quite agree that to do much would be to detract from his chances of the Pole and because of that I am not pressing the matter any further. Certainly I think he is missing the main possibilities of scientific work in the Antarctic by travelling over Shackleton's old route. However he must beat the Yankees . . .

Mawson then took his plans to Shackleton, who, in the intervals of lecturing, floating and managing small businesses and pursuing a gold mining concession in Hungary, was conceiving an enormously ambitious plan to sledge right across the continent from the Weddell Sea to McMurdo Sound, taking the Pole on the way. This was essentially the project that the German Filchner had proposed, but had abandoned when he heard of Scott's plans.*

So, once again, Scott found himself involved with the Irishman in whose character ebullient optimism and doggedness of purpose were so strangely combined. Both men were competing for funds in a limited market. Once again there was an interchange of formal letters. Shackleton wrote (21 February 1910) that he was preparing 'a purely scientific expedition', starting in 1911, to map and survey the coast of George V Land and carry out research 'in all branches of science'. This was Mawson's plan, at that time adopted by Shackleton. 'I am particularly anxious not to clash with your expedition, nor in any way to hinder your pecuniary efforts.' For this reason he was not appealing directly to the public nor to the Government but was 'being strongly supported by private individuals' – a support for which Scott was naturally hoping too. He was definitely not, Shackleton stated, aiming at the Pole, and did not intend to start until after Scott had sailed. 'The Expedition is purely *scientific*,' he reiterated, and Mawson would be its director; and he offered cooperation with Scott, or with the Americans, should either expedition be in the Antarctic at the same time.

* This sea-to-sea traverse of the Antarctic continent was not achieved until 1958, when to celebrate the International Geophysical Year Edmund Hillary followed Shackleton's old route across the Ross Ice Shelf (Great Ice Barrier), while Vivian Fuchs lead the British Trans-Antarctic Expedition, with a posse of motor sledges (Snocats), from the Weddell Sea to the Pole, and on to McMurdo Sound. The American contribution to International Geophysical Year was to establish the Amundsen-Scott Base, fully equipped, permanently manned, and air-supplied, on the site of the Pole itself. Admiral George Dufek, USN, who landed there in 1957 to inspect the site, was the first man after Scott to visit 'that awful place'. By 1971 there were forty-three occupied stations controlled by ten nations in Antarctica.

Four days later, Scott replied. He hoped, he wrote, to complete his work in the Ross Sea (i.e. get to the Pole) in one season and then to transfer his base to the west of Cape Adare. He would, he wrote, welcome cooperation in this area, but 'it should be clearly understood that my own programme for a second season will not be modified by the publication of your plans'. To this letter Scott received no reply.

Thus the matter appeared to be amicably settled, but Scott never really trusted his rival. His own target of £40,000 was not attained before the *Terra Nova* sailed, and money-raising had to continue after the expedition had reached the Ross Sea. By this time Shackleton's 'purely scientific' project had been taken over by Mawson himself, who formed an Australian expedition which reached the Antarctic in the *Aurora* early in 1912. Despite his private support, Shackleton was also appealing to the public and thus, in Markham's opinion, attempting 'to divert subscriptions from the right direction for an absurd scheme of his own'. Shackleton's ingratitude, he added, was 'scarcely human'.

While Wilson was selecting the scientists Scott himself with Evans and the expedition's secretary, a former naval paymaster called Francis Drake, were winnowing the applications and getting together the rest of the staff. This time the Admiralty raised no difficulties and three naval lieutenants came. Two were on the active list: Harry Pennell, navigator and magnetic observer, and Henry Rennick in charge of the hydrographical surveys and deep-sea soundings. The third was Victor Campbell, recently retired though only thirty-five. Two Lieutenant-Surgeons, G. Murray Levick and Edward Atkinson, were also released, together with twenty-six petty officers and seamen.

In addition, various other volunteers talked their way in, or were selected for specialist qualifications. Herbert Ponting was a skilled and experienced photographer whose pictures taken during the Russo–Japanese War, in India and in the Far East had been published in leading periodicals in Britain and America. At the other end of the scale, vis-à-vis experience, was Apsley Cherry-Garrard, aged twenty-four and a relative of Reginald Smith's. He contributed £1000 to the funds and served without pay as assistant biologist. A similar contribution came from Captain L. E. G. Oates of the 6th Inniskilling Dragoons, not quite thirty, who walked with a slight limp as a result of a wound received during the Boer War in an action which earned him a Mention in Despatches and a recommendation for the vc. His life had hitherto been devoted almost wholly to horses, dogs and sport. When posted to Mhow in South India, he took his own pack of hounds with him, and it was to take charge of the ponies that he was engaged. He came from India to join the expedition, as did Henry Bowers of the Royal Indian Marine.

Bowers was short, stocky and not very prepossessing in appearance, with red hair and a large nose which quickly earned him the nickname Birdie. It was said that after he had reported to the expedition's office on arrival, Scott turned to Wilson and said, 'Well, we're landed with him now and must make the best of it.' In a very short while he became 'a perfect treasure'. A glutton for work, always cheerful, quick and intelligent, he was so tough that he fell nineteen feet into the hold without turning a hair. 'A little man in the hold, rotund of figure and very damp and pink as to his face, with tunic unbuttoned and a peak cap tilted on the back of his head, stowing cases all day long as if his life depended on it', was how a visitor described him. All the stores, stowage and cargo were in his charge.

A *Worcester* cadet, Bowers had first joined the Merchant Navy and was then gazetted to the Royal Indian Marine as sub-lieutenant. He had navigated river vessels up the Irrawaddy, hunted gun-running dhows in the Persian Gulf, and bicycled through tropical jungles after butterflies. One of his superiors noted that when a shortage of officers obliged them to work twenty hours out of the twenty-four he really began to enjoy life, and put on weight visibly. At five feet four inches, he weighed about twelve stone.

Another former *Worcester* cadet who joined was Kathleen's brother Wilfrid, aged thirty-six. His first assignment was to go to Vladivostok to meet Cecil Meares, who was in Siberia negotiating for the purchase of ponies and dogs. Meares had gone to Khabarovsk, and thence by horse-drawn sleigh down the river Amur to Nikolievsk, covering 660 miles in seven days. Here the English manager of the Russo–Chinese Bank helped him to select thirty-four sledge-dogs and to carry out trials. A river steamer to Khabarovsk, then a train, took them back to Vladivostok where Bruce joined Meares, and twenty ponies were selected of the hardy Siberian breed.

One of Scott's fund-raising gimmicks was to invite schools to pay for a dog; many did so, at three guineas each, which can hardly have included the cost of transport. At Vladivostok, a rabid dog got in among the pack; luckily none were bitten, but to plunge these ferocious animals, unaccustomed to English dog-coddling, into carbolic baths, proved a strenuous exercise. From Vladivostok, Meares, Bruce and two young Russians, a groom and a dog-driver, escorted the animals in a Japanese steamer to Kobe, thence in a German ship to Sydney, thence to Lyttleton and finally to Quail Island, where they were inoculated ten times. Only one pony and one dog were lost on the way.

Meares had crammed a lot of travel and adventure into his thirty-three years. The son of an army officer, born in County Kilkenny while his father was serving at the Curragh, at nineteen he went to India intending to become a coffee planter, but became instead a rover, as he remained for the rest of his life. In north-eastern Siberia he traded in furs, he saw something of the Russo–Japanese War, fought in the Boer War in the Scottish Horse, and travelled to the borders of China and Tibet with an army officer, J. W. Brooke, who, on Christmas Day 1908 was murdered by members of a wild tribe called the Lolo. Meares was able to bring Brooke's body and his Chinese companions to safety. His next undertaking was to buy Scott's dogs. He and Wilfrid Bruce had not met before. 'Quite "one of the boys" but too "kid-glovey" for this job,' he wrote to his father about Bruce. Kathleen's brother had been described elsewhere as 'broad, beaming and cheerful, with always a weather eye for the girls'.

In no respect has Scott been more strongly criticised than in that of his transport plans. Divided effort, it has been said, brought him to disaster; had he concentrated solely on dogs and trained his people thoroughly in their management, he would have got comfortably to the Pole and back. His scheme of transport was, like everything Scott directed, well thought out, logical and executed with attention to detail. Motor-sledges would convey heavy equipment from ship to shore-base and on across the level Barrier as far as they could travel, establishing depots and thus sparing the animals. Ponies and dogs would take over, hauling the sledges as far as the foot of the glacier; Scott did not think that they could get beyond the lower reaches, and men alone would complete the long haul. On the way back, the cached flesh of dogs and ponies would provide the fresh meat needed to avoid scurvy.

Motor-sledges were admittedly experimental. To break new ground is always risky; in this, as in other directions, Scott was a pioneer. It is harder to understand why he placed so much reliance on ponies. Dogs had been used by almost every Arctic explorer and ponies by none until Frederick Jackson took four to Franz Josef Land. In his book, he praised their usefulness, but it is hard to see why; they floundered in soft snow up to their bellies, one had to be shot quite early on, another was found hanged by its halter and a third died of a bowel complaint. But Armitage, one of Jackson's party, thought that on a level surface like the Barrier they would do better than dogs; the Siberian pony could stand severe cold, and drag a heavier load in proportion to his weight and the amount of food he needed, than dogs could do. Moreover, ponies made better meat.

Shackleton, it is true, went all out for ponies and took nineteen, but only four survived to set out on the journey towards the Pole. Of these, one had to be shot at the second depot; another gave up at the third; and by the time the party reached the foot of the Beardmore Glacier only one, Socks, was left. Very soon afterwards he vanished into a crevasse, leaving Wild, who had been leading him, suspended by one elbow over a black chasm. On the face of it, these experiences did not confirm the superiority of ponies over teams of dogs.

Possibly bad fish lay at the root of Scott's lack of faith in dogs. He could not forget the miseries of his ailing teams, pushed to the limits of their failing strength and beyond. Had his first experience of dogs been a happier one, he might have taken a different line. As usual, he endeavoured to be fair and weigh the pros and cons. In favour of dogs he quoted McClintock, who had said that two dogs need the same weight of food as one man, and will draw a man's full load about twenty-five percent further, a light load twice as far. Added to that, the dog needs no sleeping bag, no tent, no cooking apparatus, no clothing and will draw a maximum load of about 100lbs for the expenditure of little more than half as much food as a man.

For the cons, he considered dogs fickle and unstable. When asked to draw a lightish load for short distances on good going they were excellent, but much less so when drawing heavy loads over unknown terrain and rough pressure-ridges. Men, he believed, would do as well as dogs on long journeys 'provided always that it is intended to preserve the lives of the dogs'. If not, the dog-teams showed a capacity for work 'beyond the emulation of a party of men'.

It came down, in fact, to the question of whether men were prepared to feed the dogs to each other and Scott was not sentimental about this. 'There is no real reason why the life of a dog should be considered more than that of a sheep, and no one would pause to consider the cruelty of driving a diminishing flock of sheep to supply the wants and aid the movements of travellers in more temperate climes.' It was not the killing but the cruelty that he jibbed at; the experience 'had left in each one of our small party an unconquerable aversion to the employment of dogs in this ruthless fashion'. He ended his summary with the oft-quoted words:

In my mind no journey ever made with dogs can approach the height of that fine conception which is realised when a party of men go forth to face hardships, dangers, and difficulties with their own unaided efforts, and by days and weeks of hard physical labour succeed in solving some problem of the great unknown. Surely in this case the conquest is more nobly and splendidly won.

Up to the day of the *Terra Nova*'s departure and beyond, shortage of money was a constant worry. When officers, men and scientists signed the articles there was not enough to guarantee their pay beyond New Zealand, and the pay was meagre. Some – Oates, Cherry-Garrard, Victor Campbell, Wilfrid Bruce and Tryggve Gran among them – drew nothing at all, or next to nothing. Pennell, the navigator, drew £5 a week, Rennick and the two naval surgeons £2, the petty officers fifteen shillings and leading seamen 13s 6d. Members of the scientific staff got a flat rate of £4 a week and Ponting £5. 'The fact that men are so ready to agree that this shortage [of funds] should fall on them rather than on the scientific equipment is, I think, an honour to our country,' Scott said. As leader, he topped the list with a weekly £20.

When he was packing his bags for the final departure, a newspaper reporter asked him for a last message, hoping no doubt for something inspiring on the lines of Major Darwin's remark at the farewell luncheon, 'They mean to do or die, that is the spirit in which they are going to the Antarctic.' Scott had only one thing on his mind. He told the reporter, 'There is still a deficiency in the amount required to maintain the expedition on full pay and to provide for the dependants of the crew.'

He did not sail with the *Terra Nova*, but stayed behind to raise more money and settle bills, arranging to join her at Cape Town. The Royal Yacht Squadron had elected him a member on payment of £100, which not only entitled the *Terra Nova* to fly the Squadron's prestigious burgee but exempted her from Board of Trade regulations, thus enabling Evans to have her Plimsoll line painted out and then to stow her stores 'pretty tight'. In a final ceremony on board before she sailed from the South-West India Docks on 1 June 1910, the wife of the First Sea Lord, Admiral Sir Francis Bridgeman, broke the White Ensign from her masthead, and Lady Markham the RYS burgee. Then she was towed slowly past the crowded shipping, cheered by dockers and merchant seamen and seen away with hoots and whistles from the tugs and little steamers. Ponting, standing beside the leader, wondered what their homecoming would be like. 'I don't much care for this sort of thing,' Scott answered. 'All I want is to finish the work we began in the *Discovery*. Then I'll get back to my job in the navy.'

So set forth the *Terra Nova* with her fit and eager crew, her many cases of provisions, her scientific equipment, her sledges and skis and furs and tents, the innumerable presents that had poured in (including 35,000 cigars) – with all this and high hopes, she left for the Antarctic by way of Cardiff, where she was to take on free coal and receive another £1000 and a flag bearing the Red Dragon which Teddy Evans ran up the masthead. At a civic dinner his namesake Edgar Evans got so drunk that six men were needed to restrain him and get him back to the ship. Overlooking this lapse, the *Western Mail* proclaimed that 'such seamen with faces of bronze and necks that Roman gladiators would have given the world for, were never gathered before in any ship that ever sailed from a British port'.

Scott, with his wife, left the ship at Greenhithe and had two more flags to receive. Queen Alexandra, now the Queen Mother, presented him with two Union Jacks, one to be hoisted at the farthest south attained and then brought back, while the other, a smaller one, was to be left on the spot. The new monarch, George V, King for less than one month, gave the expedition's leader a royal portrait.

Scott stayed on another six weeks before leaving for South Africa and found time to slip down, unheralded, to Outlands to say goodbye to his childhood home and carve his initials on a tree that he had planted. A premonition? In public he radiated a quiet confidence, sometimes almost breezy, but there are hints of darker thoughts in private moments.

The hardest farewell was postponed. Kathleen wrote:

Should I travel to Sydney with him, leaving my nine-months son behind? I should and I did. But looking back over my life I can think of nothing that hurt more hideously than unlocking the sturdy fingers that clung round mine as I left the laughing, tawny-haired baby Hercules for four months . . . He would not know me when I came back. He would look to someone else, maybe, for protection from me. Well! I had known, I had chosen, and joy never left me for long. In agonies and ecstasies of reciprocated love I followed my husband.

They sailed in HMS *Saxon* on 16 July 1910, seen off from Waterloo by a small party of friends and by Wilhelm Filchner and Ernest Shackleton, who waved his bowler hat to raise a cheer as the train drew away from the station. Scott wore a straw hat at a jaunty angle and, in a smart navy-blue suit, was in high spirits and looking a picture of health. Travelling with them in the *Saxon* were Ory Wilson and Hilda Evans. They reached Cape Town on 2 August 1910 ahead of the *Terra Nova*, which was overdue. Scott imagined terrible disasters and suffered, literally, from nightmares, but within a week she had arrived and he was back on the treadmill of money-raising.

He looked to the people of South Africa, Australia and New Zealand to supply the last £8000 needed to hit the target – not an exorbitant sum, he thought, to expect from the three dominions of the southern hemisphere. South Africa, in particular, seemed full of millionaires, newly enriched by the diamonds of Kimberley and the gold of the Rand, any one of whom could have found the whole sum without being obliged to sacrifice so much as a case of champagne or a box of cigars. The Governor-General, Lord Gladstone, sent a cheque for £50. Scott gave three lectures, sent letters to all the mayors and gave interviews to reporters. But South Africans were distracted by a general election, or made that an excuse for indifference. The Government set a lead in niggardliness by granting a mere £500, and from wealthy Johannesburg came a grand total of £110 5s. which included two contributions of £50 each. Cape Town did a little better with £358 5s. in cash, plus three cases of jam and eighty bottles of beer. From the whole of South Africa came a sum smaller than that proffered by the citizens of Cardiff.

In a letter to his mother, Scott looked on the bright side. They might have failed to gather in the money, but 'we leave with a large addition to our list of friends'. Kathleen, he added, was popular everywhere. Her portrait by Charles Shannon now hangs in the Johannesburg Municipal Gallery, and in 1960 a monument was unveiled in Cape Town to her husband and his men.

# 19    Furl Topgallant Sails

'We all loved him', Charles Wright wrote of Bill Wilson. Wright, a Canadian post-graduate student working at the Cavendish Laboratory in Cambridge, had applied for the post of physicist to the projected expedition and been rejected. Whereupon he and a young Australian physiographer, Griffith Taylor, walked the fifty miles from Cambridge to London in a day to persuade the Chief of the Scientific Staff to change his mind; they succeeded. 'I for one stood in awe of Scott,' Wright admitted; admiration, not awe, was his feeling for Wilson. The Scientific Director was just as enthusiastic about his colleagues and wrote to his chief from Madeira (25 June 1910) 'You have got a crew of pirates that would be exceedingly difficult to beat – or equal. I have never been with such a persistently cheery lot before.'

Like the *Discovery*, the *Terra Nova* had a leak; not such a bad one – she was an old ship and had, as it were, learned to live with it – but bad enough to demand a daily session at the hand pumps when the ship was under sail, starting at 6 a.m. and resumed every four hours throughout the twenty-four. All members of the afterguard, as the officers and scientists were called, took turns at this, and also at the much more strenuous and unpleasant jobs of trimming and stoking. Trimming involved shovelling coal from the main hold into two bunkers, one on each side of the stokehold, each holding fifty tons. When the ship reached the tropics the heat was almost unbearable; the trimmers could not stand upright, they worked in darkness save for the light of one small oil lamp; the air was foul, and in no time they were streaming with sweat and black with coal-dust all over. In spite of a thorough wash on deck after each stint, their clean clothes were blackened by coal-dust working its way out of the pores of the skin. 'The exercise is splendid' was Wilson's comment.

When, after calling at Madeira, they entered the tropics, winds grew more fitful and the engines came into use. The scientists, doctors, naval officers and general helpers found themselves transformed into stokers. Three furnaces demanded to be fed by the use of enormously heavy tools, the worst being a 'devil rake' for breaking up clinkers, which even Wilson admitted he could scarcely lift after toiling for three hours in heat so intense that Rennick fainted – but he came back to complete his four-hour watch. Frequent stings by 'stokehold flies' – drops of hot oil from the engines – plagued the men. When not shovelling coal, they had to break up large lumps with a sledge-hammer, get the fuel into a heavy iron bucket, and drag this across to the furnaces; also they had to take out ashes and heave them into a hoist. Every-thing was too hot to touch. Bathed in sweat, they worked almost naked bar-ring thick-soled boots and leather gloves. Continual noise – clattering and clanging of iron, roaring of furnaces, pounding of engines – was, Wilson con-ceded, 'somewhat trying'. He reckoned this to be the hardest work he had done in a life of unremitting toil. He appeared to revel in it, put on weight, and still had time to observe and sketch the birds, the fish and the beauties of the sky.

Hours were too precious to waste on sleep; he was called at midnight with a cup of cocoa, and again at 4 a.m. with more cocoa and a start to the day's work: 'a very good, fattening routine which gives me a very nice long day'. All the way from Cardiff to Cape Town he was working at full stretch; when not stoking, trimming, bird-collecting, skinning and sketching, to complete his report on the five-year grouse inquiry. At Madeira, he finished all the coloured grouse-skin plates and in forty-eight hours had seven hours' sleep. In his tiny cabin with no table, no chair, nowhere to spread his papers, very little light and less air, he worked standing up because he fell asleep if he sat down.

Apsley Cherry-Garrard was his assistant. He very quickly learned to catch birds by entangling them in lines, to skin them, and to classify and preserve the skins, and displayed a tireless enthusiasm almost equal to his chief's. The first to volunteer for any job, however difficult or dirty, and however seasick he felt, he was soon as much at home in the rigging as in the stokehold or on deck helping to re-stow cargo. His sight was poor and he wore glasses, but never allowed them to interfere with his activities. Harry Pennell the navigator, like Wilson always up at 4 a.m. taking stellar observa-tions, was another general favourite, 'always cheerful and genial and busy', Wilson noted, 'but never too busy to talk birds and be interested in work other than his own'. In the wardroom, Wilson wrote, there were no under-currents of tension as there had been in the *Discovery*.

The uncomplicated personality of the commander encouraged the pre-vailing attitude of hard work and hard play, as in a well-run public school. No one stood in awe of Teddy Evans, but Oates, who thought him a splendid chap, wrote that he would be sorry for the man who hesitated to obey an order. Evans led the ragging in the rowdiest mess Oates had ever been in. 'We shout and yell at meals just as we like and have a game called Furl Top-gallant Sails which consists in tearing off each others' shirts'. Wilson thought this 'excellent fun and splendid exercise in this heat' (August in the tropics). To celebrate Wilson's thirty-eighth birthday, Evans, Rennick and Bowers performed a war-dance on the main hatch. One can scarcely imagine the Owner, as Scott was called, leading the revels in this manner. Wilfrid Bruce was a trifle patronising about Evans. 'Dear cheerful soul, I have got very fond of him, but he will always be a sort of Peter Pan.'

Lawrence Oates, known as Titus or the Soldier, looked on his surroundings with sardonic humour; he said little, held dogmatically to his opinions, had no time for women and thought better of dogs and horses than of their masters. In Edward Atkinson, at twenty-eight two years his junior, he found a kindred spirit, although a less reserved one. After qualifying at St Thomas's Atkinson had served at the Royal Naval Hospital at Haslar until selected from many applicants as junior surgeon and parasitologist in the *Terra Nova*. This proved an inspired choice. Atkinson was a quiet, reliable, even-tempered man, who never shirked a duty or lost his head. 'He turns out the interior of every beast that is killed, and being also a surgeon, I suppose the subject must be interesting,' Bowers observed. Atkinson and Oates became inseparable companions.

On 25 July 1910 the *Terra Nova* anchored off the uninhabited South Trinidad Island, less than 700 miles east of Brazil, to which it belongs. The *Discovery* had also visited the island in 1901, when a new petrel, named after Wilson (*Œstrelata wilsoni*) was found. The island's many birds, secure in their mountainous terrain, had no fear of men because they had never encountered any. Terns would perch on people's heads and gannets allow themselves to be caught by hand. Wilson and Cherry-Garrard, armed with guns, went after the birds; Lillie looked for plants and rocks; Nelson and Simpson pursued fish in coral pools. 'Everything was to be captured, dead or alive, animal, vegetable or mineral', wrote Cherry-Garrard. It was unkind to allocate to Bowers, together with Wright and Evans, the insects and smaller invertebrates, because Bowers, than whom no braver man ever lived, was terrified of spiders. 'Needless to say I caught them with a butterfly net and never touched one,' he wrote to his mother. He collected fifteen species of which only five were previously known, and a new moth.

Worse than the spiders, except in Bowers' estimation, were the land-crabs which swarmed about the island in tens of thousands, pink and yellow creatures who followed the explorers' every movement with dead-looking, staring eyes, as if to say (wrote Cherry-Garrard) 'drop down dead and we will do the rest'. (They did, in fact, eat each other.) Because of them, no mammals could survive on the island. They crawled up to nibble at the intruders' feet, never taking their eyes off the men, who found them on the summit of the island, sunning themselves on bushes. While the climbers ate their lunch the crabs gathered in a circle 'waiting for us to die'.

The explorers very nearly did die, though not to feed the land-crabs; on scrambling back to the shore they found a big sea running and could not reach the boats. A lifeline attached to a buoy was secured by Bowers and the men got off one by one through heavy surf, leaving behind most of their clothes and all their equipment. When things looked desperate – one of the men had let go the rope and seemed certain to be dashed to pieces by enormous breakers – Wilson sat on a rock and ate a biscuit 'in the coolest possible manner. It was an example to avoid all panicking, for he did not want the biscuit,' Cherry-Garrard wrote.

Next day most of the clothing, equipment and collection of trophies was, with great difficulty, retrieved – all damaged by sea-water. On the summit of the island Oates had picked a pretty flower and stuck it in his hat-band; when his hat was recovered the flower was still there; Lillie spotted it, and 'it turned out' Oates wrote to his mother 'to be something not yet described, and the best thing got in the vegetable line'.

After leaving the island the ship went 'booming along' before strong westerlies, lifted by gigantic waves like a cork, followed by many birds: several species of albatross, Cape Hens, Cape Pigeons and petrels. Wilson believed that the birds flew round and round the world perpetually in these latitudes before prevailing westerly winds, landing only to breed.

On 15 August 1910 the *Terra Nova* tied up to a buoy in Simon's Bay. Wilson and Evans waved to their wives, who waved back from the bridge of the cruiser *Pandora*. 'Hurrah! parties, nibs, nobs and snobs off to welcome us,' Oates recorded, 'but they forgot to bring our letters or any bottled beer.'

In Cape Town, Scott was re-united with his colleagues, who took a few days' leave spent each after his fashion. Oates made a bee-line for the nearest pack of hounds, at Wynberg, taking Atkinson who had never been on a horse before. Wilson at last completed his grouse report with its many illustrations and got it off to Cambridge;* then he and Ory paid a visit to a whaling station in Saldanha Bay.

At Simon's Bay Wilson received the news that he was to change places with the Captain and go ahead to Melbourne in a liner, while Scott took over command of the *Terra Nova* from Teddy Evans. He was by no means pleased. The prospect of enjoying Ory's company for another five or six weeks did not compensate for banishment from the congenial atmosphere of the *Terra Nova*'s wardroom with its jolly games of Furl Topgallant Sails. Somewhat grumpily he wrote to Reginald and Isabel Smith that it was 'a great blow to be ousted unexpectedly, both to Evans and myself'. People

---

* Wilson never saw the proofs of this monumental report, one of the most thorough studies of a bird disease ever made, and amongst the best illustrated. He established as the cause of the disease the actions of a small threadworm which lies in wait in dewdrops on the tips of heather fronds on which the bird feeds. He recommended as a means of control the annual burning of about one-seventh of the heather in rotation. This is now the standard practice on well managed moors.

might interpret it wrongly. 'However it can't be helped so here I am, with my wife and her sister living in undesired comfort on shore, with the still more undesirable comfort of a liner ahead of me, instead of the happy-go-lucky attractive discomfort of the *Terra Nova*.' His sense of humour re-asserting itself, he thought that Scott's aim was to get as fat and fit as he himself had done on the voyage from Cardiff. 'But if he puts on as much as I did, a stone and a pound, in the half voyage, he will be *very* round, whereas I was only just "Cortachy" [a reference to Wilson's visits to the Smiths' Cortachy lodge] – comfortably filled out – in spite of doing everything else under the sun that people would do to get thin, or at least advise *other* people to do to get thin.'

Nor was he delighted with the prospect of having to look after Mrs Scott and Mrs Evans on board RMS *Corinthic*. Mrs Evans turned out to be a 'real brick', devoted to her husband and keen on deck games. Mrs Scott earned no such praises. Fortunately, perhaps, she was a bad sailor and kept out of his way. His tact did not work on Kathleen, who resented 'being treated as an outsider as regards expedition affairs', and Kathleen's attractions did not work on Wilson, who remained anything but her slave. His Christian asceticism and her pagan hedonism were as oil and water. 'I gather he thinks women aren't much use, and expect he is judging from long experience, so I bear him no malice,' she wrote in her diary. Here, at least, was a topic they might have agreed on. 'I hate women,' she re-affirmed, 'and wish the whole world could be populated by men and babies.' She made no secret of her boredom with her fellow-wives. 'My hatred of women is becoming a mono-mania and must be curbed.'

Wilson's main tasks in Melbourne were to select a third geologist, to con-sult with Professor Edgeworth David, and, most important of all, to persuade the Federal Government to rescind its refusal to contribute £5000 towards the expedition's funds. They had refused mainly because they had already pledged support to Douglas Mawson who was raising an expedition of his own.

Wilson disliked money-raising as much as Evans enjoyed it, but dutifully embarked on a round of interviews with politicians. The Prime Minister, Mr Andrew Fisher, he found 'a very straightforward sort of chap, quiet and rather shy', unlike the Minister for Home Affairs, Mr O'Malley, an American with a 'sandy beard, a large dicky with an enormous fixing in the centre of five opals, and a loose purple suit'. At an official garden party he managed to persuade Mr Fisher, who was looking uncomfortable in a top hat and frock coat, to think again about a Government grant. The Australian Government had given Shackleton £5000, Wilson said, so why not Scott? Shackleton's expedition, Mr Fisher explained, had been so ill-equipped that it was 'stuck', and needed the money to proceed. All the more reason to support the

*Terra Nova*, Wilson replied, which was not 'stuck', but well equipped, and needed the money for an extra, and fruitful, year's work. If two men were in a race, Fisher rejoined, and one fell and broke his leg, your duty would be to help the injured man. 'But he knew that he was talking rot,' Wilson commented.

'Horrid place Melbourne,' Kathleen considered; she was bored by the formalities and reduced, after an official luncheon party, to reading aloud to Hilda Evans at the hotel. Hilda refused to go to Government House because she got her invitation a day later than the Scotts' and thought it infra dig to accept. 'Poor silly little thing, she has rather a rotten time, but it's her own stupid little fault.'

Meanwhile Scott had been enjoying himself in the *Terra Nova*. 'My companions are delightful,' he wrote to his mother. 'There seem to be only two weak spots in the organisation and these might have been worse.' One of them was the engineer, who was discharged, the other improved. Everyone else earned glowing praises. Bowers was again a treasure, Pennell exceptionally intelligent, Oates shrewd and dedicated, Cherry-Garrard industrious and a true gentleman, as was Victor Campbell; Simpson cheerful, unselfish and able, Wright likeable and clever, and so on. He was a little doubtful about the biologist Dennis Lillie, sometimes known as 'Ouze', who, while thoughtful and imaginative, was inclined to crankiness; he believed in reincarnation, and that he had been a Persian and a Roman in previous existences. Atkinson was a skilful doctor and would make an excellent sledger, to judge by his physique. The physicist Charles Wright wrote to his father, 'The Owner has a thirst for scientific knowledge that cannot be quenched. He takes no part in the skylarking – but always looks on with a grin.'

The Owner's object in sailing in the *Terra Nova* was to get to know his men and to select the members of the two shore parties he proposed to organise. The main one would establish the expedition's base at whatever spot in or near McMurdo Sound was chosen, and carry out most of the scientific research; and from it would be chosen the men who would make the final assault on the Pole. A subsidiary party of six, called the Eastern Party, was to be landed some four hundred miles to the east in the unexplored King Edward VII Land; this, it had been decided at an early stage, was to be led by Victor Campbell. Before the ship reached Melbourne, Scott had picked the rest of his men. Bowers, originally destined to stay with the ship, was so much of a treasure that he would join the main shore party. The naval lieutenants, Pennell and Rennick, would remain in charge of the ship.

After six weeks at sea, the *Terra Nova* reached Melbourne on the evening of 12 October 1910: a wet evening with a heavy sea running. At Kathleen's insistence, Wilson embarked his trio of wives, with a sack of mail, in a motor launch and set out to search for the ship in pitch darkness. 'Bill was furious, and protested that the other women were cold and hungry, but I knew my man would expect me,' Kathleen wrote in her diary, and off they went, pitching and tossing in the heavy swell. As they approached the ship 'I heard my good man's voice and was sure there was no danger, so insisted, getting more and more unpopular . . . We at last got close to the beautiful *Terra Nova* with our beautiful husbands on board. They came and looked down into our faces with lanterns.' Wilson's version was that 'it was for them on board, Captain Scott and Lieutenant Evans, to say whether I should risk drowning their wives now, and as they seemed in favour of it I went in and they soon dropped down the side of the ship into our launch, and I went on board with the mails'. Kathleen went on board too, and 'the relief of getting back to sane folk who understood me was more than can be written about'. Wilson was equally relieved to get back to his hotel and a nightcap of cocoa with Ory, who had behaved like a brick throughout. 'In future I hope it will never fall to my lot to have more than one wife at a time to look after, at any rate in a motor launch, in a running sea at night time.'

Among Scott's mail waiting in Melbourne was a telegram, sent from Madeira on 9 September 1910, which came as a bolt from the blue. 'Beg leave inform you proceeding Antarctic. Amundsen.' No more. There is no record of how Scott reacted; curiously enough, neither Kathleen nor Wilson mentioned the telegram in their diaries. Evans later recalled, 'we considered that he [Amundsen] would go to the Pole from the Weddell Sea side'. Why this conclusion was arrived at it is hard to say – perhaps mainly wishful thinking.

While Scott made no public comment at the time about Amundsen's bombshell, the press naturally took the matter up and public opinion was aroused. With some exceptions, the Norwegian's sudden foray into the South, when Scott's expedition was already under way, was generally resented. For this, Amundsen's secrecy was mainly to blame. For secretive he had undoubtedly been. He had raised the money, and borrowed the *Fram* (without payment) from Nansen, with the publicly proclaimed intention of going to the Arctic. His crew, his dogs and his provisions had all been assembled with this avowed aim. Not only that, he had publicly stated that polar competition was a wasteful exercise. 'I most emphatically call attention to the fact,' he had told the Norwegian Geographical Society, 'that a race to the [North] Pole is not the object of this Expedition, its chief aim being to study in a scientific manner the Polar sea itself.'*

Then arrived the news that Peary and Hansen had reached the North Pole. 'It was therefore with a clear conscience that I decided to postpone my original plan for a year or two,' Amundsen wrote, 'and try to solve the last

* From a translation of the address forwarded by Markham to the RGS, on 15 October 1910, with the comment 'What an imposter!'

great problem – the South Pole.' It was also true, as he admitted, that he was heavily in debt and knew that his best chance of raising money was to bring off a spectacular triumph. 'If I was to maintain my prestige as an explorer, I must quickly achieve a success of some sort. I resolved upon a *coup*. The British Expedition had been designed entirely for scientific research. The Pole was only a side issue.' (This was untrue; Scott's intention to try for the Pole had been widely publicised and was certainly not a side issue, although he might have wished it to be.) Amundsen kept his intention so secret that only two men, his brother Leon and the ship's commander, Lieutenant Nilsen, knew of it before the *Fram* reached Madeira, ostensibly on the way to Buenos Aires and thence northwards to the Arctic; the Madeira trip was supposed to be mainly for the purpose of oceanographical research.

The Norwegians left Christiania on 9 August 1910, eight weeks after the *Terra Nova* had sailed from Cardiff. On board were ninety-seven Greenland dogs, a hut in sections, and provisions for two years. At Madeira, Amundsen revealed his plan to his crew and all gave their consent. He left his telegram to Scott in a sealed envelope to be despatched after the *Fram* had sailed. He intended to proceed straight to the Ross Sea without calling at any port at all, so that once he had left Madeira he would be *incommunicado* until his gamble had been lost or won. This non-stop voyage was a remarkable feat in itself in so small a vessel, which had been designed like a saucer to drift with the ice and not to combat the stormiest oceans in the world. Moreover, the distance from Norway to the Great Ice Barrier is over 16,000 miles – the journey was only possible because the *Fram* had diesel engines and so did not have to call in for coal. Had the secret of his true objective leaked, his backers, and even more his creditors, would almost certainly have objected, and Nansen, a friend, admirer and adviser of Scott's, might not have lent him the *Fram*.

Once Amundsen had left Madeira he vanished, bound for an unknown destination. Scott never dreamt it would be the Ross Sea. In London, resentment was tempered by doubts – wishful doubts again – as to whether the *Fram* would ever get to the Antarctic at all. Sir Clements Markham, as usual, put his opinion pithily. 'She [the *Fram*] has no more sailing qualities than a haystack. In any case, Scott will be on the ground and settled long before Amundsen turns up, if he ever does.' Markham had his own sources of information in Norway and on 15 October 1910, while the *Fram* was still at sea, reported to the RGS secretary that Amundsen had 'quietly got a wintering hut made on board and 100 dogs and a supply of tents and sledges. His secret design must have been nearly a year old. They believe his mention of Punta Aranas and Buenos Aires is merely a blind, and that he is going to McMurdo Sound to try to cut out Scott . . . If I were Scott I would not let them land, but he is always too good-natured.' Markham's

Norwegian informants may well have been right about Amundsen's 'secret design' being nearly a year old; news of Peary's triumph was published in New York on 7 September 1909 and Amundsen set out eleven months later almost to the day.

Whatever the rights and wrongs of the matter, the general view among those involved in Scott's expedition was that Amundsen's behaviour was underhand. Oates, a sportsman through and through, surprisingly dissented. He wrote to his mother, 'What do you think about Amundsen's Expedition?'

If he gets to the Pole we shall come home with our tails between our legs and no mistake . . . They say Amundsen has been underhand in the way he has gone about it but personally I don't see it is underhand to keep your mouth shut. I myself think these Norskies are a very tough lot . . . and if Scott does anything silly such as underfeeding his ponies he will be beaten sure as death.

In Wellington, Scott told reporters that he would like to send Amundsen a good-luck telegram but did not know where to send it. If, at this stage, he felt chagrin, he concealed it. He was not going to change his plans in any way, he said, or compete in a race to the Pole which would interfere with the prosecution of scientific research.

He left Australia with the financial objective achieved. Yielding to the persuasive powers of Teddy Evans, who embraced him as a fellow Welshman, the acting Prime Minister, Mr Hughes, promised half the required sum. At a dinner in Sydney in aid of the appeal a department store owner, Mr Samuel Horden, ashamed of his country's parsimony, promised a further £2500 if the Government remained so niggardly. It did, and he made good his undertaking.

In Melbourne Admiral Poore RN, in command of the Australian station, went on board the *Terra Nova* for an official inspection and inspected, in particular, the ship's cat. Nigger had joined the expedition at Portsmouth when ten days old and been adopted by Petty Officer Frank Browning, who made him a miniature hammock with two small blankets and a pillow. He was soon at home in the rigging, but needed warm baths to wash the tar off his feet. When the Admiral came round he was asleep in his hammock. He woke up, gave one look at the Admiral, stretched his paws, turned over and went to sleep again.*

---

* Nigger, who had 'the most beautiful fur', had as companions on the voyage to McMurdo Sound three rabbits, one guinea pig, one fantail pigeon and another kitten. On the voyage back to New Zealand in 1911 something on deck scared him, and he jumped into a rough sea; the *Terra Nova* hove to, a boat was lowered and he was retrieved. He often went aloft in the rigging, and one dark stormy night in 1912, returning from his second voyage south he disappeared. It was thought that he had been aloft, ice had formed on the yards, and he had slipped and fallen.

After the inspection Teddy Evans, now happily back in command – Scott, still chasing money, went on to New Zealand, via Sydney, by liner – had his moment of triumph. In his midshipman days, a senior officer had told him that he would never make a good naval officer and ought to leave the Service; that senior officer was now Admiral Poore. Evans decided to take the 400-ton *Terra Nova* out of harbour under full sail in full view of the Admiral's 13,000 ton flagship and the rest of the squadron. To manoeuvre the old sailing ship in a crowded harbour was a tricky business, but 'it came off beautifully', Wilson wrote, 'and we got all sail set and sailed down the line of battleships looking most beautiful'. When they passed the flagship everyone manned the rigging and gave a great cheer, 'a thrilling experience, and all done so quickly, and neatly and successfully'. Even the Admiral, digesting his eaten words, would have been amazed to know that one day the triumphant Lieutenant would be Admiral of the Fleet Lord Mountevans, better known to the public as Evans of the Broke.

Wilson was thankful to be on board again and to slip back into the old routine of cocoa at midnight, up at 4 a.m. to sketch the sunrise, the day spent skinning and painting birds, catching albatrosses, trimming coalbunkers, and teaching taxidermy to Petty Officer Abbott, 'an exceedingly nice gentlemanly fellow'. 'We are again a *very* merry party,' he wrote. They celebrated Evans' twenty-ninth birthday by a champagne dinner, followed by a session of Furl Topgallant Sails which left everyone practically naked. It was a wonder that the afterguard had any clothes left at all by the time they reached Antarctica.

Scott had a much less cheerful time in Sydney, making speeches, paying formal calls on notables and trying to drum up cash. Here he met the three geologists, one Australian by birth and one by adoption, who were to join the team: Raymond Priestley, aged twenty-four, from Tewkesbury; Frank Debenham, aged twenty-seven, from New South Wales; and Thomas Griffith Taylor from Essex, aged thirty. Scott's modesty and frankness went down well with the press. He made no high claims, and reporters were impressed by his sincerity and sense of purpose. As to his chances, he was realistic. 'None can foretell our luck. We may get through, we may not. We may have accidents to some of the transports, to the sledges, or to the animals. We may lose our lives. We may be wiped out. It is all a question that lies with providence and luck.'

On 27 October 1910 the Scotts reached New Zealand and were among old friends. Sir Charles and Lady Bowen (Markham's sister) were in Wellington to greet them and, in Lyttleton, Joseph J. Kinsey who acted as the expedition's agent and had become a good friend. They stayed in the Kinseys' house at Clifton on the edge of a 400-foot cliff above the sea overlooking the fertile Christchurch plains and the estuary of two small rivers, with a range of snow-capped mountains far away. 'There we were for a happy happy fortnight,' Kathleen wrote, 'working and climbing with bare toes and my hair down and the sun and my Con and all the Expedition going well. It was good and by night we slept in the garden and the gods be blest.'

The *Terra Nova* was emptied of all her stores and taken into dry dock where the leak was hunted, with success, although it could not be entirely cured. Bowers worked with systematic energy to sort out all the stores, take in new ones, and re-stow them in the right order for unloading; everything was banded, red for the Main Party and green for the Eastern one. The two huts which had come out in sections were erected on a piece of waste land by the men who would do the job when they reached winter quarters. Scientific instruments were checked and repacked and stowed. An extra-ordinary collection of objects was crammed into the little vessel. The bulk-iest items were the coal, forage for the ponies, and the three motor sledges in their wooden crates lashed to the deck. Almost the worst problem was to get in enough coal. Oates kept agitating for more pony fodder. Scott said he could only take thirty tons, Oates wanted forty-five. 'When I tackled him,' wrote Oates, 'he said not one over 30 so it's no good arguing, however we argued for one hour and he has given way which shows that he is open to reason but they will have to leave some coal behind to get the extra forage in. He told me I was a something nuisance.' No wonder; if they took on too little coal they would be stranded in Antarctica, too little pony fodder and they would not reach the Pole.

Ponies and dogs were waiting for the expedition on Quail Island in Lyttle-ton Bay, together with Wilfrid Bruce, Cecil Meares and the two young Russians, Anton Omelchenko and Dimitri Gerof. Scott went to inspect the animals and was delighted; he thought the dogs the finest lot ever got together, and Oates called the ponies first-class. (He changed his mind later and it is surprising that so experienced a horse-master did not examine their mouths more carefully, and discover the fact that some of them were much too old, and should not have been bought in the first place.) Stalls were built for fifteen ponies under the forecastle, and for the remaining four on the main hatch; but a small, overloaded sailing vessel bound across tem-pestuous oceans could not afford much comfort to ponies. The thirty-three dogs were chained to bolts and stanchions on the ice-house and the main hatch, between the motor sledges. Scott managed to get 405 tons of coal into the bunkers and main hold, twenty-five into the fore hold and thirty tons were stacked in sacks on the upper deck. Oates smuggled an extra two tons of fodder on board without the Owner's knowledge.

In the ice-house were three tons of ice, 162 carcases of mutton, three of beef, and cases of sweetbreads and kidneys; in the break of the poop a stack of petrol cases; scientific equipment overflowed from tiny laboratories;

stacks of provisions were everywhere; the wooden huts, an acetylene plant, sledges, clothing, five tons of dog food, a hundred and one other things had been squeezed in. There was scarcely room for anyone to move. 'The men were prepared to pig it anyhow, and a few cubic feet of space didn't matter – such was their spirit.'

There were, as usual, tiresome worries. Petty Officer Evans got drunk again, as in Cardiff, and disgraced the ship; he was put on a train for Port Chalmers to keep him out of harm's way. And then, the day before the final departure from Port Chalmers, the other Evans came to Scott 'excited by vague and wild grievances, the only reasonable one concerning Evans P.O. The cause of it all is not difficult to guess.'

The cause was trouble between the three wives. Hilda Evans was dreading the departure of her husband and gave way more openly to her distress than the others. Nerves were on edge. She worked her husband up to accusing Scott of various shortcomings. Tempers got heated and the three wives had a set-to described by Oates in sporting terms.

Mrs Scott and Mrs Evans had a magnificent battle, they tell me it was a draw after 15 rounds. Mrs Wilson flung herself into the fight after the 10th round and there was more blood and hair flying about the hotel than you see in a Chicago slaughter-house in a month, the husbands got a bit of the backwash and there is a certain amount of coolness which I hope they won't bring into the hut with them, however it won't hurt me even if they do.

Scott managed to placate Teddy Evans and once at sea all was well. Kathleen drew from the incident support for her anti feminism. 'If ever Con has another expedition, the wives must be chosen more carefully than the men – better still, have none.'

On 26 November 1910, the *Terra Nova* sailed for Dunedin and Port Chalmers, seen off by a multitude of well-wishers. The Scotts did not sail with her but came back in the harbour tug and had their last two days together walking over hills to Sumner with bathing suits and a razor for their luggage – 'a good merry day for our last alone'. Early on the 28 November they took the train to Port Chalmers. The Scotts and the Wilsons each had a carriage to themselves and at every stop people came to wish them luck. Next morning the Wilsons called on the curator of the Port Chalmers museum and Scott accepted a parting present of 130 grey jerseys. Then, in the afternoon, it was time for the last farewells. The harbour swarmed with tugs and small boats, their occupants waving and cheering. At last a tug took off the three wives and 'there on the bridge', Wilson wrote of Ory, 'I saw her disappear out of sight waving happily, a goodbye that will be with me till the day I see her again in this world or the next – I think it will be in this world and some time in 1912.'

Kathleen wrote, 'I didn't say goodbye to my man because I didn't want anyone to see him sad. On the bridge of the tug Mrs Evans looked ghastly white and said she wanted to have hysterics but instead we took photos of the departing ship. Mrs Wilson was plucky and good . . . I mustered them all for tea in the stern and we all chatted gaily except Mrs Wilson who sat looking somewhat sphinx-like.' After parting company with the other wives, she paid a visit to a babies' home.

The ship sailed at about 4.30 p.m. on 29 November 1910. For many of her crew, it would be a year and a half before they would see any green and living thing; five on board would never see a tree, a flower or a woman's face again.

# 20

# To One Ton Depot

For the first few days, despite the over-loading of the ship and the seasick-ness of most of the landsmen, all went well. But Scott was distressed about the ponies, packed tightly in their stalls and 'swaying, swaying continually to the plunging irregular motion', looking out with 'sad, patient eyes'. The dogs were no better off. Continually soaked by spray, they sat with wet and dripping coats in an attitude expressing cold and misery; now and again one would give a long pathetic whine. 'Such a life is truly hard for these poor creatures.'

On 2 December 1910, only three days out, they were hit by a tremendous storm. Hurricanes were frequent in these latitudes, but the *Discovery* had escaped anything so vicious. (So did the *Fram*.) Accounts given in diaries read like something out of Conrad, but the overloading and the animals made it worse.

Mountainous waves breaking over the little vessel dislodged the deck cargo and turned sacks of coal and cases of petrol, washed to and fro, into battering rams. The men striving to secure them were swept off their feet and only by a miracle not overboard. The dogs were hurled to and fro on their chains and one disappeared. The ponies' sufferings were appalling; one of them died. Seas broke over the decks with such violence that the elderly planks gave way and water poured into the waist, the cabins and the engine room.

Then the pumps choked. Coal dust mingling with bilge water and engine oil clogged into balls which lodged in the pump valves, and blocked them. Water rose to the furnaces, the fires had to be drawn and, in Bowers' words, 'we realised for the first time that the ship was slowly sinking'. Not so slowly either; an enormous sea tore away part of the bulwarks and 'the scene on deck was devastating. Captain Scott was simply splendid, he might have been at Cowes. He said quietly "I am afraid it is a bad business for us – what do you think?" I said we were by no means dead yet, though at that moment Oates, at peril of his life, got aft to report another horse dead, and more down.' Soon Bowers was diving after petrol cases. 'Captain Scott calmly told me that "they did not matter" – this was our great project for getting to the Pole – the much advertised motors that "did not matter"; our dogs looked finished and our horses were finishing.'

Scott and Teddy Evans decided to attempt to bale out the ship by hand with buckets. The afterguard, several of them hideously seasick, were set to work in two-hour watches to fill heavy buckets in the stoke-hold and hand them up two narrow iron ladders.

It was a weird night's work, [Wilson wrote] with the howling gale and the darkness and the immense sea running over the ship every few minutes, and no engine and no sail, and we all in the engine-room black as ink with engine-room oil and bilge water, singing chanties as we passed up slopping buckets full of bilge, each man above slopping a little over the heads of all of us below him, wet through to the skin, so much so that some of the party worked altogether naked . . . The ship all the time rolling like a sodden, lifeless log, her lee gunwale under water every time.

By morning the sea had begun to ease a little and the water in the engine-room, though not reduced, had been prevented from rising. Williams, the chief engineer, and Davies, the carpenter, had started to cut a hole through the engine-room bulkhead to reach the suction well of the hand-pump, which was flooded. The boilers were still hot and the men worked in sweltering conditions and up to their waists in water to drill through the metal, which took nearly twelve hours. By 10 p.m. that evening the hole was big enough for Teddy Evans to wriggle through, reach the pump-shaft and, standing up to his neck in water, clear the valves. 'To the joy of all a good stream of water came from the pump for the first time,' Scott recorded. 'From this moment it was evident that we should get over the difficulty and though the pump choked again on several occasions, the water in the engine room steadily declined.' By noon the fires were lighted, bilges sucked dry, coal and ashes cleared and 'now all is well again and we are steaming steadily within two points of our course'. The two dead ponies were lifted out through the forecastle skylight. The other ponies, while groggy, were alive, and only one dog was lost.

At any rate in retrospect, the voluntary slaves enjoyed their experience. Raymond Priestley wrote that the ship at her worst would have given Dante a good idea for another Circle of Hell 'though he would have been at a loss to account for such a cheerful and ribald lot of Souls'. Bowers ended his letter to his mother with the comment, 'Under its worst conditions this earth is a good place to live in.' Wilson, in whose character tenderness and love of nature were so strangely blended with an almost ruthless toughness, wrote, 'I must say I enjoyed it all from beginning to end.' (He was spared seasickness.)

To him had come a special experience. Just when things were at their blackest and, to top it all, the ship appeared to be on fire (a false alarm) 'there came out a most perfect and brilliant rainbow for about half a minute or

less, and then suddenly and completely went out'. No one else commented
on this rainbow; might it have appeared only to the inner eye of faith?
Certainly he took it as a message which 'seemed to remove every shadow of
doubt, not only as to the present issue, but as to the final issue of the whole
Expedition – and from that moment matters mended and everything came
all right'.

Others might have argued that from the moment when the storm hit
them a great many things, if not everything, went all wrong. Scott said
often that the outcome, however hard they strove, must ultimately rest in
the hands of providence. And on his second expedition, unlike his first, luck
deserted him. He made mistakes of course, but also those forces known to
the ancient Greeks as the Eumenides were against him. A Greek might
have seen in this tempest Poseidon's warning that the gods had not blessed
the enterprise.

Immediate stock-taking, however, showed a better situation than anyone
had expected. Two ponies lost, also one dog, about ten tons of coal, sixty-
five gallons of petrol, and a case of biologists' spirit: things might have been
much worse. Three days later the Captain was able to write, 'Everyone is
very cheerful – one hears laughter and song all day – it's delightful to be
with such a merry crew.' But he still worried about the seventeen surviving
ponies, all bedraggled and woebegone. He speculated about their psychol-
ogy. Would they remember the 'slow but inevitable torture' of this voyage?
Or did only sudden pain and shock impress themselves on equine memories?
He never grew callous; his compassion for animals deepened with the years
rather than the reverse. Many Blue Whales (*Balaenoptera sibbaldi*) were
passed, the largest creatures in existence, their blows so high as to look like
the smoke of factory chimneys; he would have been appalled had he known
that within fifty years this whole species, once so numerous, would, through
man's rapacity, have become all but extinct.

On 8 December 1910 the first berg was sighted and on the following day,
in latitude 65°8's, the *Terra Nova* entered the pack. Tabular bergs, some of
them eighty feet high, were all about them. For the next three weeks,
worry was the Captain's bedfellow. The ship had to be coaxed, zigzagged,
shoved and bashed through a great belt of floating ice, some pieces up to
thirty feet thick. Sometimes a lead opened up through which the ship
could make her way, but much more often the ice coagulated into an
impassable barrier and there was nothing to be done but bank fires, or put
them out, and wait. Which to do? Coal economy was vital. Two tons were
needed to re-heat the boilers; two tons were consumed in twelve hours by
banked fires; therefore it paid to rake out the fires for anything over a
twelve-hour delay. So at every hold-up, Scott had to guess at its duration.
No wonder he wrote 'it is a very, very trying time', and again 'it is difficult

to keep hope alive'. He kept urging himself to exercise patience, patience: never his strong suit.

Everyone else was having a delightful time. The pack, with its variety of ice formations, was full of interest and of beauty. It teemed with life: above the surface penguins, both Emperor and Adélie; seals propelling themselves over the floes; several species of albatross; skuas, Cape Pigeons, petrels of various kinds, including the loveliest of all, the pure white Snow Petrel; in the sea whales, Sea Leopards, fish of many kinds and millions of *Euphausia* or krills – reddish orange little shrimp-like schizopods – which formed the food of almost every other living creature, from seals to penguins, fish to whales. At the bottom of the food-chain were the diatoms, a kind of plankton present in such quantities as to colour the ice orange and yellow on its underside. The tow-nets of the biologists brought to the surface a great variety of marine creatures; curiously enough, Antarctic waters proved to be much richer in life than temperate or tropic seas. Beneath the placid ice floes and under calm pools, Scott noted sombrely, still chafing at the ship's imprisonment, 'the old universal warfare is raging incessantly in the struggle for existence'.

For Wilson, days in the pack seemed to fly. After his early-morning mug of cocoa he spent happy hours in the crow's-nest (a barrel lashed to the mast) watching birds and trying to capture on paper the marvellous shapes and colours of the floes and bergs that lay all about them. The 'great white South' was not white at all but kaleidoscopic in colour: the ice violet and purple in shadow, and gold, orange and rose-red where its broken edges caught the light; the sky emerald green and salmon pink, reflected in still pools between the floes. Wonderful as day-time tints were, 'no scene in the whole world was ever more beautiful than a clear midnight in the pack', Wilson wrote. The ice turned a deep purple and golden rose, the cloudless sky a lemon-green. Apart from sketching there were many tasks: shooting seals – a hateful business – and hauling them in from the floe, then skinning and flensing them; with Cherry-Garrard and Abbott, skinning penguins needed for dinner and birds caught or shot for his collection; taking his turn at the hand-pump, and so on. On Sundays, he climbed to the crow's-nest and read the Holy Communion service to himself. Everyone was busy, and no one was ill.

For light relief, there were the Adélie Penguins, like rather portly gentlemen full of their own importance and late for dinner, hurrying across the ice in their white shirt-fronts and black tail-coats to investigate the unfamiliar intruders and crying 'aark, aark' as they went. They had no fear, but an insatiable curiosity, and drove the dogs wild with lust to kill. On one occasion a little penguin became so angry with a man who tried to keep it from a sudden end in the jaws of a dog that it seized its rescuer's trousers in its beak and pummelled his shins with its flippers. The Adélies would come up at a trot when they were sung to; a group of men would gather on the poop and sing 'she's got bells on her fingers and rings on her toes, elephants to ride on wherever she goes' to a cluster of admiring birds. Meares had the loudest voice, and when he sang 'God Save the King' they dived into the water.

There sometimes lay in wait their deadly enemy, the Sea Leopard; Levick counted eighteen penguins in the stomach of a single one of these predatory seals. Comical and rather clumsy on the floe, in the water the Adélie was a different creature, twisting and turning with grace and skill, but with little avail when a Sea Leopard had marked him down. Atkinson was delighted to find a new parasite in the Adélie's intestines; it had a propeller-shaped head.

In the pack, Bowers was the boldest navigator, and sometimes alarmed the Owner by great bumps and collisions during his watch. Enormous bergs drifted silently by. Then came a gale, a long swell, and a weakening of the ice. On 30 December 1910 Scott was able to write in his journal, 'We are out of the pack at length and at last; one breathes again.' Measured in a direct line, the belt of pack-ice had been 370 miles deep and had taken twenty days to traverse. (The *Discovery* had taken less than five days.) The *Terra Nova* had used up sixty-one tons of precious coal. But now at last the open water of the Ross Sea lay ahead and 'the spirit of the enterprise is as bright as ever'. At midnight on the last day of 1910 the great snow-clad peaks of the Admiralty Range could be seen, 110 miles away and glittering in the sunlight. On New Year's Day the afterguard sunned themselves 'like rattlesnakes' on the poop, and in the evening enjoyed the best plum pudding Wilson had ever eaten, made by his parents' cook. Mt Erebus with its plume of smoke came into view. For Scott and Wilson, it was almost like coming home.

An attempt to land at Cape Crozier, where they had hoped to establish their base, was abandoned owing to rough seas. 'No good!! Alas!' Scott wrote, and Wilson was even more disappointed because they observed an Emperor Penguin chick, still in its down, stranded on a piece of ice and left behind when the rest of the colony had drifted northwards on a floe. Its 'faithful old parent' was standing near by, sound asleep. No chick in this stage of development had been seen before and 'it would have been a treasure to me', Wilson observed. But the boat would have been dashed to pieces had an attempt been made to secure it. As it was, they narrowly escaped destruction when a chunk of an overhanging cliff under whose brow they had just been rowing broke off with a noise like thunder, and crashed into the sea a couple of hundred yards behind them. The superstitious might have seen in this another warning from the watchful gods.

So McMurdo Sound it had to be, once more, for winter quarters. Rounding Cape Bird, the north-west tip of Ross Island, they proceeded down the coast and past familiar landmarks: Cape Royds, where the only change was Shackleton's hut with its squalid litter that sullied the polar purity around any human encampment; Inaccessible Island; then the lofty Cape Barne and its glacier sloping down from Mt Erebus. Scott noticed an entirely new kind of floe covered with scales, each scale consisting of little flaky ice-sheets superimposed.

They were looking for a winter base that would not, if possible, be cut off from the Barrier by open water. In a cape of moraine and rock, hitherto known as the Skuary, they found it. After a conference between Scott, Evans and Wilson this spot was chosen and re-named Cape Evans. About a mile and a half of firm ice lay between shore and open sea. On 4 January 1911 the *Terra Nova* made fast with ice-anchors and the unloading began. Across the bay stretched a panorama of ice-clad mountains which sent Herbert Ponting into rhapsodies. The ponies greeted their freedom by rolling and kicking in the snow, and Scott remarked how glad they must be to have a good scratch after enduring irritation for five weeks without being able to get at its source. He remarked also, sadly, on the suicidal behaviour of the Adélie Penguins who constantly waddled up towards the dog-teams, quite unable to comprehend their danger. 'There is a spring, a squawk, a horrid red patch on the snow, and the incident is closed. Nothing can stop these silly birds.'

The first two motors to be unloaded started up without trouble and hauled loaded sledges with gratifying speed to the base camp that was taking shape. Then the third and largest was winched on to the ice and hauled shorewards by about twenty men. Without warning it broke through the ice and sank in sixty fathoms. Scott rightly blamed himself for not having taken sufficient care to test the ice. He was in a hurry to get everything unloaded and the *Terra Nova* away to disembark Campbell's party in King Edward VII Land.

The ponies soon revealed themselves to be uneven in quality. Each displayed a separate personality. Weary Willie was self-explanatory. Christopher and Hackenschmidt fought, kicked and bolted to the very end. Chinaman ran away with Wilson until all ended together in a tangle of sledge, man and pony after sliding twenty yards.

The hut went up rapidly. It was fifty feet by twenty-five, and nine feet to the eaves, insulated with quilted seaweed, lined with matchboard, lit by acetylene gas, provided with a stove and cooking range, and divided into two by a partition made of crates (including the wine) to separate the men's from the officers' quarters, as naval tradition decreed.

Unloading began on 4 January 1911; by the 18th the hut was occupied,

the gramophone going and everyone warm and happy. Stores were stacked
in perfect order, ponies stabled; all the scientific gear installed. A grotto
had been hollowed out in the ice-clad hillside to house the, magnetic
instruments. 'Nothing like it has ever been done before,' Scott recorded,
'nothing so expeditious and complete.' As always fearing to tempt the
gods, he added, 'Our camp is becoming so perfect in its appointments that
I am almost suspicious of some drawback hidden by the summer weather.'
Wilson wrote emphatically, 'I have *never* been thrown with a more unselfish lot of men – each one doing his utmost fair and square in the most
cheery manner possible.'

Before starting on the depot-laying journey across the Barrier and
towards the Pole, Scott with Meares and a dog-team (the dogs had to be
addressed in Russian) travelled the fifteen miles south to revisit Hut Point.
He received an unpleasant shock. The window had been left open, snow
had drifted in and then frozen into a solid block of ice. The hut was un-
inhabitable. He knew who was to blame – Shackleton, who had made use of
the place three years earlier when his base had been Cape Evans. Scott was
touched on a raw nerve. 'It is difficult to conceive the absolutely selfish
frame of mind that can perpetrate a deed like this . . . finding that such a
simple duty had been neglected by one's immediate predecessors disgusted
me horribly.'

By contrast, their own dwelling was so well-found that to apply to it the
word 'hut' seemed like an insult. Bowers had been the chief architect, and
'every day he conceives or carries out some plan to benefit the camp'.
Every man was, in his own way, a treasure, the clothing and equipment
'good as good', the stores perfectly ordered and nothing had been forgotten. The cook served up seal rissoles indistinguishable from the best
beef ones. For a few days Scott's diary was almost euphoric.

On 24 January 1911 the depot-laying party got away, with all the dogs
and eight ponies, across the Glacier Tongue and on to the Barrier. Wilson
and Meares drove the dogs. With the Captain went Teddy Evans, Bowers
and Oates, Atkinson, Cherry-Garrard and Gran, the seamen Crean, Forde
and Keohane, and Dimitri Gerof, the Russian dog-driver. Two days later,
Scott with a dog-team went back to the ship across the ice to say good-bye
to Lieutenant Pennell and his crew. He expected that by the time the
depot-laying party got back to base, the *Terra Nova* would have sailed for
New Zealand after depositing Campbell and his five companions – Raymond Priestley, surgeon Levick, and three petty officers, Browning,
Dickason and Abbott – with a hut and two ponies, somewhere on King
Edward VII Land. Also on board the ship were Griffith Taylor and
Debenham who, with Wright and Edgar Evans, were to geologise in the
mountains of Victoria Land. Mail was handed over. Scott had already given

Kathleen a letter to read when she got back to England. It was more the letter of a pupil to his sage than that of a lover. Their short separation had taught him 'how much happiness you have brought me, and how much I have grown to depend on you, and how sweet to me that dependence is. I shall be thinking of the wise things you did and made me do until you brought me to a better sense of the fitness of things. You have taught me many things, and, best of all, to value things more rightly.'

Two days later the depot-laying party was on the Barrier, establishing a camp far enough from its edge to be out of danger of the ice breaking away. They called this Safety Camp, and here made their final preparations for the southward journey. Already there were doubts about the ponies. The snow was softer than anticipated, the ponies sank in with every step and floundered, and one went lame. A complete outfit of pony snow-shoes had been unloaded from the ship. Scott now discovered that all but one set had been left at Cape Evans. This set was tried on Weary Willie with results that he described as 'magical'. Yet Oates 'hasn't any faith in these shoes at all'; it was for this reason, no doubt, that they had been left behind. Devoted as he was to his charges, Oates was inclined to regard other people's ideas with suspicion. Meares and Wilson were sent back with a dog-team to fetch the shoes but, on reaching the Glacier Tongue, found that all the sea ice had broken away and that they could not reach the base at Cape Evans. 'No pony shoes – alas!' Scott wrote; he thought the ponies could have doubled their distances had they worn snow-shoes. He did not say so, but Oates was to blame for this lapse.

On 2 February 1911 the party set forth with five weeks' provisions, leaving behind two disappointed men: Atkinson with a sore heel and Crean to look after him. Each pony drew a sledge, and had a man on foot or on skis leading him. The dog-teams, which were much faster, stayed in camp each day a couple of hours or so longer and caught up the pony cavalcade at lunch time. Soon the ponies were floundering again. Scott inquired for the one set of snow-shoes and found that Oates had left it behind at Safety Camp. Tryggve Gran on his skis went back to fetch it.

As the heat of the day-time sun softened the snow, night marches were decided on in the hope of firmer going. By day the ponies were rugged-up and protected from wind by snow-walls built at every camp. They marched first in an easterly direction to clear an area of crevasses and then, at Corner Camp, headed south, averaging ten or eleven miles a day. Bowers' pony, Uncle Bill, the clumsiest and heaviest, wore the snow-shoes, and Scott thought that seven out of the eight animals, possibly the eighth also, could have used them. With restraint he remarked that it was 'trying to feel that so great a help to our work has been left behind'. Perhaps the leader should have seen to it, but he had delegated everything relating to the ponies' welfare to Oates. He found it painful to watch them panting and heaving, sometimes plunging forward in a series of jerks, and doing their best. The quiet, lazy animals came off better than the eager tryers.

At Corner Camp they were held up for three days by their first blizzard. Cherry-Garrard found it pleasantly restful to doze in his soft, warm reindeer-skin bag, lulled by the deep boom of the tent flapping in the gale and rousing himself only to eat hot meals and drink cocoa. Even Scott enjoyed an excellent meal, a quiet pipe and desultory conversation while the blizzard raged outside. But the old demon impatience soon attacked him, together with anxiety about the ponies, who grew more and more miserable. The dogs, on the other hand, appeared to be quite happy; each one dug a hollow, curled up and went to sleep, to emerge only to eat his biscuit. Sometimes two shared a hollow. It must have been irrefutable by now that dogs were very much better adapted to the climate than ponies, but if Scott realised his mistake he would not admit it.

From Corner Camp they marched due south for ten nights to make their final depot. The ponies were visibly weakening, three in particular. At Camp 11 Scott decided to send them back with their escorts and push on with the remaining five. For the next two days conditions worsened with heavy snow-drift, colder temperatures and bad surfaces. Weary Willy, led by Gran, grew wearier than ever, lagged behind, and was overtaken by the dog-teams driven by Meares and Wilson. Suddenly the dogs underwent a transformation. The wolf in them burst through its veneer of domestication and the two teams fell upon the pony which was struggling in a snow-drift. Gran, Meares and Wilson lashed about them with ski-sticks and whips and eventually got the dogs off, but not before the pony had been badly bitten. Weary Willy was led to camp and Scott with three others dragged in the loaded sledge. This, he said, brought home to them the nature of the surface and the task demanded of the ponies.

Next day Weary Willy was able to proceed, but Uncle Bill was failing. 'A good snow-shoe would be worth its weight in gold,' Scott believed. The temperature on the march fell to −21°F and they advanced less than seven miles. At Camp 15, on 17 February, Scott decided to turn back before reaching, as he had hoped, the 80th parallel. At 79° 28½'s, 142 miles from Hut Point, they built a cairn and deposited more than a ton of stores. This was One Ton Depot, whose name was to acquire so ominous a ring. Already the short season was closing in; Oates' nose was frostbitten, Meares had a bad toe and even Bowers, who went everywhere in a small green hat with a chin-strap, scorning balaclavas, got bitten ears. Scott wondered how, at his age, he would stand up to conditions on the summit. 'This cold spell gives ideas. I think I shall be all right, but one must be prepared for a pretty good doing.'

Meanwhile he wanted to get back to Hut Point where Pennell was to have left news of Campbell's party. He attached himself and Cherry-Garrard to the two dog-teams, leaving Bowers, Oates and Gran, to bring back the ponies at their own pace. The dogs were going well; Meares was a competent driver in the Russian style, and Wilson an apt pupil. Like Scott, he took a great interest in the dogs' personalities. Stareek, his leader, was a wise old man and 'quite the nicest, quietest, cleverest old dog gentleman I have ever come across'.* He looked as if he knew all the wickedness of the world and all its cares, and was bored to death by both of them. Osman was the other leader. In his team a small, hard-working dog called Mukaka was paired with a fat, lazy, greedy, black one called Nugis, who was a shirker; every now and again Mukaka jumped over the trace, gave Nugis a sharp nip and jumped back without disturbing the rhythm of the march. Wilson came to love each one of his eleven dogs and they came to know him well and answer to his voice. 'Dog driving in this orthodox manner is a very different thing to the beastly dog driving we perpetrated in the *Discovery* days.'

The two dog-teams each drawing a sledge covered seventy-eight miles on the first three days of the return journey, a distance that the ponies had needed nine days to cover outward bound. The men took it in turns to ride on the sledges and to run beside them. On the fourth day they were within twelve miles of Safety Camp, but in trying to take a short cut found themselves in a crevassed area close to White Island. Suddenly Wilson saw Meares' and Scott's dogs disappear one after the other 'exactly like rats running down a hole – only I saw no hole. They simply went into the white surface and disappeared.' The sledge hung precariously on the edge of the crevasse, resting on the snow-bridge along which it had been travelling. Osman and the two hindmost dogs remained on the brink, straining against the weight of the eight dogs who were dangling in the abyss and writhing, howling and struggling. Two of the dogs slipped their harness and fell another forty feet to a snow ledge, where they curled up and went to sleep.

* Stareek, whose name means 'old man', had been first a trappers' dog and then a mail-dog on the Amur river. 'He was not one to curry favour by extravagant tail-waggings or to go berserk with blood-lust at sight of penguins,' Debenham wrote. On occasions when a surface layer of packed snow subsided under the weight of a sledge, and air escaped with a noise like a muffled report, Stareek jumped sideways to land with all four feet on the spot, possibly hoping to discover a rabbit. On the polar journey his age told on him and he was sent back with Day and Hooper, but broke away on the first night and disappeared. Eighteen days later he reappeared during the night, a shadow of himself, having followed the men's tracks without a morsel of food for 200 miles. Astonished by his willpower and endurance, the men took him back, partly on the sledge. He recovered, and took his place as leader of a team driven by Debenham, who came to regard him as almost human. But three weeks before the *Terra Nova* sailed, Stareek quietly died.

Wilson and Cherry-Garrard came to the rescue and the four men hauled the sledge to safety, unloaded it and used it as a bridge across the chasm. Then, with the alpine rope, they hauled out the dogs two by two with great difficulty, and pressure on Osman, who was being choked by the trace looped around his chest, was relieved. Had this powerful dog not stood firm on the lip of the crevasse, the sledge must have gone through with the rest of the team.

There remained the two dogs on the snow-ledge which, measured by the alpine rope, was sixty-five feet down. Scott insisted on being lowered to rescue them despite protests from Wilson. Far from showing signs of gratitude, no sooner had they been hauled to safety than they engaged in a free fight with Wilson's team, and Scott was left dangling in the abyss while the others rushed off to separate the fighting animals. They then returned to haul up Scott who, for once showing no signs of impatience, kept muttering (Cherry-Garrard recorded) 'I wonder why this is running the way it is – you expect to find them at right angles,' and wanted to stay down and explore the crevasse. His main regret was that he had no thermometer to measure the temperature of the Barrier down a ready-made hole. Next day the party reached Safety Camp to find waiting there Teddy Evans, Ford and Keohane, but only one pony. Blücher and Blossom had died of exhaustion on the way back and Scott's party had passed unknowingly the cairns that marked their graves.

There was no news of Campbell, so after a meal and a few hours' sleep they went on to Hut Point man-hauling their sledge. The dogs were worn out and ravenously hungry, clearly underfed. Biscuit alone was not enough. Scott commented:

Meares is excellent to a point, but a little pig-headed and quite ignorant of conditions here. One thing is certain, the dogs will never continue to drag heavy loads with men sitting on the sledges; we must all learn to run with the teams and the Russian custom must be dropped. Meares is loath to run and I think rather imagined himself racing to the Pole and back on a dog sledge. This journey has opened his eyes a good deal.

The hut, now habitable again, was empty. A note pinned on the wall said, 'Mail for Captain Scott is in bag inside south door'; but there was no bag and no mail, only a fresh onion and some bread as evidence of recent human occupation. So back they went to Safety Camp, to find Atkinson, his foot healed, with Crean – and the mail. 'Every incident of the day pales before the startling contents of the mail bag,' Scott wrote.

# 21

# The Worst Journey

In the mail-bag was a letter from Victor Campbell. The *Terra Nova* had sailed along the Barrier to its eastern extremity and Pennell, like Scott himself and Shackleton, had been unable to effect a landing on King Edward VII Land. They had turned back, and at midnight on 3 February 1911 sailed into the Bay of Whales. They saw a ship, anchored to the ice, and recognised the *Fram*.

A round of courtesies followed. Campbell, Pennell and Levick had breakfast in the *Fram*, and Amundsen with two companions lunched in the *Terra Nova*; further visits were made, photographs taken, everyone was correct and polite. Amundsen offered to give Scott some of his dogs, and Pennell offered to take the *Fram*'s mail to New Zealand. There was wariness on both sides. Raymond Priestley learned that Amundsen had brought ten bitches, and that his ninety-seven dogs had increased to 116; that the try for the Pole would not take place until the following Antarctic summer; that the *Fram* had floated like a cork on rough seas; and that her crew had eaten fresh potatoes all the way from Norway (and so arrived, presumably, well stocked up with vitamins). Members of the British party were impressed and disturbed.

By a remarkably astute piece of reasoning, Amundsen had selected the Bay of Whales for his jumping-off place well before the *Fram* had sailed. Explorers had fought shy of the Barrier because it was afloat, and large chunks broke off each season and went out to sea. Amundsen noted that a bight, or bay, charted by Ross in 1841 was still in the same position when Borchgrevink landed there in 1900, and when Shackleton sailed by in 1908 and named it Bay of Whales. He drew the conclusion that the Barrier must be securely grounded at this point, possibly on submerged islets or reefs. The risk of finding his camp floating out to sea was therefore minimal. The Bay of Whales was some sixty miles nearer to the Pole than McMurdo Sound. If Shackleton had made his base there, Amundsen thought, he would have got to the Pole.

'We must at all costs get there first,' wrote the Norwegian. 'Everything must be staked on that.' There was to be no frittering away of effort in the cause of research. It was the Pole first, last and all the time. Amundsen had

brought a thoroughly professional, experienced, resolute team of men.
Each one could ski as well as he could walk. Priestley thought them 'a set of
men of distinctive personality, hard, and evidently inured to hardship, good
goers, and pleasant and good-humoured. All these qualities combine to
make them dangerous rivals.'

Above all they had dogs, plenty of dogs, and dogs as well-trained as
their masters. Nothing impressed Priestley more than Amundsen's arrival
with his team beside the *Terra Nova*. When he was abreast of the vessel he
gave a whistle, and the whole team stopped as one dog. He turned his
empty sledge upside down and left the dogs in their traces – to remain
there, without fighting, until he had finished his lunch. If Amundsen got
first to the Pole, Priestley concluded, he would owe it largely to his dogs.
The question was, could they get up the glacier? That remained to be seen.

The men in the *Terra Nova* could not but be aware that Norwegian dog-
management made British efforts appear very amateurish. As much attention was paid to the feeding and care of the dogs as to the welfare of the
men. In the *Fram* a false deck had been built above the real one with a space
between through which, in stormy weather, sea-water swished and drained
away, leaving the dogs comparatively dry; also an awning had been erected
to protect them from spray and from sun in the tropics. Their diet was a
carefully balanced mixture of dried fish, pemmican and lard, and seal-
meat while at the Bay of Whales. But no one could have called them pam-
pered; they were machines for getting the expedition to the Pole, and
Amundsen drove them until they dropped.

'There is no doubt that Amundsen's plan is a very serious menace to
ours,' Scott wrote in his diary after he had digested Campbell's news. The
Norwegians would have a shorter distance to travel, their scheme for managing their dogs seemed excellent and, above all, they could start earlier in the
season.

His [Amundsen's] proceedings have been very deliberate and success alone can
justify them. That the action is outside one's code of honour is not necessarily to
condemn it, and under no conditions will I be betrayed into a public expression of
opinion. One thing fixes itself definitely in my mind. The proper, as well as the
wiser, course for us is to proceed exactly as though this had not happened. To go
forward and do our best for the honour of the country without fear or panic.

This calm, judicial attitude was not shared by Scott's followers. Cherry-
Garrard felt a wild impulse to go straight to the Bay of Whales and have it out
with Amundsen. 'We had just paid the first instalment of making a path
to the Pole; and we felt, however unreasonably, that we had earned the first
right of way.' There was another factor too. The spirit of team-work and
solidarity amongst Scott's men had been brought to a very high pitch; they
had put aside all thought of rivalry within the team; now the serpent of

competition had entered into their Eden. Wilson alone was fairly optimistic; he thought that Amundsen had not taken into account the effect
on dogs of monotony, and of bad travelling surfaces on the Barrier. Scott
referred on more than one occasion to the effects of monotony. 'A dog must
either be eating, sleeping or *interested*. His eagerness to snatch at interest,
to chain his attention to something, is almost pathetic. The monotony of
marching kills him.' Amundsen got round this by the ingenious device of
planting frozen fish, tail upwards, at intervals along the line of march,
which served the double purpose of marking the homeward way and
interesting the dogs.

Scott had now to get everyone back to Hut Point, together with the dogs
and surviving ponies, but he had to wait for Bowers, Oates and Gran, who
were leading their animals slowly northwards from the last depot. To fill in
time, the party at Safety Camp with their one pony, took more supplies
down to Corner Camp. 'James Pigg, our own pony, limits the length of our
marches. The men haulers could go on much longer, and we all like pulling
on skis.' 'James Pigg also found the surface bad, so we camped after lunch
after doing 3 miles.' These sentences point up the absurdity of the situation
that had now been reached. The pace of the pony had become that of the
snail. The sledges had to be loaded with bulky fodder and at the end of the
march the men, who should have been resting warmly in their tents,
had to build snow-walls for ponies who constantly kicked them down.
Scott nowhere admitted it, but he must by now have realised what a terrible
mistake had been made.

He reached Safety Camp in a blizzard to find that Bowers, Oates and
Gran had arrived and that all five ponies were alive – but only just. They
were terribly emaciated. Now followed a sequence of events that was to add
up to a major disaster. To get back to Hut Point, men and ponies had to
traverse a stretch of sea ice below the Barrier's edge and march round Cape
Armitage, on the south-west corner of Ross Island. The alternative, to
cross the island itself, meant negotiating hills and pressure ridges too steep
and difficult for the worn-out ponies. This, the end of summer, was a tricky
season. Gales were increasing in frequency and liable to break up the icy
crust over the sea, even though this was quite thick; whereas frosts, severe as
they could be, were not yet severe enough to freeze the whole bay over. A
continual battle was fought in these latitudes between wind and frost for
possession of the sea.

On the last day of February 1911 the move back to Hut Point began.
Meares and Wilson led off with the dog-teams. Wilson was told to go round
by Cape Armitage if possible, but if he thought the ice unsafe to use his own
judgement. He did think so, made straight for Ross Island, and arrived
safely at Hut Point.

The others followed with the ponies and had to take the sea-ice route. They had barely started when Weary Willie collapsed. The party were obliged to camp on the spot and build a snow wall round him; after pitiful struggles, he died in the night. Scott was beginning to get despondent. The ponies' susceptibility to cold 'makes a late start *necessary for next year*'. He added, 'Well, we have done our best and bought our experience at heavy cost.'

The bill was not yet paid. While Scott with Oates and Gran stayed by Weary Willie's deathbed, Bowers with Crean and Cherry-Garrard went on ahead with the four surviving ponies and the loaded sledges. They dropped down off the Barrier on to sea-ice and started to pick their way round Cape Armitage in a black mist which pervaded everything, until they came to moving cracks which indicated that a swell was breaking up the ice. They turned back, and plodded on until they reached a snow-covered stretch of ice which Bowers judged to be safe. The ponies could go no farther, and here they camped and turned in.

After about two hours' sleep Bowers was awakened by a strange noise and went out. 'I cannot describe either the scene or my feelings,' he wrote. Everywhere the ice was breaking up and their camp was on a drifting floe. One of the ponies had disappeared, two of the sledges were on another floe and, as Bowers took it all in, their own floe split in two, by great good fortune leaving them all on the same piece.

Survival seemed unlikely, but Bowers never for a moment thought of abandoning the three remaining ponies and all four sledges to make a dash for safety with his companions. The only hope lay in heading for the land in a series of floe-hops. As soon as two floes drifted close enough together, the men hauled the sledges across and persuaded the ponies to jump. There was very little said. 'Crean like most bluejackets behaved as if he had done this sort of thing often before.' Cherry-Garrard distributed chocolate and biscuits. The ponies jumped bravely. Then came Killer Whales (*Orcinus orca*) who cruised about among the floes, 'their immense black fins sticking up, and blowing with a tremendous roar'. They soon had their eyes on the frightened ponies.

Six hours passed in this fashion before they reached the Barrier's edge, only to meet with an insuperable obstacle. A broad strip of water filled with smashed-up ice, and full of Killer Whales, intervened between the Barrier and their floe, and the Barrier itself presented a cliff twenty feet high. Crean volunteered to seek a way across, taking a note to Scott. The thing looked impossible; a single slip would have finished him, and several hours passed before his companions saw him safely up the ice-cliff and on the Barrier. 'It was not a pleasant day that Cherry and I spent there all alone,' Bowers admitted. Killer Whales were all about them, their ugly black and yellow heads at times only a yard or so away. At any moment a change in the wind might carry their floe out to sea. It resolved itself into a question 'as to whether the wind or Captain Scott would reach us first'.

The Captain won by a narrow margin. Bowers called up 'What about the ponies and sledges?' and Scott called down from the Barrier 'I don't care a damn about the ponies and sledges, it's you I want.' So, using two sledges as ladders, the two men clambered up. Bowers, however, was not going to abandon ponies and sledges whatever the Captain might say. 'I fought tooth and nail, and got him to concede one article and then another, and still the ice did not move till we had thrown and hauled up every article except the two ladders [sledges] and the ponies.' Oates was digging out a ramp for the animals to climb. And then, at this last moment, the ice started to move. The men managed to haul up the two remaining sledges before the floe drifted out of reach. After supper, Scott and Bowers went down to the Barrier's edge and saw the ponies standing disconsolately on their now distant floe, surrounded by Killer Whales. It was a gloomy moment. Bowers tried to cheer up his Captain but Scott replied, 'Of course we shall have a run for our money next season, but so far as the Pole is concerned I have little hope.' Cherry-Garrard had heard Scott say, as he helped his two lieutenants off the floe, 'This is the end of the Pole.'

Next morning, through field-glasses, Bowers saw that the ponies' floe had come to rest against a spur jutting out from the Barrier. Taking a tent and food, the whole party hurried to the spot. Bowers and Oates made their way out across the floes, reached the ponies, took one by the halter and put him at the first crack; he jibbed, and fell in. Oates had to end his struggles with a pick-axe. Meanwhile Scott had found another route and the two remaining ponies, Uncle Bill and Nobby, were brought to the brink of safety. Then Killer Whales rose out of the water to frighten Uncle Bill, who jumped sideways and missed his footing. Oates and Bowers managed to haul him out but he could not get to his feet. Three times he tried, and then fell into the water. At that moment, a piece of the Barrier broke away and Scott ordered them up. 'I can't leave him alive to be eaten by those whales,' Bowers said. Oates replied, 'I shall be sick if I have to kill another horse like I did the last.' Bowers seized the pick and struck the animal's head. 'I made sure of my job before we ran up and jumped the opening in the Barrier, carrying a blood-stained pick-axe instead of leading the pony.' Only Nobby, hauled up the Barrier edge by Scott, survived.

They had started on their depot-laying journey with eight ponies; they got back to Hut Point with two.

That the whole episode was not a chapter of accidents but part of a divine plan was the recorded conviction of two of the participants. 'I firmly believe,' Wilson wrote, 'that the whole train of what looked so like a series of petty mistakes and accidents was a beautiful pre-arranged plan in which each of us took exactly the moves and no others that an Almighty hand intended each of us to take – and no other . . . The whole thing was just a beautiful piece of education on a very impressive scale.' Bowers reached the same conclusion.

Six hours earlier we could have walked into the Hut on sound sea-ice. A few hours later we should have seen open water on arrival at the Barrier edge . . . everything fitted in to place us on the sea-ice during the only two hours in the whole year that we could possibly have been in such a position. Let those who believe in coincidence carry on believing. Nobody will ever convince me that there was not something more.

A warning from the gods – or God – in respect of hubris? 'Certainly we shall start for the Pole with less of that foolish spirit of blatant boast and ridiculous blind self-assurance, that characterized some of us on leaving Cardiff,' he concluded.

Bowers' faith in a divinity that ordered the fall of every sparrow was as absolute as Wilson's. One night when at sea – 'not in a vision, not after hearing emotional preaching etc.' – but alone on deck when asking himself, like Scott, what life was all about, Bowers felt the presence of Christ who 'came to me and showed me why we are here, and what the purpose of life really is'. It was to make a choice between the material and the spiritual; and if the spiritual were chosen, 'it will run like a silver thread through the material . . . I know my own powerful ambition to get on in this world will conflict with that pure light, but I can never forget that I did realise, in a flash, that nothing that happens to our bodies really matters'.

Three years later, recalling this experience, Bowers wrote, 'Who could refuse to stick up for such a friend, who even knew him from afar off?' On the earthly plane, love and devotion were centred on his mother. 'My love for you and the desire to remain with you always tempers my natural desire for a roving life which was born in me,' he wrote to her. 'You know at all events that your son loves and honours you above all things on earth.' His almost fanatical devotion to hard work, his passion for physical fitness – he, with Atkinson, stripped and washed in snow every morning – and even the confidences he gave only to his mother; all these might have grown, at least in part, from a sensitiveness to ridicule resulting from his ungainly appearance.

'It is ill to sit still and contemplate the ruin which has assailed our transport. The scheme of advance must be very different from that which I first contemplated. The Pole is a long way off, alas!' Scott lamented. 'Fortune is not being very kind to us.' All were now assembled (5 March 1911) at Hut Point with dogs and ponies, waiting for the sea separating them from

Cape Evans to freeze over. The heavily crevassed slopes of Mt Erebus at their back ruled out an overland journey.

Ten days later they were joined by the geologists led by Griffith Taylor, with Debenham, Wright and Petty Officer Edgar Evans, back from the western mountains and pleased with their finds. This brought the numbers in the hut up to sixteen, which meant overcrowding and no privacy. There was no equipment, and they improvised a blubber stove which covered everything with a greasy black deposit. Seal meat was their principal food. Killing the seals was a brutal business; the seal paid no attention to its executioner, who stunned it with a blow on the nose and then plunged a knife into its heart. Blizzards were frequent, but life in this dirty, dark, smoke-blackened little hut, with nothing but bare necessities, developed a strange attraction. Even Scott concluded 'We have achieved such great comfort here that one is half sorry to leave.'

At last, on 11 April 1911, he and half the party got away, leaving the rest to follow. He found the base at Cape Evans in good shape except that one of the ponies, Hackenschmidt, had died, and one dog. That left ten ponies out of the original nineteen. 'I scarcely like to express the mixed feelings with which I am able to regard this remnant.'

But he was cheered by the purposeful order of the base at Cape Evans where, under Simpson's direction, everything was clean and neat and tidy and, best of all, the scientific work was going well. Simpson's meteorological corner was full of sophisticated instruments, and the most complete set of observations as yet made in polar regions was being compiled. This time there would be no cavilling by Admiralty hydrographers. Ponting's photographs were outstanding, and remain today classics in polar photography. He had added a new word to the language, at least to that spoken by the *Terra Nova* men: to pont, which meant to pose in an often precarious position with a scene of grandeur behind. The hut was full of aids to comfort, including a device invented by Clissold the cook which rang a bell when his bread had risen to its correct height, then switched off the bell and turned on a light.

On 23 April 1911 the sun vanished beneath the horizon for the last time until August, invoking poetical thoughts from the leader. '*Impression*: The long mild twilight which like a silver clasp unites today with yesterday; when morning and evening sit together hand in hand beneath the starless sky of midnight.' He wondered whether everyone was not *too* comfortable at the base. 'I hope it will not make us slack.'

Scott wrote that the sledging season was at an end; but he had reckoned without Wilson. That extraordinary man had decided to undertake an even more extraordinary journey. He intended to go birds-nesting in the polar midwinter, in darkness, at temperatures of 100 degrees of frost, a venture that involved a final scramble down treacherous, precipitous cliffs barely scaleable at the best of times. Cape Crozier, his destination, was renowned for the ferocity of its blizzards, which swept across hundreds of miles of snow plain with nothing to break their force. He wanted some Emperor Penguin eggs. Scott twice tried to dissuade him, but when Wilson had made up his mind he was adamant. In theory, the leader could have ordered him not to go, but they were not on those terms; besides, the purpose of the egg-collecting was scientific, and as such won his support.

Unlike all other species of Antarctic bird, which migrate north to milder climates to breed, the Emperor goes south to find a level stretch of frozen sea, so bleak that it must use its own feet as a nest in which to hatch its single chick. For two months the father starves while he is incubating the egg; then the mother, well stocked with fat, returns from the sea to release the male while she feeds the chick. Born into a world of darkness, intense cold, blizzards and frozen seas, ironically the greatest threat to the chick's survival is not the climate but excess of parental love.

Wilson believed that, of all species of bird, Emperor Penguins were the most ancient and primitive. Evolved, like all birds, from reptiles, many millions of years ago they had branched off the main avian stem to become wholly adapted to a watery life, their wings turning into paddles to propel them through the sea. In the embryo of a species can often be traced its evolutionary history. A theory held at that time was that the feathers of birds had been evolved from the scales of reptiles. This theory Wilson wanted to test by collecting fertile eggs at several stages of development and examining their embryos under the microscope. The eggs, he reckoned, would be at the right stage of incubation in July. He had no difficulty in securing volunteers to go with him and invited Cherry-Garrard and Birdie Bowers.

The story of this adventure has been well told by Cherry-Garrard in *The Worst Journey in the World,* and both his companions kept diaries. Drawing two light sledges with heavy loads, 235lbs a man, they left the base on 27 June 1911. On their second night, camped on the Barrier, the temperature was already down to —56°F and later it fell to —77.5°F. Rations had been cut to the barest minimum: no sugar, no chocolate, cocoa or any 'luxuries'; only pemmican, biscuits, butter and tea. At night, instead of a pannikin of cocoa, they had plain hot water. Wilson's commitment to austerity had surely become masochistic. Even Bowers, who was all but impervious to cold, admitted, 'I was beginning to think I could stand anything, but when one has to deal with 109 degrees below freezing point I did not want to ask for more.' Sleeping bags froze so hard it was impossible to roll them up and they were carried on the sledges like three corpses; to get into them at night was purgatory. It took two men to bend the clothes the third into the required shape for getting into, and four hours to strike camp. On 1 July they advanced two-and-a-quarter miles and two-and-a-half miles next day, spending seventeen hours each day in harness. Yet when they halted they could still appreciate the marvellous aurora. Bowers wrote, 'At times we lay on our backs and looked up at what many people would call the finest sight of their lives.'

They took nineteen days to reach Cape Crozier, sixty-seven miles away. Breath and sweat froze until the travellers were encased in ice like mummies. Going out of the tent, Cherry-Garrard lifted his head to look round and could not bend it back again; he marched for four hours with his head in that position. At night they suffered agonies from cramp. Their feet and fingers blistered, and the pus inside the blisters froze. Always patient, always unruffled, always self-possessed, Wilson was the only man on earth, Cherry-Garrard believed, who could have led that journey. Bowers was his match. 'With quiet perseverance, in perfect friendship, almost with gentleness, those two men led on.'

They had to find their way between enormous pressure ridges on their right and the deeply crevassed slopes of Mt Terror, 10,774 feet, on their left. Once, advancing in blackness, the moon obscured by clouds, a little patch of sky cleared for a moment, the moon shone through and, three paces ahead, they saw a great crevasse. It was a sign; from that moment, they believed they might pull through.

Blizzards, more crevasses, probing with a pole ahead – at last they camped above the cliffs at whose foot the rookery lay. On the anniversary of Wilson's wedding day, while a blizzard raged around them, they started to build a small rock igloo, which Wilson christened Oriana Hut. When it was completed they roped themselves together and tackled the descent. They could see no more than a few yards ahead. Somehow they managed to clamber, crawl and struggle down the cliff-face, cutting steps with an ice-axe and hauling each other up and down cliffs, to reach the rookery below. And so, Bowers wrote, 'we were the first men to see the lordly Emperor Penguin nursing its eggs'.

Instead of the 2000 or so birds that had been seen in 1902, less than a hundred were on the bay ice. But there were eggs, balanced on the male birds' feet; some birds were nursing lumps of ice, believing them to be hatchable. Besides the eggs, Wilson wanted penguin blubber for the stove. What little light there was, cast by the moon, was fading. Hurriedly, they killed and skinned three penguins and collected five eggs. On the hazardous clamber up the cliffs, two were smashed; these had been held by Cherry-Garrard who, because of his poor sight, stumbled and fell more than the others.

The trio reached their hut in a blizzard. That evening a blob of burning blubber oil flew into Wilson's eye and he passed a night of agony, believing the sight to have gone. The wind rose to gale force and blew away their tent, which was pitched beside the igloo, and the hut itself filled with snow. The next day, 23 July 1911, was, Wilson observed, 'quite the funniest birthday I have ever spent'. (He was thirty-nine; Bowers brought a present of a tin of sweets.) Their hut was roofed with canvas. The blizzard swept away their hut's canvas roof and everything else, leaving them in their bags without shelter, with scarcely any food but not, in Wilson's case at least, without hope. He made plans for getting back by digging burrows in the snow to sleep in, living on biscuits. Cherry-Garrard wrote that while neither of his two companions gave up hope for a moment, he never had any hope at all. He thought about dying, peaches and syrup.

When at last the blizzard abated, they went out in the forlorn hope of finding the remains of their tent. To their amazement, it had been caught up at the bottom of a slope and was more or less intact. 'Our lives have been taken away and given back to us,' Wilson wrote. They got the primus going and had a hot hoosh of pemmican full of hairs, dirt and penguin feathers – the best meal they had ever eaten.

Bowers now proposed another visit to the rookery to get more eggs. Wilson vetoed it; he had promised Scott to bring everyone back alive. So they made a depot of everything they could manage without and started back next day. At night Bowers anchored himself to the tent so that if it went again, he would go too.

The return journey was all nightmare. On 1 August 1911, on their thirty-sixth day of travel, they reached the hut at Cape Evans. 'We were pretty tired for want of sleep,' Wilson conceded. Violent and continuous shivering had kept them awake all night and they had reached the point of going to sleep with their pannikins still in their hands. They had to be levered out of their clothing, which weighed 66lbs more at the end than at the start of the journey. 'They looked more weather-worn than anyone I have yet seen,' Scott observed. 'Their faces were scarred and wrinkled, their eyes dull, their hands whitened and creased with constant exposure to damp and cold.' Next day, Wilson and Bowers were almost themselves again; Scott believed that Bowers was the hardest traveller who ever undertook a polar journey. 'Never was such a sturdy, active, undefeatable little man.' Looking up records in the library, they found that Amundsen, while travelling to the North Magnetic Pole, had recorded a temperature of −79°F; but he had slept in igloos built by Esquimos, not in a thin canvas tent, and there had been some daylight; and his journey had lasted for five days, not for five weeks.

The three eggs, frozen but intact, got safely back to Britain and, after various vicissitudes, were examined by Professor Cossar Ewart of Edinburgh University, an expert on feathers. From these and other embryos he drew the conclusion that birds' feathers had not been evolved from reptilian scales. Negative information, but Wilson would have felt the journey fully justified; to him, a crumb of scientific knowledge was better than all the cakes of Mammon in the world.

# 22

# Winter at
# Cape Evans

'It is delightful to contemplate the amount of work which is being done at the station.' Among scientists, Scott felt in his element. His diary is full of snippets of scientific data, summaries of results, précis of lectures. The meteorologist George Simpson, whom he regarded as 'a master of his craft', was equally enthusiastic about his leader. He wrote:

One thing which never fails to excite my wonder is Captain Scott's versatile mind. There is no specialist here who is not pleased to discuss his problems, and although he is constantly asserting that he is only a layman, yet there is no one here who sees so clearly the essentials of a problem . . . He is constantly stating new problems and he seldom comes in from a walk without having made some useful observations. I must say he often sees things which have a bearing on my work which I have passed over without noting their import.

Simpson went on to give an example. The cause of the blizzards which so suddenly arose and raged with such ferocity was one of the problems he was most anxious to solve. He spent a sleepless night working out a theory, and next morning discussed it with Scott 'exactly as I should with a trained meteorologist or physicist'. They agreed that its main lines were probably correct, but next day Scott put forward a highly technical objection which, Simpson wrote, showed 'a very high power of looking at a problem in its widest aspect and could not have been made by one out of a hundred who had not specialised in physics. This is not an isolated case.' Simpson added, 'He is certainly a great man and one feels that if his polar venture does not succeed it will be through no want of thought or ability on the part of our leader.'

The leader was constantly thinking and observing. From his solitary walks, often on skis, he came back to record all things seen: three seals asleep on a floe, unusual ice formations, how an Emperor's breast reflected the faint northern light like a mirror. His almost passionate devotion to science was blended in his nature with a sensitivity to beauty and a groping towards spiritual values beyond the reach of scientific enquiry. Like others, he fumbled towards words to describe the magic of auroras.

There is infinite suggestion in this phenomenon – mysterious – no reality. It is the language of mystic signs and of portents – the inspiration of the gods – wholly spiritual – divine signalling. Remindful of superstition, provocative of imagination. Might not the inhabitants of some other world (Mars) controlling mighty forces thus surround our globe with fiery symbols, a golden writing which we have not the key to decipher?

He noted that Ponting, with all his skill, had failed to get a satisfactory photograph of a display. 'It is all very puzzling.'

In his small cabin, where the naval greatcoat he had worn as a sub-lieutenant was spread over the bunk, he sat for hours at a linoleum-covered table working out in minute detail plans for the polar journey; calculating sledge loads, drawing up tables of diets, designing improvements in equipment and dealing with a thousand and one other matters. He designed and Day made an improved ice-cutting knife, and seaman Evans produced a much improved ski-boot, at once more flexible, stronger and lighter than the standard model. Every recorded detail of Shackleton's expedition was mulled over. Scott's thoughts must often have dwelt upon that other camp some 350 miles along the Barrier, with its resolute Norwegians, and all their dogs.

Always his thoughts came back to transport. During the winter three more dogs died without apparent cause and one vanished. 'I'm afraid we can place but little reliance on our dog-teams and reflect ruefully on the misplaced confidence with which I regarded the provision of our transport.' Yet one of the dogs provided an object-lesson in polar survival. On 8 June 1911 Debenham and Gran made a short trip to Hut Point and found a missing dog, Mukaka, curled up outside the hut looking pitifully thin and weak. This dog had been injured during landing operations in January, he was lame and his hindquarters hairless, but he had continued with his team until all the dogs were brought back to base at Cape Evans on 13 May. Because of his poor condition, he had been allowed to run free; he never reached Cape Evans and was given up for lost. Somehow this half-crippled animal had kept himself alive, alone, for a month, presumably by killing a seal – there was blood on his mouth. 'Hunger drives hard' was Scott's comment. However hard it might drive a pony, no pony could kill a seal.

While he might distrust the dogs collectively, he could not resist the temptation present in almost every Englishman to turn individuals into pets. Vaida was a fierce, quarrelsome dog who lost part of his coat, and Scott began to massage his back. At first the dog growled and threatened to bite, but gradually Vaida grew to enjoy the treatment and 'now comes and buries his head in my legs whenever I go out of doors; he allows me to rub him and push him about without the slightest protest and scampers about me as I walk abroad'.

Six of the expedition's men were absent from the hut at Cape Evans:

these were Victor Campbell and his five companions who, having failed to
get ashore on King Edward VII Land, had been taken by the *Terra Nova* to
Cape Adare, where they had established their base near Borchgrevink's old
camp, erected their hut, and settled in to winter on the beach preparatory to
a summer's exploration. The Eastern Party had thus become the Northern
Party. The enforced change of plan was a bitter disappointment to Campbell, who had hoped that his party's explorations in an unknown land would
be the most important achievement of the whole expedition.

They had taken with them no dogs, but two ponies. These, Campbell
decided, would be of no use to his party in Victoria Land, where glaciers
bristling with ice-falls and crevasses fell steeply to the sea. Scott, he knew,
would be glad of them. But on arriving at Cape Evans, it was found that the
ice on to which everything had been unloaded three weeks earlier had
broken up. So the ponies were lowered overboard in a sling and towed
ashore by rowers in a whaleboat, then rubbed down and given half a bottle
of brandy each; both survived.

It had been arranged that the *Terra Nova* would pick up Campbell's
party from Cape Adare on her return from New Zealand early in 1912.
Geology, with twenty-five-year-old Raymond Priestley in charge, was to
be the main pre-occupation, and surgeon Murray Levick was to study birds
and marine life.

So the winter at Cape Evans passed, not without its agitations; another of
the precious ponies nearly died, and Atkinson lost his way and nearly
perished also. Surgeon Atkinson was always busy examining the parasites of
fish, who had a great many, mostly unknown to science. Rather touchingly,
he would come frequently to Scott inviting him to inspect under the microscope a newly discovered parasite of, quite possibly, a new species of fish.
Scott remarked how strange it was that the parasite should be discovered
more or less at the same time as its host. The interest everyone took in
scientific matters was infectious; even Bowers succumbed, and raised a
laugh by inquiring, after one of the lectures, whether the pnycnogonids were
more nearly related to the arachnids or to the crustaceans. It was a sensible
question but Bowers in the role of a biologist was unexpected.

'It is a triumph to have collected such men,' Scott wrote of his companions. The only possible exception was Nelson, the biologist, whom he
thought lazy. Once he had occasion to reprimand Tryggve Gran for, as he
thought, feigning injury to escape a duty. The young man bore no malice.
Wilson warned him that the Owner did not like to see an idle man. 'You're
Norwegian,' Wilson said, 'living up in the mountains with your thoughts.
But if you're sitting and thinking, dreaming, thinking about your family at
home, and you see Scott come along, don't sit and think. Lace your boots
over and over again, if you've nothing else to do.' Gran recalled that they

were like a family of friends and that he never heard a bad word while he was in the Antarctic. 'So, it couldn't have been better.'

On the Owner's forty-sixth birthday, his companions organised a gala dinner with champagne and toasts, after which everyone was festive and amiably argumentative. 'They are boys, all of them,' Scott wrote, 'but such excellent good-natured ones; there has been no sign of sharpness or anger, no jarring note, in all these wordy contests; all end with a laugh.' Such undiluted harmony among this isolated group of men seems almost too good to be true. (At times, nerves did get frayed; Cherry-Garrard wrote that sometimes the greatest of friends did not speak to each other for days at a time for fear of quarrelling.) Perhaps it was that very isolation from family, friends and civilisation that made such harmony possible. Here was no cause for rivalry, jealousy, intrigue, discontent; all shared equally in all that was going; they were united in a common aim. In fact they realised in microcosm that ancient and, in a larger world, forever elusive ideal of the true communist state, each man giving according to his ability and receiving according to his needs. Success was possible because their needs were small, their capacity for giving great and there were no scrimshankers. They were, of course, a most exceptional group of men: all of high intelligence, all bodily and mentally fit and able, all volunteers, all conscious of their privilege in having been selected from thousands for this great national task.

A *Discovery* custom Scott revived was the issue of the *South Polar Times*, with Cherry-Garrard as editor. As before, the Captain read aloud its contents after dinner. Wilson took immense pains over his drawings, but apologised for their quality because they were done by the light of acetylene gas, which distorted colours. He also wrote for the miscellany his one and only poem. He got Griffith Taylor to copy out the verses because he knew that, if he submitted them in his own handwriting, Cherry-Garrard would put them in regardless of their merit. In them he defined in three lines the nub of his belief about the purpose of his Antarctic adventure.

### THE BARRIER SILENCE

The Silence was deep with a breath like sleep
    As our sledge runners slid on the snow,
And the fate-full fall of our fur-clad feet
    Struck mute like a silent blow
On a questioning 'hush', as the settling crust
    Shrank shivering over the floe;
And the sledge in its track sent a whisper back
    Which was lost in a white fog-bow.

> And this was the thought that the Silence wrought
>     As it scorched and froze us through,
> Though secrets hidden are all forbidden,
>     Till God means man to know,
> We might be the men God meant should know
>     The heart of the Barrier snow,
>     In the heat of the sun, and the glow
>     And the glare from the glistening floe,
> As it scorched and froze us through and through
>     With the bite of the drifting snow.

The sun's return on 23 August was toasted in champagne, together with
Victor Campbell's thirty-sixth birthday, but as a gale was blowing the sun was
invisible and the champagne not appreciated. Three days later the sun did
appear, and Scott with Ponting climbed a berg, revelled in the first sunshine and 'felt very young, sang and cheered'. With lengthening daylight,
Oates began to work up the ponies, by means of feeding and exercise, to
their highest pitch. It became only too apparent that this was not at all high.
Jehu, one of the two who had swum ashore from the *Terra Nova*, appeared
so feeble that it was doubtful whether he would be able to start at all, and
another, Chinaman, was not much better. They were too old. It was clear
that they had not been well selected. Cherry-Garrard thought it had been a
mistake to instruct Meares to buy only white ponies, which limited his
choice; Shackleton's opinion that his own white ponies had stood up better
to the climate than the others was the reason for this injunction.

If high feeding did little for Jehu, it did too much for Christopher, a
vicious animal whose malice was matched by his strength. Only Oates
could manage him and not even Oates at times. As he grew fitter he grew
nastier, and his daily harnessing became a sort of rodeo. One foreleg was
strapped up, but he soon mastered the art of balancing on the other foreleg
while lashing out with his hind legs, so he had to be thrown.

Two men hung on to his head while the sledge trace was attached, and
then he brought his teeth into play; as soon as his foreleg was released he
leaped up and bolted, with Oates and Anton Omelchenko (an ex-jockey
from Vladisvostok) hanging on like grim death. Sometimes he escaped,
loaded sledge and all, and galloped over the floe only to lambast his pur-
suers, when they caught up with him, all over again. To break his spirit
with a whip, as many would have done, was not Oates' way. He never hit
the ponies, whether to urge them on or to punish them. Their appetites
were eclectic; ropes, head-stalls, puttees, rugs, bits of sledges, canvas, anything within reach was chewed.

Oates' devotion to these white and grey-white animals, about fourteen or
fifteen hands high, became almost an obsession. He sat with them for hours,

sometimes alone, sometimes with Anton or with Meares, watching over them, mixing hot mashes on the blubber stove he had installed, treating with skill and patience any minor injury or ailment. He shared with Bowers, Cherry-Garrard, Meares and Atkinson an area of the hut the others called 'the tenements' because of its austerity; gestures towards the sybaritic, such as home-dyed curtains over shelves, reading-lamps and pin-up pictures, excited his contempt. His bunk was fixed high on the wall so as to allow room to hang the ponies' harness underneath, where it kept relatively warm. Photographs of Oates depict strong, blunt features, crew-cut hair, a face that gives nothing away of inner thoughts or emotions. Even in his taste in reading matter, he admitted no frills. During the winter he worked his way steadily through the first volume of Napier's *History of the Peninsular War*, but never reached the second. A copy of *The Man-eaters of Tsavo* by J. H. Patterson, was also among his few possessions.

Scott had fixed the date of departure for the Pole as 1 November 1911 at the latest. They could not start earlier because the ponies would not have stood the cold. To fill in time, and perhaps stifle his impatience,* he took off with Bowers, Simpson and Edgar Evans on 15 September on 'a remarkably pleasant and instructive little spring journey' to the western mountains, mainly to inspect some stakes placed on the Ferrar Glacier the previous autumn, in order to measure its rate of flow. (It moved thirty feet in seven and a half months.) In ten days they covered 175 miles, dragging 180lbs per man.'(No dogs or ponies.) The temperature was 'not particularly high', about —40°F at the foot of the glacier; the surface was only fairly good; they 'captured' many frostbites – Simpson's entire face became blistered – and on the last day covered twenty-one miles in the teeth of a bitter gale. Nevertheless, it was all most enjoyable, and Bowers called it a picnic. He insisted on doing all the camp work; 'he is a positive wonder; I never met such a sledge traveller'.

It was probably on this trip that Scott picked his three companions for the last lap to the Pole. Uncle Bill was a foregone conclusion, although nothing had been said and Wilson himself did not take it for granted. 'Taff' Evans, too – the tried and true companion, the sterling sledger, ever ready with an anecdote, the reliable, good-natured, cheerful and truehearted man. Added to that Petty Officer Evans had, as the Captain put it, a remarkable headpiece; to his ingenuity the expedition owed many improvements in clothing, footwear, tents and general equipment. He was strong as an ox, stood up to cold, and his rank was an added advantage;

* In his camp on the Barrier, Amundsen was also impatient; determined to get away before Scott, he started on 8 September, but it was too soon. Experiencing temperatures of down to —69°F, too much for the dogs, the Norwegians made a depot of their supplies and returned to Framheim, riding on the sledges. The final start was made on 19 October, only twelve days before Scott and his party left.

one at least of the polar party, other things being equal, ought to come from the lower deck. Taff Evans would go to the Pole.

And then there was Bowers, the perfect treasure. Scott had come to rely on him implicitly. In spite of all the care taken to explain the plans, Bowers was the only man he could really rely on to grasp the details and remember them. 'The greatest source of pleasure to me is to realise that I have such men as Bowers and P. O. Evans for the Southern journey,' he wrote.

For the last weeks before departure he was busy getting his journal up to date, writing letters, and drawing up instructions for the running of the base. He had to think about money, neither a congenial subject nor a cheerful one. The expedition's funds were very low. In London the treasurer, Sir Edgar Speyer, was trying to raise more with minimal success. Kathleen Scott mentions in her diary for 13 September 1911 a distressing letter from Sir Lewis Beaumont to say that funds would run out at the end of October, and that Kinsey in New Zealand was owed £1000. She was worried, and a week later had a horrid dream, and then her son, aged two, 'came very close to me and said emphatically, "Daddy won't come back," as though in answer to my silly thoughts'. Meeting Nansen after a lecture, she felt shy, but he was immediately attracted, and during that winter their friendship grew. They discussed Amundsen. Nansen had no inkling, he assured her, of Amundsen's secret intentions. Amundsen had been evasive about his dogs and said they might be useful on the way back from the Pole – the North Pole as Nansen had believed. He thought the best plan would be for Scott and Amundsen to join forces and go on together. 'He is so simple and straightforward in his views,' Kathleen found – in this case a little over-simple, perhaps.

Towards the end of October 1911, Scott called everyone together, told them that the financial cupboard was bare and invited any who were able and willing to do so to forgo their salaries for the forthcoming year. Some had decided already to return with the *Terra Nova*: Griffith Taylor, whose leave from his university would be up; Ponting and Day, whose work would be done; and a few, such as Clissold and Forde, whose health was imperfect. Most of the others volunteered to stay another winter, if necessary without pay.

Before the departure of the Southern Party Scott, like all the others, wrote to his family and friends. 'I am quite on my feet now,' he told his wife. 'I feel mentally and physically fit for the work.' This had not been so, he knew, in London, or on the outward voyage. 'The root of the trouble was that I had lost confidence in myself.' He did not say why, and every student of his character can supply his own guess. 'Had I been what I am now, many things would have been avoided,' he concluded; what things, he did not say either.

He took comfort, he wrote, from Kathleen's courage; she would never sit down and bewail misfortune; whatever happened, she would remain 'sturdily independent and determined to make the most of the life you possess'. He wanted to come back 'having done something' but now there was 'the chance of another man getting ahead'.

I don't know what to think of Amundsen's chances. If he gets to the Pole it must be before we do, as he is bound to travel fast with dogs, and pretty certain to start early. On this account I decided at a very early date to act exactly as I should have done had he not existed. Any attempt to race must have wrecked my plan, besides which it doesn't appear the sort of thing one is out for . . . You can rely on my not saying or doing anything foolish, only I'm afraid you must be prepared for finding our venture much belittled. After all, it is the work that counts, not the applause that follows.

Kathleen he saluted as 'the antithesis of the pathetic grass widow. Bless you'.

Birdie Bowers wrote to his mother 'I cannot say too much of Scott as a leader and an extraordinarily clever and far-seeing man. I am Captain Scott's man and shall stick to him right through. God knows what the result will be, but we will do all that man can do and leave the rest in His keeping which we all are, and shall remain.'

Scott wrote on the last page of the diary that he left behind, 'The future is in the lap of the gods. I can think of nothing left undone to deserve success.'

So, on 1 November 1911, the time came for the start of the last journey.

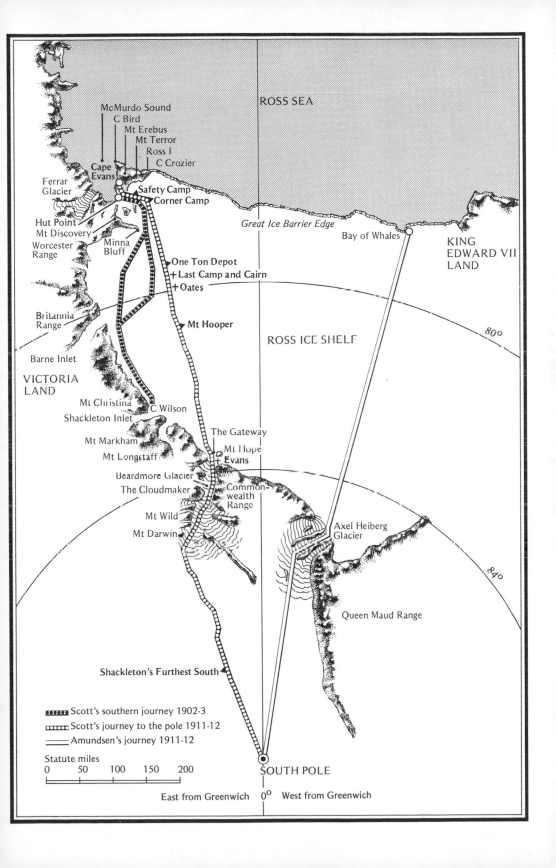

ROSS SEA

McMurdo Sound
C Bird
Mt Erebus
Mt Terror
Ross I
C Crozier

Cape Evans

Ferrar Glacier

Safety Camp
Corner Camp

*Great Ice Barrier Edge*

Bay of Whales

KING EDWARD VII LAND

Hut Point
Mt Discovery
Worcester Range

Minna Bluff

One Ton Depot
+ Last Camp and Cairn
+ Oates

Britannia Range

• Mt Hooper

ROSS ICE SHELF

800

Barne Inlet

VICTORIA LAND

Mt Christina
Shackleton Inlet

• C Wilson

The Gateway

Mt Markham

Mt Hope
Evans

Mt Longstaff

Beardmore Glacier
The Cloudmaker

Common-wealth Range

Axel Heiberg Glacier

Mt Wild
Mt Darwin

840

Queen Maud Range

Shackleton's Furthest South ◀

▦▦▦ Scott's southern journey 1902-3
▭▭▭ Scott's journey to the pole 1911-12
───── Amundsen's journey 1911-12

Statute miles
0    50    100    150    200

SOUTH POLE

East from Greenwich    0°    West from Greenwich

# 23    An Awful
           Place

The motor sledges left Cape Evans in advance of the ponies and dogs. One was escorted by Day and the other by Lashly, each walking beside his charge. Bernard Day was confident that they would reach the 80th parallel at least. Scott never hoped for that, but he desperately wanted them to succeed, because of all the time and effort they had cost, because of Day's feelings, and because he believed that in the future motor transport, its imperfections shed away, would solve the problem of polar transport. His judgement was correct; those particular motors failed, but their successors were to chug about the polar regions almost in droves.

The motors took three hours to go three miles. 'Come, come!' Scott wrote, as if admonishing a naughty child. Their speed improved, and a great moment came when Lashly drove his machine at top speed up the slope and on to the Barrier. Everyone cheered, and on went the motor in great style; hopes were high, but short-lived. The big end of one of the cylinders of Day's machine collapsed not far beyond Safety Camp, and a mile beyond Corner Camp Lashly's machine gave out as well. 'So the dream of great help from the machines is at an end.' Following directions, the four custodians of the motors – Day and Lashly were reinforced by Teddy Evans and F. J. Hooper, the steward – abandoned the machines and turned themselves into a man-hauling team, dragging their sledges forward in the van of the pony cavalcade.

Then on 1 November 1911 ten men, each leading a pony, each pony drawing a sledge, left Cape Evans in detachments. These were the leader with Wilson, Bowers, Oates, Atkinson, Cherry-Garrard, Wright, Edgar Evans, Crean and Keohane. Meares with Dimitri were to follow with the dogs. Everyone else remained at the base, the scientists to pursue their researches and make further explorations in Victoria Land. Scott expected the *Terra Nova*, when she returned in January, to bring back the Northern Party, and then Victor Campbell would take command. One of the few disappointments, as regards personnel, was Teddy Evans: 'a thoroughly well-meaning little man,' Scott had written to Joseph Kinsey, 'but rather a duffer in anything but his own particular work . . . not at all fitted to be second-in-command as I was foolish enough to name him.'

From Cape Evans there was a traditional send-off with cheers, sledge flags and photographs. Christopher ran true to form. After tying up his foreleg it took five minutes to throw him, and when released he galloped off on three legs with the sledge bumping along behind. 'Dear old Titus, that was my last memory of him,' wrote Griffith Taylor, 'Imperturbable as ever; never hasty, never angry, but soothing that vicious animal.' Progress to Hut Point reminded Scott of 'a disorganised fleet with ships of very unequal speed'. With so many things on his mind, he forgot the Union Jacks that Queen Alexandra had given him to plant at the Pole. Gran went back to fetch them on his skis.

The distance from Hut Point to the Pole and back was 1532 geographical, 1766 statute, miles. Every step of the way was to be marched on foot, with or without skis.

'It is always rather dismal walking over the great snow plain when sky and surface merge in one pall of whiteness,' Scott wrote. They plodded on across the windswept, featureless expanse of snow rippled with *sastrugi*, travelling by night for the benefit of the ponies. Temperatures never rose above freezing point and seldom above zero Fahrenheit; often the sun was obscured by a haze which made navigation difficult without landmarks; everything was grey and gloomy and spirits flagged. The grey haze of the Barrier was deceptive; *sastrugi* sometimes looked like hills; Bowers remarked that he thought he saw a herd of black cattle approaching; they turned out to be pony droppings.

Scott was beset by worries, mainly about weather and ponies. It was not long before he was asking, 'What can such weather mean?' They were getting constant snowfalls which made the surface soft and sticky and very heavy going for the ponies, who sank in to their fetlocks and beyond. 'This inpouring of moist warm air,' he noted, 'is certainly an interesting meteorological fact,' but the ponies and their leaders were unable to take such a detached view. They floundered and strained, and could average no more than ten or twelve miles a day at best. On the fifteenth day they reached One Ton Camp and had a day's rest.

Would the ponies hold out? This was the constant worry. Three were crocks: Jehu, Chinaman and James Pigg. Everyone agreed that they should have never been bought in the first place. Atkinson, leading Jehu, had doubted whether his animal would get as far as Hut Point. In the event, the ponies did all that had been hoped for and some could have done more. Jehu and Chinaman, instead of expiring at or near Hut Point, stepped out bravely and actually improved; on the eighth day out they indulged in a 'skittish little run' and Chinaman even essayed a buck. A few days later the leader was able to write, 'The ponies did excellently as usual.' Even Oates, a confirmed pessimist, grew almost hopeful, although he had described his charges as 'the most unsuitable scrap-heap crowd of unfit creatures that could possibly be got together'.

His was the credit for their recovery. After One Ton Camp the somewhat ironic situation arose where Meares, who was running short of dog-food, eyed Jehu hopefully at the end of each march wondering whether he was weak enough to be shot, whereas the others were determined to get him past the point at which Shackleton had killed his first beast. At Camp 20, on 24 November, poor old Jehu was despatched. Meares reported that he cut up well, and had quite a lot of fat. 'Jehu has certainly come up trumps after all,' was Scott's comment. 'May we all do our work as well as he did,' was Bowers'.

Four camps later, Chinaman was shot and on 1 December the unruly Christopher, who remained obstinate to the end. Bowers had become deeply attached to his own pony, and was dejected when the order was given for his execution. 'Good old Victor! He always had a biscuit out of my ration and he ate his last before the bullet sent him to his rest.' Bowers kept one of Victor's hoofs and marked the spot hoping to pick it up on the way back.

Each tent held four men who, at intervals, changed places. Cherry-Garrard remarked that he was glad when his turn came to join the Owner, who was deft, quick, tidy, and never wasted time. Each man had to shake off every particle of snow from his clothing before entering the tent, and a brush was kept to sweep the floor-cloth clear. There was never anything slovenly. Such care made all the difference to the occupants' warmth and comfort. Moreover both the Owner and Wilson were clever sledging cooks. Good cooking made the ration go farther, and even slight variations made it more appetising. Management of the primus cooker was a far from easy art, requiring fine adjustment of screws to regulate the pressure and often resulting, at low temperatures when flesh sticks to metal, in painful burns, Scott was plagued with indigestion which often kept him awake, tired out as he was. He never complained.

Depots were made at intervals of roughly seventy miles, each containing food and fuel for a week for the returning parties. Each depot was built up into a snow cairn and a flag left flying at the top. On the Barrier the pony meat was not cached – Cherry-Garrard, wise after the event, thought that it should have been. Some went into the hoosh and the rest was fed to the dogs.

'Our luck in weather is preposterous,' Scott wrote on 3 December. A full gale struck them from the south, in their faces, piling snow into drifts which buried the sledges. They marched on through a snowstorm, steering by compass, 'the conditions simply horrible', to camp near the Gateway, as Shackleton had named a chasm by the foot of the glacier where he had hauled his sledges off the Barrier. That night Bowers wrote of Amundsen, 'if he has not met with adversity he should have reached the Pole by now. I hope he has not, as I regard him as a back-handed sneaking ruffian.' Amundsen reached the Pole ten days later (14 December 1911).

The next morning (5 December) they awoke to a damp and murky blizzard. The temperature always rose just before and during a blizzard, but this time it rose exceptionally high and the snow all but melted as it fell, making everything wringing wet. The drift was atrocious. 'One cannot see the next tent, let alone the land. What on earth does such weather mean at this time of year?' Scott was afraid it meant that this was a particularly bad season. 'It is more than our share of ill-fortune,' he wrote, 'but the luck may turn yet.'

This wet, warm blizzard kept them tent-bound for four days. They lay in sopping bags in pools of water in dripping tents, the gale howling, snow and slush drifting up almost to the tops of the tents. The temperature rose to 35.5°F. 'Oh! but this is too crushing, and we are only twelve miles from the glacier. A hopeless feeling descends on one and is hard to fight off.'

When post-mortems on the polar journey came to be held, many factors were blamed for its tragic end; a long chain of mishaps could be traced back, some due to chance, some to faulty judgements; it was a tale of narrow margins only just missed. This four days' imprisonment near the foot of the glacier was a major factor. The delay made them late up the glacier, four days late at the Pole, four days late on the return journey; with those four days in hand they would have reached One Ton Depot ahead of the blizzard that held them in their last camp.

Bowers reacted typically.

When I volunteered for this Expedition I did not expect nor desire a bed of roses, nor do I now, nor for worlds would I change my position with any other man on God's earth. If I seem at times to growl at what appears the most phenomenal persistence of adversity, it is because my anxiety for the success of our object is not for myself . . . Still we are all in the same boat, the great Antarctic Expedition! None of us is more wet than the rest we are all alike and I can endure what any other man can – that is my creed down here.

On the third day of blizzard they had to go on to summit rations, the more generous allowance that should not have started until they had made their depot at the foot of the glacier and begun to climb.* This threw out Scott's carefully calculated plan. A margin had been allowed for bad weather but no one, he believed, could have expected so prolonged a

---

* The summit ration totalled 34.43oz per man and consisted of 16oz biscuit, 12oz pemmican, 2oz butter, 0.5oz cocoa, 3oz sugar and 0.86oz tea, plus a little onion powder and salt – no chocolate, raisins or cereal.

blizzard at this time of year. 'Resignation to misfortune is the only attitude, but not one easy to adopt . . . It is very evil to lie here in a wet sleeping-bag and think of the pity of it, whilst things go steadily from bad to worse.' Those wasted days could never be recalled. 'But yet, after all, one can go on striving.'

On the fourth day of blizzard they shifted the tents, which were being pressed in by the weight of wet snow and stood in pits of water. They tried to lead out a pony but he sank in up to his belly. Pony food had run out but they could not kill the animals until they had reached the glacier's foot, or the meat would be buried under wet snow. Wilson gave his pony, Nobby, all his own biscuits and lay in his bag reading Tennyson's *Maud* and *In Memoriam*. 'If the end comes to me here or hereabouts there will be no great time for Ory to sorrow. All will be as it is meant to be.'

On the fifth day the blizzard abated, they struck camp and wallowed forward through soft snow overlying the pressure ridges where land and Barrier met. They had to resort to beating the ponies who floundered belly-deep and, Wilson wrote, 'constantly collapsed and lay down and sank down, and eventually we could only get them on five or six yards at a time – they were clean done'. Yet they struggled on for eleven hours, covering five miles. Then the party camped, shot the five ponies, skinned and cut them up and made a depot. They called this Shambles Camp. Wilson was relieved not to have to watch the ponies suffer any longer. 'Thank God the horses are now all done for and we begin the heavier work ourselves.' This was on 9 December.

Two days later they were on the foot of the Beardmore. After setting up Lower Glacier depot, Meares and Dimitri started back with the dogs, taking letters. Scott told Kathleen that things were not as rosy as they might be, but that he could keep up with the rest as well as of old. Two men, Day and Hooper, had already turned back, so a party of twelve, divided into three units, set out to man-haul the sledges up the glacier towards that bitter summit over 10,000 feet above the Barrier. (Amundsen and his four companions were already there.)

The Beardmore Glacier, then believed to be the largest in the world, is over 100 miles long and in places forty miles wide. (Since then an even longer one, the Lambert, has been discovered.) It is hard to imagine the severity of that climb. They were pulling, to start with, over 200lbs per man through snow so soft that they sank in almost to the knees with every step. If the sledge stopped moving, ten or fifteen desperate jerks on the harness were needed to get it going again. Snow-blindness caused agonies on the march, and often kept its victim writhing in his sleeping-bag all night. They stumbled into crevasses, the sledges capsized and had continually to be turned over to scrape frozen snow off the runners. On 13

December – the day before Amundsen reached the Pole – in nine hours the party advanced by less than four miles.

Shackleton had found hard blue ice, giving a firm grip, on this lower section of the glacier. The four-day blizzard had smothered it in snow. 'I had pinned my faith on getting better conditions as we rose, but it looks as though matters are getting worse instead of better,' Scott observed. On that day Bowers wrote that he had 'never pulled so hard, or so nearly crushed my inside into my backbone by the everlasting jerking with all my strength on the canvas band round my unfortunate tummy'. He was quite snow-blind for four days. No wonder that 'the Owner was in a paddy with the weather'. Scott's indigestion was worse, and everyone's lips were raw and bleeding.

Gradually they drew away from the snow on to better going, over pressure ridges where the sledges slithered instead of sticking; the irrepressible Bowers actually found this good fun. 'Crossing the waves [of pressure ridges] was great sport, it was just like a scenic railway. You poised the sledge on a giddy height, aimed her carefully . . . and then down you would fly, often faster than any switchback; but also you had to haul the sledge up the other side.' On 20 December Bowers was able to record 'a great march on the most delightful blue ice surface imaginable. It was like walking over cucumber frames.' That was a record march of twenty-three miles, and still hauling uphill; at last they were making up time. At the 85th parallel, altitude 6500 feet, they were only three days behind Shackleton's dates.

On the evening of 20 December, Scott named the first returning party: Atkinson, Wright, Cherry-Garrard and Keohane. He had dreaded this moment. All had pulled to the limit of their strength, but now four good men must be deprived of their reward. 'Scott was very put about,' wrote Cherry-Garrard, who ended by having to comfort his leader rather than the other way about. Cherry-Garrard had hoped too; he trusted that he had not disappointed? 'No – no – no' replied the Captain, catching hold of the young man's arm. 'So if that is the case all is well. He told me at the bottom of the glacier that he was hardly expecting to go on himself.' The energetic young Canadian 'Silas' Wright was so disappointed that he was 'too wild to write more tonight'. He added, 'Scott a fool.' He thought Scott was being fooled by Teddy Evans. Like Bowers and others, he believed that Teddy Evans was not pulling his weight, but that when the Owner's eye was on him he put his head down and hauled with the best. But Scott was not fooled, and had no intention of taking Evans to the Pole.

Next day all three parties made a great march to establish Upper Glacier depot at about 7000 feet before the first supporting party turned back. 'Scott was fairly wound up,' wrote Bowers, 'and went on and on. Every rise topped seemed to fire him with a desire to top the next, and every rise had another beyond and above it.' At the lunch-time halt he scribbled a note to Kathleen. 'We are struggling on, considering all things, against odds . . . It is a pity that luck doesn't come our way, because every detail of equipment is right.' In the night camp he added a postscript. 'Since writing the above I made a dash for it, got out of the valley out of the fog and away from crevasses. So here we are practically on the summit and up to date in the provision line. We ought to get through.'

In camp that night the men going back gave away such of their possessions as they thought might be useful. Cherry-Garrard gave Wilson his pyjamas and a bag of tobacco as a Christmas present for Scott. Next morning he and his companions set off sadly down the glacier in a snowstorm, to reach Hut Point thirty-five days later (26 January 1912). Before they left, Scott instructed Atkinson to bring the dog-teams out to meet the returning polar party, if Meares had gone back with the ship.

Now the eight who went on had two sledges, twelve weeks' supply of oil and food and were pulling 190lbs per man. Scott's party included, as before, Wilson, Oates and Taff Evans, and Bowers had Teddy Evans, Lashly and Crean. They were still climbing, and went on climbing for another sixteen days to reach their highest altitude at 10,570 feet. Crevasses were plentiful. Bowers' team was nearly lost on Christmas Day when Lashly fell into one for the full length of his harness. 'The thing was about fifty feet deep and eight feet wide. Rather a ghastly sight when dangling in one's harness,' he admitted. It was his forty-fourth birthday and he was due for his pension – 'an undefeated old sportsman', Bowers wrote.

That Christmas Day, a strong wind in their faces, they advanced seventeen-and-a-half miles and at supper time let themselves go on 'a regular tightener'. Its contents were a fat pony hoosh with ground biscuit, another hoosh of chocolate, cocoa, sugar, biscuit and raisins, thickened with arrowroot; two-and-a-half square inches each of plum-duff; a pannikin of cocoa; four caramels each and four pieces of crystallised ginger. 'Could not hardly move' was Lashly's comment. Scott had to leave his diary writing over until next day and for once his indigestion did not trouble him. Possibly its basic causes lay in constant worry.

'Perhaps a little slow after plum pudding,' he wrote next day, camped on the 86th parallel. Although they were catching up on time, his nerves were on edge. When Bowers broke the hypsometer (instrument for measuring altitude), his temper snapped and Birdie got 'an unusual outburst of wrath . . . It is rather sad to get into the dirt tub with one's leader at this juncture.' The strain on the leader was much greater than on his followers. 'One cannot allow one's thoughts to wander as others do, and when one gets amongst disturbances, I find it is very worrying and tiring.' They were making remarkable marches over these disturbances: fourteen to seventeen miles a day when an average of ten had been the target. On 30 December they caught up with Shackleton's dates.

On the last day of the old year a minor accident occurred which was to have major repercussions. The teams halted for half a day to strip down their twelve-foot sledges, remove the worn runners, put on fresh ten-foot runners and convert their sledges into lighter ten-footers. Taff Evans, Crean and Lashly performed this task in a small tent at below-zero temperatures and without benefit of a carpenter's bench. 'Certainly P. O. Evans is the most invaluable asset to our party,' Scott considered. 'It is wonderful to see how neatly everything stows on a little sledge, thanks to P. O. Evans.' But during this operation Evans cut his hand, and it never properly healed. This was the first of the accidents that undid this burly, resourceful, experienced and reliable man.

'Last night I decided to reorganise,' Scott wrote on 3 January 1912. Five men would go to the Pole instead of four. Bowers was brought into his tent and Teddy Evans, Lashly and Crean were told to return. There is little doubt that he always intended to take Bowers, who was not in his tent because he was leading the second team. It was Oates who was the last-minute choice. To Oates, by reason of his skill and devotion to the ponies, was owed the very presence of the party on the plateau. He had proved his worth as a sledger, and he was a soldier. The navy, the army and the world of science would have their men at the Pole.

This decision has been much criticised, but it gave the party extra man-power and did not in itself make them short of food. Bowers transferred his share, and they had a month's allowance for five men to get to the Pole and back to the last depot; 'it ought to see us through', Scott wrote. But there were drawbacks. 'Cooking for five takes a seriously longer time than cooking for four, perhaps half an hour on the whole day,' he noted two days later. 'This is an item I had not considered when reorganising.' It also made things awkward for the returning party. The food was packed in units sufficient for four men for a week. The three returning men had therefore to extract three-quarters of each unit and leave one extra quarter in the bags. To say, as has been said, that Taff Evans should have been replaced is to display wisdom after the event with a vengeance. Evans was the first to crack, but displayed no sign of weakness at Camp 56. Lashly, on the other hand, like Lieutenant Teddy Evans, had been man-hauling all the way from Corner Camp. The others had been leading ponies, so Lashly and the Lieutenant had walked an extra 400 miles. They were tiring, and it was clearly sensible to send them back.

This was a bitter moment for Teddy Evans. He had always believed that he would be included in the polar party. No one else had believed it. On shipboard he was splendid, but on land he had been a failure. Moreover

Wilson had expressed doubts as to his fitness. 'I never thought for a moment he would be in the final party,' Bowers wrote, 'but he had buoyed himself up with the idea of going till the last moment . . . Poor Teddy – I am sure it was for his wife's sake he wanted to go. He gave me a little silk flag she had given him to fly on the Pole.' Lashly and Crean were both in tears when the three men turned back at 87° 32′ s, at an altitude of 10,280 feet, and 169 miles from the Pole. Achievement seemed virtually certain now, merely a matter of ten or eleven days' good sledging. No sign had been seen of the Norwegians; that they would follow Shackleton's route up the Beardmore was, for no good reason, generally assumed. So the parting was hopeful. Teddy Evans and his two companions looked back frequently until Scott's team moved out of sight, black specks on the horizon. They little thought, wrote Evans, that the three cheers they gave on parting 'on that bleak and lonely plateau would be the last appreciation they would ever know'.

'A last note from a hopeful position,' Scott wrote to Kathleen in a note for Teddy Evans to take back. 'I think it's going to be all right.' Now that they were on the plateau they hoped for relatively easy going. Instead, the surface worsened. They ran into deep *sastrugi* covered with ice crystals, which clung to the sledge runners in bunches looking like gorse, Wilson noted, making hauling hard, punishing work. Bowers had to march without skis. His party had depot'd their skis on 30 December, to lighten the loads. With his short legs, this made marching doubly hard for him. Meticulously, he took his meteorological observations at every camp; when using the theodolite he removed his gloves and mitts to fiddle with the tiny screws. Even he got frostbitten.

Nevertheless they were making progress and the sun shone. 'What castles one builds,' Scott wrote, 'now hopefully that the Pole is ours.' On 6 January 1912 they crossed the line of latitude where Shackleton turned back and were farther south, as they believed, than any man had been before. It was colder than they expected for midsummer, with fifty degrees of frost at night.

The strain that Scott was labouring under, mental as well as physical, was betrayed by a wobblyness of judgement. More than once he changed his mind; for instance, about skis. It was a mistake to have left Bowers without them; then on 7 January the other three depot'd their skis because of the roughness of the *sastrugi*, but after a mile or so the *sastrugi* levelled out so they returned to fetch them. This lost at least an hour, and every hour counted. Next day a blizzard held them in their bags, and Scott drew comfort from reflecting that Evans' hand would benefit from the rest. On 10 January they resumed the march, made a depot of one week's provisions and a few sundries (such as Wilson's pyjama jacket) and reckoned they were only ninety-seven miles from the Pole. But the surface was terrible, covered with softy sandy snow; the *sastrugi* had become confused and the steering very difficult in bad light. 'The clouds don't seem to come from anywhere,' Scott complained. 'I never had such pulling; all the time the sledge rasps and creaks. We have covered six miles, but at fearful cost to ourselves.'

This is the first clear reference to the fact that everyone was tiring. On the Barrier they had worn out the ponies; now they were wearing out themselves. 'Another hard grind in the afternoon and five (geog.) miles added. About seventy-four miles from the Pole – can we keep this up for seven days? It takes it out of us like anything. None of us ever had such hard work before . . . Our chance still holds good if we can put the work in, but it's a terribly trying time.' A day later, 'It is an effort to keep up the double figures, but if we can do another four marches we ought to get through. It is going to be a close thing.' Two days later, everyone felt chilled in the night camp, despite a higher temperature than the night before. 'It is most unaccountable why we should suddenly feel the cold in this manner.' It was, of course, a sign of diminishing vitality.

On 13 January they crossed the 89th parallel, and advanced fourteen-and-a-half miles – 'the chance holds'. Scott was getting more and more on edge. Bowers was his standby; steering in misty light under an overcast sky 'very often I could see nothing, but Bowers in my shadows directed me . . . Oh! for a few fine days! So close it seems and only the weather to baulk us.' Next day they started to descend, and made their final depot of four days' food. There was sunshine at last and they marched nearly fourteen miles. Even Scott felt almost confident. 'We *ought* to do it now.'

That was the last cheerful entry. Next day, 16 January, they made a good march in the morning and reckoned they would reach their goal next day. In the afternoon, Bowers saw something ahead which looked like a cairn. They tried to make themselves believe it was only a *sastrugus*; but half an hour later a black speck showed up unmistakeably on the snow. Nature displays nothing black at the Pole. It was a flag tied to part of a sledge. Near by was the remains of a camp and many tracks of sledges and skis. Also paw-marks of dogs – many dogs. 'This told us the whole story. The Norwegians have forestalled us and are first at the Pole.' Scott added how sorry he was for his loyal companions. He had led them into this, and, in what should have been their moment of triumph, he had failed them. 'Many thoughts come and much discussion have we had . . . All the day dreams must go; it will be a wearisome return.' Wilson allowed no trace of emotion to creep into his diary, merely noting that the Norwegians' black flag was frayed at the edges, that they were marching downhill and that there was a good parhelion in the evening.

'It was a very bitter day,' Wilson wrote on 17 January, referring to the weather; with a force five gale in their faces and fifty-four degrees of frost, they had made the coldest march he could ever remember. (He must have forgotten Cape Crozier.) Oates, Evans and Bowers all suffered from severe frostbite and they had to make an early lunch-camp because of Evans' hand. It was bitter also for the spirit. 'Great God! This is an awful place,' Scott lamented, 'and terrible enough for us to have laboured to it without the reward of priority. Well, it is something to have got here, and the wind may be our friend tomorrow.' 'A tiring day,' was Wilson's comment. He wrote calmly of Amundsen. 'He has beaten us in so far as he has made a race of it. We have done what we came for all the same and as our programme was made out.' Bowers was too busy taking sights and angles to keep up his diary, but that evening wrote a chatty letter to his mother saying that everything was fine. The great journey was done, it only remained to get back and everyone was fit and well. It was sad that they had been fore-stalled by the Norwegians, but he was glad they had done the journey in the good British way, man-hauling the loads. They formed a most congenial party and five was 'a pleasant little crowd when one is so far from home'. That night they had the fat hoosh they had promised themselves when the goal was reached and a stick of chocolate each – the funeral wake of their hopes.

They found the Norwegians' camp next morning, about two miles away. Inside the tent was a sheet of paper with five names: Roald Amundsen, Olav Olavson Bjaaland, Hilmer Hanssen, Sverre H. Hassel, and Oscar Wisting. The date, 14 December 1911, was one month and two days ago. So the Norwegians had taken twenty-one days less than the British party to reach the Pole. They had got their dogs on to the summit up a glacier they had named the Axel Heiberg. On the day Scott's party reached the Pole, Amundsen and his companions were only one week from their winter quarters in the Bay of Whales.

Everything had seemed to go as right for the Norwegians as it had gone wrong for the British. The weather was nearly always fine, there were few severe blizzards, the surfaces were generally good; on the Barrier, the dogs had even put on weight. The men, on their way back, had increased their own ration of pemmican to a pound a day each, which was all they could manage, and Amundsen wrote: 'We had such masses of biscuits that we could positively throw them about.' The journey there and back was accomplished in ninety-nine days, at an average speed of nineteen miles a day. They had their share of frostbites and narrow escapes but got back in excellent order, without sickness or injuries.

Everything was owed to the dogs, and to the men's handling of the dogs. They took fifty-two, and killed twenty-four to feed the others, and them-selves, at the head of the Axel Heiberg Glacier. (Amundsen regretted the necessity, but enjoyed the meat; during the butchering he could not take his eyes off the delicate cutlets spread out on the snow, and in the tent consumed five and wanted more.) On the Devil's Glacier the dogs flattened themselves against the ice, dug in their claws and advanced inch by inch, helped by the men, but on the Barrier 'we never had to move a foot; all we had to do was to let ourselves be towed along'. Sentences like 'perpetually fine weather', 'the sledging was ideal and the weather beautiful', 'the last eight days of our outward march we had sunshine all the time' would surely have wrung Scott's heart had he lived to read them.

Amundsen made it all sound like a picnic. No doubt, intending this impression, he glossed over minor setbacks and troubles, but minor they were. Theirs was a bold, professional and successful journey with a good share of luck. The five men, with eleven surviving dogs and two sledges, reached their *Framheim* in the Bay of Whales on 25 January 1912. (They found part of a Japanese expedition from the *Kainan Maru* camped near by.) Five days later Amundsen was off in the *Fram*, which had wintered in Buenos Aires, bound for Hobart where he handed in telegrams claiming the prize.

In the Norwegian tent, which they had named *Polheim*, Amundsen had left a note for Scott and a letter to be delivered to King Haakon. 'I am puzzled at the object,' Scott wrote, and indeed it is difficult to see in this action anything but a sly taunt, to be taken as a kind of joke perhaps. In the tent, Wilson took possession of a spirit lamp, made some sketches, and noted that tiny snow-crystals looked like miniature sea-urchins. Bowers took photographs, and then they marched seven miles south-south-east to a spot which his calculations put at within half a mile of the Pole, altitude 9500 feet. Here they built a cairn, planted 'our poor slighted Union Jacks' and the rest of the flags, photographed themselves and started for home. 'Well we have turned our back now on the goal of our ambition with sore feelings,' Scott concluded, 'and must face 800 miles of solid dragging – and goodbye to the daydreams!' They had done what they set out to do, as Wilson said; but their wreath of laurels had become a crown of thorns.

# The End
## of the Road

The five men started fairly well, hoisting their floor-cloth as a sail and scudding before the wind. Already it was getting colder; the temperature was —28°F at their second camp. They had made light of much severer temperatures than this, but now the cold troubled them. 'There is no doubt that Evans is a good deal run down.' On 23 January 1912 they had to camp early because of his hard, white, congested nose. Evans was angry with himself, 'not a good sign'. Oates' feet were always chilled. When a blizzard held them up seven miles short of the next food depot Scott wrote: 'I don't like the look of it. Is the weather breaking up? If so God help us, with the tremendous summit journey and scant food.'

At times they lost their outward track and were obliged to unharness and search for it among drifted snow-crystals and storm-tossed *sastrugi*. 'We are slowly getting more hungry.' Nevertheless, despite delays and very hard hauling on surfaces like sawdust, they made good marches: twenty-one, eighteen, twenty-two miles on two occasions. Their tiring frames were less resistant than before to injury from falls. Wilson strained a leg tendon and had to limp painfully beside the sledge without skis for several days. Scott fell and bruised his shoulder, and Evans' raw and swollen hand shed two finger-nails. Despite a surface 'white and glistening like a woodpecker's egg' (Wilson) which constantly gave way underfoot, on that day they covered nineteen miles. Then Scott and Evans fell into a shallow crevasse. It was not a bad fall, but afterwards Evans appeared 'rather stupid and incapable' on the march.

On 7 February they reached the head of the Beardmore Glacier and were at last off the hateful summit. They took a half-holiday geologising on the moraine under Mt Buckley, where Shackleton had found coal measures. Here Wilson 'had a regular field day and got some splendid things'. What they got was 35lbs of bits of rock in many of which were embedded fern-like fossil leaves and stems of plants that had been extinct for about 200,000 years.

Wilson realised their importance, but not how important they would be to palaeo-botanists, who would later examine them, and place them in a genus *Glossoptera* which flourished in warm, temperate climates in the

Later Palaeozoic times. His specimens were to furnish the first substantial evidence that Antarctica had once been clothed in vegetation. Before the evolution of mammals there were forests, lakes, rivers, and incipient deserts, since the climate was growing warmer. Those lumps of rock were perhaps the most important discoveries made by the expedition.

Their significance was greater than their finder could have realised. They furnished proof not only of profound changes in the earth's climate, but changes in its very shape and structure. Already fossils of this fern-like *Glossoptera* had been found in South Africa, India, Argentina and Australia, countries which had all formed part of the great southern continent Gondwanaland aeons ago. Wilson's finds demonstrated that Antarctica had shared this same type of vegetation and that the whole concept of a great semi-tropical southern continent – the term Gondwanaland was first used to describe it by an Austrian geologist called Suess in 1885 – was no myth. Gondwanaland was matched by a northern counterpart, Laurasia. Before that, it is now believed, a single supercontinent, Pangaea, embraced all the land surface of the earth. This was perhaps 200 million to 250 million years ago. Gradually Pangaea split and the parts drifted away from each other – India has drifted 7000 miles. Indeed they are still drifting; Europe and North America are putting about an extra inch a year between them. Wilson could not have known of this theory, which was put forward shortly after World War One, but his specimens from Mt Buckley supported it.*

Loading the rocks on to the sledge, next day the party proceeded down the glacier. To find a way between and around pressure ridges formed by tributary glaciers joining the main flow was always difficult. On 11 February, in a hazy and distorting light, they steered too far to the east and landed in the worse 'ice mess' they had ever been in. For two days, with a cheerless camp on reduced rations in between, they twisted and turned in this maze of ridges, growing more and more exhausted and despondent; the next depot could not be far away but they could not find it. Breakfast was one biscuit; they had a single meal left. At last they stumbled on the depot in a fog by sheer accident. 'The relief was inexpressible.' Scott excelled himself in under-statement when he wrote, 'There is no getting away from the fact that we are not pulling strong.' Because they were not covering the hoped-for distances they had to reduce their rations, which further

---

* Since then, many other fossil plants have been discovered in Antarctica and, to the excitement of geologists, evidence of a Palaeozoic fauna as well. In 1969 a party from Ohio State University discovered the fossil jawbone of a lizard-like reptile, *Lystrosaurus*, which flourished at the same time as *Glossoptera* plants. They were small, fast-running and lightly built reptiles, probably the ancestors of dinosaurs, and existed also in South Africa, India, and even in Russia, China and Tibet. This fossil lizard was found in the Queen Alexandra range at Coalsack Bluff. Wilson would have been looking at the eastern side of these mountains as he came down the Beardmore Glacier.

weakened them – a vicious circle. Evans was getting worse and losing heart and 'nearly broken down in brain, we think'.

On 16 February, after a 'thin' breakfast and an eight-mile morning march in thick and nasty weather, Evans collapsed with giddiness and sickness, and camp had to be made. Next day, declaring that he felt better – 'he always did' – he took his place in the traces, but his ski-boots worked loose several times, and he was left to adjust them and catch up. When he failed to do so the others went back and found him kneeling in the snow with disarranged clothing, his speech blurred and a wild look in his eyes. His companions sledged him into camp in a coma from which he never recovered, and he died soon after midnight.

A terrible thing, Scott wrote; but, facing facts, the best way out of a desperate situation. Evans was holding them back. They were down to a stark struggle for survival; the weakest had to go, or all went. A callous note crept into the diary: there was no time to mourn a steadfast companion. After a few hours' rest, they were on their way.

Wilson believed that Evans had concussed his brain when he fell into the crevasse and, weakened by his injured hand, had deteriorated day by day in the stark conditions. That he kept going for thirteen days after his fall shows extraordinary grit and willpower. Evans was the largest, heaviest man of the party and therefore needed more food than his companions to fuel his body. All were getting too little food and Evans was bound to suffer most. Bowers was the best off in this respect. Modern nutritionists, studying the case on the sketchy evidence provided in Scott's diary, have concluded that Evans' death resulted not from concussion, but from scurvy in its early stages. He showed none of the overt symptoms of this deficiency disease – Wilson would certainly have noticed them if he had – but early scurvy can lead to fragility of the blood vessels, which would have accounted for a brain haemorrhage following the minor head injury sustained on his fall. At the time of his death, all five men had been for 109 days on a diet low in all the vitamins and wholly lacking in ascorbic acid, the source of vitamin C which protects against scurvy.

They were now at the foot of the glacier where the pony meat was cached, and enjoyed their first full meal since leaving the summit. 'New life seems to come with greater food almost immediately.' Depots with adequate food and fuel at well-spaced intervals lay ahead. They should have been all right, and would have been all right had they not struck atrocious surfaces, and had they not been so nearly worn out. A covering of loose sandy snow gave them gruelling work; on the second day they advanced less than five miles. At that rate, they could not reach the next depot before running out of food. 'Pray God we get better travelling as we are not so fit as we were and the season advances apace.'

They left the glacier's foot on 19 February 1912. A week later, on the 27th, Wilson's diary ceased. Bowers had given his up on 25 January. Scott continued his ever more despondent entries until 29 March.

Six days' marching brought them to the Southern Barrier depot and here a fresh trouble came upon them, a shortage of oil. The oil allowance had been carefully calculated and two one-gallon tins had been left at each depot, sufficient for the eight days allowed to get from one depot to the next. From now on, oil was short. Probably the hot summer sun had caused evaporation even in the sealed tins, which were normally placed on top of the cairn, while the intense cold at night, now down to seventy degrees of frost, might have contracted the leather washers under the caps.*

Another seventy miles of trudging brought them to the Middle Barrier depot, and here oil was short again. Oates could no longer conceal the state of his feet. He had been marching in silent pain, his toes were black, and gangrene was setting in. Temperatures were down to −40°F, the surface was so bad that even a strong wind in the sail would not move the sledge, and every day their marches grew shorter. 'God help us, we can't keep up this pulling, that is certain. Among ourselves we are unendingly cheerful, but what each man feels in his heart I can only guess.' Putting on their foot-gear in the morning took longer and longer. The cold was piercing all their defences. Oates became unable to pull. He made no complaint and spoke little; he knew the end was near. Scott admitted that the Soldier had become a terrible burden, although he did his utmost and suffered much. 'He is wonderfully brave.'

On 7 March there is the first mention of the dogs; if Scott's instructions had been followed, they should be on their way. 'We hope against hope that the dogs have been to Mt Hooper [the next depot], then we might pull through. If there is a shortage of oil again we can have little hope . . . I should like to keep the track to the end.'

On the day of that entry the dogs, driven by Cherry-Garrard and Dimitri, were at One Ton Depot, which they had reached on 2 March to turn back for home on the 10th. One Ton Depot was seventy-two miles from Mt Hooper. On 9 March the polar party reached Mt Hooper. 'Cold comfort. Shortage on our allowance all round . . . The dogs which would have been our salvation have evidently failed.' To the end, he could not trust them. The dogs themselves had not failed, but many things had gone wrong of which Scott had no knowledge. No one, he supposed, was to blame, but it was a 'miserable fumble' – and the final blow.

A north-west wind next morning held them in camp, it was too cold to face; normally Barrier winds were southerly; now, as if God himself had

* Hodgson advanced the theory that the paraffin froze in the tins, and paraffin-ice adhering to the sides reduced the quantity that could be poured out.

turned against them, the wind was in their faces. In this bleak camp, with half-cooked food, all of them getting frostbitten, all knowing they were doomed, they discussed the situation. Oates asked for advice. He knew how much he was delaying them; perhaps, without him, they might have a slender chance. Months before, at Cape Evans, there had been a discussion about what might happen to a sledging party if one of its members were to be badly injured or to break down. Oates said that it would be the sick man's duty to eliminate himself, and that everyone should carry a revolver in case the situation arose. They carried no revolvers, but the medicine chest held opium and morphine. At this juncture Scott ordered Wilson to hand over the means of ending their troubles and Wilson complied. He kept a tube of morphine for himself and gave the others thirty opium tablets apiece. These were never used. Suicide was against the code; the Guards die, but they never surrender. So the advice to Oates was simple: just keep on. Scott did a sum. They were fifty-five miles from One Ton Depot with seven days' food; six miles a day was about the limit of their marching capacity; $6 \times 7 = 42$, leaving them thirteen miles short of the depot. 'I doubt if we can possibly do it.'

Things got worse. The north wind blew in their faces. 'A long time getting supper in the dark.' Wilson was weakening, Scott and Bowers had to make camp by themselves. The midday temperature fell to $-43°$F. 'It must be near the end but a pretty merciful end.' They would fight it out 'to the last biscuit'.

On 16 or 17 March – they had lost track of the days – Oates said he could go no farther and wanted to be left in his bag. The others refused, and he struggled on. Codes of behaviour can be cruel. He hoped to die that night, but did not; he left his opium untouched. There was a blizzard blowing in the morning. Oates made his oft-recorded remark – 'I am just going outside and may be some time' – and stumbled out of the tent. 'I want these facts recorded,' Scott wrote. 'Oates' last thoughts were of his Mother, but immediately before he took pride in thinking that his regiment would be pleased with the bold way in which he met his death.' He had borne intense suffering for weeks without complaint and did not give up hope until the very end. 'We have stuck to our sick companions to the last,' the leader wrote. 'We knew that poor Oates was walking to his death, but though we tried to dissuade him, we knew it was the act of a brave man and an English gentleman.'

They left at this camp Oates' sleeping-bag, their theodolite and a camera – but not the 35lbs of geological specimens which, at Wilson's special request, they dragged on. Scott's right foot went – 'these are the steps of my downfall'. Amputation was the least he could hope for now, 'but will the trouble spread? That is the serious question.'

On 19 March they camped with difficulty and supped off cold pemmican and biscuit. Next morning, a blizzard was blowing. Wilson and Bowers wanted to push on without the sledge to One Ton Depot, eleven miles on, to fetch food and oil, but the blizzard stopped them. They had no oil now, and only two days' food. 'Have decided it shall be natural – we shall march for the depot and die in our tracks.' They did not march again. On 29 March Scott made his last, and famous, entry. 'It seems a pity, but I do not think that I can write more. R. Scott. For God's sake look after our people.' On another page he had already scrawled, 'Send this diary to my widow.'

This was not quite the end. Nothing is more remarkable than the vitality of this forty-three-year-old man who, more than half starved and three parts frozen, lying beside his dying companions with the blizzard howling outside the small green tent, beset by the monster of despair, was able to summon strength and willpower to complete no less than twelve letters, and to complete them legibly, coherently and well. He wrote to his wife and to his mother, to his brother-in-law, to his naval colleagues Sir Francis Bridgeman and Sir George Egerton; to the Reginald Smiths, and to Sir James Barrie. There had been some quarrel or misunderstanding between him and Barrie whose cause remains unknown. Now he wrote sadly of this, asking Barrie to 'give my memory back the friendship which you suspended', to help his widow and child (Barrie's godson) and the widow of Edgar Evans. 'I may not have proved a great explorer,' he concluded, 'but we have done the greatest march ever made and come very near to great success.'

He wrote to Oates' and Bowers' mothers, and to Wilson's wife. The phrase 'His eyes have a comfortable blue look of hope' tells everything about Wilson's death; for him it had no terrors but only, as he wrote to his parents, 'an earnest looking forward to the day when we shall all meet together in the hereafter'. It was all according to God's will and all for the best. 'I have had a very happy life and I look forward to a very happy life hereafter when we shall all be together again. God knows I have no fear of meeting Him – for He will be merciful to all of us. My poor Ory may or may not have long to wait.'

Then there were business letters, as they might be called. To the very end Scott remembered his responsibilities. Duty drove his hand to write to J. J. Kinsey in New Zealand and to Sir Edgar Speyer, regretting that the expedition had been left in a muddle, thanking him for his kindness and in extenuation saying, 'But we have been to the Pole and we shall die like gentlemen.'

In his letter to Kathleen, he wrote of his hopes for his son.

I had looked forward to helping you to bring him up, but it is a satisfaction to know that he will be safe with you . . . Make the boy interested in natural history if

you can. It is better than games. They encourage it in some schools. I know you
will keep him in the open air. Try to make him believe in a God, it is comforting . . .
and guard him against indolence. Make him a strenuous man. I had to force myself
into being strenuous, as you know – had always an inclination to be idle.'

As to Kathleen herself, 'I want you to take the whole thing very sensibly,
as I am sure you will.' He would not suffer any pain; in an unusual piece of
over-statement he told her that he would leave the world 'fresh from
harness and full of good health and vigour'. When provisions were exhausted 'we shall simply stop unless we are in easy reach of another depot'.
An unemotional letter: he made it all sound as if he had done no more than
miss a train.

You know I cherish no sentimental rubbish about remarriage. When the right
man comes to help you in life you ought to be your happy self again – I wasn't a
very good husband but I hope I shall be a good memory . . . The inevitable must
be faced, you urged me to be the leader of this party, and I know you felt it would
be dangerous. I have taken my place throughout, haven't I?

There was little in the letter of regret, save for lost opportunities. 'What lots
and lots I could tell you of this journey. How much better it has been than
lounging about in too great comfort at home. What tales you would have
had for the boy, but oh, what a price to pay. Dear, you will be good to the
old Mother.' He asked her not to be too proud to accept help for the sake
of the boy. 'I haven't time to write to Sir Clements. Tell him I thought
much of him, and never regretted his putting me in charge of the *Discovery*.'
Thus at the last he recognised the thread linking a cutter race in the harbour of St Kitt's with a blizzard-bound tent in 'the heart of the Barrier
snow' near the 80th parallel South.

Finally, there was his Message to the Public, perhaps the most oft-
quoted of the expedition's many documents. By any standards this is a
clear, cogent, logically ordered statement that might have been written by a
well-fed, comfortably circumstanced individual, say a civil servant minut-
ing a file. It was Scott's apologia. He itemised the stages that had led to
disaster. The polar party had not been destroyed by faults in planning or in
organisation, but by bad weather and bad luck. It was no one's fault.

. . . but for my own sake I do not regret this journey, which has shown that
Englishmen can endure hardships, help one another, and meet death with as great
a fortitude as ever in the past. We took risks, we knew we took them; things have
come out against us, and therefore we have no cause for complaint, but bow to the
will of providence, determined still to do our best to the last . . . Had we lived, I
should have had a tale to tell of the hardihood, endurance, and courage of my companions which would have stirred the heart of every Englishman. These rough
notes and our dead bodies must tell the tale, but surely, surely, a great rich country
like ours will see that those who are dependent on us are properly provided for.

Throughout these last writings runs the same note of justification. It was as if he was addressing a phantom jury on behalf of the defence. 'Every detail of our food supplies, clothing and depots . . . worked out to perfection. . . . We have missed getting through by a narrow margin which was justifiably within the risk of such a journey.' No man can foresee all risks, guard against every contingency.

Nor did death spell failure. They had achieved their aim, the Pole: but a greater aim might be achieved by the manner of their dying. They were setting an example. Several years before, he had spoken of this to one of his naval friends. He 'only wanted to set an example of enterprise and facing risks and hardships, much needed in these days', he had told Captain Nicolson.

The example he had hoped to set was in courage, loyalty, prowess, hardihood – the Spartan virtues. But death crowned all. In his last letters, this is a constant theme. They had stuck to their sick companions, at heavy cost to themselves; they had never lost heart; there had been no recriminations. Wilson, he wrote to Ory, had never uttered 'a word of blame for leading him into this mess'; they had stuck it out to the end and died with fortitude. To Sir Francis Bridgeman, 'After all we are setting a good example to our countrymen, if not by getting into a tight place, by facing it like men when we were there.'

For ten days the blizzard raged before the last entry on 29 March 1912. Then silence, to be broken nearly eight months later (12 November 1912) when Surgeon Atkinson, leader of the search party, pulled aside the flap of the tent whose top had been spotted, all but buried in snow, by 'Silas' Wright. They saw the three men in their sleeping-bags. On the left was Wilson, his hands crossed on his chest; on the right, Bowers, toggled into the bag. Both had died peacefully, it was thought in their sleep. But Scott was lying half out of his bag, one arm stretched towards Wilson – 'one of the finest friends a man ever had', wrote Atkinson. It was a horrid sight, said Tryggve Gran. 'It was clear he had had a very hard last minutes. His skin was yellow, frostbites all over.' Gran went out of the tent, and later wrote, 'I envied them. They died having done something great – how hard must not death be having done nothing.' Petty Officer Williamson was deeply moved. 'His face was very pinched and his hands, I should say, had been terribly frostbitten . . . Never again in my life do I want to behold the sight we have just seen.'

The dead men had left everything tidy, the tent so well pitched that it had withstood winter storms, the floor-cloth spread, empty pannikins beside them. Near Scott was a little lamp made from a tin with a piece of finnesko for wick; probably Scott had used it to burn what little methylated spirit was left, in order to write until the end. He, the oldest, had been the last to die –

even after Bowers, so much younger and believed to be the toughest man who ever came to the Antarctic.

Atkinson took charge of the diaries and letters, assembled the company and read aloud the account of Oates' death, which Scott had wished to be made known, together with salient points from the diary, and the Message to the Public. Then he read the Burial Service and a chapter from Corinthians, and the bareheaded men, standing in a chilly wind with light, drifting snow, sang 'Onward Christian Soldiers', Scott's favourite hymn. The bamboos were removed, the tent collapsed over the bodies and a snow cairn built over all, surmounted by a cross of skis. There they would lie and slowly, slowly, drift northwards with the movement of the Barrier; one day they would find their last resting place in the sea.

By the side of the tent was the sledge with the 35lbs of rocks. That was all their luggage. For dying men, 35lbs is quite a lot of weight to haul.

Atkinson led his party back along the route, so far as they could judge it, that had been followed by the three companions, to look for the body of Oates, but snow had done the work of burial. They found his sleeping bag, but no more. Near the spot where they reckoned he had walked to his death, about fifteen miles from the last camp, they erected a cross with the inscription which became so famous:

Hereabouts died a very gallant gentleman, Captain L. E. G. Oates of the Inniskilling Dragoons. In March 1912, returning from the Pole, he walked willingly to his death in a blizzard to try to save his comrades, beset by hardship.

Then Atkinson with his party, leading mules that had been sent from India at Scott's request and come down in the *Terra Nova*, turned back for Hut Point. They had been prepared, if necessary, to go to the top of the Beardmore Glacier to find traces of the lost men. Now they must get back without delay to start another search; Campbell and his party, marooned for the whole winter in Victoria Land, had not returned, and were very likely dead as well.

# 25  Finale

On 18 February 1912 Kathleen Scott, addressing her absent husband, wrote in her diary, 'I was very taken up with you all evening. I wonder if anything special is happening to you. Something odd happened to the clocks and watches between nine and ten p.m.' This was the day the polar party set out on their unfinished journey across the Barrier, after Edgar Evans had died.

On 7 March came the news of Amundsen's triumph, news made worse for Kathleen by excited press reports that Scott had reached the Pole at the same time. Four days later, her young son asked her whether Amundsen was a good man. Yes, she thought so, Kathleen answered; Peter said, 'Amundsen and Daddy both got to the Pole. Daddy isn't working now.' This was the day on which Wilson distributed the opium, Oates could go no farther and Scott wrote, 'What we or he will do, God knows.'

In April came reports, cabled from New Zealand after the arrival of the *Terra Nova*, that on 4 January 1912 Scott had been safely on the summit and going strong within 150 miles of the Pole. It was generally assumed in London that the explorers were by then back at Cape Evans where they would winter, complete their scientific programme, and return for good early in 1913. Everyone was sad that Amundsen had beaten them, and Markham was incensed. Kathleen had to stop him writing furious letters to the press. She thought that her friends were afraid of her, 'I'm not going to recount what I have been feeling even if I could, it would not be pleasant reading'; but Nansen cabled a sympathetic message and, in a letter, told her that King Haakon, much as he admired Amundsen, wished that the priority had gone to Scott. (Nansen was by then in love with her, and sending her passionate and introspective letters.) She gave a party to which 110 people came. 'It seems an odd moment to give a party, but I went through it rather on principle.' In November 1912, Amundsen came to London to lecture, Markham escaped to Portugal to avoid 'the gadfly', and Kathleen went *incognito* to the lecture and found it modest, but excessively dull.

With sculpting, going to parties, dancing, and caring for her son, she filled her days to the full. 'I know you will keep him in the open air,' Scott had written, and indeed she did; he was out of doors in all weathers, generally barefoot and clothed in sleeveless tunics quite unlike the velvet suits with Little Lord Fauntleroy collars then in favour. Dutifully, she took him to see his grandmother and aunts at Henley-on-Thames, but there was an atmosphere of restraint. 'I found Mummy, Rose and Monsie sitting silently round a tea table. I tried to tell them the news and returned.' Another visit drew the comment, 'I cannot conceive how you emanated from that family. I like them, I enjoy them, we get on finely together – but how, oh how and where do *you* come in!'

There were days of depression, an undercurrent of fear. 'I wonder what your diary records today. I'm terribly depressed, you know that doesn't often happen to me. I have been entirely unable to make myself do anything or read anything all day . . . I wonder what you are doing. I'm lonely. There is absolutely nobody to talk to about it all. The young people don't care and the old people don't feel.'

The expedition was expected back in New Zealand early in April 1913, and in January she set out to meet him by way of the United States. After a few days spent in camp with cowboys in New Mexico, where she slept in the open, baked bread on a cedar-log camp-fire, and galloped over the cactus-clad range, she embarked at San Francisco in RMS *Aorangi*, expecting a long, dull voyage. On 19 February, between Tahiti and Raratonga, the captain called her to his cabin and, with shaking hands, showed her a message received by means of the still embryonic wireless. 'Captain Scott and six others perished in a blizzard after reaching the South Pole January 18th.' She thanked him, and went about her business mentally stunned, having a Spanish lesson, discussing American politics at lunch – the other passengers had not yet been told – playing deck games and drawing some comfort from a young Third Officer who 'like a big dog sits by me and is sorry'. He was there, she afterwards learnt, in case she tried to throw herself overboard; and had she believed in an after-life, she would have done so. 'But I am afraid my Con has gone altogether, except in the great stirring influence he must have left on everyone who had knowledge of him.' It was her realisation of the mental agony he must have gone through, even more than the physical suffering, that tormented her. 'I think never was there a man with such a sense of responsibility and duty, and the agony of leaving his job undone, losing the other lives, and leaving us uncared for, must have been unspeakable.'

Her brother Wilfrid was at Wellington to meet her, together with Ory Wilson, Atkinson, and Teddy Evans who had taken the *Terra Nova* down to McMurdo Sound to embark, as he had expected, Scott and his party with the rest of the expedition. There was a heart-rending moment when the ship, smartened up from stem to stern, gaily dressed with flags, with places for a banquet laid in her wardroom, nosed her way up to the edge of the ice at Cape Evans. Campbell shouted over to them the bad news. A stunned silence followed, to be broken by the rattle of the anchor and, later, by the clatter of plates as preparations for the banquet were removed.

Atkinson handed over to Kathleen her husband's diary and last letter. From the dead man's courage she drew courage for herself, and strength to face the world. With the irony of fate, the death of its leader removed the financial difficulties in which the expedition had been floundering – it was in debt to the tune of nearly £30,000. Appeals had gone unheeded, but now a public that had refused to help the living was persuaded, if with some difficulty, to give generously to commemorate the dead. After a shaky start, several fund-raising efforts were merged into a united Scott Memorial Fund to which the King and Queen each contributed £100. Before long, £75,509 had come in, debts had been paid, grants made to all dependants, and a residue of some £12,000 remained. Later this was handed over to Cambridge University and put towards the foundation of the Scott Polar Research Institute at Cambridge, officially constituted in 1926, of which Frank Debenham became the first director. Scott's personal estate, amounting to £3231, had been pledged to the expedition's funds. The honour that the King would have bestowed upon him was awarded to Kathleen, in the shape of the rank, style and precedence accorded to the wife of a Knight Commander of the Order of the Bath; she became Lady Scott and, nine years later, Mrs Edward Hilton Young, followed by yet another change of name when her politician husband was created Lord Kennet of the Dene.

Apart from Scott's widow and family, none felt more stricken than old Sir Clements, now eighty-three and plagued by gout. 'I have been quite overwhelmed with grief for the last three days,' he wrote. Scott had been right in all his calculations, and reached the Pole exactly as arranged. It was the breakdown of his two companions, unforseeable disasters, that had wrecked the plan. 'The other three could easily have saved themselves if they had bade farewell to their disabled comrades rather than perish with them. But that was impossible for such men . . . What a dear good fellow he was . . . It is heart-breaking.'

Markham himself had less than three years more to live, but it cannot be said that grief hastened his end, because this came about by accident. He was reading in bed, by the light of a candle, from a book in old Portuguese; there was electric light in the room, but typically, he preferred the old-fashioned means of illumination. The bedclothes caught fire; although the butler rushed in to extinguish the flames, the shock was too great and the old man died, unconscious, in January 1916. Over sixty books, erudite and by modern standards mostly dull, stood to his credit, and one was in the press when he died.

One of his last public functions was to attend the unveiling, in November 1915, of Kathleen's statue of her husband. (She did not go herself; she stayed in the munitions factory where her war-work lay.) Scott stands in his polar clothing, ski-stick in hand, stern and resolute, gazing out into the distance as he had so often gazed across the snows. There are two versions of the statue, one in Waterloo Place, London, in bronze, and the other, in Italian marble, in Christchurch, New Zealand, whence he and his companions had twice sailed, and only once returned.

Kathleen carved busts and statues of many others among the leaders of her day: kings, prime ministers, press barons, writers, adventurers and her old admirer Nansen, who pressed her to marry him, but was rejected as a suitor while kept as a friend. All her subjects, with the exception of a few children, were men. When she knew she was dying of leukaemia, in 1947, she chose her own epitaph: 'Kathleen. No happier woman ever lived.'

Debenham, who became Cambridge University's first professor of geography, wrote to Kathleen that, in retrospect, it was strange that a disaster to the polar party was not considered by the other members of the expedition even as a possibility, so confident were they of the ability of those five men to overcome any obstacle in their way. Yet a clear warning had been given, and it was stranger still that Atkinson did not realise its implications. The last news which those at the base received of the polar party came in notes written on 4 January 1912 from 87° 32′s, when Teddy Evans, Crean and Lashly had turned back. All was then well with Scott's team, but about three weeks later Evans, on the homeward trudge, began to display the overt symptoms of scurvy. There was nothing to be done but to push on. His condition rapidly worsened until he collapsed completely in a critical condition. They had by this time struggled to within thirty-five miles of Hut Point, Crean and Lashly dragging their officer on the sledge in a semi-conscious state.

The two seamen decided that Crean would march to Hut Point leaving Lashly with the comatose Evans. The weather was thick and very cold, they had discarded their skis earlier, so Crean had to march on foot, and if a blizzard came down he would be finished, for he could take no tent or sleeping-bag. Had these two men left Evans to die in the snow, as he implored them to do, they could have got back safely, but they never even thought of doing so. All Crean took to eat on the march was a little chocolate and a few biscuits. He had already walked for 1500 miles, hauling a sledge for most of the way. He got to Hut Point in eighteen hours, with one short pause to eat a biscuit, half an hour before a blizzard came down.

At Hut Point he found Atkinson and Dimitri with the dogs, preparing to start in about a week's time for One Ton Depot to meet the returning polar party and speed their journey home. As soon as the blizzard abated, these two men started out to succour Evans instead, taking seal meat, onions and fruit, and found him still alive; Atkinson subsequently said he doubted whether the sick man could have lasted more than another twenty-four hours. They brought him back to Hut Point, but he was too ill to be left, so Atkinson gave up his intention to go himself to One Ton Depot to meet Scott. If Evans had not succumbed to scurvy, Atkinson would have gone south as intended and might have reached Mt Hooper in time to save the four men. That is only one of the many might-have-beens.

At this stage, 19–20 February, Atkinson felt no uneasiness about the safety of the polar party, who were not expected back for at least another month. (Scott had given 27 March as his latest probable date.) But in a private memorandum written after news of the tragedy reached England, Hodgson suggested that Teddy Evans' near-death from scurvy should have given the doctor a plain and urgent warning. If Evans had been so badly afflicted, then the polar party, after a further month's sledging on the summit in the most gruelling of conditions, could not have hoped to escape.

To the question 'could any of these lives have been saved?' Hodgson returned an unequivocal yes. If, immediately after Teddy Evans had been brought in, the entire resources of the base camp had been mobilised and a six-man party, with supplies, had been despatched, they would, in his opinion, have reached the four men struggling northwards in time to have rescued them.

Actions that appear with hindsight to be expedient may at the time appear as capitulations to panic. Atkinson was a junior doctor, pitchforked by accident into the position of commander, and Scott's instructions had been clear: not to send out a relief party. Scott was not yet overdue; while Evans had been hard hit by scurvy, Crean and Lashly had shown no traces of it; too little was then known about the disease to render Hodgson's conclusion self-evident. Atkinson did not ring the alarm bell, but he did summon Cherry-Garrard from Cape Evans and instruct him to take the two dog-teams, with Dimitri and extra supplies, as far south as One Ton Depot – what Hodgson described as 'a "How do you do? Just come to help you in" sort of party'.

On 26 February 1912 Cherry-Garrard started out with trepidation, never having driven dogs in his life, nor learnt the art of navigation; the weather was thick, he could not wear his glasses because of fogging, and his destination was 142 miles away. He and Dimitri reached the depot in eight days, on 3 March, and were relieved to find that the polar party had not yet arrived, so that their supplies would be in time.

Cherry-Garrard's instructions were to get to the depot and, if there was no sign of Scott and his men, to use his own judgement as to what to do next. The matter was settled for him by a blizzard which blew for four days.

When it stopped, his dog-food was sufficient for only two more days at the depot, allowing one week for the return. He could have gone south for one more day, fifteen or twenty miles, and run the risk of missing the party, and even the route. But something was wrong with Dimitri, whose right side was getting partially paralysed; day temperatures were down to −37°F and the dogs were feeling the cold. He decided to start back for Hut Point on 10 March. The polar party were still not overdue. (They were, at that moment, at Mt Hooper, seventy-two miles away.) Having regard to the food at his disposal, and to Dimitri's ailment, and to the cold, he could not have saved Scott.

There was one thing he could have done, had he known of the urgency; he could have gone on, killed dogs to feed the dogs, and, with a lot of luck, reached Mt Hooper in time. But Scott had left instructions that the dogs were not to be put at risk because they would be needed for the sledging programme in the following year. Cherry-Garrard made the only decision he could have made in the circumstances; but the faint possibility that, had he ignored his instructions and gone south towards Mt Hooper, killing dogs as he went – and had there been no blizzards and had Dimitri got no worse, and had he not lost the way or missed the polar party in thick, over-cast weather – he might have saved three at least of his comrades, haunted him for the rest of his life.

He had a dreadful journey back, with the dogs out of hand, and Dimitri worsening, and horrible weather; and when he reached Hut Point there was more bad news. Campbell's Northern Party was stranded on the coast of Victoria Land, with no winter equipment and very little food, and no hope of relief until the following Antarctic spring. Pennell in the *Terra Nova* had picked them up from their winter quarters at Cape Adare in January 1912 and deposited them at Evans Cove, on Inexpressible Island farther down the mainland coast, to carry out a six weeks' sledging programme. He had arranged to collect them before the end of February and return them to base. Pack-ice defeated this plan. Time and again the *Terra Nova* tried to butt a way through, until Pennell had reluctantly to abandon Campbell and his men to their own devices with no hut, thin summer clothing, and only skeleton rations for six men for a month. Somehow they would have to live off the land, or rather off the sea, and use blubber for cooking, since there was no paraffin, if they were to survive.

Atkinson now began to feel anxiety about the polar party. The dogs were done up, temperatures were falling, Dimitri was still unwell, and Cherry-Garrard so exhausted that he fainted, fell, and injured a hand. That left at Hut Point only Atkinson himself and Keohane, who had come up from Cape Evans with Cherry-Garrard, on the active list. The doctor decided that he and Keohane would go south, man-hauling, as far as they could, in the hope of encountering Scott. A few days before they were due to start, the dogs 'sang' at breakfast, generally a signal of someone's approach; but no one came. Atkinson looked, and Cherry-Garrard felt, haggard with mounting anxiety. On the night of 24 March, Cherry-Garrard related, Atkinson was woken by a knocking on the window above their heads. He shouted 'Hello!' and then 'Cherry, they're in!'; a candle was lit and everyone rushed out of the hut. There was silence; no one there. The dogs slept outside; had one shaken himself and hit the window with his tail? Atkinson swore he heard footsteps; but no one came.

On 27 March 1912, Atkinson and Keohane started out across the Barrier. With only two in harness, and low temperatures, conditions were hard, but they pressed on to reach a point eight miles south of Corner Camp. By this time Atkinson was certain in his mind that the polar party must have perished. He left a depot of a week's provisions and returned to Cape Evans to find all well, although the group was much depleted; Simpson, Griffith Taylor, Ponting, Meares, Day, the convalescent Teddy Evans, Anton and two seamen had gone home in the *Terra Nova*, leaving Wright in charge of the research. Taking Wright, Keohane and Williamson, Atkinson made an attempt, late in the season as it was, to go to the rescue of Campbell's party up the western coast. They could get no farther than Butter Point.

'A man-of-infinite-resource-and-sagacity' was how Kipling described a shipwrecked mariner menaced by a whale. That description might well have been applied not only to Victor Campbell but to all the members of his party. Five were from the Royal Navy, whose resource was proverbial; the sixth, the young West Country geologist Raymond Priestley, did not lag behind. Gales having ripped their tents to pieces, they dug an igloo in the snow measuring twelve feet by nine feet and only five feet six inches high, so no one could stand upright. They made blubber lamps out of tins, and for nearly six months lived like troglodytes in a thick, greasy atmosphere of blubber smoke that saturated their worn, inadequate clothing and penetrated into the pores of their skins. They learnt to eat and even to relish blubber, normally considered revolting. Seals and penguins were not nearly as plentiful as they had hoped, and one biscuit a day was all their extra ration, save on birthdays, when the allowance was increased to two; a biscuit could be made to last half an hour.* On Sundays, each man had twelve lumps of sugar, and on the last day of each month twenty-five raisins. They were always hungry. There was a red-letter day when Browning

* These were no ordinary biscuits. Scott had them specially made by Huntley & Palmers to the following formula: flour 80lbs, rice gluten 13¾lbs, wheat meal 20lbs, sugar 7½lbs, lard 2½lbs, salt 10oz, sodium bicarbonate 2½oz, water 40lbs. They were baked to a final water content of 5% and each biscuit weighed 2oz.

killed a seal whose stomach contained thirty-six fish not too far digested to be edible.

In such conditions the six men lived out the black winter, held sometimes in their sleeping-bags for days on end by blizzards. They dreamt of food; sang old familiar songs and such hymns as they could remember; read aloud from *David Copperfield*, a life of R. L. Stevenson, the *Decameron*, and the New Testament; exchanged repartee and managed to keep cheerful, hopeful and sane.

Nor was naval discipline abandoned. Campbell drew an imaginary line to bisect the twelve foot by nine foot cave; on one side was the messdeck, on the other the quarterdeck, and nothing could be officially heard that had been spoken on the other. As a result the three officers heard many entertaining and salutary stories about officers under whom the three seamen had previously served, from which they drew the appropriate moral. Priestley believed that this arrangement greatly relieved the strain on nerves and tempers. All problems were freely discussed by everyone but, when the discussion ended, Campbell's word was law. 'No one could surpass him,' Priestley wrote, 'in cheerfulness or efficiency at work either as housemaid or cook.' In sharing their short commons, there was absolute fairness; even biscuit crumbs were divided into six equal little piles.

Their health remained remarkably good until they were attacked by ptomaine poisoning, traced to the putrefaction of seal-meat kept in a tin to thaw it out. Conditions in the igloo with men suffering from acute diarrhoea can scarcely be imagined; they had to crawl along a tunnel on hands and knees to reach a thirty-six-foot latrine pit at the other end. Frank Browning in particular was hard hit, and when in spring they set out on a 200-mile-long sledge-hauling journey down the coast he very nearly died. Food depot'd by Debenham's geological party the previous summer saved him in the nick of time. Thirty-seven days' sledging brought them to the base alive, but so thin that their limbs, Priestley wrote, were corrugated rather than rounded, and in six days after they got in he put on 35lbs. Later, one of their number, Petty Officer George Abbott, went out of his mind.

Seal-meat had protected them from scurvy. Was Hodgson right, and others after him, in singling out scurvy as the main cause of the death of the polar party? They did not die of overt scurvy; Atkinson, who saw the bodies, testified to that, and there is no mention of the conspicuous symptoms in Scott's or Wilson's diaries. But there can be little doubt that scurvy in its early stages was to blame for so weakening the men that they felt the cold more acutely, grew slower in making and breaking camp, made shorter marches, fell behind in their time-table and so were trapped by the blizzard eleven miles from One Ton Depot.

Scott went to infinite trouble to base his diets on the latest scientific information. In his day, the science of nutrition was in its infancy, and the information needed simply was not there. Recent studies* have shown that, in view of the tremendous exertions demanded of the men, the polar party's diet was deficient not only in vitamins but in energy-producing elements as well. Nutritionists now consider that the human body can do without vitamins for no more than about 120 days at most before symptoms of deficiency appear. The polar party had been on sledging diets for 150 days before the end came.

Despite all that went wrong, Scott's party had by almost superhuman efforts made up lost time, and would have come back safely had they been able to keep up on their return journey the marches they had made on their way out. So ultimately scurvy killed them, aided and abetted by injuries, extreme cold, blizzards, shortage of fuel and other factors. Scott was right to claim that 'the causes of the disaster are not due to faulty planning'. He could not have laid plans in the light of knowledge that did not then exist.

There remains the question of motive. What persuaded these men to seek out hardships so extreme that most ordinary mortals would give all they possess to avoid them? There is seldom in human behaviour such a thing as a single, simple motive, any more than there is a single, simple cause of cancer. The skein of action is ravelled up from many threads. Fame and fortune are generally given first place. Also on the list are love of country, lust for adventure, devotion to a cause, and obscurer forces like an urge towards martyrdom. Certainly there is curiosity: desire to know what lies over the next hill, at the top of the highest mountain and at the bottom of the deepest sea, on the moon, on the planets and beyond the stars. All such motives are mixed up together, and the analyst who tries to sort them out and label them is generally wasting his time.

Not only are human motives mixed, but one often masquerades as another. A lust for personal fame may put on the more noble garment of a wish to add lustre to your country's honour; indeed these two may be so closely united as to be one – how separate Napoleon's ambition from France's glory? Greed for wealth seems to be the simplest motive, but since wealth is a key to power, it is power that many of those who take the infinite pains to become extremely rich are really after. Everybody, it seems, wants power, or almost everybody, in great measure or small: to rule an empire, win a battle, command an industry, direct a newspaper, propound a philosophy, control a trade union, gain a political office, organise a demo., write a play, or simply to keep a class of children in order, or a garden club or women's institute on the right lines. Doubtless Scott was no exception to the rule of power-hunger, but it was not a driving hunger. For nearly

* In particular that made by Dr A. F. Rodgers of the Bristol Medical School and published in *The Practitioner*, 212 no. 1270, April 1974.

twenty years he had lived under a system which rations power. A naval Captain may seem omnipotent, but is at all times himself under authority. Success at the Pole would not have changed this.

Was fame the spur? The hope of going down in history as the first man at the South Pole? For this, it can be argued, he led his friends to death in the snow. Fame and its attendant flattery had touched him after his first expedition; did it impel him into his second, with much greater fame as the reward? This may have been so. Yet there was little in his nature, either of the calculation that sees fame as a bargaining counter in the market-place of life, or of the boyish immaturity that revels in fame for its own sake (as did Shackleton). Scott recoiled from the flummery attached to it, the speeches, dinners, gushing acquaintances.

In the beginning, he was pushed into the enterprise, as we have seen, by Sir Clements Markham. Thereafter, his destiny lay on a moving belt, and it moved only one way. The label 'polar explorer' was tied securely round his neck. Nothing in his conduct after the return of the *Discovery* suggests an urgent wish, or even at first a mild one, to return to the Antarctic as quickly as possible. It suggests rather a wish to enjoy his independent command, to climb up the naval ladder and to establish his first home. Certainly he was experimenting with motor sledges and had a second expedition, one day, in mind. If Markham had pushed him into the first, a combination of his friends, his wife, and the activities of Shackleton pushed him into his second attempt on the Pole. In a slang phrase, he was stuck with it. To do nothing would have been to raise the suspicion that he had funked the job. And, above all, his sense of duty was involved.

Everyone who knew Scott agreed on the strength of his sense of duty. Now it was his duty to finish the job he had begun. Moreover, he was a patriot. Today patriotism is so out of fashion that either it seems ridiculous, like frilly parasols and solar topees, or it seems downright wicked, a drug concocted by the ruling class to induce subservience in the ruled. Between Scott's generation and that of his grandchildren lies a mental gap so deep and wide that an effort of imagination must be summoned up to see things through the eyes of his contemporaries.

Those were the men of 1914 – 'the men who marched away'. When Scott's body was found, the start of the Great War was less than two years away. All the men who survived Scott's expedition were involved. In the seas off Jutland, in the Dardanelles, in the English Channel and in Flanders, they lost lives, limbs or ships, won their medals, and returned to a world that was parting company for ever with the world of their youth. Like a floe cracked by a great under-swell of storm-blown seas, past and present were drifting apart at the mercy of uncharted tides, loyalty to King and Country on one floe and loyalty to the individual – to friend, family, workmate or just oneself – on the other, separated like Bowers and his ponies by an ever widening gap inhabited by ideological Killer Whales.

Loyalty is the cement of nations. The British Empire was still a well-cemented entity in Scott's day. If the cement was beginning to crumble, few people realised it. He was under thirty when the Diamond Jubilee celebrated the zenith of the Empire. The year the *Terra Nova* sailed was the year of the greatest of the Indian durbars. To serve so great an empire was seen by those who ruled it, if not always by the ruled, as a privilege for which a price had fairly to be paid. There was nothing insincere, ignoble or ridiculous about loyalty to the nation, that is, patriotism, then; it was simply necessary, like the cement. When a building has crumbled into disparate blocks, or perhaps become a picturesque ruin, cement becomes super-fluous, and disappears. Scott's loyalty, like that of his contemporaries, was deep and genuine, one of the strands of motive making up the skein. Despite his dislike, almost abhorrence, of competition when applied to the Antarctic, he came to believe that it was his mission, however imposed, to 'bag the Pole', as Wilson had put it, for his nation. His tragedy was not only that he failed in this, but that he never really believed in its overriding importance. Nevertheless, it was his mission, and he failed, by however narrow a margin, and so faced the homeward journey a dispirited man.

Dispirited, but not defeated; there might yet be a patriotic purpose in it all. Failure could be turned to triumph by the manner in which he and his companions met their end. Examples in dying were soon to be very much needed, and who can say whether the grim finale of his last journey did not play its part in quickening the spirit of the nation in preparation for the coming test. On hearing of the disaster, Colonel Percy Bruce, one of Kathleen's many cousins, wrote to her elder brother, 'It just shows how one can face death . . . The little things, the political arguments and such like don't seem of much moment now, do they? How splendid it all is. I can't help feeling even a little proud of myself for being of the same flesh and blood even. This is indeed a case of death where is thy sting.' So felt many others as August 1914 grew near.

From first to last, the influence of Edward Wilson upon his friend and leader must not be under-estimated. Wilson was that rare phenomenon, a good man whose goodness does not provoke resentment, mistrust, or that kind of prickliness resulting from a feeling of inferiority. Perhaps it was his sense of humour that saved him from the taint of sanctimony. Scott loved him as a friend, almost idealised him as a man, and consulted him in so many ways that Wilson shares some at least of the credit, and the blame alike, for what went well and what went wrong. Everyone loved Uncle Bill, or almost everyone; among the eulogies, only one adverse comment stands out. Douglas Mawson called on Wilson when he was trying to persuade

Scott to attach his own separate project to the *Terra Nova* expedition, and stated flatly in his account of the interview, 'I did not like him.' But then Mawson was hoping for the job of Scientific Director to which Wilson had just been appointed, and Wilson did not agree to Mawson's terms.

As to Wilson's motives, there is not much doubt about those. Fame and fortune were temptations of the devil that never, so far as the record goes, tempted him. Few men can have more conscientiously striven to live as a true Christian, neither denying the world nor accepting its false values. The mainspring of his life was the worship of God through a delight in the works of God's hand. He might have written the hymn 'All things bright and beautiful'. He was an ascetic, yet there was something in him of the boisterous undergraduate; he was an artist of delicate and perceptive sensitivity, and a dedicated scientist with a passion for truth: a very complex man. In volunteering for polar exploration he was in part responding to the call of adventure, but in the main seizing an opportunity to learn more of the marvels God had created, and to spread the knowledge of them to his fellow men.

> Though secrets hidden are all forbidden
> Till God means man to know,
> We might be the men God meant should know . . .

Whatever opportunity offered he must take, for it was all part of God's plan.

'Little Bowers' was every bit as indifferent as Wilson to fame and fortune, and just as convinced of a divine plan for the world and everybody in it. He tried to explain his own motive in his last letter to his mother. 'The chief thing that impels me is the indefinable call that is as inexplicable as it is insistent. Anyway I go from here with a joyful heart that nothing on earth can take away.' Loyalty to his chief and to his country reinforced the indefinable call of the unknown. 'I am Captain Scott's man,' he had previously written, 'and I shall stick to him right through.' Without doubt, Edgar Evans shared this simple resolution.

'Titus' Oates kept his motives hidden, and the destruction of his diary ensures that so they will remain. He was bored with army life, he sought action, he shared the thirst for adventure felt by many young men of his time and class. He had no need to seek a fortune, which in any case did not interest him, and it is most unlikely that he sought fame. A certain gruffness of manner, a dislike of society, a contempt for women (other than his mother, his friend and confidante), an obsession with sport involving animals and with animals themselves, all these suggest some inner injury or apprehension, a disillusion with himself and with the world. In going to the Antarctic – he was desperately anxious to be chosen – he was perhaps running away, to seek in that austerely male companionship a sanctuary from the complexities of the civilised world. Of his leader he expressed few opinions, apart from some irritation when the Captain tried to balance the need for coal against that for pony-fodder. He was a lone wolf. His last act was a fine one, but scarcely one of self-sacrifice; he was already done for and knew it, and to walk into a blizzard seemed a fitter way for a soldier to die than to swallow the opium tablets in his wallet. Oates remains an enigma, which is no doubt what he would have wished to be. It is certain that he hated publicity. By his death, he secured it.

Charles Wright, the Canadian physicist – Sir Charles by then – after lecturing, some sixty years later, to young Americans manning the Scott Base in McMurdo Sound, was asked, in some amazement, why the bodies in the tent had not been taken back to England to be buried with full honours in a British national mausoleum. He could only reply that it had never occurred to any of the search party to do so. The bodies belonged to the Barrier – or to the Ross Ice Shelf, as it has now become – and there they should remain. On Observation Hill, overlooking Hut Point and the northern reaches of the Barrier, the expedition's survivors erected a cross made by carpenter Davies from Australian jarrah, inscribed with the names of the five men. At Cherry-Garrard's suggestion, the last line of Tennyson's *Ulysses* was chosen for their epitaph.

To strive, to seek, to find, and not to yield.

The cross still stands; aeroplanes fly to the Amundsen-Scott Base on the Pole itself in a matter of hours; and the remains of Robert Falcon Scott and his three friends move slowly down towards the sea.

# Biographical Notes

ARMITAGE, Albert, 1864–1943    His father was a doctor, who moved from Perthshire to London where he became a successful practitioner. Albert was a *Worcester* cadet and joined the P & O Line as 5th Officer in 1886. In 1894 he was released to serve as nautical astronomer to the Jackson-Harmsworth expedition to Franz Josef Land, where he was one of the land party and lived in the Arctic for two and a half years. In 1896 he returned to the P & O as chief officer, to be released again in December 1900 as navigator and second-in-command of the *Discovery* expedition. He subsequently returned to the P & O, and in 1917 the ship of which he was Captain, RMS *Salsette*, was torpedoed in the Channel with heavy loss of life. His health never fully recovered and he retired, as Commodore, in 1918. His first marriage was unsuccessful and in retirement he married again, but his health continued to be poor and he died in 1943. Skelton wrote that 'the last ten years and more of his life after leaving the P & O found him very impecunious and embittered by lack of appreciation by others'. He had one daughter by his first wife.

ATKINSON, Edward Leicester, 1882–1929    Admitted as a student to St Thomas's Hospital Medical School in 1900, he qualified in 1906 and, after a year as obstetric house physician, served on the staff of the Royal Naval Hospital, Haslar. In 1910 he was appointed to the *Terra Nova* expedition as junior surgeon and parasitologist. Quiet, unassuming and hard-working, 'Atch' was universally liked. In the winter of 1912, in the absence of Victor Campbell, command at Cape Evans devolved upon him. In World War One he served with the Royal Naval Division at Gallipoli and won the DSO, with three mentions in despatches. In 1918 he was awarded the Albert Medal for gallantry following an explosion in his ship HMS *Glatton*, when he lost the sight of one eye. He married Mary Flint Hunter of Glasgow, retired from the navy as Surgeon-Captain, and died suddenly at sea in 1929, aged forty-six.

BARNE, Michael, 1877–1961    A grandson of Sir George Seymour, under whom Sir Clements Markham had gone to sea as a cadet, Michael Barne was brought up at Sotterley Park in Suffolk, and entered the navy in 1893. In the *Discovery* expedition he served as second lieutenant. After returning to the navy he had hopes of forming an Antarctic expedition of his own and was involved in experiments with motor sledges. But these came to nothing, and former injuries to his hands from frostbite, which prevented him from handling metals at low temperatures, caused him to abandon his intention to join the *Terra Nova*. He retired from the navy soon after his marriage in 1910, to be recalled at the outbreak of

World War One as Commander of HMS *Majestic*, which was torpedoed and sunk in the Dardenelles in 1915. He then served in the Dover Patrol, was mentioned four times in despatches and awarded the DSO. After retiring again, as Captain, he devoted his life to sailing small vessels in all seas and weathers. In World War Two he re-joined the navy to command an anti-submarine patrol ship. He died in 1961, aged eighty-three, leaving one son, the elder having been killed in Burma.

BERNACCHI, Louis Charles, 1876–1942   The family were silk merchants in Lombardy. Louis' father, on a voyage for his health, took a fancy to Tasmania and acquired from its government Maria Island, some 60,000 acres in extent, on the condition that he spent £20,000 on its development within ten years. The island was uninhabited, beautiful and full of game, and the Bernacchi children enjoyed an idyllic childhood. Louis studied astronomy, magnetism and physics at Melbourne Observatory and volunteered as physicist for Borchgrevink's *Southern Cross* expedition, spending two years on the Antarctic mainland at Cape Adare. Then he was involved in the *Discovery* expedition, in which he served as physicist. After that, he led a wandering life travelling in Peru, the upper Amazon basin, Namaqualand and South-east Asia, where he dabbled in rubber plantation ventures. He married in 1906 – Scott was his best man – and in 1910 unsuccessfully contested two parliamentary seats as a Liberal candidate. In 1914 he was commissioned in the RNVR and served in auxiliary patrol ships, and in 1916 in the anti-submarine division of the naval staff; he was subsequently attached to an American destroyer squadron. He was awarded the US Navy Cross and the military OBE. After the war he returned to his rubber interests, wrote several books (including *The Saga of the Discovery*), and became a council member of the Royal Geographical Society. He died in 1942, survived by two sons and two daughters.

BRUCE, Wilfrid Montagu, RNR, 1874–1953   Kathleen Scott's favourite brother. Educated at Edinburgh Academy, he joined HMS *Worcester* as a cadet and served in the Merchant Navy as an officer in passenger liners. He joined the *Terra Nova* expedition with rather vague duties, starting with a journey to Vladivostok to help Meares take the dogs and ponies to New Zealand. Thereafter he remained with Pennell in the ship and wintered in Lyttleton. (There was a Christmas party on board with presents; his sister sent everyone a sponge-bag.) Described as 'broad and beaming', his nickname in the ship was Jumbo. In the war, as a lieutenant RNR, he served in minesweepers, and left the sea soon afterwards to marry Dorothy Boot, daughter of the first Lord Trent, and become an affluent country gentleman and pig farmer near Oxford.

CAMPBELL, Victor Lindsey Arbuthnot, RN, 1875–1956   Known in the *Terra Nova* as 'the Mate' or 'the wicked Mate', Campbell ran away three times from Eton before his father agreed to let him join the Merchant Navy. He became one of the 'Hungry Hundred', a picked batch of Merchant Navy officers brought into the Royal Navy during a period of expansion early in the 1900s. Priestley described him as 'a quiet unassuming man but imperturbable and firm'. Scott selected him as commander of the Northern Party which was to explore King Edward VII Land but which perforce became the six-man Eastern Party who, in 1912, spent seven winter months in an igloo cut off from relief and without adequate food or equipment. Campbell's staunchness, resourcefulness, humour and unfailing confidence kept up the morale of the stranded party and they returned on foot safely to the base at Cape Evans. Promoted Commander for this exploit, in World War One he saw action in the Dardenelles and won the DSO. In 1922, married to a Norwegian, he settled at Black Duck in Newfoundland, where he died, aged eighty-one, survived by one son.

CHERRY-GARRARD, Apsley George Benet, 1886–1959  A cousin of Reginald Smith's, educated at Winchester and Christ Church, Oxford, he rowed in the winning eight in the Grand Challenge Cup at Henley in 1908. Scott accepted him, on Wilson's recommendation, for the *Terra Nova* expedition, to which he contributed (as did Oates) £1000. As assistant zoologist, unpaid, he helped Wilson to skin innumerable birds, took on any odd job that was going – including editorship of the *South Polar Times* – and was with Wilson and Bowers on the winter journey to Cape Crozier; in *The Worst Journey in the World* he described the whole expedition with a literary flair lacking in most of the other accounts. His entry in *Who's Who* claimed that he 'stopped the killing of penguins on Macquarie Island, which was declared a bird and seal sanctuary by the Tasmanian Government in 1916'. He was a volunteer in World War One, commanded a squadron of armoured cars, and was invalided in 1916. A long illness followed, and thereafter he was never robust. He wrote no more books, although he contributed forewords and chapters to other people's, and lived a private life, collecting books and dabbling in painting, until his death in London in 1959. He married in 1939 but had no issue.

CREAN, Thomas, 1876–1938  Described as a great Irish giant, with a profile like the Duke of Wellington's, Crean was born in County Kerry, and joined the *Discovery* as an able seaman from HMS *Ringarooma* in New Zealand. He proved a powerful sledger and cheerful companion. On Christmas Day 1902 Barne remarked on a spirited performance in their tent by Crean, Smythe and Weller of 'what they call Romeo and Juliet'. For his heroic part in saving the life of Lieutenant Teddy Evans, Crean was awarded the Albert Medal. Wilson remarked that 'Crean, Forde and Keohane are all Irishmen but especially Crean, who is a delightful creature.' When Scott was appointed Captain of the *Bulwark*, he invited Crean to be his coxswain. In 1912 Crean bought himself out of the navy, sacrificing his pension, in order to join Shackleton in the *Endurance*. He was one of the five who, with the leader, rowed for fourteen days, after the vessel had been crushed by ice, through appalling seas in the ship's boat to South Georgia Island. With Shackleton and Worsley, he crossed the mountainous island on foot to reach a whaling station and summon aid for the rest of the crew of the *Endurance* who were stranded on Elephant Island. He died at the comparatively early age of sixty-two in his native Ireland.

DAILEY, Frederick E.,  Born in 1873, in Portsmouth, Dailey started his career as shipbuilding apprentice in HM Dockyard, Devonport, and then transferred to the navy. He volunteered for the *Discovery* as carpenter, with the rank of warrant officer, and helped to supervise the building of the vessel at Dundee. Later he served with Scott in HMS *Bulwark*, and in World War One was with Admiral Beatty in HMS *Lion*, taking part in the battles of Heligoland Bight, the Dogger Bank and Jutland. He was mentioned in despatches, won the DSC and was promoted to the rank of Lieutenant. Later he became Barrack Master of the Royal Naval Barracks at Devonport, and retired with the rank of Lieutenant-Commander. Two small islands in McMurdo Sound were called after him.

DEBENHAM, Frank, 1883–1959   Son of a parson in New South Wales and a graduate of Sydney University, 'Deb' was selected by Wilson as one of the geologists in the *Terra Nova* expedition. He was a member of the Western Party which explored parts of Victoria Land and brought back valuable finds, and he prepared the final report on maps and surveys published in 1920. After World War One, when he served with the 7th Oxford and Bucks Light Infantry, he went up to Cambridge and became a Fellow and Tutor of Gonville and Caius College and lecturer in Cartography. With James Wordie and Raymond Priestley, he founded the Scott Polar Research Institute in 1926 and became its first director, and in 1930 was appointed the first Professor of Geography in the University. He retired in 1946, having been awarded an OBE. He married in 1917 and had one son and four daughters.

EVANS, Edgar, 1876–1912   'Taff' Evans was born at Rhossili in South Wales, joined the navy in 1891, became a petty officer in HMS *Majestic* and volunteered for the *Discovery*, where he made his mark as a man of energy, humour and intelligence. Scott often commented on his resourcefulness in devising improvements in sledging equipment, on his reliable memory, his grasp of detail and his great fund of anecdotes. He was a first-rate sledger, and a tendency to get drunk when in port seems to have been his only failing. After the 1901–4 expedition he became a naval physical training and gunnery instructor, won the Royal Tattoo competitions for field gunnery in 1906 and 1907, and got married. He was one of the first to volunteer for the *Terra Nova* expedition, became Scott's right-hand man, and died on the Beardmore Glacier on 18 February 1912.

EVANS, Edward Ratcliffe Garth Russell, 1881–1957   Educated at the Merchant Taylors' School, Evans entered the navy as a *Worcester* cadet in 1896. In 1902 he persuaded Sir Clements Markham to appoint him, despite his lack of qualifications, second officer in the relief ship *Morning*, which located the *Discovery* in McMurdo Sound. On the way home after the second relief expedition in 1904, he married a Christchurch girl, Hilda Russell, who died tragically on their way back after the *Terra Nova* expedition in 1913. In 1910 Teddy Evans was planning to form an expedition of his own to reach the South Pole when he heard of Scott's intentions, placed his resources at Scott's disposal and was appointed second-in-command of the *Terra Nova*. After narrowly escaping death from scurvy on the Ross Ice Shelf he returned to naval duties. In 1917 he was in command of the destroyer HMS *Broke* which, with one other destroyer HMS *Swift*, engaged six German destroyers bent on bombarding Dover. In a roistering, old-fashioned action involving cutlasses, revolvers and hand-to-hand fighting on the fo'castle, three of the enemy destroyers were sunk and the rest retreated in disorder. The crippled *Broke*, 'her decks slippery with blood', was towed safely home and in the morning, Evans wrote in *An Adventurous Life*, 'I found over 100

German prisoners being served with a fried-eggs-and-bacon breakfast and waited on by our cheerful seamen and stokers as if they had been a visiting football team.' Evans won the DSO, rose to the rank of Vice-Admiral and was created Lord Montevans in 1946.

FERRAR, Hartley T., 1879–1932   Ferrar had only just come down from Sydney Sussex College, Cambridge, when he was appointed geologist to the *Discovery* expedition in place of the eminent Dr J. W. Gregory who had resigned. In Victoria Land he discovered fossil remains of Mezozoic flora which were among the expedition's most valuable finds. He was one of those who met his future wife, Gladys Helen Anderson, in New Zealand. He joined the Egyptian Survey Department, carrying out the first extensive surveys of the western desert, and subsequently went to New Zealand, on the staff of the Geological Survey. In 1914 he volunteered for the New Zealand Mounted Rifles, returning to his job after the war. At the age of fifty-three he died suddenly leaving two sons and two daughters.

GRAN, Tryggve, 1889–   The youngest of the team, born at Bergen in Norway, and taken on for his ski-ing expertise. He was educated in Switzerland, and had just graduated from the Norwegian naval college as sub-lieutenant in the navy when Nansen introduced him to Scott at Fefor during the motor-sledge trials. He abandoned half-formed plans of his own to get up an Antarctic expedition in order to join the *Terra Nova* without pay. He proved a cheerful, versatile and popular colleague. After the expedition he joined the Norwegian Flying Corps, and in World War One served as a captain in the Royal Flying Corps, being mentioned in despatches. Later he rejoined the Norwegian Flying Corps, and in World War Two was a prisoner of war for a short time. In 1977 he was the sole survivor of the *Terra Nova* expedition, and was living in retirement at Grimstad, Norway.

HODGSON, Thomas Vere, 1864–1926   Born in Birmingham, Hodgson started his career in a bank, but studied biology in his spare time and applied successfully for a job as assistant in the Marine Biological Association's laboratories in Plymouth. Here he remained, apart from his Antarctic interlude, for the rest of his life, becoming curator of the city's museum and art gallery. Of indifferent physique, bald and short-winded, and a 'rough diamond' according to Scott, as a biologist 'Muggins' was indefatigable, and as a companion treated as something of a joke by the young naval officers. An obituary in a Plymouth newspaper described him as 'a shy, retiring man who hid his diffidence under a mask of bluffness and a devil-may-care attitude'. His erudition was wide, his contributions to scientific journals won him distinction and he became an expert on porcelain, building up a fine collection for his museum. His health never fully recovered from the strains put upon it in the Antarctic, and he died in 1926, aged sixty-two, leaving a widow but no children.

KOETTLITZ, Reginald, 1861–1916   Of German extraction, he trained at Guy's Hospital and went into practice as a physician in Dover. In 1894 he volunteered for the expedition to Franz Josef Land led by Frederick G. Jackson, and spent nearly three years in the Arctic Circle. In the *Discovery*, where he doubled the role of senior surgeon with that of bacteriologist, he was known to his companions as Cutlets, and his somewhat stiff, humourless manner made him a butt for the chaffing of the young naval officers. After the expedition, he returned to his practice in Dover but failed to settle down, and in 1911 emigrated to South Africa. The venture proved a failure, and he and his wife died of influenza within a few days of each other at Port Elizabeth in 1916.

LASHLY, William, 1868–1940   Described by Markham as 'the best man in the engine room', and by Skelton as 'the best man far and away in the ship', Lashly joined the *Discovery* with the rank of leading stoker and proved one of the outstanding successes. He was quiet, strong, a teetotaller and non-smoker, imperturbable, good-natured and absolutely dependable. Born at Hambledon in Hampshire, he was the son of a farm worker, and a married man. After the *Discovery*, he served as instructor at the Royal Naval College at Osborne, and in 1910, by then aged forty-two, volunteered for the *Terra Nova*. He and Thomas Crean were awarded the Albert Medal for saving the life of Lieutenant Teddy Evans. At the head of the Beardmore Glacier, Wilson asked Atkinson whom he would choose to go to the Pole if an extra man were to be taken; Atkinson put Lashly first, then Crean, both ahead of Petty Officer Evans. On his return from the Antarctic Lashly was discharged from the navy with a pension and he volunteered for the Reserve next day. In August 1914 he joined HMS *Irresistible* which was sunk in the Dardenelles in 1915, and then saw further service in HMS *Amethyst*. After the war he became a customs officer in Cardiff, retiring finally to Hambledon where he called his house Minna Bluff. He died at the age of seventy, and was buried, on his instructions, with no headstone on his grave.

LEVICK, George Murray, 1877–1956   Having qualified at St Bartholomew's Hospital in 1902, Levick became a naval surgeon, and was selected in 1910 as senior surgeon in the *Terra Nova*. He was one of Campbell's Northern Party who wintered in an igloo, and as a result of his observations then and later, he wrote a standard work on Adélie Penguins called *Antarctic Penguins*. He appears to have been a quiet and unassuming member of the expedition, competent as a doctor but not forceful as a personality.

MEARES, Cecil Henry, 1877–1937   The son of an army officer and mainly Scots extraction, Cecil Meares was born in Co. Kilkelly, and at the age of nineteen became a wanderer in various Eastern countries: he traded in furs in Kamchatka and Okotz in north-eastern Siberia, and was an observer of the Russo-Japanese war. After an interlude in South Africa, where he joined the Scottish Horse and fought in the Boer War, he resumed his Far Eastern travels, and in 1908 accompanied an army officer called J. W. Brooke through the territory of the Lolo tribe, where Brooke was murdered. Meares took command and brought Brooke's body, and his Russian entourage, safely back to base. In 1910 he went to Siberia on Scott's behalf to buy the expedition's dogs and ponies. In World War One he joined the Royal Flying Corps, rising to the rank of Lieutenant-Colonel, and in 1921 took part in a British Air Mission to Japan which earned him the award of the Order of the Sacred Treasure, Third Class. After this he continued his travels, ostensibly looking for a place in which to retire; a Southern Californian newspaper described him as 'a member of the British Intelligence department and diplomatic corps through five wars'. Wilson found him 'typically a man of action and a most entertaining mess-mate and full of fun'. He finally settled, with his wife, in British Columbia, and died there aged sixty.

MILL, Hugh Robert, 1861–1950   One of a family of eleven, Hugh Robert Mill was born in Thurso, Scotland, the son of a country doctor, and a delicate child. While studying for his Doctorate of Science at the University of Edinburgh, specialising in chemistry, he worked at the Scottish Marine Station on scientific data brought back from the Antarctic by Sir George Nare's *Challenger* expedition. In 1892 he was appointed to succeed J. Scott Keltie as Librarian of the Royal Geographical Society, and became an influential figure in geographical and scientific circles in London, and the friend and helper of many explorers. In 1901 he was appointed director of the British Rainfall Organisation, holding that position until 1919, and serving actively on many councils, associations and international bodies connected with meteorology, oceanography and allied sciences. He wrote a number of textbooks, an Antarctic classic *The Siege of the South Pole*, and was the first biographer of Ernest Shackleton. Dogged all his life by ill health, his eyesight began to fail when he was in his early fifties, and before the end of a long life he became completely blind. His kindness to all who sought his help, his dry humour and a remarkable memory won him scientific distinction and a wide circle of friends.

PONTING, Herbert George, 1870–1935   An outstanding artist with the camera, Ponting began his career in the western United States in mining camps and on cattle ranches, and took up photography during travels in Japan and China. He set himself a high standard, and was a pioneer in the use of the camera as a medium of art rather than a mere recorder of events and persons. Before the *Terra Nova* expedition he had built up a world-wide reputation in this field and his work in the Antarctic greatly enhanced it. He continued his career in photography after the expedition but was less successful in several business ventures. His film of the expedition, *90° South*, remains a classic of polar photography.

PENNELL, Harry L. L., 1882–1916   As navigator of the *Terra Nova* and Lieutenant RN, Pennell won everyone's esteem for his competence, hard work, enthusiasm and ease of manner. In addition to his duties as navigator, he was an able amateur naturalist and helped Wilson and Lillie in their studies of birds and whales. A distinguished future was foretold for him in the navy, but in 1916, as a Commander, he was lost with his ship, the cruiser HMS *Queen Mary*, at the Battle of Jutland.

PRIESTLEY, Raymond Edward, 1886–1972   'Ray' Priestley was educated at Tewkesbury Grammar School and went on to Bristol University to take degrees in botany and geology. When only twenty-one, he was taken on as geologist by Shackleton in his *Nimrod* expedition in 1907–9, working under Professor Edgeworth David of Sydney University. He then continued his studies at Cambridge and Sydney Universities and in 1910 volunteered for the *Terra Nova* expedition. He was one of Campbell's Northern Party and described his experiences in *Antarctic Adventure*. After war service in Signals, he returned to Cambridge as a Fellow of Clare College, and in 1935 was appointed Vice-Chancellor of Melbourne University. Other academic distinctions followed: Vice-Chancellor of Birmingham University, chairman of the Royal Commission on the Civil Service (1953–5) and director of the Falklands Islands Base (1955–9). From 1961–3 he was president of the Royal Geographical Society. He was knighted in 1949. He retired to the neighbourhood of his native Tewkesbury and was survived by two daughters. One of his sisters married his *Terra Nova* colleague Griffith Taylor, the other Charles Wright.

ROYDS, Charles W. Rawson, 1876–1931    There was a naval tradition in Royds' family, both an elder brother and an uncle, who had taken part in an Arctic expedition in 1875, having risen to the rank of Admiral. Charles was born in Rochdale, Lancashire, was a *Conway* cadet, and went to sea in 1892. In 1899 he volunteered for the *Discovery* expedition as First Lieutenant. Cape Royds, on Ross Island, was called after him. In 1913 he was appointed Commander in HMS *Iron Duke*, which on the outbreak of war in 1914 became Admiral Jellicoe's flagship. In 1915, promoted Captain, he took command of HMS *Empress of India*, but missed the Battle of Jutland. After the war he became in turn Captain of the Royal Naval College at Osborne, Director of Physical Training and Sports at the Admiralty, and Commodore of Devonport Barracks. In 1925 he was made Assistant Commissioner of the Metropolitan Police – a controversial appointment, since some thought the job should have gone to a policeman. However he proved popular and successful, gathered in the customary honours – KBE and promotion to Vice-Admiral – but, in 1931, fell down dead, while dancing a waltz, at a charity ball at the Savoy Hotel, aged fifty-four. He married in 1918 and left one daughter.

SHACKLETON, Ernest, 1874–1922    The contradictory elements in Shackleton's character have been attributed by biographers to his genetic mixture of solid Yorkshire Quaker stock, emigrants to County Kildare, with the Celtic strains of Ireland. His father was a doctor who migrated back to England and practised at Sydenham, near London, where he raised a brood of ten whose childhood was happy, easy-going, and reasonably prosperous. (His father bred prize roses.) Ernest left Dulwich College at sixteen to become an apprentice in a merchantman, taking with him a collection of books of poetry and a Bible, which he read every night. His apprenticeship in sailing ships was hard but his nature resilient and tough. He transferred to the Union Castle line and, while serving as 3rd Officer – and through the influence of a passenger, Cyril Longstaff, son of Llewellyn Longstaff who had given £25,000 towards Scott's first expedition – was taken on as 3rd Officer in the *Discovery*. Scott selected him, with Wilson, for his southern journey across the Ross Ice Shelf, where his breakdown due to scurvy proved the turning-point of his life. Invalided home, he resolved to return to the Antarctic to prove his worth as a polar explorer. After interludes as a journalist, secretary of the Royal Scottish Geographical Society, unsuccessful parliamentary candidate and equally unsuccessful business man, the financial backing of a Clydebank ship-builder, William Beardmore (later Lord Invernairn) enabled him to form his own expedition, buy the *Nimrod*, and in 1909 attempt to reach the South Pole. He and his companions failed to do so by ninety-seven geographical miles. The ambitious aim of his second expedition, 1914–16, was to cross the Antarctic continent from the Weddell to the Ross Sea, but his ship, the *Endurance*, was crushed by ice in the former region, and her crew stranded on

Elephant Island off the tip of Graham Land. With five of his men (including Crean), Shackleton in a whaleboat twenty-two feet long made his way across 800 miles of stormy ocean to South Georgia to get help. His stranded crew were eventually rescued. Meanwhile another party under Mackintosh in the *Aurora* had gone to the Ross Sea to lay depots across the Ross Ice Shelf to the Beardmore Glacier. After appalling privations, one of the members, Spencer-Smith, died of scurvy and two others, Mackintosh and Hayward, were lost on an ice-floe carried out to sea. Shackleton sailed on his third and last expedition in the *Quest* in 1922 to explore in the Graham Land area, but died on board of heart failure on 5 January 1922, aged forty-seven, and was buried at Grytvikon, South Georgia. He 'lived like a mighty rushing wind', Mill wrote; 'I grow old and tired but must always lead on' wrote Shackleton not long before his death. He was knighted in 1909 after his *Nimrod* expedition. In 1904 he married Emily Dorman, and had two sons and one daughter.

SIMPSON, George Clarke, 1878–1965 Known as 'Sunny Jim' for his cheerful disposition, Simpson was born and educated in Derby and at Owens College, Manchester, and the University of Göttingen. After working in the Meteorological Office in London he joined the Indian Meteorological Department in 1906 and was given leave to accompany the *Terra Nova* expedition in 1910. Scott formed a great admiration for his skill as a meteorologist, his enthusiasm and hard work. He was recalled to Simla after one year's work. Subsequently he succeeded Sir Napier Shaw as Director of the Metcorological Office in London from 1920–38. He was knighted in 1938. In 1914 he married Dorothy Stephen of Sydney, and had three sons and one daughter. One of his sons was named after Scott and became Professor of Geology at the University of Exeter.

SKELTON, Reginald, 1872–1956 A Norfolk man, Skelton entered the engineering branch of the Royal Navy, and was serving with Scott in the *Majestic* when the *Discovery* expedition was formed. He was a great success, and Scott asked him to join his second expedition as second-in-command, but he was dropped, for financial reasons, in favour of Lieutenant Evans. After serving in Submarines, Skelton made rapid progress in the navy. He took part in the Battle of Jutland, won the DSO, and, back in Submarines, in 1928 was appointed Engineer Vice-Admiral and Engineer-in-Chief of the Fleet. He was created KCB in 1931 and retired in the following year. In 1905 he married Sybil Devenish-Meares of Christchurch, New Zealand, by whom he had one son and two daughters.

SMITH, Reginald John, 1857–1916 After a flying start as a King's Scholar at Eton, as a barrister and QC, Smith married, in 1893, a daughter of George Smith, senior partner in the publishing firm of Smith, Elder and Company. The following year he joined the firm, and in due course succeeded his father-in-law as senior partner. Caring deeply for literature, he established a high standard in his choice of books, never publishing an inferior work because it was likely to make money, and in his treatment of authors was exceptionally tactful, generous and helpful. So kindly were his letters of rejection, always written, often at considerable length, in his own hand, that one unsuccessful author wrote: 'If this is the way MSS are to be rejected, it should become quite a pleasure to be reckoned among the unlucky.' He was also for many years editor of the *Cornhill Magazine*.

At his shooting lodge at Invereighty, in Forfarshire, he and his wife Isabel entertained many of his authors and a wide circle of friends. In appearance he was dark and tall, almost austerely spare. In December 1916 he died when he fell from a window in Green Street, Park Lane. Not long afterwards, the house of Smith, Elder and Company was taken over by that of John Murray.

TAYLOR, Thomas Griffith, 1880–1964 'Griff' was born at Walthamstow in Essex, but his family emigrated to Australia when he was a young boy and he was educated there, graduating from the University of Sydney. In 1907 he went to Cambridge to continue his studies while working for the Australian Weather Service, and was taken on by Scott as a geologist. He was the humorist of the expedition, always ready with a quip, and he wrote amusing articles for the *South Polar Times*. He told his side of the story in *With Scott : The Silver Lining*, dwelling on the lighter side of his experiences. After the expedition he returned to Sydney as Associate Professor of Geography and moved on to North America as Professor of Geography first at Chicago and then at Toronto University. He married one of the sisters of Raymond Priestley.

WILD, Frank, 1874–1930 A descendant, as he claimed, of Captain Cook, Wild was born at Skelton in Yorkshire, the son of an itinerant preacher and schoolmaster. At sixteen he went to sea, serving as a rating on Lord Brassey's yacht the *Sunbeam*. In 1900, aged twenty-six, he joined the Royal Navy becoming seaman gunner 1st class in HMS *Vernon*. In 1901 he volunteered for the *Discovery* without much hope of being taken on, because of his small size. Small as he was, he was tough and wiry and displayed a gift for leadership. This impressed Shackleton who in 1907 invited him to join his *Nimrod* expedition, and subsequently the four-man party who discovered the Beardmore Glacier and got to within ninety-seven geographical miles of the South Pole. Almost immediately after the *Nimrod*'s return, Wild sailed with Douglas Mawson in the *Aurora* to explore the uncharted coastline of Antarctica between Adélie Land and Wilhelm II Land, discovered by Drygalski. Wild wintered with seven companions on an ice-shelf named after Shackleton and then explored some 300 miles of new coastline, while Mawson, exploring in a different direction, endured perhaps the most horrible of all Antarctic experiences as a result of which both his companions, Nimmis and Mertz, perished. Wild then accompanied Shackleton on his expedition in the *Endurance*, which was crushed in the ice and abandoned; Wild took charge of the party stranded for four months on Elephant Island while Shackleton fetched help from South Georgia. In World War One, Wild was commissioned in the RNVR and served, again with Shackleton, in the North Russian Force, and after 1919 an expedition to Spitzbergen, attaining the rank of Lieutenant-Commander. He then went to Nyasaland (Malawi) to plant cotton, but was summoned by cable to go as second-in-command to Shackleton's third and final expedition, to the Weddell Sea. When Shackleton died suddenly on board his ship the *Quest*, Wild assumed command and took his chief's body to Montevideo, Uruguay. Now nearing fifty, he returned to Africa, this time to Zululand, married, and once more tried to grow cotton. This was a disastrous failure. He took to drink, and for a while worked as bar-tender in a small country hotel. Friends found him a humble position in the reduction works of a gold-mine at Klerksdorp, Transvaal, where he died of pneumonia in August 1930, aged fifty-six.

WRIGHT, Charles Seymour, 1887–1975   The *Terra Nova*'s physicist and sole Canadian, Wright was born in Toronto and educated at Upper Canada College, and then at Gonville and Caius College, Cambridge, from 1908–10. He was athletic as a young man, energetic as an old one; Scott described him as 'good-hearted, strong, keen, striving to saturate his mind with ice problems and those of radio-activity'. He was only twenty-three when he was accepted for the expedition. A sturdy sledger, 'Silas' Wright was one of the first supporting party who hauled their sledges nearly to the top of the Beardmore Glacier before turning back opposite Mt Buckley; and in November 1912 he was navigator to the party who spotted the top of the tent in which Scott and his companions died. In World War One he served as a wireless officer, and won an MC and the Legion of Honour. From 1919 until 1947 he was on the scientific staff of the Admiralty, becoming in turn Director of Scientific Research and the first head of the Royal Naval Scientific Service. In 1946 he was made a KCB, and in the following year retired to Salt Spring Island near Vancouver, B.C. His retirement was nominal; he became consultant to the Pacific Naval Laboratory at Esquimalt and carried out research at the Scripps Institute of Oceanography and at the University of British Columbia. Towards the end of his life he revisited his old haunts as a guest of the US Antarctic Research Program's Scott Base in McMurdo Sound. His wife was a sister of Raymond Priestley; another sister married Griffith Taylor. He died in his eighty-eighth year, survived by a son and two daughters.

# Note on Sources

I am very grateful to Sir Peter Scott for giving me the run of his library and allowing me to quote from the letters that passed between his father and mother before and after their marriage, and from the diaries kept by his father on his last expedition, and for help and encouragement in other ways.

Captain Scott's niece and god-daughter, Miss Father Ellison Macartney, most kindly let me make extracts from her collection of family papers, including her uncle's early letters to his parents and part of his *Discovery* journal, and to her and her brother Mr John Ellison Macartney I am most grateful.

My thanks also go to Mrs Minna Eyre, Charles Royds' daughter, who lent me her father's journal, letters and papers; to Mr Ivo Barne, son of Michael Barne, who showed me the original of his father's journal; and to Miss Pat Wright of Ganges, British Columbia, who let me read the diaries of her father, Sir Charles Wright, which she is editing for publication.

The Librarian, Mr G. S. Dugdale, and the Archivist, Mrs Christine Kelly, of the Royal Geographical Society, were kind enough to allow me to see their collection of documents relating to the National Antarctic Expedition of 1901-4, as well as the journals of Sir Clements Markham, his invaluable *Personal Narrative,* and other material.

At the Library of the University of Cambridge I was enabled to see the manuscript of Kathleen Scott's diaries, now deposited there among the papers of Lord Kennet of the Dene. The Librarian of Greenwich National Maritime Museum made available various Markham papers including correspondence between Scott, Admiral Markham and others relating to personnel in the *Discovery* and the purchase of a ship for the second expedition, and Shackleton papers in the Invernairn collection. The Librarian of the Royal Society showed me correspondence between Sir William Huggins, Clements Markham, officers at the Admiralty and others about the handing over of the *Morning*, disagreements on the Joint Committee with the RGS, and other matters, and material dealing with criticisms of meteorological reports from the *Discovery* and with the appointment and resignation of Dr J. W. Gregory. Dr Sheila Bingham of the Dunn Nutrition Unit at Cambridge supplied valuable data on the causes of scurvy.

In the Public Records Office I was enabled to consult files relating to the purchase and despatch of the *Terra Nova*, correspondence between Scott and Admiral Wharton, and Scott's naval record.

The Director of the National Library of Australia, Mrs Pauline Fanning, went to much trouble to supply extracts from the papers of T. V. Hodgson deposited there, biographical notes on Louis Bernacchi and other material; and Miss Frances Gundry of the Provincial Archives of British Columbia was equally helpful with information concerning Cecil Meares; so also was Miss L. Kennedy of the City of Johannesburg Public Library with the career of Frank Wild. Dr Edna Plumstead of Johannesburg most kindly sent me data about the paleobotany of the Antarctic.

I am also indebted to the Librarian of the Foreign and Commonwealth Office for particulars about the Hausa Force and the Protectorate of Lagos; and to the ever helpful officers of the London Library and of the Wiltshire County Library for their invaluable supply of books. Mr John R. Murray and Mrs Virginia Murray showed me the Smith, Elder and Co. files and ledgers relating to *The Voyage of the Discovery* and to the career of Reginald Smith. There are many others who helped me with suggestions and information, and I am very grateful to them all.

For taking the onerous task of compiling an index off my shoulders, I am very deeply indebted to Mr Duncan Mackintosh, and to Biddy who helped him.

Finally there is the Scott Polar Research Institute at Cambridge, the repository of almost everything known about Scott, his companions and many other polar explorers. It would have been impossible to put pen to paper, or lay a finger on the typewriter keys, without the Institutes' assistance, and it is equally impossible to express adequate thanks to the Director, Dr Gordon Robin, for his permission to work there, and to the ever-helpful, genial and omniscient Librarian Mr Harry King, and no less erudite Archivist Mr Clive Holland, and their hospitable staff. There can be few libraries more rewarding to work in, its only fault being the temptation it offers its visitors to go on browsing among the shelves and files almost indefinitely. To Mr King I am especially grateful for checking the manuscript for technical errors.

I cannot attempt to list all the documents consulted in this library, but the following is an abbreviated list to indicate the main heads.

Collected papers of the National Antarctic Expedition 1901–4 (9 volumes)
Exchange of letters between Scott and Shackleton, 1909–10
Letters from T. V. Hodgson to his mother and sister, 1901–3
Letters from Hare, Wright and others deposited by R. Pound
Letters from Scott to J. J. Kinsey
Letters from Scott to Major Darwin, RGS, 1909–11
Papers of the Australasian Antarctic Expedition, 1911–14
Collection of letters from L. E. G. Oates to his mother
Letters from Scott to Sir Edgar Speyer, 1911
Letters from Scott to H. R. Mill re *The Voyage of the Discovery*
Letters from Markham to Scott re relief expedition etc.
Letters from Markham to Smith re Amundsen, Shackleton etc.
Memo from Armitage to H. R. Mill, 1922, re *Discovery* expedition
Medical report from Koettlitz on Shackleton, 1903
Papers of the British Antarctic Expedition 1910–13 (20 volumes)
Transcripts of tape recordings by Ontario Educational Communications
    Authority: interviews with Wright, Priestley, Gran etc.
Letter from Wilson to Shackleton, undated, circa 1910 (copy)

Letters Shackleton to Markham and Scott, 1907
Letters Wilson to Reginald Smith, 1910
Letters Cherry-Garrard to Smith, 1912
Exchange of letters between Scott and Keltie re Shackleton, 1907
Geographical Journal Jan. 1913 (Amundsen) and 1957 (obit. Campbell)
Trans-Antarctic Expedition 1955–58, Scientific Reports No. 9, 'Fossil Flora of Antarctica', E. Plumstead
MS diaries of the following:
  R. F. Scott, 1901–3 (5 volumes)
  Reginald Skelton, 1901–3
  T. V. Hodgson, 1901–4
  Frank Wild (original in National Library of N.S.W.)
  Wilfrid Bruce, 1910–13
  Frank Browning, 1910–12
  Patrick Keohane, 1910–12
  William Lashly, 1901–4, 1910–13
  George Simpson, 1910–12
  T. Griffith Taylor, 1910–13
  Thomas Williamson, 1912–13

# Bibliography

AMUNDSEN, Roald, *My Life as an Explorer* (Heinemann, London 1927)

AMUNDSEN, Roald, *The South Pole* (John Murray, London 1912)

ANDERSON, Verily, *The Last of the Eccentrics* (Hodder & Stoughton, London 1972)

ARMITAGE, Albert B., *Two Years in the Antarctic* (Arnold, London 1905)

ARMITAGE, Albert B., *Cadet to Commodore* (Cassell, London 1925)

BERNACCHI, Louis C., *To the South Polar Regions* (Hurst & Blackett, London 1901)

BERNACCHI, Louis C., *A Very Gallant Gentleman* (Butterworths, London 1933)

BERNACCHI, Louis C., *The Saga of the Discovery* (Blackie & Sons, London 1938)

BORCHGREVINK, C. E., *First on the Antarctic Continent* (Newnes, London 1901)

CHERRY-GARRARD, Apsley, *The Worst Journey in the World* (Constable, London 1922)

DUNCAN, Isadora, *My Life* (Gollancz, London 1928)

FISHER, James and Margery, *Shackleton* (Barrie, London 1957)

GREGORY, J. W., *The Great Rift Valley*, ed. A. E. Loftus (Edinburgh 1952)

GWYNN, Stephen, *Captain Scott* (John Lane, the Bodley Head, London 1929)

HAYES, J. Gordon, *The Conquest of the South Pole* (Butterworths, London 1932)

JACKSON, F. G., *A Thousand Days in the Arctic* (Harper & Bros, London 1899)

JAMESON, Admiral Sir W. S., *The Fleet that Jack Built* (Hart-Davis MacGibbon, London 1962)

KERR, Sir Mark, *The Navy in my Time* (Rich & Cowan, London 1933)

KING, H. G. R., *The Antarctic* (Blandford Press, London 1969)

LASHLY, William, *Under Scott's Command*, diaries ed. A. R. Ellis (Gollancz, London 1969)

LEWIS, Michael, *The Navy of Britain* (Allen & Unwin, London 1948)

LUDLAM, Harry, *Captain Scott. The Full Story* (Foulsham, London 1965)

MCCLINTOCK, F. L., *The Voyage of the 'Fox' in Arctic Seas* (John Murray, London 1859)

MARKHAM, Clements, *Lands of Silence* (CUP, London 1921)

MAWSON, Douglas, *The Home of the Blizzard* (William Heinemann, London 1915)

MILL, H. R., *The Life of Sir Ernest Shackleton* (Heinemann, London 1923)

MILL, H. R., *An Autobiography* (Longmans Green, London 1951)

MOUNTEVANS, Baron (E. Evans), *South With Scott* (Collins, London 1921)

MOUNTEVANS, Baron, *Adventurous Life* (Hutchinson, London 1946)

MOUNTFIELD, David, *A History of Polar Exploration* (Hamlyn, London 1974)

NANSEN, Fridjof, *Farthest North* (New York 1897), abridged version ed. Denys Thompson (Chatto & Windus, London 1955)

PONTING, Herbert, *The Great White South* (Duckworth & Co., London 1921)

POUND, Reginald, *Scott of the Antarctic* (Cassell, London 1966)

PRIESTLEY, Sir Raymond, ADIE, R. J., ROBIN, G de Q, eds., *Antarctic Research* (Butterworths, London 1964)

PRIESTLEY, Raymond, *Antarctic Adventure. Scott's Northern Party* (T. Fisher Unwin, London 1914)

ROSS, Sir James Clark, *A Voyage of Discovery & Research in the Southern & Antarctic Regions, 1839–43* (John Murray, London 1847)

SAVOURS, Ann, *Scott's Last Voyage* (Sidgwick & Jackson, London 1974)

SCOTT, Kathleen, *Homage : a book of sculptures* (Geoffrey Bles, London 1938)

SCOTT, Kathleen, *Self Portrait of an Artist* (John Murray, London 1949)

SCOTT, R. F., *The Voyage of the Discovery* (Smith, Elder & Co., London 1905)

SCOTT, R. F., *Scott's Last Expedition* (Introduction by J. M. Barrie, Smith, Elder & Co., London 1913)

SCOTT, R. F., *Diaries in Facsimile, 1910–12* (6 vols) (University Microfilms, London 1968)

SEAVER, George, *Birdie Bowers of the Antarctic* (John Murray, London 1938)

SEAVER, George, *Scott of the Antarctic* (John Murray, London 1940)

SOUTH POLAR TIMES. Vols 1 and 2, 1901–3 and vol 3, 1910–1911 (Smith, Elder & Co., London 1907 and 1911)

SHACKLETON, Ernest, *The Heart of the Antarctic* (Heinemann, London 1909)

SHACKLETON, Ernest, *South : the story of Shackleton's 1914–1917 expedition* (Heinemann, London 1970)

SMITH, Humphrey Hugh, *A Yellow Admiral Remembers* (Arnold, London 1932)

SORENSEN, Jon, *Fridjof Nansen* (Allen & Unwin, London 1932)

TAYLOR, T. Griffith, *With Scott : the Silver Lining* (Smith, Elder & Co., London 1916)

WESTER WEMYSS, R. E. Baron. The Life and Letters of Lord Wester Wemyss by his widow, baroness V. Wester Wemyss

WILSON, E. A., *Diary of the 'Discovery' Expedition to the Antarctic 1901–4*, ed. Ann Savours (Blandford Press, London 1966)

WILSON, E. A., *Edward Wilson's Birds of the Antarctic*, ed. Brian Roberts (Humanities Press, New York 1968)

WILSON, E. A., *Diary of the 'Terra Nova' Expedition to the Antarctic 1910–12*, ed. H. G. R. King (Blandford Press, London 1972)

# INDEX

# INDEX

# Elspeth Huxley

One of Britain's distinguished authors, Elspeth
Huxley has written more than thirty books, the
best known of which include *White Man's Country:
Lord Delamere and the Making of Kenya; Red
Strangers;* and an autobiographical trilogy, *The
Flame Trees of Thika; The Mottled Lizard;* and
*Love Among Daughters.* She has also written
biographies of David Livingstone and Florence
Nightingale.